# Being Useful

# Being Useful

## Policy Relevance and International Relations Theory

*Miroslav Nincic and Joseph Lepgold, Editors*

*With a Foreword by Alexander George*

*Ann Arbor*

THE UNIVERSITY OF MICHIGAN PRESS

Copyright © by the University of Michigan 2000
All rights reserved
Published in the United States of America by
The University of Michigan Press
Manufactured in the United States of America
∞ Printed on acid-free paper

2003  2002  2001  2000    4  3  2  1

*A CIP catalog record for this book is available
from the British Library.*

Library of Congress Cataloging-in-Publication Data

Being useful : policy relevance and international relations theory /
    Miroslav Nincic and Joseph Lepgold, editors ; with a foreword by
    Alexander George.
        p. cm.
    Includes bibliographical references and index.
    ISBN 0-472-11072-1 (cloth : alk. paper) — ISBN 0-472-08656-1
(paper : alk. paper)
        1. International relations—Philosophy.  2. Policy sciences.
    I. Nincic, Miroslav.  II. Lepgold, Joseph.

JZ1305 .B448  2000
327.1'01—dc21                                              00-025981

*To the memory of*
*Kenneth Organski*
*and*
*Richard Sinopoli*

# Contents

Foreword      ix
*Alexander George*

Introduction: Scholarship and the Contours of
Policy Relevance      1
*Miroslav Nincic*

**Part 1. Theory of Relevance**

    **A. Relevance and the Ivory Tower**

Policy Relevance and Theoretical Development:
The Terms of the Trade-off      21
*Miroslav Nincic*

Counselors, Kings, and International Relations:
From Revelation to Reason, and Still No Policy-
Relevant Theory      50
*Arthur A. Stein*

Scholars and Statesmen: Framework for a
Productive Dialogue      75
*Joseph Lepgold*

    **B. Relevance and the Corridors of Power**

How Social Science Can Help Policymakers:
The Relevance of Theory      109
*Ernest J. Wilson III*

In Pursuit of Praxis: Applying International Relations
Theory to Foreign Policy-Making      129
*Bruce W. Jentleson*

**Part 2. The Relevance of Theory**

### A. The Relevance of the Domestic Context

Domestic Political Consequences of the Cold War's End:
The International Impact on America's Foreign
Policy Capacity                                                    153
  *Robert J. Lieber*

Putting Theory to Work: Diagnosing Public Opinion on
the U.S. Intervention in Bosnia                                   174
  *Eric V. Larson*

### B. The Relevance of Related Approaches

Ethnic Fears and Security Dilemmas: Managing
Uncertainty in Africa                                              237
  *Donald Rothchild*

Military Diffusion, the Information Revolution, and
U.S. Power                                                        267
  *Emily O. Goldman*

From Sea-Lanes to Global Cities: The Policy Relevance
of Political Geography                                            295
  *Donna J. Nincic*

### C. The Relevance of Rationality

Agreement through Threats: The Northern Ireland Case    325
  *Steven J. Brams and Jeffrey M. Togman*

The Outcome of the Negotiations over the Status of
Jerusalem: A Forecast                                            343
  *A. F. K. Organski*

**Conclusion**

Policy Relevance and Theoretical Development in
International Relations: What Have We Learned?                   363
  *Joseph Lepgold*

Contributors                                                     381

Index                                                            383

# Foreword

*Alexander George*

The editors of this volume have suggested that I address the following questions in this foreword: (1) Why should academic specialists care about the issue of the policy relevance of scholarly research on international relations; and what benefits do I think the development of international relations would gain from work that might help to bridge the theory-policy gap? (2) How have my own research interests over the years reflected a desire to bridge the gap? (3) Is it really possible to bridge the theory-policy gap; and what lessons have I learned from a lifetime of trying to do so?[1]

## I

In my view, research that aims to develop policy-applicable knowledge and theory is not at all inconsistent with efforts to develop international relations theory. Rather, quite the opposite! Such efforts are indispensable for the further development and refinement of international relations theory.[2] Why? Because structural-realist theory, the dominant international relations theory in American political science, while certainly necessary, is insufficient by itself either for *explaining* foreign policy decisions and outcomes of interactions between states or for *conducting* foreign policy. Indeed, Kenneth Waltz himself emphasized and made it clear that his structural-realist theory is *not* a theory of foreign policy. Waltz warned against expecting his theory to "explain the particular policies of states" and regarded it as an error "to mistake a theory of international politics for a theory of foreign policy." Waltz also acknowledged that structural-realist theory "makes assumptions about the interests and motives of states, rather than explaining them." That Waltz regards structural-realism as a theory of constraints on foreign policy rather than a theory of foreign policy is made clear in his observation that "what it [structural-realist theory] does explain are the constraints that confine all states."[3] In this sense and to a degree, structural-realist theory is indeed policy-relevant.

But we are left with a large vacuum in international relations theory that must be addressed if one is interested in developing more and better knowledge that will be of some use for the explanation and conduct of foreign policy. This is a challenging task, and, as this book illustrates, specialists in international relations are usefully responding to it in different ways.

## II

My own efforts over the years to fill the vacuum of international relations theory and to bridge the theory-policy gap have focused on only one of the paths outlined in this book. For most of my career, which includes twenty years spent with the RAND Corporation before coming to Stanford University in 1968, I have pursued a research program that focuses on problems of international conflict avoidance, management, and resolution. I have found an analytical historical approach, combined with cognitive psychology and social psychology, particularly useful, though this is by no means the only way to study these problems. I have been particularly interested in how lessons of historical experience can be correctly drawn and cumulated into policy-relevant theory.

This research strategy required me to develop better ways of doing historical case studies, to raise the standards for case studies, and to develop and explicate procedures for doing multiple case studies of a given phenomenon — such as deterrence, coercive diplomacy, crisis management, or security cooperation — in ways that would reflect scientific consciousness and produce systematic findings that could be cumulated within a theoretical framework.[4]

Quite early in pursuing this research program, I concluded that it would be necessary to move beyond structural realist, rational choice, and game theories. These deductive approaches to theory development "black-box" both the process of policy-making and the strategic interaction between states that leads to outcomes; that is, they deal with these processes by assumption. Instead, I felt it necessary for my purposes to engage in direct but admittedly difficult empirical study of decision-making processes and strategic interaction between actors. However, in agreement with the editors of this book as well as with many other scholars, I do not regard deductive and empirical ways of developing international relations theory as antithetical; efforts to link them more closely can be productive and should be pursued.[5]

To fill the vacuum in international relations theory to which I have alluded, I do not believe it would be useful to try to develop a very general theory of foreign policy, or "statecraft" as historians used to call it. More useful contributions are made by focusing specifically on each of the many generic problems encountered in the conduct of foreign policy — such as problems in deterrence, coercive diplomacy, crisis management, war termination, preventive diplomacy, crisis avoidance, mediation, conciliation, cooperation, and so on.

## The Needs of Policymakers

To deal effectively with each of the generic problems identified here, policymakers need four types of knowledge. First, they need a *general conceptual model* that identifies the critical variables of a strategy for dealing effectively with the phenomenon in question, whether it be deterrence, crisis management, coercive diplomacy, conciliation, or something else. Such a conceptual understanding identifies the general logic associated with successful use of that policy instrument. However useful it is as a conceputal model, it is not itself a strategy but merely the starting point for constructing one that will fit the particular situation that confronts the policymakers.

Second, therefore, the policymaker must tailor the general concept into a *specific strategy.*

Third, the policymaker needs a *correct image of the adversary* whose behavior the strategy is designed to influence. Policy specialists and academic scholars agree on this fundamental point: in conducting foreign policy one must try to see events — and, indeed, assess one's own behavior — from the perspective of the adversary. Only by doing so can the decision maker diagnose a developing situation accurately and select appropriate ways of communicating with and influencing the adversary. Faulty images of each other are a source of major misperceptions and miscalculations that have often led to major errors in policy, to avoidable catastrophes, and to missed opportunities.

Fourth, the policymaker needs *generic knowledge* of the conditions that favor effective use of a strategy in different circumstances. Developing empirically grounded knowledge of the conditions under which a strategy is likely to succeed or fail helps to bridge the gap between scholarly studies undertaken by research specialists and the needs of policymakers.

I quickly discovered during the course of interviews with policy specialists several years ago that their eyes would glaze as soon as I used the word *theory;* but they nodded approvingly when I spoke of the need for generic knowledge! I wondered why this was so, and the answer was obvious and important. Policy specialists recognize that generic problems exist in the conduct of foreign policy—for example, the task of deterrence emerges repeatedly over time with different adversaries and in different contexts. Therefore, policy experts readily agree that general, or generic, knowledge about the uses and limitations of a particular strategy or instrument of policy, derived from proper study of past experience, can be very helpful when one considers possible uses of that strategy in a new situation. Systematic assessment of past experience with a particular instrument of policy should lead to formulation of *conditional* (as against very general probabilistic) *generalizations* that identify the conditions and circumstances under which a strategy is or is not likely to be successful.

## III

Some years ago I came to the conclusion that it is more appropriate to speak of *bridging* the gap between theory and practice than of *eliminating* it. The choice of words reflects an appreciation of the limitations as well as the uses of policy-applicable theory and generic knowledge. Scholarly knowledge of this kind can have only an indirect and limited impact on policy-making. Since I also claim that generic knowledge is often critical for sound policy, I need to explain this apparent contradiction.

Generic knowledge provides essential inputs to policy analysis within the government and serves as an aid to the judgment that policymakers must exercise in dealing with specific situations. Generic knowledge cannot substitute for policy analysis or for the policymaker's judgment. Even the best theoretical conceptualization of a strategy and the most highly developed generic knowledge of it cannot substitute for competent policy analysis within the government, in which analysts must consider whether some version of the strategy is likely to be viable in the particular situation that they confront. Similarly, generic knowledge cannot substitute for the judgment policymakers must exercise in deciding whether to employ that strategy in a particular situation, since that judgment must take into account other relevant considerations not encompassed by generic knowledge of the strategy.[6]

It is in this sense that scholarly knowledge has an indirect and often limited impact on policy. Nonetheless, as I have argued, well-developed generic knowledge of different instruments of policy is capable of making a critically important contribution to policy-making.

How, then, can generic knowledge *aid* (not substitute for) policy analysis and the decision maker's judgment? First, it can assist in making a sound diagnosis of a problematic situation; then, and only then, it can help to determine whether an effective policy response is possible in that particular situation and what form it should take. Thus, policy-relevant theory and knowledge contribute to two essential tasks of policy-making: the *diagnostic* task and the *prescriptive* one.

I place particular emphasis on the diagnostic contribution policy-relevant theory and generic knowledge are capable of making rather than on their ability to prescribe sound choice of policy. Correct diagnosis of a policy problem and of the context in which it occurs should precede and, as in medical practice, is usually a prerequisite for efforts to make the best choice from among treatment options. This analogy with medical practice is an apt one since the policymaker, like the physician, acts as a clinician in striving to make a correct diagnosis of the problem before determining how best to prescribe for it.

The science of microbiology and its relationship to medical practice offers a highly relevant model for thinking about the relationship of theory and practice in international relations. Consider the relationship of smoking cigarettes (and exposure to other carcinogens) to cancer. Statistical-correlational studies have long convinced most of us that some kind of causal relationship does exist. Microbiologists have been working for years — lately with considerable success — to identify the intervening causal processes. Why is this important? Finding the causal link creates opportunities for developing new intervention techniques for halting the development of cancers.

The medical analogy, once again, is highly germane for the development of policy-relevant knowledge of international relations. Knowledge of causal mechanisms offers foreign policy practitioners opportunities for identifying possibilities for using leverage to influence outcomes of interaction with other actors. Of course, the success that microbiology is having in identifying causal mechanisms operative in many diseases cannot be easily duplicated in the study of international relations. Nonetheless it is heartening that in recent years political scientists and some philosophers of science have increasingly emphasized the importance of trying to identify causal mechanisms.

What, then, are some of the implications of the preceding observations for at least some research on foreign policy? One implication is that theory and generic knowledge do not need to satisfy the high degree of verification that science attempts to achieve. Just as intelligent people are generally able to manage the many chores of everyday life reasonably well without benefit of knowledge that meets the highest scientific standards, so too can intelligent policymakers use knowledge of the different generic problems of statecraft when it is available. In other words, when scientific knowledge is not attainable, we can at least strive to produce usable knowledge.

A second implication is that scholars should include in their research designs variables over which policymakers have some leverage. A third implication is that too strict a pursuit of the scientific criterion of parsimony is inappropriate for developing useful policy-relevant theory and knowledge. The policymaker has to deal with complex situations that embrace many variables; he or she will get more help from rich theories, by which I mean theories that embrace many relevant variables. Such theories must meet two criteria: their contents must be at least plausible, and they should contain indications of the particular conditions under which their propositions are likely to hold. At the very least, such theories and generic knowledge serve as a sophisticated checklist that reminds policy specialists of the numerous conditions and variables that can influence their ability to achieve desired outcomes. But when more fully developed, such rich theories of generic problems identify the conditions that favor (although they do not guarantee) the success of a policy option. Hence the objective of this type of policy-relevant knowledge is to produce conditional generalizations and usable knowledge.

As requested by the editors, I have described the type of research I have engaged in over the years to help fill the vacuum in international relations theory. I would not want to leave the impression that development of generic knowledge of instruments of foreign policy is the only or the most important way in which scholarly research can contribute to policy. Scholars can and indeed do make other types of contributions, some of which are discussed in this book. For example, well-informed, objective analyses of problems having to do with the impact of nationalistic, ethnic, and religious conflicts on intrastate and interstate relations, nuclear proliferation, environmental and ecological problems, population and demographic trends, problems of food production and distribution, water scarcities, sanitation, and health problems are an essential part of knowledge required for the conduct of foreign policy.

Still another type of useful scholarly contribution lies in the activity of policy-relevant forecasting, a topic that has received attention in the past but which remains in need of much additional research and reflection. Forecasting efforts occupy a central role in policy-making. Policy-making in the State Department requires forecasting, but the general inadequacy and sporadic nature of its policy-planning efforts over the years is well known. What can academic scholarship provide to improve matters? Some years ago Herbert Simon wrote about the importance of "design theory" and "design exercises": his initiative remains to be pursued.[7] Intelligence specialists within the government have made progress in developing the concept of *analytical* forecasting, again an essential refinement that should be pursued.[8] Policy-relevant forecasting, it should be recognized, often requires the development and proper use of area knowledge as well as substantive expertise in the subject matters being addressed.

These are by no means easy requirements to achieve. Given the global scope of American foreign policy interests and the very large number of countries on which specialized information and expert judgment is needed, there is a shortage of qualified area experts outside as well as within the government.

An encouraging development is the striking performance in making predictions by means of an expected utility model developed by Bruce Bueno de Mesquita and associates. It should be noted, however, that the model requires input from area experts and, hence, is dependent on the informed sophistication of traditional area experts.[9]

In addition, scholars can — and indeed do — make a variety of other types of contributions. Among these are the development of better concepts and conceptual frameworks that can assist policymakers to orient themselves to the phenomena and problems with which they must deal. Although scholars may not be in a good position to advise policymakers how best to deal with a specific instance of a general problem that requires timely action, they can often provide a useful, broader discussion of how to think about and understand that general phenomenon — such as, for example, the problem of ethnicity and nationalism.

A recent example of an important effort to mobilize scholarly knowledge and resources in order to deal with an overwhelmingly important policy problem is the Carnegie Commission's study of preventing deadly conflict. This recently concluded three-year study not only drew on available scholarly knowledge; it also stimulated important new scholarly efforts to fill the gaps in such knowledge. It is a fine example of a collaborative effort of high-level policy influentials and scholars to analyze the sources of deadly conflicts and to identify and evaluate tools for preventing or limiting them.[10]

Among the many virtues and contributions of the present book is its depiction of various ways in which policy relevance may be conceived in the field of international relations, and its mapping-out of approaches for developing policy-applicable theory and knowledge.

NOTES

1. In responding to these questions I have drawn from two recent publications: *Bridging the Gap: Theory and Practice in Foreign Policy* (Washington, D.C.: United States Institute of Peace, 1993) and "Knowledge for Statecraft: The Challenge for Political Science and History," *International Security* 22, no. 1 (summer 1997), 44–52.

2. For a sophisticated statement of the need for political scientists to give more emphasis to policy-relevant research on important policy problems, see Peter C. Ordeshook, "Engineering or Science: What Is the Study of Politics?" in Jeffrey Friedman, ed., *The Rational Choice Controversy* (New Haven: Yale University Press, 1995), 175–88. Ordeshook summarizes his views as follows: "Until the 'engineering' component of the discipline assumes a central role, research — whether theoretical, empirical, or any other combination of the two — will continue to generate an incoherent accumulation of theorems, lemmas, correlations, and 'facts' " (175). In several unpublished papers, David Dessler has made similar observations regarding the need to infuse a "pragmatic" dimension into international relations theory.

3. Kenneth Waltz, *Theory of International Politics* (New York: McGraw-Hill, 1979), 121–22.

4. For this purpose, I developed the "method of structured, focused comparison" during the course of my research on substantive problems of deterrence, coercive diplomacy, and crisis management. An early description of this method appears in Alexander L. George, "Case Studies and Theory Development: The Methods of Structured, Focused Comparison," in Paul G. Lauren, ed., *Diplomacy: New Approaches in History, Theory, and Policy* (New York: Free Press, 1979), 43–68. A restatement and further development of the method is in preparation and will appear in a book coauthored with Andrew Bennett (forthcoming, MIT Press). We have written a number of draft papers for this project; they are available on http://www.georgetown.edu.bennett.

5. This position is similar to that expressed by some leading proponents of rational choice and game theories. In one study, Robert Bates and his coauthors combine and integrate these theories with detailed case narratives. These authors argue that rational choice theory does better when it is integrated with in-depth historical case studies. Indeed, they insist that combining deductive and empirical approaches is essential and fruitful: "Narrative supported by theory, we believe, is stronger than narrative alone; and theory supported by narrative is better than mere theory" (Robert Bates et al., *Analytical Narratives* [Princeton University Press, 1998]; the quotation is from the introductory chapter [8]).

6. I have emphasized the importance of developing a better understand-

ing of the relationship of analysis to the various types of judgments policymakers typically have to make (see chapter 2 in *Bridging the Gap*). Deborah Larson and Stanley Renshon are currently collaborating in a study of the relationship between analysis and judgment.

7. Herbert A. Simon, *The Sciences of the Artificial* (Cambridge: MIT Press, 1969).

8. See, for example, Joseph Nye, "Peering into the Future," *Foreign Affairs* 73, no. 4 (July/August 1994), 82–93. See also my article on policy-oriented forecasting in Nazli Choucri and Thomas W. Robinson, eds., *Forecasting in International Relations* (San Francisco: W. H. Freeman, 1978).

9. For a recent description of this forecasting technique and its performance, see Bruce Bueno de Mesquita and Frans N. Stokman, eds., *European Community Decision Making* (New Haven: Yale University Press, 1994).

10. Carnegie Commission on Preventing Deadly Conflict, *Preventing Deady Conflict* (New York: Carnegie Corporation of New York, December 1997).

# Introduction: Scholarship and the Contours of Policy Relevance

*Miroslav Nincic*

Political science's roots in societal and international challenges would scarcely be surmised from current academic postures toward policy-relevant scholarship. The notion that work steeped in practical needs reflects compromised academic aspirations, that it is incompatible with the growth of innovative and epistemologically laudable theory, pervades many departments of political science. The attitude is reflected in the discipline's leading journals, and it has shaped the professional reward structure of major research universities. Dissident voices are sometimes heard. Karl Deutsch, former president of both the American Political Science Association and the International Political Science Association, argued that "insofar as political science is a science, it is an applied one. Its tasks are practical, and its theories are both challenged and nourished by practice."[1] Eugene Meehan complained that, within political science, "teachers have trained teachers to train teachers to train teachers, and so on ad nauseam . . . The result is scholasticism pure and simple, minimally committed to the development of knowledge that relates to the reasoned pursuit of reasoned goals."[2] But these seem to be exceptions, and if some feel that policy relevance is a worthwhile scholarly objective, their voices have become increasingly faint.

Theory and research are judged on the basis of their coherence, analytical complexity, and especially the sophistication of the conceptual and research tools employed, not on the basis of their practical value. In support of this, it is observed that, much as the progress of the natural sciences would suffer if concrete applications rather than the expansion of disinterested knowledge were the guiding objective, so explanation and interpretation of the political world might be hobbled if tethered to policy agendas. Additionally, it is sometimes implied that an insistence on the applicability of knowledge could blur the line between science and partisanship, to the certain detriment of the former.

Even if the desirability of relevance is not questioned, it is occasionally viewed as an objective beyond plausible reach. In some views, the nature of the social sciences, the conceptual and methodological foundations on which they rest, place their findings outside the conceptual frame of reference of most government leaders. Even when training is not a barrier to effective communication, decision makers operate under time constraints that make it unlikely that they could digest and incorporate scholarly findings into the formulation and implementation of practical policy. And, as Charles Lindblom has pointed out, policymakers must combine analytical and political problem solving, where the political involves the accommodation of interests involved in a policy rather than the intrinsic structure of the issue requiring resolution; whereas the scholar is likely to help only with the analytical, having no particular grasp of the political.[3]

Still, and for two reasons at least, it is hard to argue that an understanding of international relations and foreign policy should be pursued with no regard to practical relevance. To begin with, the justification for a field of study is strengthened if it may help inform policy on matters of consequence. A promise of pragmatic utility is not the only justification for academic inquiry, but knowledge should be more than just a foil for academic debate and a vehicle for the promotion of academic careers. Beyond this, it is possible that the quality of knowledge, even of a very general and theoretical sort, would benefit if it were grounded in practical challenges — that relevance may be a path to understanding, as well as vice versa. These points will be further discussed in this volume, but it may be stated, even now, that questions about the role of policy-relevant knowledge should at least be regarded as open and subject to examination in the manner of any analytical challenge. This is the objective that the editors and authors assign themselves.

The essays in this volume address the desirability of policy-relevant knowledge and its challenges and possibilities, and they provide illustrations of bodies of knowledge from which useful practical implications can be drawn. However, an overarching issue, one requiring resolution before other matters can usefully be addressed, concerns not the substance of policy-relevant scholarship but the relation of those who produce it to the broader community of which they are a part. In this regard, two issues in particular merit consideration in this chapter. The first concerns the danger that work with a policy orientation will seek to shape the ends that political activity should pursue, entangling it with values rather than facts, thus undermining the mission of empirical scholarship. The second asks who should be considered appropriate judges of the scholarly product — academic peers or the society whose needs policy-relevant work seeks to address? Before describing the substance and structure of the book, these two issues should be addressed.

## Policy Relevance, Scholars, and Society

### Societal Ends and Policy Means

Explicitly or implicitly, a number of observers are concerned that policy-relevant work may violate an ideal of education and scholarship, one associated with the liberal conception of the democratic state. As philosopher Michael Root has argued, the preference for a value-neutral state — that is, one committed to procedures of democratic decision making, but not to the promotion of one view of the public good over another — is a core component of the liberal creed.[4] Often, within this creed, commitment to value-neutrality is extended to the pursuit of knowledge, which, it is felt, should encourage epistemologically proper methods of inquiry but should not promote a particular set of social values via this inquiry. The latter are grounded in moral feelings with no truth-value, whereas only a concern with statements possessing truth-value is the proper province of scholarship in a liberal society: "The liberal state is forbidden to use the law; the liberal schools are forbidden to use the classroom or curriculum; and the liberal social sciences are forbidden to use teaching or research to endorse one conception of the good over the other."[5]

An implication often drawn from the liberal ethos is that, while political science may properly concern itself with the analysis of means, any discussion of ends is outside its province. In George Herbert Meade's words, "science does not attempt to formulate the end which social and moral conduct ought to pursue."[6] The decision about what should be promoted must, in this view, flow from democratic procedures of aggregating societal preferences, not from the wishes of scholars.

If science should concern itself only with means, not goals, one may fear that those who advise on how ends are to be promoted cannot be value-neutral. By charting optimal courses of action, they cannot, in the nature of things, avoid urging certain ends over others, and thus certain values over others. The solution to the problem is sometimes sought in a restricted definition of the analyst's role, in injunctions to the effect that such a person must act as an agent, not a principal. Alexander George and Richard Smoke, foremost theorists of usable knowledge for foreign policy, have maintained:

Policy science, as we would define it, is itself value free, although in a different sense from the value-freedom of empirical theory. The policy theorist, acting as such, accepts the values of the constitutionally authorized decision-makers of his nation and offers contingent advice: "if you want to accomplish x, do y in your policy."[7]

This solution to the ends-means problem may seem simple and workable, but it is quite elusive. It assumes that a meaningful distinction can be drawn between the ends and means of political action, that science can help society select the latter without influencing its feelings regarding the former. Actually, this can rarely be done. The distinction is tenable only with regard to "pure" ends, those that can be defined as objectives in and of themselves, not as a means for attaining any other, more general or more elevated goal. A set of pure ends surely exists, but it is also (1) a set with very few members and (2) a set whose members are self-evidently, axiomatically, desirable. Objectives of this sort may include justice, welfare, felicity, that is, goals that virtually everyone would embrace and whose meaning is definable only in the most abstract terms. Lacking a firm empirical content, they are of very limited analytical use. By the same token, social scientists have no incentive to either urge or discourage their pursuit, and, in the abstract sense given to such objectives, no argument would surround the need to understand how they should be attained.

But once one moves even slightly away from what amount to trivial statements of pure ends, almost every goal is, at some remove, subordinate to them by an assumed, direct or indirect, instrumental relation. In other words, virtually every nontrivial societal goal is ultimately an instrumental goal, so that virtually all political arguments and policy debates, even with a relatively broad common frame of political values, actually involve means. Democrats and Republicans, liberals and conservatives, hardly ever argue about pure or ultimate ends, only about the proper methods of proceeding toward them. No one disputes the need to reduce poverty, but sharp debate surrounds the desirability of doing so via government or market forces. There is rarely dissensus on the need to improve primary and secondary education, but not everyone concurs on the type of knowledge that should be conveyed to youth, or whether this is best done by private or by public schools. Everyone agrees that peace is desirable; not everyone concurs on the proper mix of force and diplomacy it sometimes requires.

In this sense, it is emphatically not the case that ends are value-laden and sharply debated while means are value-free and uncontroversial. As a rule, it is precisely the other way around: virtually everyone seems to subscribe to the same restricted set of noninstrumental aims, hence no special value judgments are involved in their consideration. There are, however, many possible ways of attaining these ends; and much value judgment (and consequent debate) is associated with the evaluation of these means. Because quarrels almost always involve ways of attaining ends, the injunction that policy-relevant work must be value-free is quite inconsistent with a recommendation that it concern itself with means alone, while leaving discussion of ends to the democratic process. It is also vacuous, because no one wishes to debate ultimate ends, but short of these the distinction between ends and instruments is, most of the time, meaningless.

To illustrate the argument, George and Smoke, in a direct continuation of the above quotation, find it necessary to introduce a few qualifications to their principle of value-free policy research:

> When necessary, the policy analyst should indeed urge that the objectives of current or contemplated policy be redefined to make them more consistent with what he perceives to be the more final goals of the policy maker. However, he does not assert his own "final" goals or values (except perhaps negatively by declining to assist in implementing certain policies).[8]

Quite apart from the admission that it is, after all, acceptable for scholars to try to influence "final" goals negatively (logically no different a matter from trying to do so "positively"), the authors recognize that policy scientists can legitimately engage in goal manipulation—it all depends on the level of the goal.

All of this might lead one to suggest that no policy-relevant work is desirable within the academic community, but barring scholars from a discussion of both ends and means places restrictions on the academic enterprise that are disturbingly broad, and that bear no correspondence with actual academic practice—past, present, or, in all likelihood, future. The sensible conclusion, it seems, is to place no constraints whatsoever on what the social sciences can properly concern themselves with. This does not eliminate the possibility that work with a policy orientation may fall short of certain ideals of scientific inquiry. Consciously or not, scholars in this area may be found to interpret facts in light of values, or to twist analyses to encourage acceptance of objectives. How much of a problem this is apt to be, and whether such problems are proper to policy-relevant work or are shared by scholarship of a less applied sort, will be further discussed elsewhere in this volume.

## The Issue of Peer Evaluation

Another argument against work that seeks to inform policy is that such work may vest power to evaluate scholarship in the hands of people other than academic peers, threatening, again, the epistemological integrity of the social sciences, which have, in fact, been criticized for failing to ignore the political and ideological fads that engage parts of the lay public.[9] By contrast, in recent times the natural sciences have staunchly resisted evaluation of any sort other than peer review, a steadfastness deemed crucial to their record of achievement. By "speaking truth to power," it might be argued, scholars respond to the concerns of either the lay public, or policymakers, or both, implicitly agreeing to allow these segments of society to judge the quality of their contributions, and impeding the growth of innovative and empirically verifiable knowledge.[10] The risks may seem substantial, but the issue is not clear-cut: it all depends on which aspect of the scientific product is externally evaluated.

It is unacceptable to place the authority to evaluate scholarship's epistemological merit in any hands other than those of scientific peers, since such merit can be judged only according to the canons of scientific inquiry, and only by those who have mastered and accepted these canons. This much is beyond debate, but it does not exhaust the issue, since the purpose of scientific inquiry cannot be reduced merely to a demonstration of epistemological virtue. Its ultimate mission is to answer meaningful questions about the natural or social world, and any judgment on the value of a scholarly product must, in addition to epistemological considerations, be concerned with the significance of the questions it addresses. This significance may, of course, be grounded in the applications to which the new knowledge can be put, but it may have nothing to do with practical considerations. According to sociologist Scott Greer, three sorts of problems, or questions, typically engage the attention of social scientists,[11] and the appropriate judges of the importance of the issues addressed may depend on the category of question involved.

A first category involves policy issues, that is, social problems to which some practical urgency attaches — practical because the problem is, in principle, amenable to solution; urgency because some segments of society at least care that it should be resolved sooner rather than later, while the extent of the perceived urgency is an approximate measure of the value that is placed on finding a solution to the problem. The second category of problems are those of general social philosophy, originating from a need to conceive of social existence in terms of a meaningful system of institutions and relations, and to harmonize that philosophical cognition with actual experience. Here, scholarly problems usually originate from a discrepancy between accepted worldviews and actual evidence. The purpose of the inquiry, then, is to resolve this cognitive dissonance, either by integrating the new evidence or new ideas within the existing frame of reference, or by creating a new, more satisfactory frame of intellectual reference. The third class of problems consists of those intrinsic to developing scientific disciplines. These involve the internal consistency of scientific theories, as well as their match with observable evidence; consequently, the problems to be resolved, under this heading, stem from challenges to the validity of existing theories or to their empirical accuracy.

These categories are not mutually exclusive, and some combinations of all three may drive an individual scholar, or even an entire disciplinary research program — but any one of them can lend significance to scholarly inquiry. For present purposes, it is important that the appropriate judges of the importance of the questions addressed by scholarship may vary according to the category of question involved.

The third class of issues — problems intrinsic to developing scientific disciplines — is rarely recognized outside the scholarly community, and the scientific importance of the questions addressed cannot easily be judged by those who have not mastered the requisite theories and who lack the training needed to interpret the implications of relevant evidence. Consequently, the importance of this sort of scholarship typically must be judged internally, by the peers of those conducting the inquiries. But the same conclusion does not to apply to the other two classes of problems.

To begin with, scholars are not the only acceptable judges of the importance of the issues of general social philosophy they choose to address. Gaps between social and political worldviews and actual practice may be recognized at various levels of society, and such awareness can be as meaningfully rooted in the daily experience of ordinary citizens as in the academically sanctioned writings of professional social scientists. By the same token, many, though not all, segments of the lay public can evaluate the success of intellectual efforts at resolving the gaps. This is to say not that anyone could produce a satisfactory resolution of such discrepancies, but that many people other than the peer reference groups can form a reasonable opinion of the value of scholarly efforts of this sort. Consequently, it is hard to justify a determination to exclude nonpeers from evaluating the importance of social scientific attempt to deal with problems of general social philosophy — even if they cannot say much about their epistemological merits.

This also applies to the first of Greer's three categories of problems addressed by social scientists — those relevant to policy. It is hard to believe that the only, or even the most appropriate, judges of the practical urgency of policy issues are to be found in the scholarly community. It could be argued that those who stand to be affected by a policy are in approximately as good a position to estimate the urgency of the problems it addresses, and that, consequently, segments of the lay public may legitimately judge the practical value of the scholarly effort, assuming it is epistemologically sound. It could further be argued that those who are charged with implementing a policy — that is, the society's policy-makers — are apt to have a pretty good idea of the feasibility and implications of possible solutions, at least as good an idea as most professional academics. Under the circumstances, it is reasonable to open the process of assessing the value of policy-related inquiries undertaken by social scientists to members of nonpeer groups.

In any case, the example of the natural sciences does not provide a satisfactory parallel with regard to the role of nonpeer groups. The closest analogues to policy-related questions within the natural sciences would be those involving the technological implementation of knowledge produced by basic science. While some members of the lay public may be in a position to estimate the value of such applications, very few could judge the feasibility of developments that lead from scientific principles to practical applications; in most cases, only engineers and technicians are capable of forming valid opinions in this regard.

Although there may be limited similarities between policy and technology, analogies between the social and natural sciences break down completely where other categories of issues are concerned. If it is possible, within the social sciences, to speak separately of general problems of social philosophy and of the substantive problems intrinsic to developing scientific disciplines, this is because there is assumed to be a class of theoretical questions validly addressed by both scholars and nonscholars, and another falling within the latter's exclusive province. While this may be an appropriate view, it is hard to find a parallel in the natural sciences — where virtually all theoretical matters, because of the highly specialized conceptual foundation and intellectual tools involved, are within the domain of none but those who have mastered them professionally. Consequently, it is understandable that the scope for nonpeer evaluation should be much more restricted in the natural than in the social sciences — with regard to the *importance,* as well as the soundness, of scholarship.

Thus, as long as primarily epistemological matters are not involved, a concern that policy-relevant scholarship will be impaired through the intrusion of nonpeer evaluation is an overblown concern. The only remaining worry is that epistemological questions themselves may come to be resolved on nonscientific grounds, an issue that will be further discussed in the following essay.

In any case, our sentiments about policy-relevant scholarship may vary somewhat according to the precise manner in which relevance is conceived. Accordingly, we require a brief overview (to be expanded later in this volume) of the various ways in which relevance may be conceived in the field of international relations.

### Forms of Policy Relevance

Like pure theory and research, policy-relevant work can concern itself either with the process or the substance of policy. Process theory aims to further the quality of policy-making in general, not to attain specific policy outcomes. For example, Alexander George, in *Presidential Decisionmaking in Foreign Policy: The Effective Use of Information and Advice,*[12] links certain deficiencies in the policy-making process to distortions in the flow of pertinent information within the policy-making body, and he examines ways of organizing the process so as to minimize such distortions and improve the quality of policy analysis and decision. Another example is provided by Philip Zelikow in "Foreign Policy Engineering," in which he identifies the components of "policy engineering": the business of establishing links between the ends and means of policy. A condition for making policy more effective is to recognize the major phases of that process and the informational needs that are proper to each. His contribution is to devise a schema that makes this apparent.[13]

Process theory is clearly relevant, and those whose contributions lie in that area do work that is both interesting and valuable, but the focus of this volume is on the purposes rather than the mechanics of foreign policy-making. Consequently, our principal concern is with *substantive* theory, by which we mean issue-specific theory, which identifies the casual forces behind classes of outcomes surrounding the issue of interest. Its goal is to provide general propositions about the relation between variables that have a bearing on desired outcomes, so that, as long as appropriate initial conditions are identified in concrete applications, policymakers are given guides to action that are superior to the trial and error of experience, to dubious historical analogies, or to simple bureaucratic habit.

The question, then, is, How can substantive theory be policy relevant? While the question will be addressed in somewhat greater detail in the following essay, knowledge can be said to be policy-relevant if it establishes the range of possibilities for policy and/or identifies the consequences of various courses of action. Thus, the forms of policy relevance depend on which of these two functions is being addressed.

*The range of possibilities.* Two mutually compatible levels of relevant scholarship can be identified. The first establishes *instrumental* relations describing the link between contemplated policies and desired outcomes. Instrumental relations need not be offered in a simple bivariate form; ideally, they would specify the qualifying conditions (ceteris paribus) that mediate the link between policy and outcome. The second form of relevance, within this category, establishes the broader *context* within which the instrumental relations operate. This may be done by identifying the conditions that shape the status of the policy instruments (e.g., are they, in fact, available?) and of the pertinent ceteris paribus conditions. In other words, these variables are treated as endogenous to the theoretical system when contextual relations are established, while instrumental relations view them as exogenous. The context of policy can also be clarified via predictive knowledge, to the extent that it helps anticipate the future status of policy instruments, or that it provides an ability to anticipate the policy objectives that will be pursued in the future.

*The consequences of choice.* In addition to knowing what can be attained and how, it is necessary to be aware of the impact one's policies are apt to have on needs and objectives other than that which is the policy's proximate purpose. Most policies involve direct costs occasioned in producing the policy and usually (though not always) expressed in monetary terms. In addition, policies can imply a range of secondary costs, often in the form of opportunities forgone because of the policy, and sometimes as a consequence of attaining (rather than simply pursuing) the policy's primary objective. Any light shed by scholarship on either direct or secondary costs should encourage a more informed pursuit of the national interest via instruments of foreign policy.

Thus, policy relevance is a broader concept than its most obvious, instrumental form alone would suggest. Because of this, any discussion of the promises and pitfalls of a policy science within the field of international relations must cast a correspondingly wide net; and so we will examine the issue from a variety of perspectives.

## The Volume's Structure

**Theory of Relevance.** The volume's first part is divided into two sections. The first, "Relevance and the Ivory Tower," discusses the desirability of, and possibilities for, relevant knowledge. The second section,

"Relevance and the Corridors of Power," illustrates the sorts of substantive scholarship that may help illuminate the range of possibilities and the consequences of choice.

*Relevance and the Ivory Tower.*   The essay entitled "Policy Relevance and Theoretical Development: The Terms of the Trade-off" discusses the consequences for international relations theory of asking that it should be useful to policy. Assuming, as was done in this introduction, that policy relevance does no necessary violence to the proper relationship between academia and society, the next question is whether it impairs scholarship's ultimate responsibilities to itself. Since explanatory theory is the ultimate aim of science, the issue boils down to the consequences of relevance for the field's ability to produce such theories. The essay distinguishes an explanatory theory's *soundness* (in an epistemological sense) from its *value* (the desirability of explaining that which the theory purports to explain). After further articulating the various forms that relevance can assume, it inquires if and how they could impair either of these two properties. The essay concludes that policy relevance is much less likely to undermine the quality of theory, in terms of either soundness or value, than is often assumed.

Arthur Stein's "Counselors, Kings, and International Relations: From Revelation to Reason, and Still No Policy-Relevant Theory" asks why there has been so little effort to generate theoretical knowledge with applications to international relations and foreign policy. Both the discipline's professional structure and the nature of the subject matter would have led one to expect that such theory should be plentiful. According to Stein's introspective essay, the explanation is multifold. Partly, it is to be found in what he deems the field's devotion to faddishness, which discourages theoretical development of any kind, whether relevant or not. Partly, it stems from the fact that many scholars study nonmalleable variables, resulting in findings of limited use to decision makers. They also emphasize the casual forces behind outcomes, rather than the consequences that the outcomes themselves produce, leaving policymakers with little grasp of the aftermath of various courses of action. Academics also often shrink from articulating the policy implications of their own findings, if these findings are not politically palatable, and they allow their preferences to shape academic discourse on matter of policy (decreasing their credibility with government officials). Despite these problems, Stein anticipates that relevant knowledge will continue to develop, along with the growth of the field of international relations.

In "Scholars and Statesmen: Framework for a Productive Dialogue," Joseph Lepgold discusses the circumstances accounting for the communications gap between scholars and policymakers, and the ways in which it could be bridged using existing professional networks and institutions. The aim is to build an ability to analyze the strategic context facing policymakers, and to do so accurately enough to help them sort through competing causal claims. He distinguishes several types and levels of theory with regard to their ability to promote this goal.

*Relevance and the Corridors of Power.*    The two essays in this section each address the prospects for policy-relevant knowledge, as the issue is viewed by policymakers. The essays are from two scholars who have occupied senior positions in the nation's foreign policy apparatus, and who discuss the practical issues involved in conveying academic knowledge to Washington, D.C.

Ernest Wilson, whose background includes a position on President Clinton's National Security Council staff and directorship of the policy-planning office at the U.S. Information Agency, identifies, in "How Social Science Can Help Policymakers: The Relevance of Theory," the kinds of knowledge that government officials are most eager to have. He points out that the great bulk of foreign policy activity includes not major changes to the existing attitudes toward other nations, but "modest adjustment to current standard operating procedures to meet slightly new conditions." Under the circumstances, he distinguishes four major categories of academic knowledge that policymakers desire, and he discusses the likelihood that various levels of theory would, in fact, produce the requisite types of knowledge.

Bruce Jentleson, who, in addition to a prolific record of scholarly publication, has served in a senior capacity on the State Department's policy-planning staff, provides specific illustrations of the manner in which theoretical knowledge was used in the policy process. His contribution, "In Pursuit of Praxis: Applying International Relations Theory to Foreign Policy-Making," examines two case studies of efforts at bridging the theory-policy gap, both observed during his tenure at the State Department. The first deals with the Clinton administration's efforts at defining an overarching post–Cold War paradigm for international relations based, partly at least, on theoretical propositions about international peace and cooperation. The second involves the Middle East Multilateral Arms Control and Regional Security negotiations (an attempt to establish what scholars call an "international security regime"). He discusses the link between the explicit theories of academics and the implicit theories that often guide the thinking of practitioners, and he examines ways of linking the two.

The essays within part 1, in addition to the introductory essay, provide theoretical prisms through which to consider the issue of policy relevance, and some background for thinking about the practical obstacles, from the demand side, of rendering scholarship usable to those who are in a position to act on it. Ultimately, however, most of the answers to questions about the feasibility of relevance must be provided by the body of substantive knowledge that the field is capable of producing, and the second part of this book, "The Relevance of Theory," provides a sampling of suggestions in this regard.

**The Relevance of Theory.**   Few of the contributions in the second part seek to provide specific policy prescriptions, attempting instead to shed light on the sorts of considerations to which policymakers must be attentive. For the most part, the essays direct attention to the nonobvious, and in some cases neglected, areas of political sciences from which useful insights may be drawn. Even where insights are of a reasonably apparent nature, the specific manner in which they can be applied may not have occurred to the reader, and most probably not to the policy-making community. This part is organized around three sections.

The essays in "The Relevance of the Domestic Context" discuss the ability of theories that deal with the internal setting of foreign policy to provide decision makers with a sense of what domestic policies would allow. In "Domestic Political Consequences of the Cold War's End," Robert Lieber explains how the scope and direction of U.S. foreign policy is constrained by national political conditions. In turn, the domestic setting is shaped by the international system (the "second image reversed"), especially the character of foreign threats. The more clearly this interaction is understood by decision makers, the firmer is their grasp of the contours of domestically permissible foreign policy. In this case, the Cold War's demise has fostered the reassertion of the Madisonian features of U.S. democracy and its associated limitations on strongly centralized political authority. Lieber draws parallels with the aftermath of the Civil War and the end of the World War I, and he suggests certain implications for the conduct of U.S. foreign policy.

In "Putting Theory to Work," Eric Larson of RAND examines how theories of public opinion, in which political science has invested much, may inform the choices of decision makers, Larson's model — approximating an ideal of "rational" public behavior — identifies the domestic political constraints, in the form of varying levels of public support, on U.S. military intervention abroad. By providing a model of the determinants of popular support for intervention, illustrated with evidence on the peacekeeping operation in Bosnia and capable of assessing the robustness of public support to worse-than-expected

outcomes, he demonstrates that theory can be used as a valuable diagnostic tool. He also demonstrates that the model could be generalized
to other, more costly, interventions.

The next section, "The Relevance of Related Approaches," turns
to specialized fields of political science for suggestions that might be
policy-relevant to international relations. Donald Rothchild, who has
produced some of the best scholarship on diagnosing and resolving ethnic conflict in Africa, applies some of his insights to the problems of
international conflict, in "Ethnic Fears and Security Dilemmas." The
parallel between the security dilemma of nationalities within "soft,"
multiethnic states and that experienced by nation-states in the quasi
anarchy of the international system means that a better understanding of
the former yields an improved grasp of the latter. Moreover, the external spillover effects of ethnic conflict imply that more effective approaches to interethnic conflict resolution also help mitigate its international ramifications. Rothchild examines the implications of his analysis
for U.S. policies aimed at addressing both the internal and external
consequences of interethnic conflict.

A frequent task of policy-making is to keep definitions of policy
objectives, estimates of their costs, and notions of appropriate tools in
harmony with the evolving technological context of their pursuit. The
challenge may be especially great for national security policy, given the
dependence on rapidly evolving technologies. Projected transformations
in U.S. conventional force posture to accommodate a whole new generation of systems, based largely on state-of-the-art information technology,
promises to change the nature of warfare — possibly leading to war goals
defined by the imposition of paralysis, rather than pain, on enemies.
Referred to as the revolution in military affairs (RMA), this transformation has so far claimed the attention of few political scientists. Emily
Goldman, in the essay "Military Diffusion, the Information Revolution,
and U.S. Power," relies on propositions from organizational theory to
examine some of the consequences of the RMA, especially assuming a
significant international diffusion of its innovations, for the future conduct of U.S. foreign and defense policy. In this way, she demonstrates how
anticipatory thinking based on tools of empirical social science can provide a road map for thinking about the consequences of policy.

In earlier times, reference to geographical context provided much
that was considered important to gauging the scope of any nation's
opportunities in world politics. Nevertheless, spatial variables central
to the work of such scholars as Halford MacKinder, Nicholas Spyk-
man, and Harold and Margaret Sprout have occupied few contemporary analysts. A belief that geography has been made irrelevant by the

reach of modern weaponry, the computerization of international securities markets, the ease of communication, and the speed of travel has led to a virtual eclipse of geopolitical approaches to international relations. Nevertheless, Donna J. Nincic argues, in "From Sea-Lanes to Global Cities: The Policy Relevance of Political Geography," that the discipline's ability to account for the international context of foreign policy-making would benefit from greater attention to spatial considerations. As an illustration, she shows how an emphasis on the earth's physical contours highlights the importance of major sea-lanes of communication (SLOCs) to U.S. national security. At the same time, a concern with a nation's control of its geographic space lends a clearer interpretation to the emergence of the world city as a key actor in the global political economy, one that nations cannot deal with via traditional policy approaches.

The last section of part 2, "The Relevance of Rationality," contains two contributions that search for relevance within one of the most influential (and at the same time most controversial)[14] approaches to the study of political life. This approach is based on the assumption that political actors are guided by principles of rationality, defined as in microeconomic theory by an inclination to maximize expected utility. These two essays illustrate the approach's potential as a source of predictive and other insights into the dynamics of international conflict and negotiation. It may help interacting policymakers draw the logical implications of the assumptions they make about each other's behavior.

Possibly the most developed framework for the study of political interaction within the context of this approach is furnished by game theory, one of whose most eminent exponents within political science is Steven Brams of New York University. In his essay with Jeffrey Togman, "Agreement through Threats: The Northern Ireland Case," we are given a heuristically valuable insight into the nature, and possible future, of the Northern Ireland conflict, based on an application of the theory of moves (TOM), a variant of game theory developed largely by Brams.[15] The conflict over Northern Ireland between Great Britain and Sinn Féin/Irish Republican Army (IRA) is analyzed as a $2 \times 2$ game. The unique Nash equilibrium is shown not to predict recent behavior of the Sinn Féin/IRA; rather, its moves are consistent with an assertion of its threat power, according to TOM. They show how game theory and TOM can shed light on the possible paths to peace and the obstacles that may be encountered. In turn, this can help decision makers predict the dynamics of conflicts and the possibilities of resolution.

Kenneth Organski, employing a political forecasting model successfully used in analogous applications by Bruce Bueno de Mesquita and others,[16] seeks to forecast the course of negotiation on the future of Jerusalem. His essay, "The Outcome of the Negotiations over the Status of Jerusalem," describes his attempt to predict, in 1995, what would have been the results of secret negotiations between the Palestinian National Authority and the Rabin administration over the final status of Jerusalem. Although Rabin's assassination made it impossible to verify the predictions, subsequent revelations concerning the talks demonstrated that Organski's prediction, while perhaps surprising, was very close to the mark. In turn, this strengthens the case for expected-utility models as diagnostic tools, designed to anticipate the outcome of processes of interactive decision making.

In a concluding essay to the volume, entitled "Policy Relevance and Theoretical Development in International Relations: What Have We Learned?" Joseph Lepgold summarizes the suggestions and insights offered in this book. He evaluates how far it has led us toward a goal of useful, as well as epistemologically sound, knowledge, indicating what further obstacles must be overcome on this path and suggesting ways in which this may be achieved.

NOTES

1. Karl W. Deutsch, *Politics and Government* (Boston: Houghton Mifflin, 1974), 7.

2. Eugene J. Meehan, *The Foundations of Political Analysis: Empirical and Normative* (Homewood, Ill.: Dorsey Press, 1971), 244.

3. Charles E. Lindblom and David K. Cohen, *Usable Knowledge* (New Haven: Yale University Press, 1962), 11.

4. Michael Root, *Philosophy of Social Science* (Oxford: Blackwell, 1993), especially chapter 1.

5. Quoted in Root, *Philosophy of Social Science,* 16.

6. "Scientific Method and the Moral Sciences," in *Selected Writings* (University of Chicago Press, 1964), 256.

7. "Theory for Policy in International Relations," *Policy Sciences,* December 1973.

8. George and Smoke, "Theory for Policy," 619.

9. For example, Joseph Ben David, *Scientific Growth* (Berkeley: University of California Press, 1991), 365–85.

10. Joseph Ben David, "Innovations and Their Recognition in Social Science," *History of Political Economy* 7, 4 (1975): 434–55.

11. Scott Greer, *The Logic of Social Inquiry* (Chicago: Aldine, 1969).

12. Boulder: Westview, 1980.

13. Philip Zelikow, "Foreign Policy Engineering: From Theory to Practice and Back Again," *International Security,* spring 1994: 143–71.

14. For a good overview of some of the issues and arguments, see Jeffrey

Friedman, ed., *The Rational Choice Controversy* (New Haven: Yale University Press, 1996).

15. Steven J. Brams, *Theory of Moves* (Cambridge: Cambridge University Press, 1994).

16. Bruce Bueno de Mesquita, "Political Forecasting: An Unexpected Utility Model," in Bruce Bueno de Mesquita and Frans H. Stokman, eds., *European Community Decision Making: Models, Applications, and Comparisons* (New Haven: Yale University Press, 1994).

# Part 1
# Theory of Relevance
## A. Relevance and the Ivory Tower

# Policy Relevance and Theoretical Development: The Terms of the Trade-off

*Miroslav Nincic*

## I. The Source of Concern

Knowledge is policy-relevant if it clarifies the range of choices available for the attainment of policy objectives, as well as the consequences of opting for certain policies rather than others, so that implications for the attainment of desired outcomes can be drawn. Some scholars feel that the major mission of the study of international relations is, precisely, to chart the paths to a better world. One author estimates that "many, perhaps most, international relations theorists are motivated by a desire to improve the working of the international system, judged by many to be poor . . . there is a long-run desire to understand the system in order to improve policy."[1]

At the same time, much interesting and valuable knowledge has no direct and immediately discernible bearing on policy objectives, and by no means everyone agrees that the explicit pursuit of policy relevance is a desirable academic endeavor. In one view,

> it would be tragic if International Relations, having fought so long to establish itself as a serious, indeed indispensable, area of scholarly enquiry, should at the very point of success throw it away through an inability to resist the siren song of policy relevance.[2]

The preference from this perspective is for basic theory, whose purpose is the creation of knowledge as an end in itself, independent of the uses to which it might be put. Objections sometimes spring from a concern that relevance may place science at the service of political and partisan interests, twisting knowledge to conform to unscientific ends. A mild form of this fear is that "once there are external influences on the choice of problems (and hence of results) the 'objectivity' of science loses an important dimension."[3] Even if the academic enterprise were not to be thus corrupted, it is often feared that the growth of knowledge may be hobbled by the stifling consequences of pragmatic agendas. Hans Morgenthau, for instance, questioned "whether scientific creativity can flourish if the scientific mind is tied to a practical purpose extraneous to itself, and is thereby deprived of the uncommitted speculative curiosity from which great scientific discoveries of the past have flourished."[4]

These are considerable issues, and questions regarding the role of knowledge and the interplay between the pure and the applied must be addressed. Accordingly, I will inquire whether the pursuit of relevance is, in fact, detrimental to the growth of knowledge, specifically to the development of sound theoretical thinking about international relations and foreign policy.

I will deal with policy-relevant theory (PRT), which is distinct both from what might be called idiographic policy analysis (IPA) and from basic theory (BT). IPA, often found in such journals as *Foreign Affairs* and *Foreign Policy,* generally attempts to specify the circumstances that may produce specific policy outcomes, such as, for example, a political arrangement between Israel and the Palestinians, or the success of a particular set of international trade negotiations. It seeks to provide as full a picture as possible of the circumstances surrounding some policy challenge, as well as informed speculation about the consequences of hypothetical courses of action. It may, but need not, encourage a given course of action. IPA is often both valuable and sophisticated, but it focuses on the singular, and while it may invoke generalizations as part of its explanatory effort, it rarely aims to produce any — its focus being confined to the case at hand. By contrast, PRT seeks to produce general propositions involving relations between categories of phenomena and with a bearing on *classes* of policy outcomes. The relation between PRT and IPA is that the former may produce the generalizations that policy analysis relies upon, while the latter may provide empirical foundations for these generalizations. BT, like PRT, seeks to produce general propositions about international relations, but the former does so with no reference to their potential applications. Accordingly, the difference between the two is neither one of level nor, necessarily, one of method — merely one of purpose.

Although PRT has not been the dominant part of the field of international relations, it does account for a significant portion of the efforts in the field, and illustrations are not hard to find. Alexander George and Richard Smoke's *Deterrence in American Foreign Policy*[5] derives, on the basis of intensive case studies, the requisites for the deterrence of limited conflict, and it draws the appropriate implications for the practice of extended deterrence by the United States. Joseph Nye's *Bound to Lead*,[6] analyzing the foundations of national power, articulating the evolving forms of international interdependence, and drawing implications for the international role of the United States, provides an illustration of policy-relevant theorizing. A recent article by David Lake and Donald Rothchild,[7] explaining the bases for ethnic violence, the associated development of security dilemmas, and the implications for an international role with regard to such conflicts, is another example. Most of the work on the theory of nuclear deterrence produced between the late 1950s and early 1980s furnishes further instances of this type of work. Other examples readily suggest themselves.

One reason why PRT has not been more central to academic work is linked to the concern that the pursuit of policy relevance may harm the growth of empirical knowledge, of which theory is in many ways the foundation. Because of this, we must ask whether the development and quality of theory in international relations might suffer from an attempt to have it provide guidance for practical policy. A starting point is to define what we mean by a theory, and to discuss how its quality should be evaluated. Having discussed what is implied by the notion of a good theory, I will examine the ways in which it can be made policy-relevant. On this foundation I will then inquire whether relevance must exact a price in terms of theoretical quality.

## II.  The Measure of a Desirable Theory

Theory is a set of general propositions about the same subject, connected by relations of conjunction and implication, that, by imbedding knowledge in a meaningful structure, allows relevant properties of that subject to be explained and predicted.[8] While there are many conceptions of the items that should be placed on a scorecard of theoretical worth, no consensus defines a common set, particularly not in the social sciences.[9] Nevertheless, I will not stray too far from most perspectives by suggesting that the desirability of theory can be judged at two levels.

We may begin by asking how well it discharges its missions of explanation and prediction. A theory constructed to do well in this regard will generally conform to the internal canons of scientific inquiry—to the extent that it does, it may be considered a *sound* theory. Beyond that, we may ask, How *valuable* is the theory's contribution to knowledge? This question has both a qualitative and a quantitative aspect, for a valuable theory could be one that (a) accounts for many phenomena or (b) accounts for few but very important phenomena. A theory that does neither cannot be considered valuable, no matter how sound it is. At the same time, it is unlikely that an unsound theory could be particularly valuable, except in a limited, heuristic sense. Accordingly, soundness is a necessary but insufficient condition for value, while the latter has no necessary relation to the former.

## Sound Theories

Since a sound theory is one that competently discharges its mission of explaining and predicting, an examination of soundness must begin with a discussion of these two functions. There is little controversy about the meaning of prediction: it is the business of anticipating a future condition, by establishing a link between it and an antecedent condition.[10] The antecedent condition may be as simple as a prior value of the property that is being predicted, or it may involve a complex pattern of multivariate causation, but the meaning of prediction remains relatively uncontroversial.[11] The relation between explanation and prediction is more complex, as are their respective places in empirical theory. The logical structure of the two may be quite similar, but this is not necessarily the case, since prediction need not assume prior explanation. For example, the ability of ancient astronomers to anticipate the movement of celestial bodies far outstripped their ability to explain why these movements occurred as they did. With regard to everyday experience, most people could predict that speaking on one end of an open telephone line would result in their words being reproduced at the other end, while lacking a grasp of the processes involved. Of the two, therefore, explanation tends to be the more demanding task and, by extension, the more ambitious scientific achievement.

Although explanation remains an elusive concept, it is adequately captured by the dominant, nomological-deductive[12] view, the concrete expression of which depends on whether the question answered by the explanation implies a singular empirical statement (e.g., "Why do Britain and France never wage war against one another?") or an empirical generalization ("Why do democracies never fight?"). Explaining a singular statement requires that it be identified as a specific instance of a general proposition. Here, the argument that explains the statement needs, among its premises, at least one generalization (G), or "covering law," and at least one singular statement (I), specifying an initial condition. From these, the singular statement or conclusion (C) that we seek to explain is inferred. For example:

Democracies never fight each other (G)
Britain and France are democracies (I)                    (1)
_____
Britain and France never fight each other (C)

If the word *cause* must be part of our notion of explanation, we may say that the cause of our conclusion is provided by the initial condition, given the operation of the covering law (Britain and France don't fight each other because they are democracies, whereas democracies never fight each other). Explaining singular statements is the business of IPA, which, while resorting (explicitly or implicitly) to generalizations in the form of covering laws, seeks to articulate a catalog of pertinent initial conditions and to draw the policy-relevant conclusions that are implied. By contrast, PRT's mission is to provide the generalizations that serve as the covering laws for the explanations and recommendations that IPA offers.

General propositions can be produced in two fundamental ways. Sometimes, a general proposition can be explained in terms of a covering law of an even higher degree of generality, as well as at least one antecedent condition of a similar level of generality, in which case this is simply an extension of the previous explanatory model. For example:

Governments responsive to public opinion do not fight other
governments so responsive (G)
Democratic governments are responsive to public opinion (I)    (2)
_____
Democratic governments do not fight each other (C)

Sometimes, however, the generalization will be explained without recourse to an initial condition, on the basis of two or more generalizations that constitute the premises of the argument producing this generalization as a conclusion. This is a purely logical argument of the form

Democracies must comply with public opinion (G1)
Democratic public opinion disapproves of war against
democracies (G2)                                              (3)
_____
Democracies don't fight each other (C1)

Here, no initial condition is needed, and the cause is provided by the conjunction of the two premises (democracies don't fight each other because, as democracies, they must comply with popular preferences, whereas public opinion disapproves of fighting other democracies).

Thus, whether a singular or general statement is to be explained, explanation requires theoretical generalizations, and these are, precisely, the defining components of theory. It is also apparent how a prediction differs from an explanation. Aside from the fact that prediction (unlike explanation) involves some reference to the time of the assertions contained in the premises, explanation rests on at least one theoretical generalization linking an antecedent and consequent condition, while prediction requires, in principle, no more than the observation of some empirical regularity (France and Britain will not fight each other because, since the Napoleonic wars, they have never done so; my voice will be reproduced at the other end of the telephone line because this has always been the case, for me and everybody I know).

While an ability to predict says little about a capacity to explain, the obverse rarely applies: in the vast majority of cases, we are well placed to predict that which we are in a position to explain. This is true of the examples above, and it is far easier to find instances confirming the rule than disconfirming it. Of course, if we have been able successfully to predict an outcome on the basis of some theoretical generalization, we then have excellent grounds for believing that this generalization is, indeed, a proper basis for the explanation. The bottom line is that, while even prediction alone may be very useful, a theory that allows no more than this is a comparatively modest accomplishment (no matter how sophisticated the analytical tools that are marshaled for this purpose), while the production of generalizations capable of explaining is a more ambitious and valuable attainment.[13] Because of this, and while predictive power alone may characterize an adequate theory, the measure of a superior theory is its ability to *explain* classes of phenomena that we have some reason to care about. Accordingly, I am adopting a conception of theoretical purpose that is closer to the "realist"[14] than to the "instrumentalist" position in the philosophy of science.[15]

Although explanatory ability, like the aptness to predict, could be judged in a case-by-case, post hoc manner, it would be far better if a theory's soundness could be determined ex ante, on the basis of its intrinsic attributes. In these terms, and while there is room for debate around the edges, two key attributes stand behind a theory's explanatory ability: (1) the truth of its premises (are they empirically correct?); (2) its completeness (in the sense that no propositions crucial to the task of explanation are missing). While it seems sensible that explanatory arguments based on general propositions should involve true propositions, and that no important premises should be left out of the argument, both requirements require further discussion.

*True generalizations.*    Truth, at least from the perspective of the "corre-spondence theory"[16] of truth, refers to the coherence between an idea (in our case in the form of a premise) and observable data, but the implications of a requirement that the premises of theoretical arguments should be true depend, to some extent, on whether the argument behind the theory is deductive or inductive. Although an inductive argument is sometimes thought of as one that moves from the specific to the general, while a deductive argument proceeds from general premises, this is not a strictly accurate basis for distinguishing between the two (except, for example, in the case of induction by enumeration). From the point of view of formal logic the distinction is simply this: a deductive argument is one whose premises fully support its conclusion, while the premises of an inductive argument support the conclusion, but less than fully.[17] A mathematical derivation is, for example, a deductive argument; most reasoning by analogy, as well as most statistical arguments, are examples of inductive arguments.

If the premises of a deductive argument are true, then as long as the argument is logically valid (e.g., a valid syllogism) the conclusion is implied by logical necessity. In other words, in a valid deductive argu-ment, true premises necessarily imply a true conclusion; but the con-verse does not apply, for a deductive argument containing one or more false premises may, nevertheless, produce a true conclusion. For exam-ple: all left-handers are Republicans; Newt Gingrich is left-handed; therefore, Newt Gingrich is a Republican. From a deductive point of view, this argument is perfectly valid, and the conclusion is undeniably true; nevertheless, both of its premises are false. The problem is that there is nothing in the process of deduction itself that can tell us whether a true conclusion was produced by false premises — a situation that is obviously perilous to explanatory endeavors.

With regard to our discussion of the respective merits of prediction and explanation, we should consider the argument occasionally made by social scientists of a deductive bent — which often invokes in its support Milton Friedman's much-quoted article on "The Methodology of Posi-tive Economics,"[18] according to which the value of a theory is deter-mined by how useful it is at predicting certain outcomes, whether or not the assumptions behind the successful predictions are correct. Since, as we have seen, it is logically possible for false assumptions to yield accu-rate predictions, the statement is not completely indefensible, but two observations impose themselves. The first is that it is much more likely that an accurate prediction would be produced by a valid argument based on true premises than by one incorporating false premises, since the latter's truth could be merely coincidental. Because of this, attentiveness to the accuracy of one's assumptions is likely to enhance the quality of one's predictions. The second observation is that, even though false premises may coincidentally yield correct predictions, they certainly provide no basis for *explaining* the outcomes they seek to predict and must be viewed as a less ambitious achievement than arguments that, proceeding from true premises, provide both an explanation and a prediction of some relevant outcome.

The premises of an inductive argument typically involve statements that are, explicitly or implicitly, conditional or probabilistic. Accordingly, and unlike the deductive case, true premises need not produce true conclusions in an inductive argument — all that can be said here is that true premises are more likely to yield true conclusions, and vice versa, although rigorous statistical research methods will often give us a reasonably good idea of the probability that our conclusions are, in fact, true. Thus, while we cannot be sure that true premises lead to true conclusions, we may less often be led to true conclusions by false premises; and our ability to both explain and predict, on the basis of generalizations inductively produced, becomes a matter of degree.

Whether primarily deductive or inductive, the explanatory value of the theory benefits from true premises: in the deductive case, it ensures a true conclusion; in the inductive case, it makes it much more likely. Under the circumstances, the empirical correctness of the premises of a theoretical argument are an important condition of the theory's ability to do an adequate explanatory job.

*Theoretical completeness.*    A complete theory is one that omits no general propositions necessary to explain the phenomenon it addresses. Nevertheless, the pursuit of completeness requires careful judgment. In international relations, as elsewhere in the social sciences, consequences rarely possess a single cause or lack secondary effects; and, in a world of intricate causal patterns and multiple layers of implication, boundaries tracing perfectly complete theories can rarely be drawn. Moreover, as parsimony, or the dismissal of considerations that are extraneous or barely apposite, is equally a measure of good theory, the typical strategy is to stay well within these hypothetical boundaries.

With these caveats in mind, it is desirable that theories should have no debilitating gaps. Full explanations are obviously preferable to partial explanations, and the predictions they yield are correspondingly more accurate. Thus, for example, if the probability of peace between two countries does not wholly hinge on their domestic political arrangements, but is also affected by the extent of their economic interdependence and their relations with third parties, then a theory focusing exclusively on the first circumstance would be glaringly incomplete. Explanatory incompleteness can assume two forms. The omitted influence may have a bearing on the phenomenon to be explained while, at the same time, being unrelated to other influences with a similar bearing (e.g., in statistical analysis, the case of orthogonality). If so, the explanation will be impoverished by ignoring this influence, but the partial impact of the causal factor(s) encompassed by the theory would not necessarily be biased empirically — it is just that the picture would be incomplete. If, however, the influences included were related to those that were not, even this partial picture could be distorted, for what is attributed to the first may actually be reflecting the operation of the latter. Consequently, and while an elegant theory is preferable to one that is cumbersome, other things being equal, aesthetic appeal cannot be weighed equally with completeness. A sound theory, one that does a good job of explanation and prediction, is likely to be based on true premises and to encompass all pertinent causal propositions.

## Valuable Theories

Because a theory can be both commendably sound and disappointingly banal, it must be evaluated not only in terms of its epistemological virtues but also by the value of the increment in knowledge it seeks to provide. Value, in turn, has both a qualitative and a quantitative dimension, since a theory may be valuable because of (1) the *scope* of the phenomena it accounts for and (2) the *significance* of the phenomena it addresses.

*Theoretical scope.*   A complete theory is one that neglects no significant component of the explanation behind an outcome; a theory of great scope is one from whose premises many implications may be drawn. Theories that correctly account for many phenomena that had previously been poorly understood, or that adumbrate new paths to explanation, are obviously better than those that illuminate a very narrow range of questions, or questions to which we already had satisfactory answers. Accordingly, the theory's scope is a first measure of its value.

This criterion is consistent with Imre Lakatos's dictum that bodies of related theory ("research programs") should be evaluated in terms of how "progressive" or "regressive" they prove to be.[19] In Lakatos's view, theories are rarely rejected because some of their premises appear untenable. Rather, most have a "hard core" of assumptions and hypotheses considered irrefutable, in the sense that they cannot be questioned without opting out of the research program. The hard core is shielded by two sorts of rules. The first (the "negative heuristic") defines this core by specifying which assumptions and hypotheses are unassailable. The second (the "positive heuristic") indicates how the research program may expand and develop, consistent with the hard core's assumptions.

Thus, the research program establishes a "protective belt" of generalizations and assumptions, subject to a range of permissible modifications in light of the evidence. If observational data is at odds with the hard core, the explanation and the remedies are to be found in the protective belt. By adjusting the protective belt, a theory can thus be modified to yield a product that continues to resemble itself, but without some of the problems and inconsistencies of the original theory — permitting it to remain part of the research program, with a family resemblance ensured by the negative heuristic shielding the hard core. For example, Marxism may be considered a research program, one that in many eyes entered a degenerative phase some time ago. As its initial predictions of rising rates of surplus value extracted from labor in response to declining profit rates, and of a correspondingly intensifying class conflict, failed to be vindicated by the early part of the twentieth century, Lenin's *Imperialism*[20] sought to show that profit rates could be maintained without increasing rates of surplus value extraction, by means of imperialist expansion. Additional assumptions thus managed to rescue the essence of Marxist political economy from falsification by events. Political realism can also be considered a research program, whose neorealist variant, as devised by Kenneth Waltz,[21] was intended to develop an additional layer of assumptions (an expanded protective belt) designed to cope with flaws in the classical realism of authors such as Hans J. Morgenthau.[22]

But how far can one go in adapting the protective belt? In other words, when does a theory become too burdened with ad hoc assumptions and exceptional conditions to justify any further fidelity to its basic premises? According to Lakatos, as long as the new assumptions *expand* the range of phenomena that the theory can claim to explain. A research program that continues successfully to account for novel phenomena is a "progressive" program and should be kept alive; one that does not is a "degenerating" program and should be abandoned. Similarly, when two competing research programs are compared within the same field of inquiry, the one that is more progressive — that is, which explains what the other does and then some — is to be preferred. In our case too, and in a related vein, a theory with a wider explanatory reach is to be considered preferable to one with a narrower reach, other attributes being equal.

*Significant theory.*    In addition to conditions of scope, a theory's importance is also defined by what may loosely be termed its *significance:* the
knowledge it provides must be knowledge worth having. For this to be
the case, and as we are dealing with empirical theory, its concepts must
refer to world states that exist or that could exist, and for which an
acceptable operational definition is provided; in other words, the concepts must be empirically meaningful.[23] The "righteousness" of policy
is not an empirically meaningful concept; the "cost" of a policy is.
Beyond this, judgments about a theory's significance are rooted in
values and expectations rather than in the canons of scientific inquiry,
and because the knowledge produced in international relations, especially that cast in quantitative and formal terms, is sometimes charged
with triviality, we must begin with an overview of the foundations on
which such charges rest.

There are at least two forms that triviality can assume. If a theoretical argument involves a question whose answer we have no reason
to care about, we are in the presence of a pure form of triviality. The
reasons for our indifference may be pragmatic, resulting from a perception that the answer fails to affect our well-being in any discernible
fashion, but knowledge need not be useful in order to be worth having.[24] The justification for the humanities rarely rests on pragmatic
grounds, and even scientific results need not include implications for
action to be considered important. Most people would regard as meaningful theories that contribute to our understanding of human evolution, although it is unlikely that many practical implications could be
drawn from even the best evolutionary theories. Similarly, geological
theories on continental drift would hardly be judged trivial, even
though they contain few guides to action. Thus, even relatively "useless" knowledge may be considered important if it addresses questions
that culture, human experience, or natural curiosity lead us to seek to
answer. If we simply do not care, the knowledge is intrinsically trivial,
no matter how sound the theory behind it, or how broad the scope of
meaningless phenomena it addresses.

In addition to intrinsic importance, there is another standard
against which the significance of conclusions is sometimes measured,
related to how surprising they are in terms of initial expectations. Generally, the interest that a statement of theoretical relation, like a statement
of fact, generates is inversely proportional to its antecedent plausibility — since it is usually deemed more important to demonstrate the
unexpected than to confirm the self-evident. It may be objected that,
while it could seem trivial to confirm what most people would have in

any case expected, it is often a good idea to do so — simply because the contrary finding, though unlikely, would be extremely interesting.[25] For example, although most people would yawn at the finding that U.S. presidents disliked communism, it would be highly intriguing to discover that, contrary to expectations, this was not necessarily so. The argument makes a point, but it assumes that the question to which the anticipated answer is provided is of considerable *intrinsic* importance; otherwise, it could not be considered important, even if its antecedent plausibility had been very low. Triviality (T), therefore, *jointly* depends on the intrinsic significance of the question (S) and on the antecedent plausibility of the answer (A): it is inversely proportional to the former and directly proportional to the latter (if a formal expression of the relation is desired, it is $T = AS^{-1}$).

Having defined *desirable theoretical knowledge* as that which is both sound and valuable, with each of these qualities being further defined by two properties, we may ask how these qualities could be undermined by adding, as an additional desideratum, that the theory be policy-relevant. This implies an overview of the forms that relevance can take, since its implications for the growth and quality of theory may depend on the type of theory we have in mind.

## III.  Types of Relevance

According to a rather extreme view, the virtues that produce a good political theory are coextensive with those making it policy-relevant (although the obverse need not be true). Since the task of empirical theory is to provide general propositions about the link between causes and effects, then, in a world defined by complex and extended patterns of causality, every bit of sound knowledge provides a better understanding of the range of choices and of the consequences of various courses of action. Should this improved understanding appear minimally useful at present, it may prove so subsequently, in light of some theoretical discovery or empirical development making it possible and desirable to act on the acquired understanding. From this perspective, it makes little sense to distinguish relevant knowledge from *any* sound and valuable knowledge. Thus, William Fox could ask:

> Why should anyone expect an international relations theorist to be useful? Isn't his function to be omniscient and disinterested? The answer to the second question provides the answer to the first. By not allowing his interests to cloud his vision, the student of interna-

tional relations can make the observations of world politics which permit him to advance disinterested theories to account for and explain these observations. Thus, these interested conclusions help the policy-maker act with greater rationality.[26]

This is a facile and untenable position. While it can certainly be argued that those qualities that make a theory sound and valuable may be necessary to making it useful, they are not sufficient. Much solid, acquired knowledge has no discernible utility, and, while it is not logically precluded that it might prove useful in the indeterminate future, the contingency is often too remote to merit serious consideration.[27] A more realistic view of the relation between theory and relevance requires that we identify some internal properties of theories that might help us determine, ex ante, just how relevant they are apt to be. Since theory is policy-relevant in terms of establishing the range of possibilities and explaining the consequences of various choices, degrees of relevance may be assessed by asking how well these two functions are accomplished.

### The Range of Possibilities

By articulating the range of possibilities available to a nation pursuing its international objectives, policy-relevant theory can serve as a foundation on which foreign policy agendas can be established, as well as a backdrop against which to judge the performance of policymakers. Since recognizing the range of the possible requires a grasp of the causal processes behind the set of desired outcomes (what can realistically be attempted given the available policy instruments), it calls for an understanding of the links between instruments and objectives, which can be examined at two levels: (1) the level of instrumental relations and (2) the level of contextual relations.

*Instrumental* relations describe the expected impact of policy tool(s) on desired outcomes; as such they are the most directly relevant form of knowledge. Examples would include a set of theoretical propositions describing the consequences of economic sanctions wielded against a certain class of countries on the likelihood that they would abandon an objectionable policy, or else a general argument about the impact of policies designed to accelerate the transition from authoritarian rule to democracy on the likelihood of aggressive external behavior by the nations concerned. To qualify as instrumental, the relationship between policy and outcome need not be of a simple, bivariate form—ideally it would specify the controlling, ceteris paribus conditions that qualify the link between policy and outcome.[28] In the case of the economic sanctions, internal support for the targeted country's government, and the availability of alternative trading partners, could determine whether the sanctions would, in fact, cause that government to change its behavior. Similarly, the geopolitical circumstances of nations undergoing democratic transformation might also affect their peaceable or bellicose inclinations.

*Contextual* relations extend our grasp of the causal processes behind desired policy outcomes by accounting for the values of those variables that, within the instrumental relationship, appear as independent variables. This is consistent with Alexander George's concept of "contingent generalizations," whose purpose is to "identify how relevant situational variables change and vary according to circumstances."[29] If theoretical models were limited to establishing the impact of independent variables, in the form of both direct policies and pertinent control variables, then such variables would remain exogenous within the model's structure. By making them endogenous, relevance could benefit on at least two counts. To begin with, those who wish to act on the basis of the theoretical knowledge could anticipate the values of the control variables, which would give them a better grasp of the impact their policy is likely to produce. In the case of economic sanctions, policymakers could benefit by having a better idea of what determines the target nation's chances of gaining access to other markets and suppliers, a circumstance that could undermine the sanctions' effectiveness. Similarly, because it is difficult to predict the impact of democratization on the external behavior of nations if the pattern of their regional rivalries is neglected, an ability to anticipate these patterns yields a better idea of the effect, on regional peace and security, of a policy designed to encourage democratization in the area.

Contextual knowledge is not limited to making endogenous the ceteris paribus conditions that mediate the relation between instrument and outcome; it includes the circumstances that shape the accessibility or malleability of that policy instrument. Trade sanctions could induce another nation to change objectionable policies, but anticipated domestic economic costs may make it difficult for the initiator to resort to sanctions. By implication, the chances that the policy could, indeed, be pursued increases with an understanding of how to mitigate its domestic costs.

Contextual relevance may also assume a *predictive* form, exemplified by propositions that help anticipate the future status of the instruments employed for the pursuit of currently accepted policy objectives. For instance, forces promoting international economic interdependence might increase the future vulnerability of certain countries to economic sanctions. A declining national tolerance for governmental secrecy may make the use of covert operations in support of democracy abroad more difficult in the future than in the present.

Predictive relevance can assume yet another form. Because the challenges of foreign policy change along with evolving international and domestic circumstances, an ability to anticipate objectives that will be sought in the future improves the probability that they would be attained. Thus, knowledge about the determinants of the availability of natural resources could indicate that global supplies of oil will fall short of international demand at some future point, suggesting, in turn, that new policy challenges will have to be confronted. The nation may have to position itself to gain access to oil in open, perhaps increasingly fierce, competition with others. Alternatively, it may have to decrease its reliance on foreign sources of oil, perhaps by more vigorously developing other sources of energy.

### The Consequences of Choices

It is not enough to explain what can be attained and how. It is also necessary to know what impact one's policies may have on objectives other than the directly intended outcome. In this regard, we may share the social scientists' view of purpose, according to which "it is their business to determine reliably the immediate and remote costs and consequences of alternative courses of action, and to make these known to the public."[30] We may also concur with the sentiment that "the practical utility of social research consists not only of finding means to achieve stated goals, but also of discovering unanticipated consequences and ramifications of policies and other social actions."[31]

Most policy endeavors entail *direct* costs associated with producing the policy, which are often measurable in monetary terms (as in the case of the budgetary outlays attendant on military preparedness). Many policies involve a range of *secondary* consequences as well — resulting from the policy, but not directly involved in producing it. Typically this includes a number of opportunities forgone. In the case of economic sanctions, the policy may deprive the sanctioning state of whatever benefits it derived from commercial or financial interaction with the target nation. Economic sanctions could also hurt other nations whose economies are linked to the target's, encouraging their retaliatory activity against the initiator. Secondary consequences may also flow from the actual attainment of the policy objective. For example, U.S. victory over Iraq in the 1991 Gulf War shifted, temporarily at least, the local balance of power in favor of Iran — another nation with whom the United States maintained hostile relations.

Secondary consequences encompass benefits as well as costs. Military growth, along with its associated technological developments, may produce breakthroughs that come to benefit the civilian economy (as was the case with computers and numerous advances in metallurgy). Economic sanctions designed to weaken an adversary's economy may also strengthen the initiator's broader diplomatic position (assuming that a significant portion of the international community agrees with the need to confront the sanction's target).

There are, therefore, various ways in which theory can be relevant, and they are not limited to establishing direct relations between policy instruments and outcomes. Not every facet of relevance must be represented in a theory that claims to have practical significance, but the implications for theoretical development may depend on the forms of relevance at issue.

## IV.  Theory and Relevance: The Terms of the Trade-off

Having identified the ways in which theory can be policy-relevant, we must ask whether we should aim to make it so. Since the benefits of relevance are evident, the major uncertainties involve the price it exacts, and for our purposes the question is whether a goal of relevance would impair other qualities of theory, particularly its soundness and value. Clearly, this is a relative matter, since the impairments we fear are assessed relative to an ideal of disinterested scholarship — the ideal to which policy-relevant work usually is compared by its critics. Thus, the question resolves itself into one of whether PRT is likely to do as well with regard to soundness and value as would theoretical investigations unfettered by policy concerns, that is, BT.

Two sources of potential problems should be distinguished. The first is epistemological: Is there something about the logic of inquiry proper to the two sorts of theory that favors the soundness and/or value of one over the other? The second concern is better captured by the sociology of knowledge than by scientific epistemology; it springs from the possibility that the professional incentives by which the two sorts of scholars are driven may favor the soundness and/or value of the work produced by either. These are logically distinct categories of concern, and both may affect the relative quality of theory produced.

Figure 1 catalogs the possibilities for theoretical impairment; an answer to the question about the relative performance of PRT and BT, qua theory, requires a comparison in these terms. A first observation is that neither type of theory is relatively more likely to encourage a logic

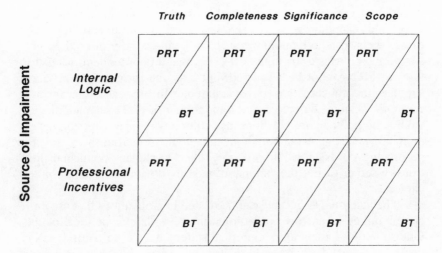

Fig. 1. Attributes of theory

of inquiry injurious to theoretical soundness. In both cases, the irreducible function of theory is to explain: an ability that is independent of whether the phenomenon to be explained involves a policy outcome or not. As has been pointed out, "relevance is a perspective applicable to the focus of research and not to the epistemic quality of the inquiry."[32] But it cannot be assumed that there is nothing about the logic of inquiry of either PRT or BT that could affect the *value* of their respective contributions. It is also quite conceivable that the professional incentives and culture proper to the two theoretical styles could differently affect their soundness and/or value. Because of this, a closer examination of likely performance requires a discussion of how the two types of theory are likely to fare with reference to their truth, completeness, scope, and significance.

## Truth and Relevance

If the substance of a conclusion is more important to a scholar than its empirical correctness, the argument's premises may be distorted, consciously or not, to justify the desired inference. The incentive to distort could spring from some partisan objective, or it could be fueled by ideological blinders. Inducements to delude could infect most forms of relevance, but one suspects that they are most to be feared in the instrumental case, for it is there that desired outcomes are involved most directly. Incentives to mislead might also be found in discussions of direct and secondary costs, if a scholar's commitment to certain policies causes their costs to be minimized (or if it causes the projected costs of competing policies to be inflated). The possibility of tendentious distortions in PRT cannot be dismissed, but a search for concrete instances suggests the concern may be overstated.[33] In any case, this form of corruption cannot be considered a monopoly of PRT, since ideological values and political predilections may color any scholarship that engages political values. A statement about the viability of socialism or, say, the peacefulness of Islam would probably reflect a scholar's political inclinations, whether or not the statement had any obvious bearing on policy choices.

The incentive to deceive can be rooted in motivations that are more closely linked to narrow professional interests than to political beliefs. One sometimes encounters empirical statements whose truth, one suspects, is distorted, consciously or not, by a desire to create maximum scholarly impact, to the scholar's greater glory, by challenging a broadly held assumption, by seeming to fill a widely lamented gap in knowledge, or by scoring points in a visible academic debate. However, the character of the incentives involved gives no reason to think that such statements are more likely to mar policy-relevant work than scholarship guided by politically disinterested motives.

Truth may also suffer from problems that have no basis in an incentive to distort. Quite often, in inductive work, the problem stems from a necessarily arbitrary operational definition of theoretical terms. Thus, whether it is true that democracies do not fight each other may depend on whether or not one accepts the (by now fairly standard) definition of war as an interstate conflict involving at least 1,000 battle deaths.[34] Similarly, statements about international inequality that are true when national wealth is measured in conventional GNP-per-capita terms may have to be modified if a broader measure of quality of life is substituted.[35] The problem here is not that truth is misrepresented, but that sometimes it is difficult to agree on its exact boundaries. Similar problems may be produced by imperfect measuring instruments and procedures, which, if the measurement error should be systematic rather than random, may bias the generalizations produced by the research. But there is no reason to think that systematic, though wholly unintended, measurement errors are more apt to impair the truth of theories that seek to be relevant than the truth of those that do not.

Truth may also be undermined by simplifications designed to foster theoretical parsimony and elegance, a problem more often encountered in deductive than in inductive work.[36] A simplification that strips away redundant layers of meaning, or that ignores idiosyncratic deviations from common tendencies, is a necessary part of theory-building, to which the growth of knowledge owes much. But when simplifications play havoc with the truth of the premises employed, the implications for explanatory generalizations are debilitating, even where interesting conclusions follow as valid deductions from premises of dubious truth. An illustration is provided by realpolitik's claim that the pursuit of power is a dominant aspiration of states, one that pervades their conduct of international affairs. In the "classic" realism of Hans J. Morgenthau, the power drive is rooted in one of those "elemental bio-social drives by which in turn society is created."[37] In the neorealism of Kenneth Waltz, this need flows from the anarchic structure of the international system, and the pervasive security dilemma this creates.[38] Certain predictions, especially about the way in which nations distribute and manage power, follow naturally from this premise, and gratifyingly elegant models of international politics are derivable on this basis. But the truth of their assumptions is tenuous. As an empirical matter, one can identify many nations that, linked to other members of the international system by objective conflicts of interest, are sharply attentive to power considerations. But it is equally easy to compile long lists of countries that are by no means troubled by security fears, and whose policies indicate no great concern with power. Yet, so influential is political realism and so convenient are its assumptions for theory-building that there has been almost no effort to establish the empirical correctness of the premises undergirding it; and given the ultimate implausibility of many of these premises, one may assume that their truth is suspect.

Significantly, realism's simplifications are unrelated to attempts at relevance, since, while Morgenthau was concerned with the practical applications of his precepts, Waltz has displayed no great interest in policy implications — a pure theory of international relations being his apparent objective. On the whole, one suspects that misleading simplifications, with their corresponding impairment of explanatory ability, are likely to occur wherever parsimony is more valued than truth. It is likely that deductive research compares unfavorably with inductive work on this basis, but not that the problem weighs more heavily on PRT than BT.

## The Goal of Completeness

An emphasis on relevance could limit the comprehensiveness of theoretical explanation, but the magnitude of the problem depends on how broad a conception of relevance is adopted, as well as on the pattern of incentives behind the analytical endeavor. The highest probability of theoretical constriction comes with a view of relevance limited to its instrumental version, and with an overriding concern for the effectiveness of the policy involved. In this regard, one might worry that the policy instruments covered by instrumental relations could be determined by the scholar's estimate of how effectively they could be acted upon, neglecting those which, while causally significant, are not particularly malleable. Recourse to certain policy instruments could be precluded by domestic politics or cultural constraints, or they might not be affordable in terms of their direct costs and secondary consequences, but this does not make them less necessary to a theoretical explanation of the desired outcome. Scholars might also be led to emphasize policy instruments that promise to have the greatest causal impact on the desired outcome, disregarding those whose influence is less dramatic, with similar costs to theoretical completeness. Accordingly, if the analyst is guided by a narrow notion of practicality rather than a broad conception of social causality, the explanatory structure behind the policy recommendations may be weakened by significant gaps.

If afflictions of this sort are possible, the problem is not rooted in the nature of PRT. Because soundness is a necessary, albeit insufficient, condition for theoretical relevance, and since theory must be reasonably complete in order to be sound, a proper view of the analyst's purpose precludes omissions of this sort. Analytical deformities in the name of practicality are more likely to characterize the thinking of actual policymakers, perhaps also of practitioners of IPA, but there is less reason to expect them in policy-relevant theory — as long as the scholar's incentives are dominated by professional incentives that reward soundness, without penalizing valuable and relevant theoretical work. In a satisfactory program of policy-relevant theorizing, the instrumental relations would encompass a comprehensive statement of links between policies and outcomes, an adequate survey of pertinent contextual considerations, as well as a discussion of direct and secondary consequences. The influences that, in a vision bounded by narrow practicality, might be neglected become variables whose values are explicitly accounted for.

On grounds of both truth and completeness, risks to soundness cannot be entirely neglected, but they appear modest, and, where they cannot be dismissed, their source is more likely found in misguided professional incentives than in the logic of inquiry inherent in relevant theory. By the same token, there is little to suggest a bias toward incompleteness in the case of BT, particularly in general propositions empirically derived on the basis of an examination of observational data, as in the statistical models whose success is partly measured in terms of variance explained. Somewhat firmer grounds for concern may be found in purely deductive work, where elegance and parsimony are sometimes purchased at the price of theoretical completeness. But the problem, if indeed there is one, is not grounded in the logic of deduction per se, but in incentives that are more aesthetic than epistemic.

### Relevance and Valuable Theories

The first issue is whether PRT asks questions that are intrinsically at least as meaningful and interesting as those addressed by scholars with a commitment to disinterested theory. There is firm ground for assuming that this is the case. A question that claims the interest of a policy-relevant theorist typically involves the pursuit of some desirable objective, and, while it is logically possible that objectives of trifling importance would be addressed, the contingency is remote. Lacking much incentive in the form of professional rewards to be relevant (these rewards unambiguously favoring basic theory), scholars usually embark on such work because of the importance attached to the issues involved, an importance measured by the consequences of failing to attain the policy objective.

However, because intrinsic importance need not be gauged exclusively in pragmatic terms, issues addressed within BT may be even more significant than those examined in a policy-oriented context. Not only is this conceivable in principle, but it is sometimes assumed that the really important scientific questions can only be tackled with a wholly disinterested frame of mind. Abraham Flexner expressed a widely held view when he maintained, decades ago in a subsequently much-quoted article, that "throughout the whole history of science most of the really great discoveries which had ultimately proved to be beneficial to mankind had been made by men and women who were driven not by the desire to be useful but merely by the desire to satisfy their curiosity."[39]

I think, however, that this rests on a somewhat romanticized view of scholarly curiosity and of the manner in which questions are selected for scientific examination in the academic community. In most of the social sciences, where professional recognition depends partly on the apparent sophistication of the research tools and conceptual categories employed, questions are often selected according to the tools and concepts that can plausibly be employed in their analysis. These are not criteria that have much bearing on the intrinsic importance of the issues addressed, and some loss may be expected here. Often too, issues are selected because, for whatever reason, a critical mass of colleagues has already decided to deal with them. Partly, this stems from an understandable conviction that a question addressed by a large number of colleagues is one that must be worth addressing. Partly, it springs from the fact that an intensely studied issue implies the easy availability of empirical information (say, a useful data set) upon which research can readily be conducted. Partly too, it is because incorporation into a vigorous stream of scholarship stands to promote the visibility of associated work by embedding it in a lively pattern of mutual citation, promoting the professional visibility of participating scholars. These are circumstances better explained by the sociology of knowledge than by the canons of scientific method, and experience indicates that either significant or trivial issues may occupy scholarship in the process.

Issues that are not currently very meaningful may become so subsequently, in the light of novel information or emerging needs, but one must be leery of a justification for apparently trivial work that rests on the possibility that some value may someday be discovered for its findings. To be at all plausible, the justification requires that the currently trivial does, in fact, often prove significant with time. Whether or not this is true of the natural sciences may be debated, a debate complicated by the difficulty of disentangling the various strands of scientific work, both pure and applied, that precede most useful discoveries in these areas. In the social sciences, however, instances of trivial work for which value has later come to be found do not readily come to mind — what was trivial a decade (or more) ago is likely to be every bit as trivial today.

In the field of international relations, charges of triviality are also directed at conclusions that appear self-evident. Here, the claim of banality can be refuted if the importance of a correct answer is great enough to make *any* uncertainty intolerable, and it can further be mitigated in inverse proportion to the conclusion's antecedent plausibility (not all expectations are equally firmly held). Controlling for intrinsic importance, the task is to decide whether policy-relevant thinking is more or less prone to confirming the expected than is basic-theoretical work. Largely, the issue is one of asking what incentives either style of thought might have to offer conclusions of high prior plausibility, incentives that are extraneous to the issue's intrinsic importance.

For PRT, it might be feared that political rewards — in forms ranging from public acclaim to access to power — may sometimes be proffered to scholars who prove the obvious, because even that which is apparent may be hotly denied in political debates. But again, actual instances do not suggest themselves, and it is hard to be impressed by an abstract possibility with so few empirical referents. As far as BT is concerned, no specific grounds for the banality of high antecedent plausibility come to mind, although, once again, this could well be the by-product of academic agendas within which the significance of substantive conclusions matters less than the current appeal of the analytical methods employed.

## Relevance and Theoretical Scope

The scope of what we seek to explain is restricted by the questions we choose to ask, so it would be good to know whether disinterested scientific curiosity yields a greater range of questions than do policy-relevant interests. By definition, the questions generated by the latter are limited by the outcomes that are to be influenced, and this may constrict the field of theoretical investigation in several ways. Policy objectives are guided by narrow current interests and values, and these are bounded by a variety of shifting and parochial considerations and, occasionally, by ideological agendas.[40] PRT's explanatory reach could be limited in the process, but the gravity of the problem depends on the type of relevance at issue.

One could argue, on behalf of PRT, that concerns are greatest where theories focus on instrumental relations alone, and that, if broadened to encompass necessary contextual relations, as well as direct and secondary consequences, theoretical edifices explaining very many things may arise. To this, however, it could be retorted that the starting point is always given by the policy objective, and that the theory's scope cannot extend very much beyond its confines. Assuming that this is so, the criticism does not distinguish PRT from BT, since there is no reason to think that basic theory's explanatory structures are less firmly rooted in the outcomes it seeks to explain. The only issue that really matters is whether either type of theory concerns itself with a larger range of outcomes than the other, a question whose answer would require careful examination of the two bodies of scholarly literature, and I have no a priori basis for predicting what conclusions would be reached.

Under this general heading, it must be observed that degenerative theory, that which keeps expanding its protective belt of ad hoc assumptions and auxiliary hypotheses with no corresponding increase in the range of phenomena accounted for, is unlikely to be compatible with policy-relevant work. Here, pragmatic incentives make an understanding of policy outcomes (both the causes and implications) the principal justification for theoretical development, and the measure of its success is whether, with regard to these outcomes, it explains the range of the possible and the implications of choices. Where observational data indicate that the theory is failing in its task, it will probably be modified or abandoned. Concerns that are extraneous to its objectives — for example, the faddishness or sophistication of the analytical tools used — are unlikely to sustain an unsuccessful theory. Therefore, considerations that sometimes ensure the longevity of degenerative theory are less likely to afflict PRT than BT, and the former's explanatory scope may benefit accordingly.

## V.  Conclusion

The issue of relevance, its desirability and feasibility, will continue to be debated in political science and political philosophy,[41] as well as in the subfield of international relations, and no resolution should be expected in the foreseeable future. Nevertheless, certain beliefs must be challenged. Even with an explanatory conception of theory's purpose, we find nothing alarming about asking that it should be policy-relevant, since there is little reason to assume that PRT must fare less well than BT, in terms of either soundness or value. The possibility that relevance would corrupt knowledge by twisting it to conform with ideological biases, as at one time the natural sciences were hobbled by being tethered to theological agendas, may reasonably be set aside, simply on grounds of implausibility. Similarly, it is not likely to be placed at the service of narrow partisan objectives. In a liberal society, few instances can be found of theoretical knowledge that is corrupted in such a fashion, and, in a competitive marketplace of ideas, they are easily detected and denounced when they do appear.

Other threats may be entangled with a quest for relevance, but they are hardly insuperable; in any case, similar problems afflict BT. Truth, completeness, and explanatory scope could, in principle, suffer from the professional incentives of relevant theorists, if these were to lead them to generalizations that favor simple, direct, and immediately workable guides to action, of the sort that may be most appealing and comprehensible to policymakers. But in the nature of things, this is a problem more plausibly encountered in IPA than in PRT. Moreover, the structure of professional rewards facing the scholar unburdened by a concern with relevance seems at least as often to be based on criteria external to the quality of the explanations offered. Whatever qualms about relevance one may entertain, they tend to be rooted in assumed professional incentives, not in the nature of the explanatory enterprise. Moreover, these incentives are often compared to an overly idealized conception of the drives behind the development of basic theory.

In an observation as apposite to the field of international relations as to other behavioral sciences, Abraham Kaplan observed that inquiry related to practice has the advantages of providing anchorage for our abstractions, and data and tests for our hypotheses. For behavioral science the advantages are especially great, counteracting the tendency to empty verbalizations characteristic of some sociologies, or the self-contained formalism of certain economic theories.[42]

In a similar vein, Joseph Ben David, a distinguished sociologist of science, has observed that an intellectual grounding in the world of practice may lead to considerably more innovative and interesting work than scholarship shaped exclusively by the ethos of ivory towers:

> Practice . . . is an invaluable guide in locating relevant problems — rather than finding illusory ones, which happened not infrequently in the history of academic thinking . . . The problems of practice are always real, and it usually possesses a tradition which is the result of a long collective process of trial and error and which may suggest the way toward new theory and new methods.[43]

Thus, it could be argued that the pursuit of useful knowledge may produce theory of a better quality, because empirically more meaningful and more focused on the truth of its premises than a program of knowledge-creation dominated by the reward structure of disinterested theory.

There are indications that political science, the source of most international relations theory, may be becoming more alert to the benefits of responding to practical challenges. After several decades during which the discipline was enamored of deductively sophisticated, although often substantively tenuous, conceptions of theory, as exemplified by the rational choice approach, faint glimmers of introspective criticism can be discerned. An illustration is provided by the controversy sparked by the publication, in 1994, of *Pathologies of Rational Choice Theory,*[44] in which the authors took this orientation to task for failing to yield empirically meaningful and sustainable findings. Many of the reactions from within the ranks of the approach were understandably defensive, but not all. In an especially thoughtful response, Peter Ordeshook, a leading practitioner of rational choice theory, candidly admitted that "the substantive relevance of much formal rational choice analysis is tenuous, and its empirical content lacks coherence."[45] The solution, in his view, is to recognize the relation between pure theory ("science") and applied theory ("engineering"), and to have the engineering component play a greater role in the process of knowledge production. Urging that we abandon the image of science as "an enterprise directed by academics armed with theorems and lemmas or by experimentalists scurrying about in white smocks,"[46] he observes:

> Science proceeds less coherently, through induction and infer-ence, informed by attempts to be practical and to manipulate real things . . . Out of such a process come ideas about what is generaliz-able, what is best understood by existent theory, and what is an anomaly that warrants further investigation . . . the practical appli-cation of theory and experience feeds back on our awareness of theoretical inadequacies and on our identification of phenomena that warrant generalization and theoretical understanding.[47]

The point is not to criticize the rational choice approach, which remains an important contribution to social science, but to suggest that any form of social theory may benefit from an attentiveness to real-world problems. It may be time to shed the notion that a quest for policy relevance represents compromised academic aspiration, and to entertain the possibility that a response to practical challenges may not only im-prove our ability to attain national and international objectives, but also yield a more meaningful and credible theoretical edifice.

NOTES

1. Michael Nicholson, *Causes and Consequences in International Relations* (London: Pinter, 1996), 171.

2. Christopher Hill, "Academic International Relations: The Siren Song of Policy Relevance," in Christopher Hill and Pamela Beshoff, eds., *Two Worlds of International Relations* (London: Routledge, 1994), 21.

3. Jerome R. Ravetz, *The Merger of Knowledge and Power* (London: Mansell Publishing, 1990), 25.

4. Hans J. Morgenthau, *Science: Servant or Master* (New York: New American Library, 1972), 88.

5. New York: Columbia University Press, 1974.

6. Joseph S. Nye, Jr., *Bound to Lead* (New York: Basic Books, 1990).

7. David A. Lake and Donald Rothchild, "Containing Fear," *International Security* 21, no. 2 (fall 1966): 1–34.

8. A good and somewhat related conception is provided by Abraham Kaplan, who defines theory as "more than a synopsis of the moves that have been played on the game of nature; it also sets forth some idea of the rules of the game by which the moves become intelligible." *The Conduct of Inquiry* (San Francisco: Chandler, 1964), 302.

9. For discussions of the components of good theory, see Ernest Nagel, *The Structure of Science: Problems in the Logic of Scientific Explanation* (New

York: Harcourt, Brace and World, 1961), chapters 5 and 6; Johan Galtung, *Theory and Methods of Social Research* (New York: Columbia University Press, 1967), chapter 6; Karl Popper, *The Logic of Scientific Discovery* (New York: Harper, 1968), chapter 3.

10. For a discussion of the relation between explanation and prediction, see Kaplan, chapter 40; also Michael Nicholson, *The Scientific Analysis of Social Behavior* (London: Pinter, 1983), chapter 9.

11. For a good discussion with regard to international relations, see Nazli Choucri and Thomas W. Robinson, eds., *Forecasting in International Relations: Theory, Methods, Problems* (San Francisco: W. H. Freeman, 1978).

12. See, especially, Carl G. Hempel, *Aspects of Scientific Explanation* (New York: Free Press, 1965): part IV.

13. As Stephen Toulmin points out: "Scientists are interested in 'forecasting techniques' only incidentally, and any more satisfactory sense of prediction takes for granted the idea of explanation, rather than defining it." *Foresight and Understanding: An Enquiry into the Aims of Science* (New York: Harper and Row, 1961), 99.

14. Realism in this sense has nothing to do with political realism (realpolitik).

15. The distinction is discussed in A. F. Chalmers, *What Is This Thing Called Science* (Stratford: Open University Press, 1978), chapter 10, and Ernst Nagel, *The Structure of Science: Problems in the Logic of Scientific Explanation* (New York: Harcourt Brace, 1961): 129–52. For a particularly well-argued statement of the realist position, see Richard W. Miller, *Fact and Method: Explanation, Confirmation and Reality in the Natural and Social Sciences* (Princeton: Princeton University Press, 1987).

16. As opposed, in particular, to the "coherence theory" of truth, a perspective with fewer adherents within the theory of knowledge. See Robert Chisholm, *Theory of Knowledge* (Englewood Cliffs, N.J.: Prentice Hall, 1989), and Laurence Bonjour, *The Structure of Empirical Knowledge* (Cambridge: Harvard University Press, 1985).

17. See, for example, William H. Brenner, *Logic and Philosophy* (Notre Dame: University of Notre Dame Press, 1993), chapter 4, and Milton Hobbs, *The Objectives of Political Science* (New York: University Press of America, 1993), chapter 1.

18. In Milton Friedman, ed., *Essays in Positive Economics* (Chicago: University of Chicago Press, 1953), 3–43.

19. Imre Lakatos, "The Methodology of Scientific Research Programs," in Imre Lakatos and A. Musgrave, *Criticism and the Growth of Knowledge* (Cambridge: Cambridge University Press, 1970).

20. Vladimir I. Lenin, *Imperialism: The Highest Stage of Capitalism* (New York: International Publishers, 1939) (first published in 1917).

21. Kenneth N. Waltz, *Theory of International Politics* (Reading, Mass.: Addison-Wesley, 1979).

22. Hans J. Morgenthau, *Politics among Nations: The Struggle for Power and Peace* (New York: Knopf, 1948).

23. Milton Hobbs, *The Objectives of Political Science* (New York: University Press of America, 1933), 10–13.

24. For a provocative discussion of this issue, see Bertrand Russell, "Useless Knowledge," in Bertrand Russell, ed., *In Praise of Idleness and Other Essays* (London: Allen and Unwin, 1935), 9–29.

25. This is discussed in Nicholson, *Scientific Analysis,* 95–100.

26. William T. R. Fox, *The American Study of International Relations* (Columbia: University of South Carolina, 1968).

27. As Nico Stehr points out: "Social science research which is not explicitly designed to generate practical knowledge may in fact succeed in producing such knowledge. But efforts which are from the beginning aimed at producing such knowledge claims have a much better chance to succeed because such research efforts do not have to rely on fortuitous "local" circumstances in order to achieve a fit with practical conditions of action." *Practical Knowledge: Applying the Social Sciences* (London: Sage, 1992), 121.

28. For the importance of controlling variables in policy-relevant thinking, see Johan Galtung, "Science as Invariance-Seeking and Invariance-Breaking Activity," in Johan Galtung, ed., *Methodology and Ideology,* vol. 1 (Copenhagen: Christian Ejlers, 1977): 72–97.

29. "Theory for Policy in International Relations," *Policy Sciences,* December 1973.

30. George A. Lundberg, *Can Science Save Us?* (New York: Longman, 1947), 29.

31. Joseph Ben David, *Scientific Growth: Essays in the Social Organization and Ethos of Science* (Berkeley: University of California Press, 1991), 402.

32. Philip H. Melanson, *Political Science and Political Knowledge* (Washington, D.C.: Public Affairs Press, 1975), 130.

33. On this point, see Stehr, *Practical Knowledge,* 147–49.

34. A discussion of some of the empirical issues involved in the debate on the democratic peace can be found in Michael E. Brow et al., eds., *Debating the Democratic Peace* (Cambridge, Mass.: MIT Press, 1996).

35. David Morris, *Measuring the Condition of the World's Poor: The Physical Quality of Life Index* (New York: Pergamon, 1979).

36. Richard Miller defines a "bias toward the superficial" characteristic of much deductive work in the social sciences. This bias is reflected in "an unjustified preference for theories denying the operation of causal factors which are relatively hard to observe [arising from] at least three aspects of deductivism: the rejection of the hedges and defense on which deeper theories usually depend; the neglect of causal depth in assessing explanations; and the neglect of the actual context of scientific development in the choice among hypotheses." *Fact and Method,* 262.

37. Morgenthau, *Politics among Nations,* 39.

38. Waltz, *Theory of International Politics.*

39. Abraham Flexner, "The Usefulness of 'Useless' Knowledge," *Harper's Magazine* 179 (1939), 535.

40. Hill, "Academic International Relations," 7–9.

41. In the area of political philosophy, see Jeremy Waldron, "What Plato Would Allow," in Ian Shapiro and Judith Wagner DeCew, eds., *Theory and Practice* (New York: New York University Press, 1996), 138–77, and Jeffrey C. Isaac, "The Strange Silence of Political Theory," *Political Theory,* November 1995, 636–88.

42. Kaplan, *Conduct of Inquiry,* 399.

43. David, *Scientific Growth,* 35.

44. New Haven: Yale University Press, 1994.

45. Peter C. Ordeshook, "Engineering or Science: What Is the Study of Politics," in Jeffrey Friedman, ed., *The Rational Choice Controversy* (New Haven: Yale University Press, 1996), 175.

46. "Engineering or Science," 180.

47. "Engineering or Science," 180, 181.

# Counselors, Kings, and International Relations: From Revelation to Reason, and Still No Policy-Relevant Theory

*Arthur A. Stein*

"The inseparable conjunction of counsel with kings" predates the rise of the analytic mind (Francis Bacon, quoted in Goldhamer 1978, 7). Even when political leaders believed in "divination, oracles, avenging deities, and other manifestations of the supernatural," they looked to masters in rites and rituals to advise them on affairs of state (Goldhamer 1978, 230). As reason replaced revelation as the basis for decision, kings turned to counselors with new bases of expertise, drawn from different ranks within society.[1]

In the modern world, leaders constantly seek knowledge and expertise even as they and others belittle the quality and relevance of the scholarly product. They lament that "those who can't, teach," to deride and discredit both the concrete policy recommendations of academics and the abstract scholarship produced in much of the academy.[2] Yet in many areas, especially technical ones, the importance of policy expertise, and with it professional policy training, has grown. During the twentieth century, the social sciences solidified their intellectual autonomy and developed professional degrees and programs for the education of practitioners. In international relations, this meant the development of professional training programs for the foreign service and related careers.[3]

As research has become more important to policy formulation, academics have become important policy players. Scholars in some disciplines advise government officials; in some fields they can move smoothly between government and the academy. The Council of Economic Advisors, for example, institutionalizes the policy relevance of economics and is statutorily presumed to provide a governmental platform for academic economists.[4] There is nothing comparable for scholars of international relations, although academics have become more prominent in the ranks of foreign policy advisers and have largely replaced lawyers as the profession from which such advisers are drawn.

In this essay, I argue that international relations theorists, despite their obvious interest in current events and relevance, and despite the importance of the knowledge they possess, do not directly address the needs of policymakers. I locate the problem in the nature of the field, its current level of development, and the nature of policy relevance.

**There Should be Policy-Relevant Theory**

There is every reason to expect the field of international relations to be policy-relevant. It is not plagued by the kinds of problems that make scholarship irrelevant. It does not separate policy and theory institutionally and so force ideas to move so slowly from one isolated scholarly community to another that theoretical scholarship remains unknown to policymakers. It does not focus solely on theoretically generated questions. Its intellectual agenda, unlike those in many disciplines, is driven as much by questions of immediate policy concern as by issues that emerge purely from the intellectual evolution of a scholarly paradigm, the need to develop a general perspective and address anomalies unexplained by current theory.

Field Organization and Policy Relevance

Professionalization has typically meant separate training programs for practitioners and theoreticians, but in international relations the two remain in the same tent. Unlike basic scientists and engineers, or psychoanalysts and clinical psychologists, they generally share a single institutionalized path for training, research, and teaching. The economists who teach in economics departments often bear little resemblance to those who teach in business schools, and the training of graduate students in economics is quite different than that of MBAs.[5] But in political science and international relations, the division between theory and application is minimal. Although graduate professional programs in public administration and international relations exist, they are few in number and count predominantly political scientists among their faculties. Many scholars who study mainly policy and address primarily policy audiences teach in mainstream political science departments. Moreover, even though there are no policy positions in foreign affairs that require political scientists, those who have held such posts have sometimes been eminent ones (Kissinger, Brzezinski).

## Focus on Real-World Events

International relations should also be policy-relevant because its students are interested in, if not preoccupied by, the real world — perhaps too preoccupied for the field's own good. To develop as a science, natural or social, inquiry must focus on analytic rather than practical questions. It must focus on theory development and assessment and their attendant requirements of abstraction and methodology. The scientist's audience is other scientists working on similar questions. That is how science evolves. Whatever its speed, intellectual progress proceeds linearly. Eventually, cumulative knowledge about how some facet of the world works may make policy intervention possible, but that is a by-product, one often deferred for a long time and not readily predictable from initial lines of inquiry. The distinguished social scientist Donald Campbell made the point directly by holding that social scientists should avoid reading the daily newspaper. It was his way of stressing that social scientists should look primarily toward the theoretical development of their respective fields. Their task, like every scholar's, is to push back the frontiers of knowledge. Although that knowledge is about the world, a focus on daily events would only deflect them from their core activity.

But international relations theorists in the twentieth century have been overwhelmingly preoccupied with the real world, often shifting the focus of their scholarly inquiry as a function of current events. The world of the 1920s and early 1930s, with its emphasis on such international institutions as the League of Nations, led scholarly attention to international law and political economy, and to the league's specific attempts to use international agreements to constrain and even outlaw war. Within a few years, however, the overwhelming post–World War II desire to avoid nuclear war swept away these subfields.[6]

In the last half of the twentieth century, every important historical development has left a new literature in its wake, often one financed by government and private foundations. Not a few subfields have drowned in the process. The postwar fear of nuclear weapons generated deterrence theory.[7] The creation of the United Nations led scholars to focus on international organizations. The Korean War spawned a literature on limited war. The creation of the European Economic Community generated a subfield on regional integration, and the Cuban missile crisis spawned an industry devoted to the study of crises. The war in Vietnam brought new interest both in how wars end and in their domestic consequences. In the 1970s, the combination of détente, oil crisis, and the collapse of Bretton Woods led to the brief demise of security studies and the birth of international political economy. At the same time, the failure of the United Nations and the seeming end of integration in Europe led to the disappearance of regional integration studies and the virtual disappearance of work on international organizations. The collapse of the oil market, U.S. rearmament, and heightened fears of war led to a brief eclipse of international political economy and an equally brief renaissance of security studies in the middle 1980s. But the end of the Cold War created tough times for security analysts, as ethnic conflict and terrorism have become the prime foci of the early 1990s. Renewed momentum toward European integration and the seemingly renewed relevance of the UN simultaneously led to the reemergence of the moribund subfields of international organization and regional integration.

Indeed, international relations as a field is so responsive to new real-world developments that its very core remains in flux. Extended great-power trade and cooperation brought arguments that the increased costs of great-power wars may have caused their extinction. That there has actually been no such war in the half-century after World War II generated debate about whether there has been a fundamental change in international relations (Mueller 1989; Kaysen 1990). The emergence of the multinational corporation led to discussions in the early 1970s of diminished sovereignty and to predictions that transnational relations would replace international ones.[8]

Ironically, scholars may have contributed to the field's lack of cumulation and intellectual progress by responding to every twist and turn on the international scene.[9] The regular shifts in focus have contributed to the field's retardation rather than making it more useful to policymakers. Responding to real events is no guarantee of developing policy-relevant theory, and it risks creating the academic equivalent of generals who prepare to wage the last war. Indeed, the ability of scholars to be caught napping is best illustrated by the end of the Cold War and the collapse of bipolarity, which was widely believed to be stable and enduring.[10]

Yet faddism is an inadequate explanation for shifts in scholarly inquiry and the lack of progress. One root of the problem lies in the very nature of the phenomena that the field studies. Other areas of political science analyze department variables that recur and sustain continuous interest. Students of U.S. elections are certain to see another election. International relations scholars are not assured of much. A war between the great powers may be followed by a period of peace that is longer than a scholar's career. A superpower confrontation like the Cuban missile crisis may never recur. Critical phenomena do not occur with regularity and may not return with sufficient frequency to sustain interest and funding or provide sufficient data.[11] As a result, scholars respond to new historical developments.

Moreover, fads can arise even in fields with a consistent focus. That economists consistently focus on firm profits and market competition has not prevented business management's many gurus from preaching pseudoscience and creating or following crazes with pernicious consequences.[12]

Scholarly focus shifts in response to changing political developments for three reasons. First, many scholars who are genuinely interested in the real world want their work to address contemporaneous concerns. Second, government — a major source of demand for scholarly product — has interests of immediate policy relevance.[13] Third, the private foundations that support scholarship often have agendas that shift with the times. In the wake of détente, for example, the key foundations supporting international relations scholarship abandoned certain lines of inquiry. The Ford Foundation, for example, decided it would no longer fund security studies. Ironically, the fear of Reagan's rearmament program in the early 1980s brought many foundations back to supporting work on national security and on the Soviet Union. Yet that interest cooled once more with the end of the Cold War. Whether because of supply (the natural interest of scholars) or demand (governments and foundations with money), international relations scholars focus on real-world concerns and should presumably be policy-relevant.

Despite the field's overwhelming concern with the real world and despite the absence of a rupture between theoreticians and engineers, international relations remains a field that most find has little to say to policymakers. It seemingly has all the ingredients for policy relevance. Its practitioners are interested in the real world and are encouraged and supported to study current events. Social engineers and theoreticians cohabit departments and schools. Yet international relations theory remains a disappointment to policymakers, and this is a source of frustration for scholars.

## The Problem

That leaders have turned to advisers and intellectuals for millennia does not belie the problem. Nor does the advent of political science, which long postdates the existence of policy counselors. In whatever era, however, the question is whether advice is grounded in some body of expertise — whether it is rooted in tested and accepted knowledge-claims. Foreign policy, no less than medicine, must distinguish between the quack and the physician.

Whatever its weaknesses, the field of international relations can have some policy relevance. All knowledge about how the world works is relevant.[14] Any knowledge of means/ends relationships matters. Atheoretical work can be policy-relevant. Purely descriptive studies can be useful. Policymakers would have found it helpful, for example, to have a study showing that the Soviet Union was typically cautious in crises and withdrew at the first sign of serious opposition. Even if no theory explained the pattern, simply describing it might have been useful.[15]

Medicine illuminates the range of useful knowledge available to those who would act. Doctors can sometimes treat symptoms, such as pain, without treating or even understanding the etiology of a disease. They excise tumors, for example, without knowing what causes them or if the surgery will work. Doctors can also diagnose a disease and detail its likely prognosis without being able to intervene. Such prognosis even without control, help, or relief of underlying causes can still be useful. Yet, even when doctors know both the cause and the evolution of a disease, they cannot always control or reverse it — a case exemplified by the plaintive desire for a cure for the common cold.

International relations, like medicine, can be useful even when it cannot explain and cannot offer the hope of cure or control. Yet there remains a deeper problem.[16] For a set of reasons developed below, the propositions developed in the field are not particularly relevant to the making of foreign policy.

### Researching the Exogenously Nonmanipulable

Although the most useful knowledge pertains to levers that are directly manipulated by policymakers, many international relations theories do not involve such manipulable exogenous factors. Recent scholarship on the implications of the end of the Cold War provides an example. One implication of realist arguments about the stability of bipolar worlds, for which the Cold War is an exemplar of stability assuring an extended peace between the superpowers, is that the end of the Cold War should bring conflict and instability. It should bring back the bad old days of European chaos, leaving us hankering for the good old Cold War.[17] Despite this argument's importance, one can only imagine the Oval Office reaction to a briefing on how the multipolarity of the future will be more unstable than the bipolarity of the past. There is nothing that any chief executive of any nation can do to alter such historical developments. Nothing in the theory provides a way to make multipolarity more stable or to bring back bipolarity.

Knowing the relative stability of different systems is interesting and may be useful to those seeking to alleviate systemic problems, but provides little guidance by itself. It is equivalent to the information offered by a weather forecaster, who need not know the etiology of weather patterns, who cannot control them, and whose predictions have substantial variance and little predictability. Although we cannot control the weather, we still find it useful to know that it might rain. But the utility of the weather forecast is conjoined with our having umbrellas and raincoats — protections not discovered, created, or provided by weather forecasters. International relations forecasts of increased instability under multipolarity are equivalent to imperfect weather forecasts without umbrellas or raincoats.

Work at the systemic level of analysis is of limited utility to policymakers, who necessarily work at the individual and national levels. Political leaders interact with other leaders and develop policies to deal with other nations, whose actions and reactions they must assess. Systemic scholarship, however interesting, remains of limited utility. It deals at a level of aggregation not commensurate with that at which policy takes place, and it involves independent variables that are not manipulable policy levers. Systemic characteristics are a product of the actions and interactions of states — no one state's choices mold the system.[18] Policymakers can create neither bipolarity nor multipolarity, because foreign policy operates at the individual and national levels. International relations theory deals with broad sweeping patterns; while such knowledge may be useful, it does not address the day-to-day largely tactical needs of policymakers.[19]

### Not Researching the Levers of Policy

Not only have scholars analyzed much that is in no way manipulable by politicians, but they have often failed to study the implications of those levers actually available to elites. A simple catalog of policy measures makes the point.

The positive actions states take toward each other include recognition, economic and military aid, the extension of commitments, and a variety of other measures culminating in full alliances. The consequences of many of these are often unstudied. Then, too, those scrutinized are not always relevant or important to policy. We know little about the political consequences of one nation's recognizing or not recognizing another. Most studies of foreign aid deal with its determinants; few examine its consequences. Nations commonly sell weapons as a way of improving and strengthening bilateral relations, but little research has addressed the actual impact of these transactions. Even analyses of the consequences of alliances and deterrence commitments have been limited by a primary focus on their relationship to war and successful deterrence. Although important, this does not tell policymakers all they need to know.

Governments signal displeasure with each other by withdrawing ambassadors and recognition, isolating other states diplomatically, displaying military force, and imposing economic sanctions, and by threatening, warning, and actually using force. Analysts have totally ignored some of these policy levers and have adequately studied only the impact of economic sanctions.

Most scholars focus on the extremes of the cooperation/conflict continuum. Since their interest lies in war and peace, they study war and alliances. But much of international relations occurs between the extremes; most policy choices do not involve declaring war or joining an alliance. The full range of policy instruments remains to be adequately conceptualized and studied.[20] There are different kinds of alliances, but we have no labels to distinguish them.[21] Similarly, there is a need to distinguish along the conflict continuum, between enemies and rivals, for example. Neither scholars nor policymakers have an adequate vocabulary for discussing the range of relationships. Moreover, scholars have inadequately studied the ramifications of using the levers that do exist.

## Academic Discourse and the Policy Problem

The problem of policy relevance is also a function of how the academy differs from the policy world; the very nature of the scholarly enterprise and its institutional organization impede policy relevance. Scholars focus narrowly, with the consequence that what a policymaker needs to know is to be found across disciplines and fields. Moreover, scholars focus on the general and generic, and policymakers are interested in the particular.

Because scholars focus on dependent variables, on explaining some phenomenon, they debate the relative importance of different explanations. As a result, literatures cluster around common dependent variables. The core debate in international relations about the causes of war involves disputes about the relative importance of different explanatory variables. This can be policy-relevant if policymakers want to achieve or avoid or change the dependent variable.

But because policy entails the choice of particular instruments, it requires knowing the consequences of specific policy choices, information that, even if available, will likely be found across many literatures.

The consequences of any policy X are not to be found in any literature focusing on X. Rather, they are found in the disparate literatures that each focus on one of X's particular consequences, whether Y or Z or something else. This is a general problem for any field's policy relevance: it cannot provide useful information about the consequences whose determinants are the focus of inquiry. Gathering information on wars' consequences is much harder than finding out about their origins, for studies of wars' effects are spread across entire disciplines, including a small body of work on the international systemic consequences of war. But ascertaining the impact of war requires assembling information from all the areas of research in which it appears as an independent variable (Stein 1980).

This problem is exacerbated when policymakers want to know about not only their envisioned objectives but the unintended consequences of their choices. The effect of war on domestic politics, which is of keen interest to politicians, is detailed in literatures focusing on specific aspects of domestic politics. War appears as an independent variable in a host of disciplines and literatures, including those on the growth of government, inflation, divorce, and social cohesion.[22]

The organization of scholarly activity is problematic for policy relevance for still another reason, its focus on generic rather than particular knowledge. Science values general theory, which strives to replace proper names with analytic constructs (Przeworski and Teune 1970). Among the social sciences, which have not moved as far down this intellectual path as other sciences, economics has made the greatest advances in this direction. Economists do not teach courses on General Motors or Intel. They do not even teach courses on the automobile or computer industries or, for that matter, on the U.S. economy. Rather, they teach theories of the firm and of markets. Students analyze supply and demand rather than particular products or commodities. They are educated to apply what they learn in general courses on micro- and macroeconomics to specific information on their own, to discover the vagaries and particularities of soybeans or computer chips on the job. It is not surprising, therefore, that the business school curriculum only slightly overlaps that of graduate economics training. And it is not surprising that professional schools fill in the particulars through the use of case studies.

In political science, the movement toward general theory has not yet had the same curricular and intellectual impact. Along with courses on theory, most departments continue to teach U.S. foreign policy and the institutional politics of particular nations. Political scientists still use proper names. Nevertheless, the eclipse of area studies and the emphasis on general theory has begun. Yet governments continue to be organized along area-study lines, and policymakers need particularistic information.

A poignant illustration of the problem occurred when the chief architect of a U.S. bombing campaign of North Vietnam asked his professional school mentor, the scholar who had taught him deterrence theory, for counsel on signaling American intentions, but the teacher could not help as his former student had hoped.[23] He needed too much specific knowledge about Vietnam to apply the general model. Ironically, critics of U.S. policy in Southeast Asia had decried the hawks' intellectual commitment to nonspecific propositions without any knowledge of Vietnamese history and culture. Applying general arguments about signaling and even about war's costs and benefits often require knowing how particular actors look at the world and how they assess their costs and benefits. Distressingly, the inability to ascertain the values that underlie other leaders' choices sometimes results in frustrated analysts and policymakers characterizing what they do not understand as crazy and irrational. Many U.S. scholars and political leaders labeled Saddam Hussein a nut when they could not reconstruct (or did not share) the value system in which his choices were perfectly rational and understandable. Marrying the general to the particular is necessary for true policy relevance, but the combination is rarely found in the academy.

The policy inadequacies of generic knowledge-claims is greater when international relations are actor-specific. In other fields, correlational analysis can be the basis for important public policy choices even absent precise causal links. The strong correlational link between smoking and lung cancer involved enough observations that the inference was strong enough to adopt a national health policy aimed at changing the public's attitude toward smoking even though tobacco companies could counter, as they did for many years, that the etiology of lung cancer remained a mystery and that correlation was not causation. That a substantial number of individuals who smoked heavily lived long lives without developing lung cancer provided adequate grounds not to act.

In contrast, the number of available observations of international relations is quite small, and correlations in the social sciences are much smaller.[24] Correlational knowledge that 9 percent of a large population will get some disease may be enough to warrant a policy intervention. But when one scholar found a .3 correlation between alliances and war (meaning that in his data 9 percent of wars could be explained by alliances), his initial conclusion, that NATO should be disbanded, was based on too little data and too weak a link to carry much policy weight.[25] There was no large population of alliances to strengthen the basis for the inference, and the data could not be used to infer that 9 percent of all alliances end in war. Most problematic, however, was the use of aggregate correlational data to draw an inference about one particular entity. In a small $N$ world, the ability to make policy prescriptions for particular actors from poor data is virtually nil.

In their world of general theory, social scientists do not often supply the particularistic information demanded by policymakers. Someone designing a public health policy does not care if a given individual will get lung cancer but about lung cancer rates for the entire population. In contrast, a policymaker devising a foreign policy cares very much about the likely responses of particular countries to particular circumstances. Generic patterns matter only if they give clues to specific situations. But an international relations theorist's generic policy observations are not specific to any actor, which is the interest of the policymaker. The proposition that states balance against the most immediate and proximate threats without regard to ideology would be the basis to conclude that the new Iranian government of 1979 would eventually turn to the United States as the only great power capable of balancing the clearly more direct threat of the Soviet Union. Such analysts waited in vain for Iran to turn to the United States in the 1980s. Similarly, the commonly and strongly supported proposition that leaders who lose wars get replaced provides little comfort to U.S. policymakers still dealing with Saddam Hussein as president of Iraq at the end of a decade that began with the defeat inflicted upon Iraq by the United States. Generic probabilistic knowledge-claims are less useful than particularistic knowledge. A regional specialist's knowledge of Iranian mullahs or Iraqi politics would likely have been more accurate and more useful to U.S. policymakers, even if that knowledge was neither theoretically well grounded nor generalizable. In many areas, in-depth experiential knowledge dominates general theorizing and statistical generalizations for the formation of policy.

### High-Stakes Public Policy and Social Science

International policy choices can have great consequences, ones that may be neither limited nor reversible. Bad foreign policy advice can result in otherwise avoidable wars. This makes the burden for both counselors and advisees a heavy one. They must weigh recommendations carefully. Even broad consensus does not exempt prescriptions from careful scrutiny and possible rejection.

Scholarship develops and cumulates over time. One era's truth is revised and modified, if not turned on its head.[26] The character of the scientific revolutions in the development of the hard sciences should give scholars pause before they rush to make policy pronouncements.

Over a substantial period, a general scholarly consensus on what I call *nuclear stability theory* drew from both historical experience and theoretical models of deterrence to conclude that nuclear weapons stabilized world politics. Mutual assured destruction, in which both the United States and the USSR could withstand an initial strike and still hold sufficient weapons for retaliation, provided a robust and stable deterrence. Yet only a brave few have been willing to venture forth on this foundation to argue that nuclear proliferation might stabilize world politics, should not be opposed, and should perhaps be encouraged. A bolder position, though unvoiced, might be that the superpowers should manage proliferation and provide sufficient survivable forces to new nuclear powers to assure stability and avoid the unstable transition period to mutual assured destruction, the time during which not all nations in a region have yet developed sufficient survivable nuclear capability and those with small vulnerable forces have strong incentives for first-strike preemption.

Few are prepared to extol the virtues of nuclear proliferation, and no one is ready to recommend that great powers encourage and underwrite the process. Policymakers would be appalled, but it is not the expected political response alone that leads scholars to shrink from the consequences of their own work. In 1964, Karl Deutsch and J. David Singer developed their famous argument that multipolarity is more stable than bipolarity. Their case was coherent, logical, and sustained by multiple arguments. But they shied away from the obvious policy implication of their own work and ended with an almost comical retreat from the intellectual ground they had so elegantly staked. Almost three decades later, John Mearsheimer drew on arguments about the stability of the bipolar nuclear world to conclude that analysts would soon look back nostalgically to the stability of the Cold War. Clearly, he argued, the multipolar future would be less stable. But since nuclear weapons had been a stabilizing force in themselves, he pointed out, the world would get a chance to find out whether the stabilizing consequences of nuclear weapons or the destabilizing consequences of multipolarity were more important. Mearsheimer predicted nuclear proliferation and recognized its generally stabilizing impact, yet pulled back from recommending proliferation. Indeed, he shifted the analytic focus of his argument to conclude with a set of ad hoc observations about the undesirability of nuclear weapons in the hands of unstable regimes.[27]

*Nuclear stability theory* is an example of a long-term scholarly consensus that had no impact on policy.[28] Scholars themselves drew back from the obvious policy implications of their work. They went through extensive mental contortions to sustain a belief in the undesirability of nuclear proliferation. This may have reflected their underlying values, an unwillingness to oppose government policy, or a fear of the consequences of being wrong. Ironically, the first scholarly and analytic critique of *proliferation stability theory* came after more than two decades of a policy-irrelevant consensus. Only in the post–Cold War world did there develop a legitimate intellectual debate in which both sides drew on powerful analytic arguments to sustain their respective views on nuclear proliferation. Such a shift in scholarly outlook is one reason not to accept even those policy prescriptions with a broad scholarly consensus behind them.[29]

## Politics and Policy

Foreign policy, like other public policies, entails choosing ends as well as means, yet science, which analyzes means/ends relationships, has little to say about the latter.[30] Social scientists making policy pronouncements have at best the expertise to address means/ends relationships. When they discuss desirable objectives, their opinions should carry no more weight than that of any other voter. How, then, are scientists to separate their own policy preferences from their policy prescriptions?[31] It is no wonder that social scientists (who mask their policy preferences in expertise) and policymakers (who worry as much about the political as the policy risks of their programs) so suspect one another.[32]

U.S. security policy during the Cold War rested on the country's nuclear weapons, and the continued development of that arsenal and the desirability of negotiated nuclear agreements both depended critically on scientific advice. Yet despite the relatively well developed body of accepted knowledge claims in physics, the relationship between scientists and government was amazingly conflictual:

> At the root of the progressive decline of the president's science advisory apparatus has been a progressive loss of faith in the process by both sides: by scientists in the ability of the government to make proper choices based upon the evidence, rather than partisan pressures; and by presidents in the capacity of scientists to give objective advice, uncolored by personal views. (Herken 1992, 217)

Physicists were disappointed when their views were ignored, but policymakers often found the scientists' views a reflection less of science than of political belief. Yet throughout the Cold War, presidents have had to rely on the technical knowledge of the scientific community even as the problematic relationship between scientists and foreign policy affected scientific advice on national security issues.[33] During the late 1930s, physicists saw their sole advisory problem as an inability to get their views about the implications of scientific developments to the president of the United States. Beginning with the National Defense Research Council's creation as the United States neared entry into World War II, a variety of institutions were established to bring scientific advice to the president.[34] The President's Science Advisory Council, born in 1957, set up the first direct channel between scientists and the White House, although it and the post of science adviser were abolished in 1973.

Like scientific counsel, foreign policy advice is encumbered by scholars' implicit preferences and their disdain, nonetheless, for the political. The theorists' policy irrelevance is magnified by their paucity of empirically verified knowledge-claims and the uncertainty of and variance in their findings. Like physicists, political scientists have strong political beliefs and constitute a comparable aviary of hawks and doves. As noted above, their views can even keep them from recommending policies that flow logically from their scholarship. And they, too, proffer their recommendations with a concern for policy rather than political optimality. In fact, they often decry the impact of politics upon policy.[35]

## Process-Oriented Prescription

Much of the important policy-relevant work in the field has focused not on substance but on process — on the *how* rather than the *what* of foreign policy.[36] Its aim, to improve the quality of decision making by improving the way decisions are made, reflects the more general intellectual developments of the last centuries. Across an array of disciplines, scholars have focused on improving the quality (read rationality) of human decision making. Early developers of probability theory hoped to improve their gambling fortunes. Logicians wanted to help people reason better. Decision theory, in all its manifestations across disciplines, is one of the great achievements of the last century and a half (Nozick 1993). As developed in philosophy and economics, this typically formal work tells reasoners what to do rather than what to avoid; it stresses how to be rational. Individuals, presumed to be self-interested, can learn to apply the tools of decision making to improve their outcomes.

Such studies of decision making, built on the presumption that individuals are crippled decision makers, have been largely normative, with an emphasis on increasing their rationality. Decision theory can, therefore, be seen as a tool. Just as the telescope and microscope allow people to see things beyond their normal eyesight (the simple observational mechanism they are stuck with), such tools as probability theory, logic, decision theory, and game theory can improve the choices that individuals would otherwise make.[37]

The self-conscious use of decision theory by self-interested individuals becomes *self-validating*.[38] Once normative tools are used self-consciously to make choices and guide behavior, they can be employed as positive explanations by scholars interested in explaining behavior. Models of choice that began as normative guides to improve behavior become positive explanations for it.

In contrast, psychological studies of decision making have analyzed how individuals failed to match the requirements of the rational actor model. Cognitive psychologists have shown how people misassess probability and how decision is affected by the ways in which choices are framed. They have also demonstrated that biological (hardwired) inference shortcuts often lead to decisions that violate statistical inference and how crisis and stress reduce the effectiveness of individual and group decision making.

The normative implication of psychological explanations of actual decision-making processes is that an awareness of these psychological pressures and forces can make individuals better decision makers. In fact, such a normative argument permeates this work. Through role-playing and crisis simulation, people can learn how to fight groupthink and premature closure.

Psychological studies of actual decision making are, therefore, *self-falsifying* once known. They presume that self-awareness vitiates the implications of psychology, that knowledge will lead people to avoid pitfalls they might otherwise fall into.[39] The normative implication of positive knowledge of how people make decisions is that people will no longer make decisions in those ways once they become self-aware.[40]

Scholarship on foreign policy process has taken two tracks. One is directed at optimality; it is *formal, normative, and self-validating*. Awareness of these arguments leads people to use them, and so the normative becomes the positive. A second track focuses on the constraints and limitations to rationality in foreign policy decision making. This path is empirical and positive, but its knowledge claims are *self-falsifying*. Awareness of the ways in which individuals actually make decisions leads them to avoid pitfalls and do better.

## The Limits of Policy Relevance

In addition to the policy inapplicability of extant theory, formal work on the logic of decision making tells us that there are limits to the policy relevance of theory. The tools of strategic choice (commonly known as game theory) seem to provide the optimal policy tool for decision makers. The models incorporate the preferences of those who need to make a choice with whatever knowledge is available about the preferences of others. Foreign policy is, after all, inherently strategic. Leaders are making choices on behalf of states in a context of interaction with other states. Such models, then, are perfectly suited for use by both decision makers and analysts interested in explanation. That such tools were created with a normative intent, as tools to improve decision making, only reinforces their prospective decision-making utility. Ironically, developments in the field of strategic choice suggest the limitations of the models themselves. These results suggest that the informational requirements for applying theories of choice are immense and unlikely to be met in any real-world situations. Moreover, the models are plagued with incompleteness and indeterminacy.

In cases where a government needs to know the choices that another government will make, for example, the literature on social choice provides an indication of both what information is required and the limits of what we can infer from that knowledge when that other state is not a unitary actor. The other state may consist of different branches of government, different political factions, different governmental agencies, or even a number of high-level officials who will jointly make decisions. Such cases can be modeled, but they very quickly reach the limits of the tractable and knowable. Formal results, such as Arrow's impossibility theorem, establish that even a knowledge of the preferences and the rules of decision making may not be enough to determine the social choice without a more exact specification of the process. When dealing with a nonunitary actor, the aggregation problems associated with arriving at a collective choice bedevil attempts to assess the basis of others' choices and the nature of their likely reactions. The implications of Arrow's impossibility theorem led one scholar to conclude that international relations theorists had no choice but to treat states as unitary integrated actors, as if they were a single person with a utility function (Bueno de Mesquita 1981, 11–18).

Finessing the aggregation problem by treating states as unitary actors only simplifies the analytic problem somewhat. Applying strategic interaction models in such cases still requires a knowledge of the other actors' complete options and their preferences. Knowing their preferences is an exceptionally strong requirement that extends beyond the typically discussed notion of knowing the intentions of other states.[41] One needs to know how others evaluate the full range of outcomes, including ones that will never be reached. The existence of incomplete information typically generates situations with multiple equilibria and takes the analysis into a realm in which there are competing equilibrium concepts. In such cases, strategic interaction models provide no further clue for making decisions — they are incomplete and indeterminate.[42]

Formal work in decision theory, and in social and strategic choice, delineates both the informational requirements for decision making and the limitations of advice given the available information. It tells us that even as we accumulate knowledge about how the world works, there are inherent limits to our ability to generate unique optimal policy prescriptions.[43]

## Conclusion

Policymakers will always turn to advisers and new ideas. Public policy is purposeful behavior sustained by some objective and some sense of appropriate means. In that sense, it is always rooted in ideas. As John Maynard Keynes put it:

> The ideas of economists and political philosophers, both when they are right and when they are wrong, are more powerful than is commonly understood. Indeed the world is ruled by little else. Practical men, who believe themselves to be quite exempt from any intellectual influence, are usually the slaves of some defunct economist. Madmen in authority, who hear voices in the air, are distilling their frenzy from some academic scribblers of a few years back. I am sure that the power of vested interests is vastly exaggerated compared with the gradual encroachment of ideas. (1936, 383)

If ideas are indeed the cornerstone of policy, then knowledge rooted in theory and empirical observation is better than a hunch without any foundation in theory or empirical regularity, even though well-grounded choices may still involve mistakes. It is better than studying entrails or turning to the stars. Policy errors arise even in fields far more scientific than international relations, those with better and more plentiful data and with possibilities for experimentation. Policy decisions about medical treatments cannot always be made from animal models and experiments. Additional data sometimes leads to complete reversals in medical recommendations. The medicine practiced in earlier centuries was often wrongheaded and caused mischief and tragedy. But even though it consisted of knowledge-claims rooted in an analytic logic and subject to empirical falsification, it took generations before individuals going to a physician for help could be certain of receiving treatment that was more beneficial than harmful.

Closer to home, the field of economics has clearly grown in its understanding of the way the economic world works. Harry Truman, who regularly heard economists demur from offering clear-cut advice by noting "on the one hand" and "on the other hand," said he wanted "a one-handed economist." Some are now prepared to say that we have finally entered the world of that one-handed economist (Mueller 2000; but see Lal 2000). Politicians following the advice of economists today are more likely to benefit than in times past, although harmful economic advice was peddled in some subfields (e.g., development economics) as recently as the 1970s.

The changing nature of the policy role of international relations is likely to follow that of other fields, especially other social sciences. The advisers to the throne who proffered policy advice in times past were as likely to offer quackery as sound counsel. The ability to sell unproven home remedies without much theoretical and empirical validation remains even in developed fields.[44]

International relations as a field remains at an early stage of development. Its data are sparse, its theoretical disputes still largely unresolved, its advice still of the two-handed variety. It is not yet a rigorous discipline from which the uncredentialed can be readily ascertained. There are too many practitioners practicing without a license, and even those with credentials carry a small tool kit with little to offer and little of that assured. At the moment, it is not clear whether the policymaker who seeks scholarly advice benefits upon receiving it. But, within the limits of the knowable, that will change.

NOTES

My thanks for the support of the UCLA Academic Senate and the University of California Institute on Global Conflict and Cooperation. My thanks to the editors and Amy Davis for their advice and counsel.

1. Residual uses of the supernatural continued well past the Enlightenment. The Nazis consulted astrologers, as did Nancy Reagan. Goldhamer (1978, 141) points out that the conflict between the analytic and intuitive mind in politics has always existed, labeled by such dichotomies as "Mind versus Heart, Rational versus Traditional, Modern versus Ancients, Reason versus Intuition, Calculation versus Judgment, Scholar versus Actor, Theory versus Practice and Experience, Book Learning versus Common Sense." He goes on to note (142) that the scholar "has a somewhat ambiguous status" and is "just as likely to be rejected by the intuitive and practical man as by the theoretician and calculator."

2. Edwin Meese III, White House counsel to Ronald Reagan, described

an expert as "somebody who is more than 50 miles from home, has no responsibility for implementing the advice he gives, and shows slides" (Simpson 1988, 20).

3. Princeton University's Woodrow Wilson School was originally founded in 1930, the Fletcher School of Law and Diplomacy in 1933, Johns Hopkins School of Advanced International Studies (SAIS) in 1943, Harvard University's John F. Kennedy School of Government (founded as the Graduate School of Public Administration) in 1936, and Columbia University's School of International and Public Affairs (founded as just the School of International Affairs) in 1946. In contrast, Columbia University's other socially relevant professional schools were founded much earlier: the School of Journalism in 1912, the School of Social Work in 1898, and the School of Public Health in 1919.

4. One exception came when President Reagan long delayed appointing a council chair, was quite willing to go outside the academy to find one, and considered the possibility of abolishing the office.

5. There has also been a temporal component to this divide in economics. In some periods, abstract theory and formalization were unwelcome. This was the charitable reason for Harvard's failure to offer Paul Samuelson a job (Silk 1976; Samuelson 1992). In the 1990s, pure theory was again increasingly downplayed by many economics departments that instead stressed the importance of empirical application.

6. See the discussion of the impact of World War II on scholarly research interests in Stein 1980.

7. For popular treatments, see Kaplan 1983 and Herken 1985. Governmental assistance for the development of deterrence theory extended to very abstract theoretical enterprises, including mathematics and game theory, that might be only remotely applicable to the real world. For a discussion of game theory's normative roots and the governmental financing of its development, and for additional cities, see Stein 1999.

8. Vernon 1971; Keohane and Nye 1972; Chayes and Chayes 1993. The counterattack emphasized the continued centrality of nation-states and saw the prospect for war as defining international relations. Waltz's (1979) *Theory of International Politics* should be read as an example of the empire striking back to reaffirm the central core of international relations theory. Even its title suggests a rebuke to alternative formulations. Attacked, proponents of the position quickly retreated from their excessive optimism, although not so fully as to extinguish all debate. Keohane and Nye's delineation of "complex interdependence" was a dramatic retreat from transnational relations. The 1990s version of the debate included Mearsheimer's (1994) attack on the utility of international organizations and the responses to him from the advocates of "liberal institutionalism."

9. The field of economics came under increasing criticism from the 1970s to the 1990s for a focus defined by theoretical concerns internal to the field rather than by external economic developments. Important economic trends in productivity and wages, for example, were little understood by modern economists and, more important, seemed of little concern and interest to many of them. In contrast, John Maynard Keynes, earlier in the century, was dramati-

cally affected by and interested in such real-world developments as the Great Depression of the 1930s.

10. The failure to predict the end of the Cold War suggests a problem for the field's policy relevance, but not for international relations theory as such, despite the claims of many that international relations theory must be rethought and reconstructed. The end of the Cold War, as well as its unpredictability, are both fully explainable within the core realist tradition. Realism is a typical equilibrium argument in which perturbations are exogenous shocks (Stein 1993). The theory has greater difficulty with explaining the Soviet Union's retreat from its empire without a fight, though a consistent story for this could be developed within the framework of the theory. More problematic for realism is the failure of the exogenous shock of the Soviet Union's implosion to have resulted in the reequilibrium dynamics central to the model's operation.

11. This poses a special problem for scholars who must invest their human capital in areas that may literally disappear, at least for substantial periods of their intellectual lifetimes. In some cases, a focus of inquiry can disappear almost entirely, as happened with the end of the Cold War and the collapse of the USSR when those whose expertise involved the Cold War, deterrence, weapons systems, and the Soviet Union itself were forced to find alternative areas of study. When currents shift, scholars must decide what to do. Often, bitter generational battles can ensue. Peace scientists were aghast to see the eclipse of their field and the emergence of international political economy. One eminent peace theorist reacted with horror to young scholars studying the trade in commodities by noting at one international meeting that coffee was less relevant than nuclear weapons, which remained the central problem for international politics. He decried the diminution of intellectual talent that still focused on the planet's core concern, the avoidance of nuclear war.

12. See Micklethwait and Wooldridge 1996. One painful example was the downsizing fad begun by the best-seller *Reengineering the Corporation,* which, most soon came to admit, did not work as advertised. Faddism also exists even in the hardest sciences. One physicist describes it this way: "It is easy to jump on the latest bandwagon when your mind is in one of its usual states of hibernation and you don't have any decent ideas of your own. This is particularly true in my own field, cosmology, where definitive experimental tests of theories are slow in coming. So you can calculate to your heart's content without fear of being proved wrong in the near future" (Rothman 1989, viii).

13. A few isolated bureaucratic agencies have, during certain periods, been willing to support basic research without any sense of immediate or even potential utility.

14. Lindblom and Cohen (1979, 5–6, 8, 29) argue that professional social inquiry includes the entire panoply of academic social science and can affect social problem solving quite indirectly.

15. Analogously, technical analyses of the stock market, which are atheoretical trend-trackers, remain useful. Medicine also finds a correlational knowledge of factors dubbed *markers* to be useful for diagnosis even absent theories causally linking them to underlying diseases. Purely descriptive work can also

have profound theoretical consequences. Margaret Mead's description of the gender relationships on a single island was of great theoretical importance because she depicted something that should not have existed if Freudian theory were correct.

16. Below, I offer a set of reasons why much international relations research is not particularly relevant to the making of foreign policy. But there are also more general problems that make the social sciences of limited use in solving social problems (Lindblom and Cohen 1979).

17. This argument was most forcefully made in a popular magazine and in an applied journal by John Mearsheimer (1990a, 1990b).

18. This can be illustrated using an analogy common to the field, that of states as firms. Just as firms cannot affect the market's structure, for it remains outside them and results from the cumulative combination of firms' behaviors, so states cannot affect the structure of the international system.

19. This is Kissinger's position about the utility of international relations theory.

20. The emergence of events-data studies in the late 1960s and 1970s was one response to the failure of international relations scholars to study the bulk of international relations that occur in between the extremes of alliances and war. Compiling databases of international events and coding them on a scale of cooperation and conflict was a way of broadening the empirical reach of the field. Unfortunately, too many empirical studies focused on descriptive statistics, and the entire exercise ultimately got bogged down in methodological disputes. Later, the recognition of the need for broader data could be seen in the development of a behavioral component for the Correlates of War data project.

21. The term is not always applied consonantly. The characterization of a "special relationship" between the United States and Britain signaled that Britain was closer than America's other allies. But the term has also been used to signal the U.S. commitment to Israeli security absent an alliance (though many consistently and incorrectly call Israel a U.S. ally). The problem is similar to that which exists in interpersonal relationships as new terms are periodically required to distinguish different degrees of commitment (*significant other* joins *fiancé* and *spouse*). Our vocabulary, in international as well as other relations, is inadequate for the range of observable relationships.

22. For a longer intellectual history of the study of the impact of war and its evolution in this century, see Stein 1980.

23. The relationship, between Thomas Schelling and John McNaughton, is discussed in Kaplan 1983, 332–36).

24. There are generic empirical problems inherent in international relations. There are too few countries and, happily, too few wars and alliances on the dependent side, for adequate empirical analysis. But the number of independent variables is large, and so significant findings are hard to come by. Not surprisingly, the scientization and mathematization of the field have emphasized formal studies and simulation rather than empirical work.

25. When the paper was subsequently published, the policy prescription was substantially toned down.

26. The change to viewing the earth as round rather than flat marked a significant shift with important consequences, as did the change from believing that the sun moved around the earth to the other way around. Such dramatic changes are also found in the social sciences. Economic theory once held that printing money would lead to lower interest rates; later theory held that printing money led to higher ones. Plausible theory and historical experience both underlay the comparable certainly with which the two arguments were propounded. But one economist notes that a Rip van Winkle who went to sleep in 1870 and awoke in the 1990s would find that the economic theory he knew before nodding off remained perfectly adequate — that he could do without the intellectual twists, turns, and diversions of the intervening century (Lal 2000).

27. Mearsheimer's analysis, until the very end, is purely systemic. The ad hoc arguments at the end bring in domestic politics; they are unsubstantiated, undeveloped, and outside his analytic framework. The theory about nuclear stability does not hold that possession of nuclear weapons by sober states is stabilizing. Rather, the point of that argument is that possession is stabilizing since it makes states sober in the realization that no objective is worth the cost. To argue that unstable regimes should not have nuclear weapons is wholly outside the argument and inconsistent with the whole thrust of the nuclear stability hypothesis.

28. The scholarly work on deterrence stability was consistent with a finite-deterrence strategy and not with large-scale deployments driven by war-fighting doctrines. Yet both U.S. procurements and U.S. targeting plans reflected warfighting doctrines held by the military and did not reflect the scholarly consensus.

29. A scholarly consensus, especially as regards an uncertain future, is also harder to find than most imagine. Paul Ehrlich of Stanford, in discussing the National Academy of Sciences, said it "would be unable to give a unanimous decision if asked whether the sun would rise tomorrow" (quoted in Simpson 1988, 139).

30. See the classic statements by Max Weber.

31. Lindblom and Cohen (1979, 11) point out that political scientists will push for analytical problem solving even when there are conflicting values.

32. The distinction between political and policy risk comes from Lamborn 1985.

33. This paragraph draws upon Herken 1992.

34. This was not the first time that war spurred institutional development in the relationship between the state and science. The National Academy of Sciences was created during the Civil War, and the National Research Council was established in 1916.

35. The disdain of the foreign policy advising elite for domestic politics is sometimes articulated in the strongest terms. George Kennan, an intellectual architect of containment, complained about the ability of democracies to respond early and smoothly to foreign policy challenges. A comparable complaint

was later voiced by Oliver North, who felt frustrated by the Reagan administration's inability to awaken the public to the challenge he believed Nicaragua posed.

36. Henry Kissinger (1979) argues in his memoirs that the same can be said of what one learns in government service: "High office teaches decision making, not substance."

37. For an extended discussion of this and the use of strategic interaction models in international relations, see Stein 1999.

38. An interesting example comes from the government's sale of cellular phone rights. All the bidders hired their own game theorists, and most accepted the recommendations they received from them. Not surprisingly, the bids did not meet the projections made by non–game theorists prior to the bidding. One bidder who did not follow the advice did not do as well (Koselka 1995).

39. This is the claim of psychoanalysis, with its core presumption that patient awareness is the key to treatment.

40. Much the same can be said about organizational process models of decision making (more typically called bureaucratic politics). The presumption here, too, is that awareness of how organizational dynamics impair decision making can itself improve the quality of decisions. The process literature often portrays itself as offering an alternative explanation to purpose. Yet much of it focuses on policy implementation rather than adoption, and that which focuses on the latter is descriptive rather than theoretical and constitutes a supplement rather than an alternative to purposive explanation. For one of the few attempts to integrate organizational with cognitive process in an explanation of foreign policy choice, see Gronich 1991.

41. A sense of the magnitude of the problem for those wishing to apply these tools is provided by scholarly disagreement about the exact nature of past historical episodes. If scholars with access to the documents of all parties cannot agree long afterward about the nature of the strategic game that states thought they were engaged in, then policymakers in the midst of a crisis have a much more difficult time.

42. The strategic interaction literature is full of competing equilibrium concepts and paradoxes in which plausible decision criteria generate different choices. Indeed, one general implication of work in decision theory and social choice theory is that the imposition of too many criteria for any choice generates at some point a null set — that is, there is no choice that meets all conditions. Selection requires relaxing one or more of the desired criteria. But relaxing different criteria will lead to a different choices. Often, relaxing any one criterion generates a feasible set rather than a unique outcome.

43. For an excellent introduction to the utility and potential of strategic choice for international relations theory, see Lake and Powell 1999. For my views of the strengths and limitations of the approach, see Stein 1990, 1999.

44. An interesting example comes from Arthur Laffer's marketing of supply-side economics and the Laffer curve. His specific argument was scoffed at by mainstream economists, who complained not only about his argument but about his credentials and lack of a Ph.D. in economics.

REFERENCES

Bueno de Mesquita, Bruce. 1981. *The War Trap.* New Haven: Yale University Press.

Chayes, Abram, and Antonia Handler Chayes. 1993. On Compliance. *International Organization* 47:175–205.

Deutsch, Karl, and J. David Singer. 1964. Multipolar Power Systems and International Stability. *World Politics* 16:390–406.

Furner, Mary O. 1975. *Advocacy and Objectivity: A Crisis in the Professionalization of American Social Science, 1865–1905.* Lexington: University Press of Kentucky.

Goldhamer, Herbert. 1978. *The Adviser.* New York: Elsevier North-Holland.

Gronich, Lori Helene. 1991. Expertise, Naivete, and Decisionmaking: A Cognitive Processing Theory of Foreign Policy Choice. Ph.D. diss., UCLA.

Herken, Gregg. 1985. *Counsels of War.* New York: Alfred A. Knopf.

———. 1992. *Cardinal Choices: Presidential Science Advising from the Atomic Bomb to SDI.* New York: Oxford University Press.

Kaplan, Fred. 1983. *The Wizards of Armageddon.* New York: Simon and Schuster.

Kaysen, Carl. 1990. Is War Obsolete? *International Security* 14:42–64.

Keohane, Robert O., and Joseph S. Nye Jr., eds. 1972. *Transnational Relations and World Politics.* Cambridge: Harvard University Press.

———. 1977. *Power and Interdependence: World Politics in Transition.* Boston: Little, Brown.

Keynes, J. M. 1936. *The General Theory of Employment, Interest, and Money.* London: Macmillan.

Klotz, Irving M. 1986. *Diamond Dealers and Feather Merchants: Tales from the Sciences.* Boston: Birkhäuser.

Koselka, Rita. 1995. Playing Poker with Craig McCaw. *Forbes* 156, no. 1: 62–64.

Lake, David A., and Robert Powell, eds. 1999. *Strategic Choice and International Relations.* Princeton: Princeton University Press.

Lal, Deepak. 2000. The World Economy at the End of the Millennium. In *Politics, Prosperity and Peace: Essays in Honor of Richard Rosecrance,* ed. John Mueller. The Political Economy of Global Interdependence, ed. Thomas D. Willett. Boulder: Westview Press.

Lamborn, Alan C. 1985. Risk and Foreign Policy Choice. *International Studies Quarterly* 29:385–410.

Lindblom, Charles E., and David K. Cohen. 1979. *Usable Knowledge: Social Science and Social Problem Solving.* New Haven: Yale University Press.

Mearsheimer, John J. 1990a. Back to the Future: Instability in Europe after the Cold War. *International Security* 15:5–56.

———. 1990b. Why We Will Soon Miss the Cold War. *Atlantic* 266, no. 2: 35–45.

———. 1994. The False Promise of International Institutions. *International Security* 19:5–49.

Micklethwait, John, and Adrian Wooldridge. 1996. *The Witch Doctors: Making Sense of the Management Gurus.* New York: Random House, Times Books.

Mueller, John E. 1989. *Retreat from Doomsday: The Obsolescence of Major War.* New York: Basic Books.

———. 2000. The Rise of the Politically Incorrect One-handed Economist or Je Lepšie byt' Bohat a Zdrav, ako Chudobn a Chor. In *Politics, Prosperity and Peace: Essays in Honor of Richard Rosecrance,* ed. John Mueller. The Political Economy of Global Interdependence, ed. Thomas D. Willett. Boulder: Westview Press.

Nozick, Robert. 1993. *The Nature of Rationality.* Princeton: Princeton University Press.

Przeworski, Adam, and Henry Teune. 1970. *The Logic of Comparative Social Inquiry.* Comparative Studies in Behavioral Science. New York: Wiley-Interscience.

Rothman, Tony. 1989. *Science à la Mode: Physical Fashions and Fictions.* Princeton: Princeton University Press.

Samuelson, Paul A. 1992. My Life Philosophy: Policy Credos and Working Ways. In *Eminent Economists: Their Life Philosophies,* ed. Michael Szenberg. New York: Cambridge University Press.

Silk, Leonard. 1976. *The Economists.* New York: Basic Books.

Simpson, James B., comp. 1988. *Simpson's Contemporary Quotations.* New York: Houghton Mifflin.

Stein, Arthur A. 1980. *The Nation at War.* Baltimore: Johns Hopkins University Press.

———. 1990. *Why Nations Cooperate: Circumstance and Choice in International Relations.* Ithaca: Cornell University Press.

———. 1993. Disequilibrium and Equilibrium Theory: Explaining War in a Theory of Peace, Explaining Alliances in a Theory of Autonomy. Paper presented at the annual meeting of the American Political Science Association, Washington, D.C.

———. 1999. The Limits of Strategic Choice: Constrained Rationality and Incomplete Explanation. In *Strategic Choice and International Relations,* ed. David A. Lake and Robert Powell. Princeton: Princeton University Press.

Vernon, Raymond. 1971. *Sovereignty at Bay: The Multinational Spread of U.S. Enterprises.* Harvard Multinational Enterprise Series. New York: Basic Books.

Waltz, Kenneth N. 1979. *Theory of International Politics.* Menlo Park, Calif.: Addison-Wesley.

# Scholars and Statesmen: Framework for a Productive Dialogue

*Joseph Lepgold*

On its face, intellectually powerful theory should be useful to policymakers. Indeed, it is more counterintuitive that better theory would *not* be useful to policymakers than the reverse. Reflecting this premise, many international relations (IR) theorists and at least some practitioners prefer a productive dialogue.[1] Far more, however, downplay the prospects for policy-relevant IR theory. This essay explores how this debate might be reframed in ways that will generate more productive conversations on the problem of policy relevance. It concludes that while there are some obstacles, the theory-practice dialogue in IR can be improved in ways that advance the agendas of both theorists and policymakers.

I make three arguments that bear on these issues. First, while there is a communications gap between many IR theorists and practitioners, there is a far wider range of IR activities and groups than the simple theorist-practitioner dichotomy suggests. Second, the institutions and professional networks that support the varied activities of these groups have already created the framework for a transmission belt that could be used to link theory to practice more easily and visibly. Third, these groups share a basic goal: to develop an ability to analyze the strategic context facing political leaders precisely enough to evaluate competing causal claims. With these points in mind, I also argue that theory can be useful to policymakers in various ways, and that different theories will contribute more to some than to others.

Of course, people who are profoundly skeptical of theory are unlikely to be enthused about efforts to make theory relevant to policy choices. But the issue for theorists who feel otherwise is what *they* can do to further this purpose. A generation ago, Abraham Kaplan suggested a solution:

The criticism that a plan of action is 'all right in theory but it won't work in practice' . . . must be properly understood. The theory may specify conditions which are not fulfilled in the particular case before us; the criticism then amounts to saying that the proposal is a good solution, but to another problem. A theory may even involve conditions which can never be fulfilled, because of the idealizations involved — perfect elasticity, frictionless motions, and the like. Then the criticism in question can only be to the effect that for the case at hand the assumed condition is an oversimplification, and that in this case the theory will not help to provide even an approximate solution. But unless in some cases the plan of action is of some use in solving our problem it is hard to know what is meant by the concession that it is 'all right in theory.' Theory is *of* practice, provided only that the mode and contexts of its application are suitably specified.[2]

The task, then, is to specify more completely and precisely the defining characteristics of different theoretical arguments and the varied situations that confront policymakers.

This essay explores how Kaplan's strategy might be pursued, given the contemporary organization of the IR field in the United States. The first section of this essay reviews and reframes the notion of a theory-practice gap. The second section discusses different ways in which theory can be useful to policymakers and suggests how better specified theories could help fulfill these purposes. The third section applies the argument to a question that has grown in significance over the last generation: When do international regimes facilitate the achievement of national policy objectives?

### Rethinking the Theorist-Practitioner Gap in International Relations

Many people believe that "much of today's [IR] scholarship is either irrelevant or inaccessible to policymakers," and that there is, as an almost inevitable consequence, a "chasm" separating the "two cultures" of IR theorists and officials.[3] One reason often given for this gap is that theorists and officials have different professional incentives. They often frame questions differently, face different kinds of deadlines, and usually seek different kinds of answers. While officials often feel pressured to make complex decisions quickly, "[scholars'] product is published knowledge, and their audience and judges are their colleagues. They are not necessarily concerned with the application of their knowledge."[4]

Little in the modern academic incentive system rewards applied work: "the reward structure of the academy does not promote policy research . . . [it] is not likely to get a scholar academic tenure."[5]

This difference in incentives is accentuated by policymakers' desire for precise predictions about the results of possible policy choices.[6] They want to know that if condition Z exists, or that if they do X, Y is likely. Few existing theories provide this kind of knowledge.[7] Without it, officials are often reluctant to make risky choices based on academic advice. Theorists, meanwhile, often worry that practitioners' preoccupation with predictability might lead them to conflate correlation with causation. For instance, U.S. officials find the argument that democracies do not fight among themselves appealing because they think it helps them produce a result they like, even if neither they (nor anyone else) understands precisely why it works. Theorists, by contrast, have devoted much effort to analyzing whether or why this relationship holds.

A second reason often given for a gap is that officials care about variables they can control or influence in the short to medium term.[8] Theorists, on the other hand, often have not framed their questions so as to focus on manipulable variables. Admittedly, this can be hard to do. Many scholars are interested in phenomena that are inherently abstract or otherwise not easily manipulable, and the explanatory variables they use may not provide the manipulable tools policymakers want. For example, while theorists may identify competing ethnic identities as a key factor in the outbreak of communal violence, this variable provides officials little useful leverage. An answer that might satisfy a scholar may be of little use to officials seeking to forestall such violence.

A third problem is a perception that knowledge too often fails to accumulate because academic debates rarely seem to get resolved. For instance, prior to the Gulf War and the U.S. intervention in Haiti there was much discussion as to whether economic sanctions can change behavior in target states. Despite much research and continuing practical interest in the issue, however, this debate remains unresolved.[9]

A fourth problem is that IR theory and research agendas often mirror contemporary events rather than reflect on them from a distance. For example, the Liberal reaction to Realism stemmed partly from the presumed decline of U.S. economic power and the oil crises of the 1970s, while the rise of Structural Realism in the 1980s reflected a renewed Cold War.[10] IR study in the United States is especially prone to faddishness because major foundations fund many key conferences and research projects, and in doing so they often react to the latest turn of world events.[11]

Theories that reflect events this closely carry two costs. One is that theorists lose their comparative advantage; they become little more than commentators on current events, but often without the detailed substantive expertise of journalists or historians.[12] A second is that they can help practitioners only when they have some distance from current developments. Much theoretical work in political science has been prompted by real-world issues that suggest intellectual puzzles. Especially in IR, one would expect a close commingling between discussions within a scholarly field (what Lakatos calls a discipline's internal history) and discussions of substantive, nondisciplinary issues that affect scholars' interest in various theoretical problems (its external history).[13] As noted below, the development of international regime theory in the 1980s in part reflected a waning focus on deterrence and a shift toward policy issues that put institutions closer to center stage. A good IR theory, however, should identify and explain patterns that transcend particular issues, actors, and historical eras.[14] In doing so, it should explain and help anticipate major changes in world politics. Theory offers little explanatory power if it must be reinvented each time issues, actors, and eras change.

All of these are genuine problems. But what needs to be done to make existing theory more visibly and easily useful to policymakers — identifying the defining conditions of different theoretical arguments more precisely and systematically — would accelerate rather than slow down theoretical growth. Moreover, a framework for connecting theories to specific policy problems already exists. There appear to be four groups of literatures and professional activities in the field. These activities are supported by institutions and professional networks that create a potential transmission belt that runs from "pure" theory to "pure" policy-making. The two intermediate types of activities involve people who have mixes of theoretical and applied interests. Since there is less professional distance between any two adjacent types of activities than across the whole spectrum, a series of bridges exists across much of it. These IR activities can be arrayed as shown in figure 1.

*Group 1: General Theory.*    General theory aims to subsume under a coherent explanation a broad array of empirical phenomena; it is typically not attached to specific categories of issues, temporal domains, or spatial domains. It corresponds to what Miroslav Nincic calls *basic theory* in his chapter in this volume. Because general theories seek to transcend substantive contexts, they often take a deductive form. Rational choice approaches exemplify a Group I theory that focuses on the processes and outcomes of strategic interaction. Group I work asks such questions as: When do actors cooperate?[15] To what extent are actors' preferences endogenous to strategic interaction, and to what extent are they exoge-

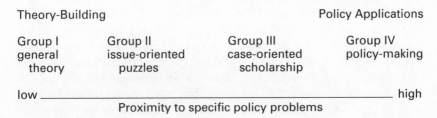

| Theory-Building | | | Policy Applications |
| --- | --- | --- | --- |
| Group I<br>general<br>theory | Group II<br>issue-oriented<br>puzzles | Group III<br>case-oriented<br>scholarship | Group IV<br>policy-making |

low _____ high
Proximity to specific policy problems

**Fig. 1. Professional IR literatures and activities**

nous?[16] In the United States, such work is typically published in such IR journals as *International Organization, International Studies Quarterly,* and *World Politics,* and in such general political science journals as the *American Political Science Review.*

*Group II: Issue-Oriented Puzzles.* This type of literature analyzes particular classes of puzzles that are tied to specific categories of issues, temporal domains, and spatial domains. Puzzles are phenomena for which there is no adequate (or at least widely accepted) explanation.[17] In Group II work, unlike Group I theories, the range within which explanatory variables vary is typically restricted (though this is often implicit rather than explicit), and research questions are generally tied to specific empirical referents. Group II literature is designed to account for a pattern evident in a specific set of cases rather than to account for a wide variety of outcomes with a single explanation.

Group II comprises two kinds of IR literatures. One is area studies; it is based on the assumption that certain mixes or ranges of variables distinguish regions from one another. This work sometimes borrows from that in Group I. One scholar, for instance, has explored why Arab leaders who value their sovereign autonomy have also at times identified with a wider, pan-Arabic referent group that had incompatible preferences.[18] Some area specialists in the United States move in and out of government positions over the course of their careers and share ideas in various ways through professional networks.

A second kind of Group II literature explores theory-driven puzzles. While this work implicitly shares the area specialists' assumption that certain mixes or ranges of variables distinguish one set of problems from others, the models in this type of literature tend to be grounded more explicitly in theories that apply across actors and regions. Alliance behavior, for example, has been explained by Group II models that claim leaders balance against external threats, against internal as well as external threats, and by models that see actors' learning rather than extant material conditions as the source of policy choices.[19]

Journals specializing in Group II work include *Latin American Research Review, International Security, Security Studies, Global Governance,* and *Political Science Quarterly.* Group II and Group I publication outlets overlap: *World Politics* and *International Organization* examine some region or issue-specific puzzles, while *International Security* at times focuses on issues of wider scope. But what distinguishes Group II work is a focus on puzzles that originate in and apply to substantive referents, rather than arguments that seek to transcend such referents.

*Group III: Case-Oriented Scholarship.* The work in this group seeks to explain certain types of policy-relevant events or situations. Specialists in this role recognize that the logic underlying policy may need to be fleshed out in a generalizable way, so that lessons can be learned and needless trial and error avoided.[20] Yet their interest in generic knowledge is largely instrumental. For instance, a former U.S. official wrote a book on how military power can be effectively used in the post–Cold War world. He borrowed some classic work on force and diplomacy from Group I and Group II scholars such as Thomas Schelling and Alexander George,[21] but focused on a policy audience. Group III publication outlets include journals such as *Survival* and *Orbis,* as well as many products of think tanks.

Group III work is produced largely in think tanks, at least in the United States, where Group I and Group II work dominates within most university faculties. It is also produced in universities with public policy or international affairs programs, which focus on professional training rather than generic knowledge for its own sake. Think tanks operate at the boundary between government and the part of the academic community with a sustained interest in policy.[22] They draw into dialogue people that "cross the conventional boundaries between types of expertise and experiences. University professors sit [a]round the table with military officers and diplomats, with journalists from the quality press, businessmen and bankers, politicians and their research assistants."[23] As a result, think tanks and policy programs are the major places where people move back and forth from more theoretical to more applied activities and roles.

Think tanks come in many varieties. Some cover much of domestic and foreign policy, while others specialize in military strategy, international trade policy, or region-specific issues. Research associates at think tanks typically examine the concepts that underlie policy using approaches drawn from such fields as political science and organization theory. They remain involved with policymakers through seminars or through publications that officials (or more often their staffs) read, yet they try to remain detached from day-to-day concerns. Their distinctive product is a longer-term perspective on events and their implications than most day-to-day policy literature can afford.

*Group IV: Policy-Making.*    The IR literature in this group, found in such places as *Foreign Affairs, Foreign Policy,* and op-ed pieces in major newspapers, tends to focus directly on specific policy problems. It corresponds to what Nincic calls idiographic policy analysis and is designed for an audience that sees practical experience and the specific context in which a problem arises as the key factors that must be brought to bear in analyzing it.[24] Nevertheless, career policy professionals are more likely to use ideas from Group II and Group III work than are political-level officials. This reflects severe limits on top officials' time, but also different training and intellectual habits, with career officials likelier to be exposed to theoretical work.[25]

These four activities can be linked productively in several ways. Group I theories, for instance, can be used to speak directly to policy issues, or they can be used to reframe Group II puzzles in ways that reflect connections among various IR puzzles. The latter, in turn, might allow those in Group III to see more easily which areas of Group II research apply to specific sets of policy problems. Group II puzzles can similarly speak directly to policymakers, or, to make them more accessible to officials, they can be interpreted through those in Group III. When this type of dialogue between Groups II and III takes place, the result can be what Nincic calls policy-relevant theory. The point to bear in mind is that all four types of literatures can help policymakers understand the "real world."

Consider, for example, how one particular Group I theory, rational choice, has addressed the problem of policy relevance. Rational choice has had a major impact in political science and economics. It is designed to explain value-maximizing choice (i.e., preferences over policies), given actors' preferences over outcomes and their perception of the strategic situation they face. It does not constitute a general theory of politics, since it does not explain why people value particular outcomes, norms, or other objectives as ends in themselves. For these reasons and others, it is highly controversial within parts of political science.[26] But it does account for policy choice, strategic interaction, and the outcomes that stem from such interactions in a theoretically powerful way.

Rational choice work can give policymakers two kinds of useful knowledge. First, it can tell them how best to achieve their objectives, if they know the preferences and power positions of the relevant actors. In game-theoretic terms, this amounts to specifying any equilibria that exist in a strategic situation.[27] By this criterion, the approach has succeeded: in 1989, a CIA official said that spatial models had generated correct predictions in 90 percent of the instances with which he was familiar.[28] Rational choice has been applied to issues as diverse as the future of Hong Kong, the prospects for stability in northeast Asia, and the likelihood of peace in Northern Ireland.[29] Successful prediction of this kind amounts to a direct connection between Groups I and IV. Second, by providing a general theory of strategic interaction, rational choice can situate within a common, intuitively plausible intellectual framework Group II debates that deal with particular types or conditions of strategic interaction. Theory in this sense organizes existing knowledge of a particular type.[30] Further, understanding such commonalities in strategic interaction might allow those in Group III to better locate and frame for policymakers the puzzle-oriented research they need. Formal analysis offers an intellectually consistent and replicable way to make these connections, one that can be communicated credibly among officials.

None of this implies that the *only* way to communicate IR theory to officials more productively is to focus on building highly general theories first. To the contrary, the process of more precisely specifying the empirical and theoretical assumptions that define Group II puzzles should proceed in any case. I take this up in the next section, where I argue that it has been common in IR to confuse distinctive prevailing conditions with different causal mechanisms. As a result, many IR debates have been intellectually unproductive. A more precise specification of the assumptions underlying Group II puzzles may thus be necessary even in the absence of a widely accepted Group I theory, both to improve the connection to policymakers and as a step toward energizing conversations about what a general theory relevant to the kinds of puzzles at hand would look like.

With this in mind, IR policy practitioners (those who read or produce work in Groups III and IV) can use insights or empirical findings from Group I or Group II work in five ways. First, officials may want to identify how different actors — themselves included — are framing questions, since foreign policy controversies often turn on the analytical assumptions that define different intellectual traditions and worldviews.[31] Clearer insight into one's own views and those of others could help many officials identify not only which perspectives they find most persuasive in general, but also which sets of assumptions appear to fit best the specific policy issue at hand. Second, some theory-driven puzzle work will help officials identify the strategic situations they confront, giving them a sense of the possibilities and constraints in that context.

Third, still other theories are designed in ways that can help officials assess the possible utility of different long-term policy goals. To take the application discussed in the third section of this essay, of what long-term use are international regimes? Fourth, there are groups of theories that can help people identify and select strategies for achieving preferred outcomes, including the variables that are manipulable in certain situations and the risks of alternative strategies.[32] When it comes to questions of choosing a bargaining strategy, expected utility theory, a variant of rational choice approaches, provides many examples of the direct Group I-IV connection.[33]

Fifth, there is a wide range of theories that speak to very focused questions about how one conceptualizes and measures different key variables. Such theories can help officials and analysts interpret facts and decide which data are important to track.

Different theoretical literatures will thus be useful in distinct ways. Officials concerned about their short-term bargaining options, for instance, may not find much that is useful in work on the democratic peace or structural arguments at the level of the international system. But policymakers also could use analyses that help them plan for the future, diagnose strategic situations, and understand how other actors view the world. Depending on the specific question, different theories can be helpful in each of these ways.

This array of activities and uses of theory indicates that specialists in case-oriented scholarship (Group III work) can help link insights from Group I work, area studies, or theory-driven puzzles to policymakers' concerns. Group III work can benefit from Group II's efforts to provide empirical referents and findings for larger theoretical questions, and from Group I's interest in processes common to various substantive problems. Correspondingly, Group II work may benefit from studies that are knowledgeably grounded in specific and practically relevant referents. Yet the Group I and Group II literature can focus on explaining causation without necessarily exploring directly its policy implications. A distinct role for Group III specialists is to help transmit ideas from the left side of the continuum in figure 1 to the right side, and vice versa. While many in Group III have social science training, they use that knowledge primarily to structure and inform policy choices, not to extend disciplinary knowledge.[34]

The link between theory-building and policy applications, however, functions differently depending on whether the ideas come from area studies or more abstract work. This is not problematic where a direct Group I-IV link has succeeded, as it has among consumers of expected-utility work in the policy community. But the issue of abstraction does affect the Group II-IV link. Specialists in area studies often exchange views in various governmental, nongovernmental, and policy venues. Yet the communication problem between officials and scholars who focus on theory-driven puzzles is deeper. Theoretical work is based on an epistemology in which policy problems have no intrinsic interest unless their implications are generalizable.[35] Many officials find such an approach too abstract. Area studies, by contrast, emphasize how many causes combine in complex ways to shape actors' behavior. This is how many officials think; they want to understand cases in contextual detail.[36]

While little can be done directly to narrow this gap in professional cultures, the way theory-driven puzzle work is packaged *can* change. Many such arguments that are in fact highly conditional are presented as if they are generic; the defining empirical conditions that affect relationships among the variables are left unidentified. If these arguments were better specified, it would be easier to fit puzzle-specific research to real-world cases, and to use theory in a number of distinct ways. More precisely specified arguments would also help policymakers better use area-studies work. Much like officials, area specialists have a causal perspective that drives the interpretation of context. But it often remains implicit.[37] Laying it out would help those interested in policy applications to approach area-studies work more critically. Finally, more explicitly specified arguments would help attenuate some unproductive debates within Group II, by getting people to see that the distinctive patterns in various puzzles often reflect distinctive mixes of initial conditions, not different kinds of causes. I turn next to how these goals can be achieved.

### Making Puzzle-Driven Theories More Policy-Relevant

I have argued that Group I IR theories can be used in two ways: to speak directly to policy issues, depending on the type of knowledge officials need, or to reframe Group II debates by highlighting generic patterns of choice and outcomes. Yet in the absence of a widely accepted Group I theory, more precise specification of the empirical and theoretical assumptions that define Group II puzzles should proceed. How can this be done?

By their very nature, Group II theories are built to examine distinctive theoretical and empirical puzzles. Not surprisingly, scholars disagree about the defining features of these puzzles — specifically, about the nature, frequency, and importance of different sets of issues, the salience of certain kinds of actors, the political arenas that matter in policy-making, the compatibility of actors' preferences, and so on. While such disagreements are natural, they need to be explicitly discussed.

Two kinds of underspecification need to be avoided. First, empirical assumptions about the operative ranges of the explanatory variables often remain implicit. As a result, scholars do not recognize that apparent disagreements about causation often reflect different empirical assumptions. For instance, Realists and Liberals implicitly agree that the compatibility of preferences drives the strategic importance of power and whether people care more about relative or absolute payoffs; yet they typically disagree about how compatible preferences in fact are. Implicit empirical assumptions may also obscure the effects of threshold changes in the values of the variables. Within a certain range of preference orderings, one may need threats to deal with another actor, but within other ranges one may need to reassure him instead. Clarity about the location and effects of thresholds between these ranges has theoretical and practical importance. When Soviet leaders in the mid-1980s came to have new expectations about the effects of continuing to operate under the existing system, for instance, international alignments were thrown into flux.[38]

A second problem arises when theorists do not specify the effects of restrictive theoretical assumptions on outcomes. Of course, restrictive assumptions are necessary; only a limited number of variables and relationships can be examined in any one argument. Such restrictions are based on ceteris paribus assumptions that the excluded factors remain constant during the period of observation or do not affect outcomes. Theory-driven puzzles would be clarified if they discussed more systematically the nature of the contingent generalizations that rely on such assumptions. In particular, cases where excluded variables can be assumed to interact with those in a model must be singled out from those where there are no presumed interaction effects.[39]

These kinds of issues affect not just the internal validity of the resulting models (the degree to which relationships hold as stipulated within a sample of cases), but also their external validity (the degree to which they can be generalized beyond these cases).[40] Those who offer case-oriented scholarship use context-specific expertise to extrapolate Group II inferences to what officials want to know. Since no two cases are identical, a question arises: To what extent are cases used to support a particular Group II model similar to those on officials' desks? To answer the question, those who specialize in Group III applications must assess the degree to which the model can be generalized beyond the cases that give it internal validity. To do this, they must be able to evaluate which excluded factors interact with those in the model — and thus need to be included — and which can be ignored.[41] Their work becomes easier if the assumptions in theory-driven puzzles are made explicit.

Unfortunately, this too seldom occurs. Many Group II models reflect puzzles that have emerged from prominent historical cases, without the contingent statements that would distinguish what is unique about the case from what is generic to the model. Arbitrarily restrictive assumptions about the values of the variables are thus often implicitly embedded in theoretical concepts. For instance, a spiral model (one reflecting the lessons of 1914) claims that threats reinforce security dilemmas and are self-defeating. A Munich-syndrome model claims that threats establish credibility and induce adversaries to retreat. But neither indicates when and why other cases fit these patterns.[42] If the issue of which argument is correct is truly an empirical one,[43] underspecification creates a false theoretical problematic. Similarly, underspecified arguments make the context-dependent nature of power unintelligible. Much work has shown that the relevant sources of power depend on the issues and actors involved.[44] Obscuring these distinctions yields a misleading view of the conditions under which power affects behavior.

One way to incorporate scope conditions explicitly into the contingent generalizations that dominate Group II theories is by analyzing typologies.[45] A *type* is a group of cases in which the values of the variables are strongly associated. A typology asserts that the relevant variables occur together in fairly few combinations.[46] For example, it is often claimed that war stems from misjudgments about capability or resolve. Yet we may be able to match more precisely certain kinds of perceptual errors and causal effects. Misperception of another's resolve may be common in authoritarian systems, where the analysis or flow of information is politically hampered. Errors about capabilities may be common when actors' relative power positions are shifting rapidly. As these examples suggest, typologies present a systematic way to be precise about mixes of variables.

Too heavy a reliance on typologies could, however, impede the development of more powerful Group II theories. As Achen and Snidal note, "if generalizations are not required to apply to all cases, we can specify contingent conditions to protect any favored generalization, so long as it can be plausibly supported in *some* cases."[47] Theory-driven puzzle work must therefore ultimately move beyond unconnected typologies and seek to explain how different mixes of variables and the distinctive outcomes they produce are related to major underlying dimensions of variation in world politics. And formal theory, as a Group I approach, does examine the implications of different combinations of preference orderings, power positions, and time horizons, using a consistent set of analytic assumptions.

Nevertheless, as previously argued, the process of more precisely specifying the empirical and theoretical assumptions that define Group II puzzles should proceed apart from any particular consensus among theorists as to the merits of rational choice approaches. Typological analysis is one way to do this. It can help clarify the defining features of theory-driven puzzles, both for those who focus on policy applications *and* for those mainly concerned with other intellectual puzzles. Making these distinctions explicit would not only help policymakers identify the Group II work they can use; it might also stimulate conversations about the dimensions and causal processes of world politics that transcend particular puzzles.

One objection to this line of argument may come from scholars who deny that their understanding of specific puzzles — whether based on particular regions, periods, or types of issues — could be enhanced by looking for theoretical dimensions that reflect larger patterns. They seem to believe that efforts to explain these more general patterns deny the importance of their expertise. This is not so. Debates between proponents of general social science theories and regional or substantive specialists often portray them as competitors, when they in fact are highly complementary. While some cases *are* highly unusual, practitioners and theorists need a way to evaluate and compare them systematically. Precisely defined typological arguments that can be linked to more general theories would fulfill both needs.

It might also be argued that it is difficult to specify scope conditions precisely in theory-driven puzzles, since manipulating initial conditions through controlled experiments is impossible. But theorists can recognize and identify the distinguishing features of the cases they examine even if they cannot manipulate those conditions. And having done so, theorists can precisely articulate the corresponding assumptions about the range in which the factors actually vary.

Practitioners would benefit from more explicitly specified theories in each of the five ways discussed in the first section of this essay. First, a better awareness of the theoretical and empirical assumptions in different intellectual traditions and perspectives can help officials see how actors frame issues and define strategic situations. This would clarify the terms of some policy debates, and, to the extent that one's own preferred strategy depends on another's definition of the situation, such clarity would help policymakers deal with other actors.

Second, arguments that clearly specify prevailing empirical conditions can help officials identify the strategic situations they face. Such work will illuminate groups of similar cases, minimizing people's tendencies to draw lessons from only the most readily available and visible examples.[48] For instance, if certain types of miscalculations were found to be closely linked with specific types of wars under certain external or domestic conditions, officials might find it easier to diagnose the nature of a nascent crisis more precisely than if all they had at hand was a universal "wars stem from misperception" generalization.[49]

Third, once policymakers understand the strategic context and the assumptions of other actors, more precisely specified theories can help them assess the possible utility of different policy goals. With respect to international regimes, for instance, officials might want to know the kinds of problems they are most (and least) helpful in addressing. They might also want to know whether an institution could help to transform the strategic context itself in some issue area. Or, to take another example, it is commonly asserted that democracies do not fight one another. Since democratization can be a slow and uneven process, what aspects of the process are most conducive to reducing armed rivalry, and which are relatively less so?

Fourth, given a particular set of preferences over outcomes and a clearer understanding of the strategic situation they face, more precisely specified theories can help officials make better strategic choices. This can occur in two steps. To begin, such arguments can help officials see more clearly what aspects of the environment are nonmanipulable, which aspects are more subject to their control in the short to medium term, and how the two are linked. An enhanced ability to control one's environment may be the clearest benefit of precisely defined scope conditions.[50] One may, for instance, be able to select a bargaining strategy with some confidence if one can assume that others' preferences for outcomes will remain the same. Expected-utility arguments, which make this assumption, are then useful in assessing options.[51] Constructivist arguments, by contrast, contend that actors' preferences can change as a result of social interaction.[52] If the situation instead fits these assumptions, policymakers' bargaining options beyond the short term are simultaneously broader and less certain than under conditions that fit the rational choice assumption of stable preferences over outcomes.

Having made these judgments, policymakers can then take a second step. They can use more precise theoretical and empirical assumptions to identify the risks of alternative strategies. Since such risks will be minimized if options fit the situation, contingent propositions about the effectiveness of various strategies are most useful to officials.[53] For instance, what is the risk that trying to topple a government through economic coercion will instead strengthen it? Officials are aware of this risk, but it would be useful to know how it differs across types of cases. The sanctions literature, which often treats the feasibility of economic coercion as an either-or issue, is generally unhelpful in inferring degrees of risk.[54]

Fifth, well-specified theories can help officials and policy analysts interpret facts and decide which data are important to track. Different theoretical arguments identify different meanings and operational indicators for key concepts. The social power literature, for example, claims that capability indicators mean little outside a strategic context and set of policy goals; Realists typically make the opposite assumption.[55] The better the rival arguments are specified, the easier it is to test them against one another, assemble a cumulative body of evidence, and identify the practical policy implications.

One must remember, of course, that well-specified arguments are no panacea in solving foreign policy problems. People differ in what they believe constitute problems to be solved and can disagree about how to solve a problem even if they define it similarly. Social science can clarify issues and choices for officials but rarely can identify specific answers.[56]

I have argued so far that if theory-driven puzzles were more precise, practitioners would find them more useful. But would the price be weaker theory? This is a common belief among theorists who see themselves and policymakers as inhabiting separate worlds. But if we instead see the way in which the adjacent groups in figure 1 overlap, the trade-off between theory that is more policy-relevant and theory that is better on its own terms disappears. This is because policymakers as well as theorists need to analyze the strategic context in which action occurs precisely enough to evaluate competing causal assertions. Even if they are indifferent to policy relevance, theory-driven puzzle specialists could find that greater precision would allow them to work out the implications of their own assumptions more carefully. Once a basic set of models relevant to some puzzle is properly specified, for instance, the generalizations can be refined by assessing them according to various cases within each type.[57] Furthermore, precise identification of the contingent statements under which arguments hold would promote the internal disciplinary progress of puzzle-specific work by clarifying the nature of empirical and theoretical disagreements, thereby attenuating some unproductive debates. There is, in short, no inherent trade-off between good theory and policy-relevant theory.

Better-specified arguments would also help those focusing on general theory and those interested in specific puzzles discuss how various issue-oriented puzzles are linked. As I have argued, many IR models reflect distinctive cases. Yet these models presuppose the existence of a set of logically interdependent principles that explains them.[58] A long-range theoretical task is to situate typologies as specific instances of more general arguments. While people might naturally begin to build theory by generalizing inductively about problems they care about, at some point Group II puzzles might be recast as parts of larger arguments. This would involve elaborating a set of theoretical assumptions about the relationships among variables that lets their values move beyond the restrictive ranges that defined earlier work. Some Group I work on international collaboration and regimes, as explained below, has already moved in this direction. This work has some direct policy implications and, insofar as it affects the identification and framing of Group II puzzles, indirect policy implications.

The next section discusses what officials can learn from IR theory about a question that interests many of them: When can international regimes serve policy objectives? A Group I literature about regimes is emerging, yet most of the theoretical work in this area is cast in terms of specific puzzles. In these cases, I argue that more precisely specified theories would help people better diagnose strategic situations, assess the value of different long-run policy goals, and make policy choices.

### From Theory to Policy: Using International Regimes

As global issues have mushroomed over the past few decades, international collaboration and rule-making have proliferated. The growing importance and complexity of international trade, protection of the biosphere, and the proliferation of dual-use technologies exemplify such issues. As discussed earlier, the prominence of issues that might call for action through regimes has affected scholars' interest in theoretical puzzles. By *regimes* I mean rules, norms, and institutional forums that allow actors to bargain in regular ways to coordinate their behavior.[59] Theory-driven puzzle work (Group II) and some general theory (Group I) have tried to understand how and when regimes shape international behavior.[60] Group III work, such as that of the Commission on Global Governance, has focused on the role or design of regimes in addressing types of substantive problems.[61]

A policy debate on the value of regimes has arisen alongside this scholarly discussion.[62] It has focused on these issues: Should institutionalized cooperation be a long-term U.S. goal? If it might be so, can specific institutions, such as a reformed UN or an enlarged NATO, be used to promote U.S. objectives? How then might they do so? Policy practitioners who want to consider these issues need to ask three major questions. First, what strategic situation do we face? Specifically, officials might ask whether actors' preferences are compatible enough to make institutionalized cooperation useful. Theory-driven puzzle work might help them here by offering a view of actors' preferences and the prospects for satisfactory institutional solutions. Those who focus on Group III and Group IV activities then need to ask whether these assumptions fit existing or foreseeable conditions. Second, what long-term value might lie in working within an institution in this area? By codifying norms and expectations, can international institutions change governments' behavioral incentives, as some Group II work suggests?[63] Third, what policy options regarding regime participation will help us achieve desired outcomes? Here, officials may ask how a regime's rules can be shaped to maximize its usefulness. Officials may also want to know how different actors are framing questions about the uses, limits, and risks of regimes, so that they can adjust their strategies accordingly.

This section is organized in two parts. I first briefly examine some Group I work on international collaboration, to assess how it might speak directly to policymakers and to examine how these ideas may help to reframe Group II debates more productively. Such reframing should affect the way in which the puzzle-oriented literature can help those in Groups III and IV to diagnose strategic situations, assess the expected value of strategies for achieving policy goals, and so on. Second, setting aside the possible value of Group I work in these senses, I analyze Group II puzzles that deal with regimes independently, to see how they might be framed so as to be most useful to policy practitioners.

## How Can the Group I Literature Help Policymakers?

Because sustained cooperation is unlikely if actors define utility in relative terms, Group II work on regimes has been preoccupied with whether states are absolute or relative gains seekers.[64] The question has no single answer. Actors at some times seek to improve their own welfare, irrespective of others'; at other times, they care about their relative standing. One might instead assume, as some Group I work does, that how actors define utility depends on specific features of their environments.[65] As in economic models, what varies across strategic situations (i.e., markets or international systems) in this kind of argument is not units' preferences over outcomes, but the constraints under which actors try to realize them.[66]

This formulation has direct implications for policy choices. If states receive higher relative returns from cooperation than their partners, and the strategic environment allows those gains to be converted into a usable military advantage, collaboration will often be imprudent. Geographic or technological conditions that provide an offensive military advantage illustrate this type of situation, since military investment and battlefield success are directly linked. Conversely, when force is unlikely to be used, states need not compare their returns from cooperation to others'.[67] Arguments that highlight such prevailing conditions could help those in Groups III and IV to diagnose strategic situations and assess one key risk of participating in regimes.

This formulation also implies a way to bypass a false problematic that has marked much of the Group II conversation about state preferences. If we assume that policymakers think of utility absolutely or relatively depending on the strategic setting they face, rather than generically across environmental contexts, issue-specific puzzles should be defined in terms of the specific types of environmental constraints that affect the definition of utility and how they produce this effect. The more explicit and precise this link becomes, the more productive Group II conversations about collaboration can become. It should also make it easier for those in Group III to identify Group II work that policymakers can use, an issue to which I return below.

Rational choice Group I scholars have also examined why and how regimes arise. They see the existence and nature of regimes as an endogenous function of actors' instrumental, utility-maximizing behavior, given substantive preferences and environmental constraints. For example, James Morrow argues that international collaboration raises four kinds of policy problems: the monitoring of behavior, the sanctioning of misbehavior, reconciling different preferences over solutions (distributional problems), and how knowledge about possible solutions is to be shared (informational problems). In dealing with the latter two, Morrow notes that while actors would often prefer some regime solution to none — a preference that would suggest honest, full pooling of private information — distributional conflicts give actors incentives to dissemble.[68] But the relative importance of these two problems differs across strategic situations. Where information problems outweigh distributional problems, what he calls "communicative equilibria" should result: actors can be expected to pool information fully and honestly. Where distributional problems loom larger but Pareto-superior solutions exist, actors can be expected to agree on some coordination strategy or to delegate leadership duties to some specific agent.[69]

This argument makes a limited but useful contribution to policy specialists by suggesting generic types of bargaining strategies, given the salience of informational problems and conflicts over issues. It may not tell officials more than they would know intuitively, but intuition is not always explicit and easily communicable. It does, moreover, suggest variables that policy specialists would want to track, and it points to something that can be manipulated: negotiating strategies and specific moves. It may also have a bearing on puzzle-specific regime work by emphasizing that convergent preferences over regime outcomes cannot be taken for granted. I return to this issue below.

## What Can the Current Group II Conversation Tell Practitioners?

Leaving aside for purposes of discussion whether the following Group II puzzles involving regimes could be reframed by being placed within a rational choice or other Group I framework, the Group II → IV link can be analyzed independently. I do so in two steps: I first survey some Group II debates and then show how defining initial conditions more precisely could help policy specialists.

Liberal Institutionalist, Realist, and Constructivist schools have made the major Group II arguments about regimes. Institutionalists see many situations in which actors have compatible preferences but cannot achieve them due to deficient information and high transactions costs. Uncoordinated action thus often leads to suboptimal results. Regimes can lower actors' transaction costs through routinized rules and decision procedures, and can inhibit defection by providing information about others' behavior.[70]

Realists largely disagree with this reasoning. They tend to see international issues as conflicts of purpose and power, not as cases of market failure. Except where a hegemon can provide goods cheaply and easily to weaker states, thereby attenuating competition within that group, they see collaboration as likely to be episodic at best. As a result, Realists argue that "what is most impressive about international institutions . . . is how little independent effect they seem to have on state behavior."[71] Since self-help forces states to focus on relative payoffs, they are wary of any policy constraints that could benefit a potential rival more. Even commercial cooperation can be impeded, since capabilities are assumed to be fungible across issue areas.[72]

In contrast to both Liberal Institutionalists and Realists, Constructivists see regimes as more than instrumental in nature. States are seen to exist within an international society; the preferences and identities of its members are seen to grow and change through a process of interaction, in which regimes may play a key part. For Constructivists, regimes embody a shared sense of meanings, both causal and prescriptive.[73] People can be socialized to new roles, objectives, preferences, and senses of legitimacy or community through norm-governed interaction.[74]

How well do these arguments speak to the three policy questions identified above? Consider first Institutionalism. It pinpoints several ways in which regimes can have long-term utility, as well as aspects of the environment that may make these functions valuable. Officials can ask: (1) Would information provided by a regime alter payoffs or time horizons in beneficial ways? (2) Would a regime be an efficient way to deal with substantively related issues? Because officials often lack the information or analysis they need to cope with an uncertain environment,[75] Institutionalism encourages them to ask when information deficits should be addressed collectively.

Institutionalism offers another way to match policies and strategic situations. If actors wish to avoid a specific outcome, the desired behavior is largely self-enforcing and only modest regulation is needed. But if they want to achieve a specific outcome where uncoordinated behavior will be unlikely to produce it, more careful monitoring and sanctioning are needed.[76] The difference between the kind of regime needed to reduce the risk that nuclear weapons can be launched without proper authorization (an objective presumably shared by central state officials) and that needed to stem the flow of ballistic missile technologies (a collective action problem) captures this point. Institutionalists highlight the latter (mixed-motive) situations, which constitute most strategic situations in world politics.

Precise definition of strategic situations can also help people assess policy risks. A key risk in taking part in a regime is that preferences will diverge too much to make a Pareto-superior equilibrium unstable. Yet Institutionalists have done little to identify when this risk will be high. Mixed-motive situations are indeed common, as Institutionalists claim, but the category includes quite distinct sets of preference orderings. Institutionalists see the degree to which preferences overlap as a variable, which implies that the degree and importance of institutionalization in world politics vary as well.[77] But in basing their argument on the ceteris paribus premise that agreements can be mutually beneficial, Institutionalists have posited a restrictive set of initial conditions. Functional theories about institutions tend to assume convergent interests,[78] thus downplaying such risks.

Institutionalism pinpoints several potentially manipulable variables, any of which might be strategically useful. It encourages officials to ask questions such as these: How can information best be pooled? How can regime obligations be defined so that behavior becomes significantly transparent and thus predictable? How can negotiations efficiently cluster issues? Since effective regimes often have narrow membership,[79] a regime's constituency is a key manipulable variable.

What do Realist arguments on regimes offer those in Groups III and IV? Realists assume an unvarying strategic environment, one leaving little room for states to act noncompetitively. The case of benevolent hegemony is the only major exception to this presumption. Realists conclude that long-term cooperation is unlikely and carries major policy risks, and that even narrow regimes based on shared aversions are exceptional.[80] But few officials live in such a uniform environment. To assume that regimes are always risky or useless is to build a theory around a set of fairly atypical cases. Ironically, today's Neorealists make an error identified by Arnold Wolfers, an earlier Realist: when analyzing the impact of regimes on policy, they substitute a sweeping generalization for careful empirical analysis.[81] On the other hand, a good understanding of Neorealists' theoretical and empirical assumptions might help officials identify instances in which relative gains-seeking *does* pose high risks. Such knowledge might also help officials understand how other actors are framing analyses of specific cases or policy problems.

Finally, how can Constructivism speak to those interested in policy applications? It highlights situations in which transnational communities of norms and beliefs exist and can affect how governments interact. U.S. officials, for instance, may not care on principled grounds that many states regard U.S. nonproliferation policy as hypocritical (i.e., Washington opposes most but not all states' efforts to acquire nuclear weapons), but this attitude may hinder them when they try to strengthen pacts such as the Nuclear Nonproliferation Treaty.

Constructivism also pinpoints potentially manipulable variables. One scholar suggests that institutions may actively "teach" norms and thereby change behavior, noting UNESCO's successful advocacy of a coordinating role for governments in scientific research.[82] A community of policy experts may thus be able to manipulate institutional machinery to spread ideas and policy priorities. But Constructivists have not explained how such shared understandings arise, what it takes to sustain them, and the conditions under which they are likely to change. The theoretical literature has thus given policymakers little help in assessing the risks of working within a self-defined community *if* such behavior is based on an assumption of stable preferences over outcomes.

In sum, while Group II work on regimes has offered insights on strategic diagnosis, manipulable variables, and the long-term value of regimes, initial conditions in these models have not been specified as precisely as policy specialists might wish. I next consider how a research program of the kind outlined in the second section of this essay would allow those who focus on policy applications to use Group II work better.

## Toward More Policy-Relevant Group II Conversations

*What Defines the Relevant Strategic Situation?*    The issue here is how states' strategic settings can be elaborated so that the *resulting* concern for relative gains, and therefore the prospects for cooperation, can be understood.[83] Policy specialists might prefer a narrow specification of the context, to ensure internal validity in the specific cases they care about. Theorists would likely prefer a broader specification. This trade-off can be handled in a way that benefits both groups. One could identify a set of policy issues (e.g., global trade within certain sectors) and use available theory (e.g., strategic trade theories, or assumptions about the sources and kinds of market failure) to indicate the conditions under which collective-action problems call for a regime.[84] Or one could make contingent assumptions about actors' environments (e.g., a world in which states are predatory traders but conceal such intentions so they can benefit from others' concessions) and then link these features to actors' preferences within an issue area. If officials care about a certain case and it fits to some extent a model's specification of the strategic environment, policy implications follow. Either way, this approach categorizes the generic mixed-motive category into more refined yet still theoretically useful types of contexts. It would be diagnostically more useful to policy specialists than many present Group II discussions and would help them address a question that Institutionalists have largely bypassed: Why are regimes created in some issue areas rather than others?[85]

*What Kinds of Long-Term Value Can Regimes Provide?*    While Institutionalists have highlighted the benefits of information in addressing some collective-action problems, those interested in specific cases and issues might wish to explore more precisely the links between transparency and collaboration. What kinds of behavior can shared information induce, and how much can such information change people's preferences? On the one hand, the existence of regimes per se does not necessarily mean that states use them to avoid uncertainty and pursue efficiency.[86] At the same time, it is the *degree* of certainty and efficiency available within a regime that must be compared with the situation that would exist were there no rules or regularized communication.

One intriguing experience in this regard concerns the apparent success of the International Science and Technology Center (ISTC). The ISTC is a formal, Moscow-based regime that funds alternative projects for under- and unemployed Russian weapons specialists so as to discourage them from working for rogue states such as Iran and North Korea. It supplies its members (the major OECD countries) with data on the activities of Russian weapons facilities where ISTC projects are located and data on the projects funded by specific ISTC members, so that they can coordinate their efforts.[87] Whether this regime may be a template for other arms proliferation problems—an issue of keen policy interest[88]—could depend partly on Group II work that would explore whether private trafficking in weapons technologies is a generic problem, and the conditions under which pooling data about countermeasures is an effective response.

Most ambitiously, actors involved in a policy issue may constitute an epistemic community. These groups share four things: (1) policy values in an issue area; (2) causal beliefs linking policies and outcomes; (3) notions of what constitutes valid knowledge in that area; (4) a specific policy agenda.[89] Such groups have influenced policy-making in areas as diverse as pollution control in the Mediterranean, regulation of global trade in services, and efforts to stabilize the nuclear arms race.[90] What accounts for such successes? It would seem that policy problems and solutions have been framed so as to be accessible to those with more as well as less applied IR roles. This may be valuable in formulating and especially in legitimating policy across a wide range of constituencies.

But consider what a policymaker might want to know if she were considering whether to invest in such deep collaboration. For an epistemic community to be sustained, assuming shared normative and policy goals, people must agree that a given set of empirical and causal relationships holds. In technical areas, experts must shape and validate a consensus that $X \rightarrow Y$ under certain conditions, and they must interpret these assertions for traditionally trained officials. U.S. and European scientists, for example, agreed in 1988 that depletion of the ozone layer was caused by CFC gases that led to harmful health effects.[91] If these conditions are met, puzzle specialists, case analysts, and working officials can be linked around arguments that tell them how to analyze and address certain problems. But how likely is it that all of these conditions will simultaneously be satisfied? This is an issue that Group II work on regimes could examine, and one that more applied IR professionals would likely care about.

*What Policy Options Will Promote Our Objectives?* More precisely specified arguments can help officials in both of the steps they take in making strategic choices. Consider first the identification of manipulable variables. One such variable is the breadth of a regime's membership. As membership grows, Group II work contends that it becomes harder to reach agreement, monitor regime rules, and sanction noncompliance.[92] Yet broad participation is desirable in regimes that deal with such global problems as oceans management. Based on a study of negotiations over a regime to deal with global warming, James Sebenius has suggested a way to deal with such trade-offs. He urges that when a universal regime is desirable but hard to achieve, agreement might first be reached among a small group on basic principles. Progressive rounds of customized small-group negotiations would take place among the core group and selected other states, with incentives offered for their adherence, until something near universality is reached.[93] In thinking about such questions, practitioners might benefit from contingent propositions that link breadth of regime participation to such variables as issue type or other features of the strategic context.

Another potentially manipulable variable is the strength of a regime's rules. Strength refers to the uniformity of behavior demanded: strong rules impose uniform standards of behavior, while weak ones contain many exceptions or escape clauses. The more that strong rules are needed to control actors' behavior, given some set of policy objectives, the harder a regime is to create and maintain. Classical collective security illustrates this. A uniform pledge of protection to all states against aggression might deter some aggression that would otherwise occur, but the very uniformity of action required to be broadly dissuasive is difficult to achieve, given temptations to renege. Collective security in this form is thus fairly implausible, though less demanding kinds of multilateral conflict management options may be more workable. On the other hand, strong rules allow states to calculate gains and losses from transactions across many situations and partners, thus obviating a need for case-by-case reciprocity.[94] Group II work that linked the strength of regime rules to problems in maintaining uniform behavior and the corresponding benefits of strong institutions could help policy specialists think through these trade-offs.

Consider finally the identification of policy risks. If practitioners assumed that how actors define utility depends on the type of strategic situation they face, the risk that taking part in a regime will lead to harm from relative-gains seekers should vary situationally. More precise identification of strategic situations would thus improve risk assessment. Studies that examined relative growth rates under differing conditions and types of regimes, and then assessed the Realist proposition about the likelihood and results of such gains, could help policymakers decide whether or when such fears are warranted.

It may also be risky to try to work within a self-defined transnational community when policy views and values are changing, or to try to change such values and views when they are firmly rooted. What those who focus on policy applications might find useful here are contingent propositions about the kinds of factors that cause shared understandings to arise within a group, the kinds of groups within which such processes occur, and the conditions under which such views and beliefs change.

This is just a sample of the ways that better-specified theories could help those who specialize in Group II, Group III, and Group IV work on regimes to interact more easily and productively. Even useful theory may, of course, go unused. Cultural differences between those who focus on theory-building and policy-making may impede extensive sharing of ideas. But their basic interests in understanding the world are *not* so different. With case-oriented scholarship as a bridge, theories of the kind discussed in this paper should travel to practitioners. The roads that link these groups may need repair, but they already exist.

## Conclusion

The broad skepticism about the possibilities for policy-relevant IR theory is unwarranted. There is a wider range of IR groups in the United States than the "theorist-practitioner" dichotomy implies, and the infrastructure that supports their activities has created a framework for useful exchanges. But to realize this potential, officials must be able to link theory more effectively and easily to the issues they face. At present, this is difficult to do. Too often, empirical and theoretical restrictions are built implicitly into theoretical models, and key elements of the strategic context are left undefined. This has two negative effects. First, practitioners who might want to use existing theories often find that they shed little light on the kinds of questions they face. Second, many theorists mistakenly think they disagree about basic causation, when in fact they disagree about empirical issues. More precisely specified theories would address both problems.

Such arguments would allow those who specialize in case-oriented scholarship to realize their potential as intermediaries between theory-driven puzzle specialists and policymakers. Many of those who produce this literature have academic training, and others are former officials; they thus are well situated to translate well-specified arguments into the "engineering" terms working officials need. But to do this, they need arguments that carefully lay out empirical and theoretical assumptions. As the regimes examples illustrate, work that carefully specifies the values of the variables is easier to apply to real-world cases. Better specified propositions might also facilitate a set of general theoretical assumptions about the relationships among variables that would allow their values to move beyond the restrictive ranges they assume in many existing theories. Such a general theory could speak directly to policy needs, or it could be used to reframe Group II puzzles in ways that officials would find easier to use. Thus, what needs to be done to make theory more useful for policymakers will accelerate theoretical growth.

The point here is not to blur the line that sets apart those who focus on theory-building and those who focus on policy applications. This line is genuine and important. There is a real division of labor among the IR communities. But as in any interdependent relationship, different comparative advantages are precisely what give each group incentives to interact with others. It is odd, after all, to think that understanding the world better should *not* have important policy implications. If theorists clarify their assumptions about the world and communicate them clearly, they will improve their own work and have more to share with those who act.

NOTES

This chapter is a revised and expanded version of "Is Anyone Listening? International Relations Theory and the Problem of Policy Relevance," *Political Science Quarterly* 113, no. 1 (spring 1998): 43–62.

1. Alexander L. George, *Bridging the Gap: Theory and Practice in Foreign Policy* (Washington, D.C.: U.S. Institute of Peace, 1993); Alexander L. George, "Bridging the Gap"; Gen. John C. Galvin (ret.), "Breaking Through and Being Heard"; Edward Kolodziej, "What Is the Challenge and Will We Accept It?" and Joseph Kruzel, "More a Chasm than a Gap, But Do Scholars Want to Bridge It?" all found in *Mershon International Studies Review* 38, supplement 1 (April 1994); David D. Newsom, "Foreign Policy and Academia," *Foreign Policy* 101 (winter 1995–96).

2. Abraham Kaplan, *The Conduct of Inquiry* (New York: Chandler, 1964), 295–96, emphasis in original.

3. The quoted phrase is found in Newsom, "Foreign Policy and Academia," 64. For the reference to a "chasm," see Kruzel, "More a Chasm than a Gap," 179; for the "two cultures" notion, see George, *Bridging the Gap,* chapter 1.

4. James L. Adams, *Flying Buttresses, Entropy, and O-Rings: The World of an Engineer* (Cambridge: Harvard University Press, 1991), 4041, quoted in Philip Zelikow, "Foreign Policy Engineering: From Theory to Practice and Back Again," *International Security* 18, no. 4 (spring 1994): 150.

5. Kruzel, "More a Chasm than a Gap," 179.

6. Mark H. Moore, "Social Science and Policy Analysis," in Daniel Callahan and Bruce Jennings, eds., *Ethics, the Social Sciences, and Policy Analysis* (New York: Plenum Press, 1983), 274.

7. Jon Elster, *Nuts and Bolts for the Social Sciences* (Cambridge: Cambridge University Press, 1989), 8–10; Kaplan, *The Conduct of Inquiry,* 347–51.

8. Moore, "Social Science and Policy Analysis," 275–76.

9. See, for example, the very different arguments in Klaus Knorr, *The Power of Nations* (New York: Basic Books, 1975); Lisa Martin, *Coercive Co-*

*operation* (Princeton: Princeton University Press, 1992); Gary Clyde Hufbauer and Jeffrey J. Schott, *Economic Sanctions in Support of Foreign Policy Goals* (Washington, D.C.: Institute for International Economics, October 1993), 64–85; R. Harrison Wagner, "Economic Interdependence, Bargaining Power, and Political Influence," *International Organization* 42, no. 3 (summer 1988).

10. Joseph S. Nye Jr., "Neorealism and Neoliberalism," *World Politics* 40, no. 2 (January 1988): 235–37.

11. Christopher Hill, "Academic International Relations: The Siren Song of Policy Relevance," in Christopher Hill and Pamela Beshoff, eds., *Two Worlds of International Relations* (London: Routledge, 1994), 7.

12. Hill, "Academic International Relations," 10.

13. Imre Lakatos, "The Problem of Appraising Scientific Theories: Three Approaches," in Imre Lakatos, *Mathematics, Science, and Epistemology,* Philosophical Papers vol. 2, John Worrall and Gregory Currie, eds. (Cambridge: Cambridge University Press, 1978), 115–16.

14. Alan Lamborn, "Theory and the Politics in World Politics," *International Studies Quarterly* 41, no. 2 (June 1997): 187–214.

15. See, for example, Kenneth A. Oye, ed., *Cooperation under Anarchy* (Princeton: Princeton University Press, 1986); Arthur A. Stein, *Why Nations Cooperate* (Ithaca: Cornell University Press, 1990); Robert Jervis, "Realism, Game Theory, and Cooperation," *World Politics* 40, no. 3 (April 1988).

16. For the Constructivist position, see Alexander Wendt, "Anarchy Is What States Make of It," *International Organization* 46, no. 2 (spring 1992), and Michael Barnett, "Institutions, Roles, and Disorder: The Case of the Arab States System," *International Studies Quarterly* 37, no. 3 (September 1993). For a recent statement of the choice-theoretic position, see Bruce Bueno de Mesquita and David Lalman, *War and Reason* (New Haven: Yale University Press, 1992).

17. James N. Rosenau, "Before Cooperation: Hegemons, Regimes, and Habit-Driven Actors in World Politics," *International Organization* 40, no. 4 (autumn 1986): 852, 871.

18. Barnett, "Institutions, Roles, and Disorder."

19. Stephen Walt, *The Origin of Alliances* (Ithaca: Cornell University Press, 1987); Stephen R. David, "Explaining Third World Alignment," *World Politics* 43, no. 2 (January 1991); Dan Reiter, "Learning, Realism, and Alliances: The Weight of the Shadow of the Past," *World Politics* 46, no. 4 (July 1994).

20. Davis Bobrow, "The Relevance Potential of Different Products," *World Politics* 24, supplement (spring 1972): 223.

21. See Richard N. Haass, *Intervention* (Washington, D.C.: Carnegie Endowment, 1994).

22. Donald M. Snow and Eugene Brown, *Beyond the Water's Edge: An Introduction to U.S. Foreign Policy* (New York: St. Martin's Press, 1997), 239.

23. William Wallace, "Between Two Worlds: Think Tanks and Foreign Policy," in Hill and Beshoff, eds., *Two Worlds of International Relations,* 146.

24. Bobrow, "The Relevance Potential of Different Products," 223.

25. George, *Bridging the Gap,* 4, and chapter 1, 147–48, footnote 2.

26. See Donald P. Green and Ian Shapiro, *Pathologies of Rational Choice Theory: A Critique of Applications in Political Science* (New Haven: Yale University Press, 1994).

27. Michael Nicholson, *Rationality and the Analysis of International Conflict* (Cambridge: Cambridge University Press, 1992), 60–61.

28. Bruce Bueno de Mesquita, "The Benefits of a Social-Science Approach to Studying International Affairs," in Ngaire Woods, ed., *Explaining International Relations since 1945* (Oxford: Oxford University Press, 1996), 67.

29. See, among many others, Bruce Bueno de Mesquita, David Newman, and Alvin Rabushka, *Forecasting Political Events: The Future of Hong Kong* (New Haven: Yale University Press, 1985); Bruce Bueno de Mesquita and C.-H. Kim, "Prospects for a New Regional Order in Northeast Asia," *Korean Journal of Defense Analysis* 3 (1991): 65–82; Steven J. Brams and Jeffrey M. Togman, "Agreement through Threats," in this volume.

30. Bueno de Mesquita, Newman, and Rabushka, *Forecasting Political Events,* 7.

31. Robert Jervis, *Perception and Misperception in International Politics* (Princeton: Princeton University Press, 1976), 143–65; Hill, "Academic International Relations," 21; George, *Bridging the Gap,* xviii.

32. On the usefulness of identifying manipulable variables, see Stephen Walt, "The Renaissance of Security Studies," *International Studies Quarterly* 35, no. 2 (June 1991): 212; on policy risk, see Alan Lamborn, *The Price of Power* (Boston: Unwin Hyman, 1991), chapter 3.

33. For example, see Bruce Bueno de Mesquita and Frank Stokman, eds., *European Community Decision Making* (New Haven: Yale University Press, 1994); Bruce Bueno de Mesquita, "Multilateral Negotiations: A Spatial Analysis of the Arab-Israeli Dispute," *International Organization* 44, no. 3 (summer 1990): 317–40.

34. Moore, "Social Science and Policy Analysis," 290.

35. Robert L. Rothstein, *Planning, Prediction, and Policymaking in Foreign Affairs* (Boston: Little, Brown, 1972), 134.

36. Jack Snyder, "Science and Sovietology," *World Politics* 40, no. 2 (January 1988): 170; Zelikow, "Foreign Policy Engineering," 145.

37. Snyder, "Science and Sovietology," 175–76.

38. See Joseph Lepgold, Bruce Bueno de Mesquita, and James Morrow, "The Struggle for Mastery in Europe, 1985–1993," *International Interactions* 22, no. 1: 41–66.

39. Lamborn, "Theory and the Politics in World Politics," 16.

40. See Donald T. Campbell and Julian C. Stanley, *Experimental and Quasi-Experimental Designs for Research* (Boston: Houghton-Mifflin, 1963), 5–22, for a discussion of the internal and external validity of various kinds of research designs.

41. Campbell and Stanley, *Experimental and Quasi-Experimental Designs for Research,* 17.

42. Robert Jervis, "Models and Cases in the Study of International Conflict," in Robert L. Rothstein, ed., *The Evolution of Theory in International Relations* (Columbia: University of South Carolina Press, 1991), 64, 67.

43. Dean G. Pruitt, "Stability and Sudden Change in Interpersonal and International Affairs," *Journal of Conflict Resolution* 13, no. 1 (March 1969): 35.

44. Lamborn, "Theory and the Politics in World Politics"; Robert A. Dahl, "The Concept of Power," *Behavioral Science* 2, no. 3 (July 1957); David Baldwin, "Power Analysis and World Politics: New Trends versus Old Tendencies," *World Politics* 31, no. 2 (January 1979). For an expected-utility formulation, see Bruce Bueno de Mesquita, "Risk, Power Distribution, and the Likelihood of War," *International Studies Quarterly* 25, no. 4 (December 1981): 541–68.

45. Alexander George and Richard Smoke make this argument in *Deterrence in American Foreign Policy: Theory and Practice* (New York: Columbia University Press, 1974), 632–42.

46. Arthur Stinchcombe, *Constructing Social Theories* (Chicago: University of Chicago Press, 1968), 44, 47.

47. Christopher H. Achen and Duncan Snidal, "Rational Deterrence Theory and Comparative Case Studies," *World Politics* 16, no. 2 (January 1989): 157, emphasis in original.

48. Alexander L. George, *Presidential Decisionmaking in Foreign Policy: The Effective Use of Information and Advice* (Boulder: Westview, 1980), 240–42, 244–45.

49. Paul Diesing, *Patterns of Discovery in the Social Sciences* (Chicago: Aldine-Atherton, 1971), 190; Alexander L. George, "Case Studies and Theory Development: The Method of Structured, Focused Comparison," in Paul Gordon Lauren, ed., *Diplomacy: New Approaches in History, Theory and Policy* (New York: Free Press, 1979), 59.

50. Paul Davidson Reynolds, *A Primer in Theory Construction* (Indianapolis: Bobbs-Merrill, 1971), 91.

51. For an example, see Bueno de Mesquita, "Multilateral Negotiations: A Spatial Analysis of the Arab-Israeli Dispute."

52. See, among others, Wendt, "Anarchy Is What States Make of It"; Martha Finnemore, "International Organizations as Teachers of Norms," *International Organization* 47, no. 4 (autumn 1993).

53. George, *Bridging the Gap,* 120–25.

54. One exception is David Baldwin, *Economic Statecraft* (Princeton: Princeton University Press, 1985).

55. Compare Dahl, "The Concept of Power"; Baldwin, "Power Analysis and World Politics"; and Lamborn, *The Price of Power,* with Robert Gilpin's noncontextual definition: "In this book, power refers simply to the military, economic, and technological capabilities of states." See his *War and Change in World Politics* (Cambridge: Cambridge University Press, 1981), 13.

56. Charles E. Lindblom, *Inquiry and Change: The Troubled Attempt to Understand and Shape Society* (New Haven: Yale University Press, 1990), 4, 149–50; Morris Janowitz, "Military Institutions, the Draft, and the Volunteer

Army," in Bernard Barber, eds., *Effective Social Science* (New York: Russel Sage Foundation, 1987), 75–76.

57. Diesing, *Patterns of Discovery in the Social Sciences*, 189.

58. John C. McKinney, *Constructive Typology and Social Theory* (New York: Appleton-Century-Crofts, 1966), 36; Diesing, *Patterns of Discovery in the Social Sciences*, 189.

59. See Stephen D. Krasner, "Structural Causes and Regime Consequences: Regimes as Intervening Variables," in Krasner, ed., *International Regimes* (Ithaca: Cornell University Press, 1983), 1; James D. Morrow, "Modeling the Forms of International Cooperation: Distribution versus Information," *International Organization* 48, no. 3 (summer 1994): 408.

60. See, among many other works, Krasner, *International Regimes*.

61. See *Our Global Neighborhood,* report of the Commission on Global Governanace (Oxford: Oxford University Press, 1995).

62. See, for example, Alberto R. Coll, "Power, Principles, and Prospects for a Cooperative International Order," in Brad Roberts, ed., *Order and Disorder after the Cold War* (Cambridge: MIT Press, 1995); Gareth Evans, "Cooperative Security and Intrastate Conflict," *Foreign Policy,* no. 96 (fall 1994): 3–20; and various essays in Chester A. Crocker, Fen Osler Hampson, and Pamela Aall, eds., *Managing Global Chaos* (Washington, D.C.: U.S. Institute of Peace, 1996).

63. Robert Axelrod and Robert O. Keohane, "Achieving Cooperation under Anarchy: Strategies and Institutions," in Oye, ed., *Cooperation under Anarchy,* 252.

64. See Robert O. Keohane, "The Demand for International Regimes," in Krasner, ed., *International Regimes;* Robert O. Keohane, *After Hegemony* (Princeton: Princeton University Press, 1984), 66; Joseph M. Grieco, "Anarchy and the Limits of Cooperation: A Realist Critique of the Newest Liberal Institutionalism," *International Organization* 42, no. 3 (summer 1988): 485–507; John C. Matthews III, "Current Gains and Future Outcomes: When Cumulative Relative Gains Matter," *International Security* 21, no. 1 (summer 1996); various essays in David A. Baldwin, ed., *Neorealism and Neoliberalism* (New York: Columbia University Press, 1993).

65. Powell, "Anarchy in International Relations Theory," 337.

66. Robert Powell, "Absolute and Relative Gains in International Relations Theory," *American Political Science Review* 85, no. 4 (December 1991): 1304.

67. Powell, "Absolute and Relative Gains," 1316.

68. Morrow, "Modeling the Forms of International Cooperation," 393.

69. Morrow, "Modeling the Forms of International Cooperation," 413.

70. Keohane, *After Hegemony,* 97; Kenneth A. Oye, "Explaining Cooperation under Anarchy: Hypotheses and Strategies," in Oye, ed., *Cooperation under Anarchy,* 20.

71. John J. Mearsheimer, "The False Promise of International Institutions," *International Security* 19, no. 3 (winter 1994–95): 47.

72. Mearsheimer, "False Promise," 20–21; Grieco, "Anarchy and the Limits of Cooperation," 498.

73. Friedrich Kratochwil, "The Force of Prescriptions," *International Organization* 38, no. 4 (autumn 1984): 705. See also Friedrich Kratochwil and John Gerard Ruggie, "International Organization: A State of the Art on the Art of the State," *International Organization* 40, no. 4 (autumn 1986): 763–71.

74. Among others, see Wendt, "Anarchy Is What States Make of It," and Finnemore, "International Organizations as Teachers of Norms."

75. Janice Gross Stein, "Detection and Defection: Security 'Regimes' and the Management of International Conflict," *International Journal* 40, no. 4 (autumn 1985): 608.

76. The distinction is between what Arthur Stein calls a dilemma of common aversions and a dilemma of common interests. See Arthur A. Stein, *Why Nations Cooperate* (Ithaca: Cornell University Press, 1990), chapter 2; see also Robert O. Keohane and Joseph S. Nye Jr., "Two Cheers for Multilateralism," *Foreign Policy* 60 (autumn 1985), 155–56, and Stein, "Detection and Defection," 607–8.

77. Robert O. Keohane, "Neoliberal Institutionalism: A Perspective on World Politics," in Keohane, *International Institutions and State Power* (Boulder: Westview, 1989), 2–3.

78. Lisa Martin, *Coercive Cooperation* (Princeton: Princeton University Press, 1992), 40; Stephan Haggard and Beth A. Simmons, "Theories of International Regimes," *International Organization* 41, no. 3 (summer 1987): 509.

79. Keohane and Nye, "Two Cheers for Multilateralism," 158–59.

80. Stein, "Detection and Defection," 608.

81. Arnold Wolfers, "The Actors in International Politics," in Arnold Wolfers, *Discord and Collaboration* (Baltimore: Johns Hopkins University Press, 1962), 22.

82. Finnemore, "International Organizations as Teachers of Norms," passim.

83. Powell, "Anarchy in International Relations Theory," 337.

84. For an application in international trade, see Mark Zacher and Brent Sutton, *Governing Global Networks* (Cambridge: Cambridge University Press, 1996), chapter 2.

85. Haggard and Simmons, "Theories of International Regimes," 508.

86. Haggard and Simmons, "Theories of International Regimes," 508.

87. Glenn E. Schweitzer, "A Multilateral Approach to Curbing Proliferation of Weapons Know-How," *Global Governance* 2 (1996): 27, 33.

88. Schweitzer, "A Multilateral Approach," 35–38.

89. Peter M. Haas, "Introduction: Epistemic Communities and International Policy Coordination," *International Organization* 46, no. 1 (winter 1992): 3.

90. Haas, "Epistemic Communities," and other articles in this special issue; Peter M. Haas, "Do Regimes Matter? Epistemic Communities and Mediterranean Pollution Control," *International Organization* 43, no. 3 (summer 1989).

91. Haas, "Do Regimes Matter?" 401. For the ozone example, see Richard Benedick, *Ozone Diplomacy* (Cambridge: Harvard University Press, 1991), chapter 9.

92. Axelrod and Keohane, "Achieving Cooperation under Anarchy," 234–38; Keohane and Nye, "Two Cheers for Multilateralism," 157–58.

93. James K. Sebenius, "Designing Negotiations toward a New Regime: The Case of Global Warming," *International Security* 15, no. 4 (spring 1991).

94. John Gerard Ruggie, "Third Try at World Order? America and Multilateralism after the Cold War," *Political Science Quarterly* 109, no. 4 (fall 1994): 560.

# B. Relevance and the Corridors of Power

# How Social Science Can Help Policymakers: The Relevance of Theory

*Ernest J. Wilson III*

This essay grows in part from my frustration with policymakers when I was an academic, and my even greater frustration with academics when I was a policymaker. From my campus perch in faraway Ann Arbor, Washington decision makers seemed distant, insufficiently aware of the latest empirical data or scholarly debates, and far too focused on the short term and the immediate. From my White House chair, my former university colleagues seemed out of touch with reality, dangerously naive, and hopelessly long-winded. There seemed to be big gaps between the promise and performance of the contribution social science could provide to practical policy-making.

Since I was serving in the first full post–Cold War administration (Clinton I), there was added frustration because of the palpable need for fresh perspectives on the radically changed international system, on the one hand, and the modest provision of fresh perspectives from the foreign policy bureaucracy, the political appointees, or academics.

Now back on campus at the University of Maryland, College Park, and with better perspective on both sides, I am struck by how much the gap expresses an imbalance between the basic needs of policymakers and the production of university-based scholarly work. It is a kind of imbalance between the demands of officials and the supply of analysis, and the challenge especially of trying to match demand and supply during difficult periods of transition in the international system.

These concerns are of course not restricted to college faculty and the White House. In the current transitional period there is renewed and widespread interest in new analytic perspectives, and in the scholarship-government nexus. On the academic side, for example, the Association of Professional Schools of International Affairs (APSIA) is as active as the Council on Foreign Relations or the Policy Planning Staff at the

Department of State in exploring the implications for their traditional tasks of the massive and unexpected international changes brought about by the collapse of the Soviet Union and the near disappearance of the great global ideological division of our time. Once-secure academic areas like "security studies" are fundamentally questioned (Klare 1994). In such times existential questions come to the fore — "As society changes, how does my role also change?" Even in the classic international relations field of security studies, prominent observers have noted that "few diplomats, negotiators, and arms control policy makers seemed to find much utility in the theoretical writings of scholars; few scholars found much promise in the practitioners' experience" (Thompson and Jensen 1991, xii).

Beyond global changes, one prominent practitioner-scholar has also noted the changes taking place within the academy and their consequences for practice. Complaining that "much of today's scholarship is either irrelevant or inaccessible to policy makers," David Newsom (1996) concludes that "the growing withdrawal of university scholars behind curtains of theory and modeling would not have wider significance if this trend did not raise questions regarding the preparation of new generations and the future influence of the academic community on public and official perceptions of international issues and events." Reaching a similar conclusion, a survey of APSIA schools reported that the schools "will be looking for faculty with more applied/policy making experience than has been the case in the past. It is likely that an increasing number of future APSIA faculty members will be 'scholar-practitioners' with solid academic credentials as well as extensive policy experience in the public and/or private spheres" (Goodman, King, and Szabo 1994, 20).

My purpose in this essay is to provide a balanced assessment of the potential contributions that social science theory can make to the practice of foreign policy, particularly during a period of dramatic geopolitical and economic transition. As Newsom notes, the potential contributions are not trivial, especially in these turbulent times at home and abroad when good conceptual guidance can be a valuable practical resource and guide through the uncertainty of the future.

## Assumptions

In this essay I make several assumptions. First, the subject of this inquiry is not how scholars can learn more about foreign policy in order to write better scholarly tracts. Rather, my topic is the contribution of social science theories and practices to improved foreign policy-making.

Second, I believe the current state of affairs is suboptimal for both sides. On the one hand, social science research and writing in the academy is less policy-relevant than it could be; on the other, policy-making is less coherent, conceptual, and "contextualized" than it could be.

Third, I concentrate less on abstract categories called *theory* and *practice,* and more on the actual observed behavior of practitioners and theoreticians as observed in action.

Fourth, I assume that the work of scholars can and should *complement* but in no way replace the ongoing work of the many excellent analysts within the foreign policy community, including in-house policy staffs, the intelligence agencies (from whom analytic reports are commissioned), and a welter of foreign and domestic agencies like the Bureau of Intelligence and Research (INR) at the State Department. Outsiders underestimate the enormous amount of time and energy devoted to producing and exchanging information and analyses in government, through agency-agency bilateral consultations, or larger interagency meetings, drafting sessions, and so forth.

I suggest a way of reformulating the problem to make it easier for scholars to "speak truth to power," especially in those relatively new and unfamiliar global policy areas that increasingly impinge on U.S. interests, from problems like the energy crisis, environmentalism, and the information revolution that seem to pop up quickly on the screen of senior policymakers, and for which policymakers are less well prepared than for other more traditional areas of foreign policy.

As Newsom and others indicate, suboptimal policy outcomes typically reflect a mix of mismatched perceptions of "relevance," very different incentive structures and practices, and long-standing cultural differences between the academy and the bureaucracy. In my experience in both cultures, the single most compelling problem is the misperception scholars have about the relations between the *supply* of policy-relevant analyses and counsel by outside scholars, and the daily needs of policymakers on the *demand* side. Until those misperceptions are recognized, addressed, and resolved, the academy will not be as useful to policymakers as it should be. In brief, scholars are often naive and inattentive to the demand-side needs of the equation.

## What Is "Foreign Policy"?

One cause of the problem of mutual misperception is an overly narrow definition of *foreign policy.* As described by academics (especially perhaps among theorists), *foreign policy* seems to mean grand strategy. Their interest is in the high politics of boldly charting new directions, helping design new and innovative definitions of world order, or explaining how the "Prince" should calculate his nation's interest (i.e., relative vs. absolute gains). Considerable attention is given to continuing security issues of defense and deterrence (George 1993). Certainly, with the demise of the previous organizing principles — containment and the Cold War — there is a genuine need for well-informed thinking on grand strategy. Newsom himself assumes this meaning when he writes: "Challenges to conventional wisdom and provocative explorations of international issues are part of the domain of the scholar and teacher and are precisely what is often missing in the official policy world" (Newsom 1996, 52). While true, foreign policy advice as challenging and "provocative explorations" captures only one part of the picture. That is not what most foreign policymakers need most of the time, nor what most scholars do.

In reality, foreign policy like domestic policy consists mainly of modest adjustments to current standard operating procedures to meet slightly new conditions. Most real-world foreign policy occurs at the rather more mundane end of the spectrum — where State Department country desk officers and deputy assistant secretaries do the day-to-day work of government. Here in the weeds and trees (not yet the forest), even assistant secretaries can toil. Sometimes senior people from assistant secretaries on up get to do "high policy," but it is decidedly not a daily occurrence *but intermittent and unpredictable.*

The conventional uninformed academic view seems to be the perspective of the seventh and eighth floors in the State Department, where Cuban missile crises, decisions to commit troops, and the search for new paradigms occupy the attentions of the few people in the rooms at the top.

However, in terms of the total time and effort devoted to foreign affairs by federal agency staff, perhaps 90 percent is devoted to the implementation of current policies to fit new circumstances. The remaining 10 percent is reserved for high policy of the type often contemplated in the academic journals. The 10 percent is often important for the long-term steering of government, but as important as it is, it should not overshadow the quotidian requirements of governing. What policymakers actually do shapes what policymakers actually need. This essay seeks to restore balance by insisting that both are important elements of policy, and that both can be helped by social science theory.

## The Importance of the Demand Side: What Policymakers Need

The starting point for a discussion of the academic-practitioner links should be the needs of the makers of foreign policy. Too often scholars start with their favorite scholarly debates within the academy and how they should be given greater attention by policymakers. Instead, academics interested in policy influence should begin by asking, "What do real government officials need on a daily and weekly basis?" That question more than anything determines the frequency, depth, and usefulness of the links between the two communities.

My experience at the White House on the NSC staff, in directing the policy planning office at the U.S. Information Agency, and working closely with state, Department of Defense (DoD), and other agencies, is that policymakers have a variety of needs that scholars could help meet. These are the need for more and better (1) information and analysis, (2) feedback and interpretation, (3) project packages, (4) political support, and (5) contextualization. Clearly, these categories overlap, but they are quite distinct needs.

### Foreign Policymakers Need Current Information and Analysis

Most of the time, most policymakers want very concrete kinds of information. They seek better information and analysis of events, people, and maybe a trend or two. What is happening on the ground this week in country X? Who is up and who is down in country Y? What are the views of a scholar just returned from region Z? What are European views of NAFTA? On the more analytical side, policymakers want to know, for example, whether our democracy programs are working in the field. What is the latest thinking about the Internet and security? There are a lot of scholars (especially area specialists) and a lot of government officials for whom tracking and analyzing country-level developments (or concrete topics like energy or the environment) are their bread and butter, where they share a professional interest in a country or region. This is probably where policy intellectuals most interact with government officials. The classic example is the briefing the State Department's INR Bureau organizes for new ambassadors going out to their posts, usually with a combination of panelists from the universities, from state and other departments, and from the intelligence agencies.

### Policymakers Need Feedback

Smart policymakers also need, on occasion, to test their tentative conclusions and potential recommendations with knowledgeable people outside the interagency regulars. This kind of evaluative feedback is extremely important as officials move from gathering information and analysis to formulating options for action. Scholars and outside analysts often provide this service through small seminars organized by Washington think tanks like the Council on Foreign Relations or the Carnegie Endowment. The products of these seminars are not theories as such; rather, the most useful products are analytic checklists of issues and of key actors that policymakers should keep in mind as they do their daily work, as well as key conceptual distinctions and analytic questions to pose at critical decision junctures.

## Policymakers Need Project Packages

There are critical moments in the trajectory of a public issue when the design of foreign policies requires that one asks large, conceptual questions as a guide to practical programmatic choices. For example, to design AID or USIA projects to support democracy, one should first define what one means by *democracy*. What is the nature of democracy in developing countries? What is the role of civil society in central and western Europe? What are the societal origins of the dynamics of conflict and violence? Which variables are susceptible to policy influence in the short to medium term, and which ones are structural and fixed? The motivating question behind each question is, "What policies and instruments can the U.S. government put into place to promote the forces of democracy?"

For example, the National Research Council has held a number of exploratory brainstorming sessions with leading scholars, researchers, and policymakers on topics such as conflict management and the transition to democracy (National Research Council 1991). The academics describe the state of the theoretical and empirical work in the field, the officials describe their practical problems and concerns, and together they discuss ways the U.S. government could gain practical purchase over such issues through new programs and policies.

Sometimes overlooked when considering channels of influence through which social science theories make themselves felt are the abundant commissioned studies contracted from think tanks, universities, and consulting firms by various foreign policy agencies. While the State Department uses this mechanism on occasion, it seems a more common practice for USAID and the DoD. The quality of the studies is not always guaranteed, but they are sincere efforts to match theory and practice. USAID has used brainstorming sessions to help policymakers frame requests for proposals sent out to universities and private consulting firms that result in substantial contracts in areas like democracy building in central or eastern Europe or in Africa. The DoD often contracts with RAND and others to analyze theories of communication within and between societies and their implications for information warfare. These are partly pragmatic exercises, partly efforts by the contracting agency to get outside experts and scholars to help them systematically think through tough areas of international policy. For example, is the development of democracy historically driven as much by elections as by assertive groups in civil society? Are enhanced communications patterns the cause of or concomitant to economic development? These are not trivial topics, and they are driven by profound theoretical debates.

### Policymakers Need Political Support

A related but analytically distinct requirement of policymakers is to win friends and influence people who are in a position to help or hurt the administration and its policies. To do their job well policymakers need political support from outside policy intellectuals and opinion leaders. From the perspective of the policymaker, the purpose of these interactions is mainly to convince others of the rightness of a policy; to ascertain from the key domestic players what will play in Congress, in the think tanks, and among key domestic interests; and to seek substantive policy inputs. For this, government strategists occasionally invite outside policy influentials and the heads of major organizations to panels at the secretary of state's forum or to smaller meetings. Sometimes, academic policy intellectuals help to organize such sessions and are invited to attend. Sometimes, but all too rarely, officials test these ideas beyond the beltway, outside Washington (Clough 1994; Destler and Yankelovitch 1994). Throughout, the process involves give and take; policy intellectuals seek to influence the substantive ideas of the insiders, while the officials seek to convince the outsiders.

### Policymakers Need Contextualization

Especially in periods of rapid change across many levels, policymakers need access to work that sets familiar problems or new unexpected challenges into an analytic framework that helps them make better decisions. *Contextualization* differs from *policy packages* in that the latter are deliberately initiated from within government as a guide to help design a particular set of activities contemplated by the policymaker. They are much more instrumental and focused.

By contrast, providing context is more abstract and general, not necessarily tied to a set of particular programs or agency. Contextualization can provide better decision-making frameworks, defined as ones that

> define the *kind of problem confronted* (is it important or unimportant, strategic or commercial, worth a lot or a little attention?);
> identify *core attributes and dimensions;*
> describe the *component parts;*
> identify boundaries and explain *links with related issue areas;*
> *set the problem in context* by explaining the broader context and background from which it emerges;
> identify the key institutional *actors,* public, NGO, and private;
> improve the appreciation for the *range of options* realistically available;
> improve the *selection of the most effective options;*
> know more surely what the *consequences* of these options may be.

Some of the problems that arise are long-standing and familiar ones that are nonetheless rendered more uncertain by the new global context in which they are occurring (such as the familiar problems of ethnopolitical violence in Bosnia or Rwanda), but which occur in a very different international political and value context. Other problems are newer, such as the sudden occurrence of energy crises, terrorist attacks, environmental problems, or the many challenges of the information revolution. I say more about the newer challenges below.

### What Is IR Theory?

It is equally useful to disaggregate and define what we consider *theory.* By *theory* I mean a rigorous, logically integrated set of assumptions and hypotheses that claim to explain some clearly defined aspect of the world through statements linking cause and effect.

### From Theory to Policy

In its broadest terms, one can imagine a series of concentric circles where something called *theory* is produced and distributed (this section has benefited from discussions with my former NSC colleague Jeremy Rosner). In this schema, the most theoretical work is done on the outer circle, and the most policy-relevant work in the inner circle: the farther from Circle One, the more abstract and academic the work is; the closer to Circle One, the inner circle, the greater the likelihood that the "theory" supplied will be a theory "consumed" and acted upon by a policymaker. The criteria for assigning a work to one circle or another include the balance between general English and specialized jargon; the balance between the abstract and concrete; and whether it is the author's intent to provide practical solutions to practical problems, or to concentrate on theoretical conceptual puzzles (Nincic, personal communication).

The purpose of work in the farthest circle, Circle Four, is to develop, test, and debate theories within the academy. The current debates over the calculation of relative and absolute gains, and realist versus institutionalist views of the world system, fit here (Niou, Ordeshook, and Rose 1989). The articulation and testing of theories about international cooperation, the conditions under which democracies go to war, or have more or less harmonious trade relations, or cooperate or fail to cooperate (Axelrod 1984), might also be conducted here. This kind of work is published in journals that policymakers almost never read, such as the *American Political Science Review,* and presented on panels they never attend. At the next level (Circle Three) is work published in the leading subfield journals that a government specialist might occasionally read, such as *International Security* or the *Journal of Democracy,* or a regional journal like *Asia Survey.* These probably have some impact on functional or regional specialists in government. At Circle Two are the small number of general foreign policy journals like *Foreign Policy* or *Foreign Affairs,* where coherent principles, arguments, and hypotheses about the way a system works — "theories" — are occasionally put forward (one thinks of such important recent efforts as Huntington's [1996] "Culture Clash" theory, or those of Fukuyama [1992] or hegemonic decline theorists). Theoretical work here is less heavily footnoted, and often more clearly written, targeted to an audience of policy influentials. This is public rhetoric in a strict and positive sense. Finally, at the first level are arguments made in general publications like *Atlantic Monthly, New Republic,* and the op-ed columns of major daily newspapers. Sometimes these are boiled-down theories originally constructed at Circle Four and then picked up by the public intellectuals, policy entrepreneurs, and political opportunists that abound in Washington. Rarely does the original Circle Four theorist write a Circle One piece himself or herself. But Circle One work is often done with the busy policymaker in mind, with all his or her time constraints and information overload. An example is the success Robert Kaplan had in popularizing theories relating environment degradation and social violence developed by scholars at the University of Toronto (Kaplan 1994).

If this description of weighted policy impacts is useful, then pure theory of the kind valued at APSA meetings is not particularly valuable to senior officials at the State Department, the DoD, or the NSC. A theoretical insight becomes valuable to the degree it is translated and filtered into terms policymakers find directly relevant to decisions they need to make next week. By the time the translation is complete, the theory is often reduced to checklists and virtual bumper stickers — "democracy reduces the chances of war, so the United States should promote democracy abroad"; "environmental degradation in Africa causes social dislocation"; "ethnic conflicts are becoming more salient in a post–Cold War world"; the world is still a dangerous place, so don't slash the defense budget."

Beyond print journals there are a variety of other channels of influence linking academic theorists and policy practitioners. I submit they include, in roughly descending order,

> theories students are taught in professional or graduate school, theo-
> ries they take with them to senior government jobs years later;
> theories that policy intellectuals bring with them from the think
> tanks and universities when they become government officials;
> "theories" advanced in the Circle Two and Circle Three journals;
> small seminars in the think tanks;
> individual scholars invited in for "policy advice"; and
> theories described in Circle Four journals.

There are three caveats. Arguably, the most serious abstract thinking and discussions about broad strategic priorities are driven mainly by the empirical observations and analysis of the most senior policy officials as they watch the world around them. The wrenching changes we see in the world today do not always need the subtle analyses and values of theorists to be brought to senior policymakers' attention. They read the cable traffic, receive intelligence briefings, travel abroad, and watch CNN.

Second, the angst of the academic IR theorists and their occasional searches for relevance are institutionally misplaced. In fact, these issues are dealt with daily by faculty, deans, and students of public and foreign policy schools. Their professional life is filled with asking, teaching, and writing about the theory–policy–relevance problem by breaking big policy problems into bite-sized chunks that public officials can possibly solve. Department-based IR theorists are usually less "applied" and take less active interest in applied policy-making perspectives than do theorists based in policy schools.

Finally, despite the 90 percent/10 percent split between daily policy-making and more rare and rarefied "high strategy," and despite caveats one and two above, the United States very much needs good, creative, theoretically driven, strategically sensitive social science to help it make the difficult transition to a non-bipolar, post–Cold War global system. To this degree Newsom and others are correct. The United States badly needs bold, clear, and policy-relevant work that draws officials' attentions to the shape of the new forests as well as to the details of the trees and weeds. On this point the interests of scholars and practitioners coincide, and social science and policymakers can both benefit from this kind of thoughtful analysis and serious reflection.

## New Issues: Where Social Science and Practice Intersect (Mapping)

This author's experience in government and universities suggests there is a particularly crucial area where the conceptual capacities of social scientists and the pressing, practical concerns of policymakers converge strongly. These are policy topics where the application of social science methods to difficult policy problems can be especially fruitful — the emergence of new and unfamiliar global challenges that are suddenly thrust onto the agenda of senior policymakers, and which may threaten national security, but for which there is not a great deal of accumulated senior-level policy experience. This would include the international energy crisis of the 1970s; the policy challenges of the environmental movement in the 1980s; the global information revolution; and the tangled intersection of emergency humanitarian relief, development assistance, and peacekeeping.

We can contrast these issues with other more settled and familiar policy areas — much of domestic politics; bilateral relations with neighboring countries; trade in manufactures; negotiations on chemical weapons; consular issues; and so forth.

If social science analysis and theory are indeed relevant to public policy, then they should be able to shed light on this new class of problems. Indeed, such an approach could simultaneously address these emerging problems directly relevant to the demand-side needs of practitioners who need help setting emerging issues in context, as well as intellectually engaging to scholars.

### What Do All These Issues Share?

The emergent global policy problems like the environment or energy — what might be called E-Issues — share certain conceptual, political, and institutional features (Wilson 1987; Choucri 1993).

1. *These challenges seem to arise very quickly on foreign policy agendas.* We speak of the energy *crisis* or the information *revolution,* denoting the pace with which E-Issues pop up on the agenda of policymakers.

2. *The magnitude and the direction of change are highly uncertain.* E-Issues are characterized by substantial debates on the extent of the problem, with some foreign policy traditionalists minimizing the impact, and others exaggerating it.

3. *Their societal and national security impacts are highly uncertain, and the winners and losers are not immediately apparent.* Does the information revolution create huge unemployment at home, or does it create vast new employment opportunities? Will higher environmental costs hurt all manufacturers, or selected ones in the Northeast? Is the information gap between rich nations and poor growing or shrinking, and what are the implications of each for U.S. interests?

4. However, *the stakes of "E-Issues" do appear high for key political officeholders.* Presidents, prime ministers, and secretaries of state do not wish to appear incompetent when confronted with puzzling new policy problems.

5. These issues are *cognitively difficult and complex.* Bytes and bits, RAM and ROM; the ozone layer and AIDS epidemics; nuclear power and solar power—These are tough issues to analyze and to master intellectually.

6. While typically involving remarkable *technological innovations,* the issues are simultaneously *deeply embedded* in profound societal values and complex networks of global and national relationships. The pace of technological change in information technology (IT) means that government policy is often two steps behind the market. As Barber demonstrated in *Jihad vs. McWorld* (1995), these technologies can fundamentally challenge basic beliefs of culture and community. Some influential intellectuals in the developing world view CNN and videotapes as assaults on their way of life.

7. Perhaps the most difficult challenge for analysts and policymakers alike is that *these issues transcend traditional bureaucratic and disciplinary boundaries.* E-Issues cannot be confined to a single authority but are the partial responsibility of a variety of government bureaucracies, independent agencies, and private companies. Analytically, such issues also flow across disciplinary and scholarly boundaries. Engineering, economics, political science, history, and the humanities can all claim to contribute to our understanding of E-Issues. In bureaucratic terms, for example, responsibility for energy policy before the creation of the Department of Energy on the heels of the oil import crises of the 1970s fell to the Bureau

of Mines, the Nuclear Regulatory Commission, the Middle East Bureau at the State Department, and Exxon. What agency is responsible today when an environmental crisis hits? Whoever is responsible for creating coherent policies from these subdomains needs the skills and perspectives of engineers, private sector marketers, community groups, national security advisers, and so forth (Lindberg 1977).

Are these challenges genuinely different, or are they simply new instances of familiar problems? One can contrast our effort here to specify a particular *class* of policy problems—which we are calling E-Issues—with a related but somewhat different effort by scholars to identify regular stages through which all policies are alleged to pass, whether E-Issues or more normal ones. Marvin Soroos, in *Beyond Sovereignty,* provides a nine-point checklist of policy stages. He includes (1) recognition of a policy problem; (2) specification of procedures; (3) understanding of goals and principles; (4) formulation of policy alternatives; (5) consideration of policy alternatives; (6) decision on a policy; (7) implementation of the policy; (8) evaluation of the policy; (9) decision on the future of the policy (Soroos 1986, 88). Certainly, E-Issues are especially interesting in phases 1 to 3. But Soroos's approach does not address the particularities of E-Issues or distinguish between them and other classes of policy issues. All the seven issues combine in issues like the information revolution to challenge the traditional capacities of public officials (and private managers as well) to master the matter quickly and effectively. Too much is emerging too quickly from too many different directions. For the information revolution, for example, digitalization, data compression, and falling costs are changing the underlying technology at such a dizzying pace that product cycles shrink from years to months, much faster than government regulations and other public policy actions can keep up with the changes. International commercial competition is exploding, even in once monopolistic, trade-sheltered areas like telephone service, leading in the short term to unemployment in a politically salient sector of the economy.

Out of this confusing stew decision makers seek ways to identify relatively permanent markers and signposts that can guide their action. As I indicated above, most public officials are responsible for tracking developments in one country or activity; they manage one office, one bureau, one agency. All of these are small pieces of a larger picture; foreign policy managers need to know how their narrow responsibilities on their own turf fit into the evolving new whole. Given these conditions, and the needs of policymakers, what can social scientists provide?

## Providing Context: Mapping as a Social Science Strategy

Addressing these challenges requires the analyst to think outside the box, that is, to reconceptualize issues beyond the necessarily narrow boundaries of bureaucratic demands and organizational standard operating procedures. It means looking beyond the conventional short-term definitions of what constitutes a policy problem, and scanning the environment broadly looking for medium- to long-term connections that may not be immediately visible in the day-to-day conduct of foreign policy. These are skills and intuitions that researchers and analysts outside the government are most likely to bring to bear. They do not come automatically, however, to all policy scholars, since they also require a synoptic vision beyond the conventions of a single academic discipline. The approach that best meets these conditions is intellectual mapping. By *mapping* I mean the identification and explication of the defining dimensions of a new problem, its constituent elements, and its general contours and boundaries.

In a volume published by the Institute of Peace, the authors recognize that this kind of intellectual mapping is a useful technique in the early phases of the emergence of a policy field. They recognize that developing an intellectual map takes place "when work has begun but there remains overlapping and conceptual confusion. People then stop for a bit to see where different areas converge and diverge" (Thompson and Jensen 1991). Their analysis of the shifts occurring among national security studies and peace studies after the Cold War is illuminating. While they concentrate mainly on academic discourse, and not on policy practices, this kind of exercise of tracking where different subcomponents converge and diverge is useful, I maintain, for both scholars and practitioners.

For scholars, mapping is useful mainly because it helps them to recognize the larger picture of which their current academic interest might be only one part. Mapping can show the forest as well as the trees of a new intellectual area. Mapping helps press the "so what" question, by struggling to define the big picture and offering up large important issues of problem definition and conceptual stance, to prevent the policy-maker from getting mired in microstudies of one subcomponent of the problem. And studies of subcomponents can be informed by their awareness of other related issues that may affect the subcomponent. Mapping helps identify emerging areas requiring empirical investigation, and at the same time it directs the more ambitious to develop hypotheses and to apply and test theories, work they might not otherwise do in the absence of preliminary mapping.

For practitioners, mapping can meet some of the needs identified previously in this essay, by improving problem definition, enhancing the analysis of both core attributes and critical linkages with other issues, and providing contextualization.

While analytic and conceptual, mapping is typically pretheoretical. Unlike theory, mapping does not necessarily posit coherent statements systematically relating cause and effect. But mapping and theory are related. In these new E-Issue areas, until the intellectual mapping tasks are achieved, good policy and good theory are harder to achieve. Whether trying to understand international terrorism, global warming, or large regional migrations, both scholars and practitioners benefit from this kind of work defining and identifying core components, key dimensions, external parameters, and policy linkages. Therefore, we anticipate synergies between policymakers and scholars as both try simultaneously to get their arms around the emerging challenge. In the following sections I very briefly map some of the core elements, key linkages, and boundary conditions of the information revolution; this approach could equally be applied to the energy crisis or environmental policy or other E-Issues.

## The Information Revolution as E-Issue

One major reason government officials find the field of international information and communication policy a headache is that until recently it did not exist as such, which makes it difficult to manage. It also makes it a classic candidate to be described as an E-Issue.

Similarly, prior to the energy crisis of 1973, "energy policy" did not exist as a distinct and integrated field. Rather, it was at most the intersection of coal policy, nuclear policy, oil import policy, policies toward domestic production, and so forth (Lindberg 1977). In the same way, "information policy" as such did not exist until recently; previously, there was broadcast policy, encryption policy, telecommunications policy, and so on.

In terms of the history of "information" and foreign policy, perhaps the most salient areas of concern to foreign policy experts were intelligence, on the one hand, and the public diplomacy functions of the U.S. Information Agency, the Voice of America, and Radio Free Europe/ Radio Liberty (RFE/RL), on the other. Most often there was little connection between the two poles: one side was open-source and public;

for the other, information was closed and classified. At the open end, government sent out information to influence foreign publics and governments, through public diplomacy, government-owned and operated radio and television broadcasts, and international visitor exchanges (Snyder 1995). At the other end of the spectrum, the intelligence community brought in information from countries around the world. The two occasionally converged, as with the revelation of CIA support for RFE.

Then, in the late 1980s and especially the early 1990s, a series of simultaneous technological and commercial revolutions erupted in the information and communications industries, changes that would rock the world of policymakers. First, there were big changes within the traditional and familiar open-closed dimension, both in trade craft of the intelligence community with the growth of new forms of encryption and with the rise of satellite communications as intelligence-gathering media. Challenges came to the world of public diplomacy with the rise of the media alphabet soup, for example, CNN and MTV, and of course with the arrival of the Internet (Wilson 1997).

Second, and more radically, changes occurred beyond the traditional open-closed policy dimension. Globalization and technological innovation greatly enhanced the role of private sector investors and operators. For the first time, private firms began investing in public communication infrastructures, as governments sought to privatize their telephone companies and invite foreign satellite and cell-phone providers into their once-protected national markets. Private markets have become much more important for policy, and officials now need to pay close attention not only to the traditional open-closed policy dimension, but to the public-private dimensions as well. However, this new dimension (public-private) is far less familiar to the day-to-day conduct of information policies than the old dimensions.

Another impact of privatization and globalization is to shift substantially the traditional roles of federal agencies (Rutkowski 1995). Previously in the United States, private sector issues were important domestically in broadcast licensing and regulations, but rarely bled over into foreign affairs. Today, by contrast, the domestic and foreign are merging. More and more, the regulation and monitoring of private U.S. markets by the Federal Communications Commission (FCC) and the Justice Department expand to include responsibilities for monitoring international private transactions. At the same time, agencies like the USTR that traditionally handled trade matters and thorny problems where the private sector intersected with the public, and rarely if ever managed telecommunications and IT matters, has now become a lead player in the IT-telecoms field. The bureaucratic losers are traditional foreign affairs agencies like the State Department, shoved more and more into the background during difficult bilateral and multilateral IT negotiations.

In effect, all the agencies are forced to respond to new and unfamiliar challenges from new issues and new actors. The old signposts and policy maps are no longer adequate.

### Mapping the Effects of the Information Revolution: An E-Issue

Figure 1 shows the kind of contribution that social science thinking can provide policymakers, giving them a broader and more nuanced understanding of complex, emerging E-Issues, in this case, the information and communication revolution. Along the x-axis — open to closed — are traditional concerns of Washington policymakers, especially information gathering and evaluation, and information broadcasting and export. Government was mainly interested in its own agencies' activities in IT.

With the information revolution, a new dimension has suddenly appeared on the screen of Washington policymakers. In addition to the traditional concerns about openness and confidentiality in the public sector (e.g., in the broadcasts of Radio Free Europe), officials must

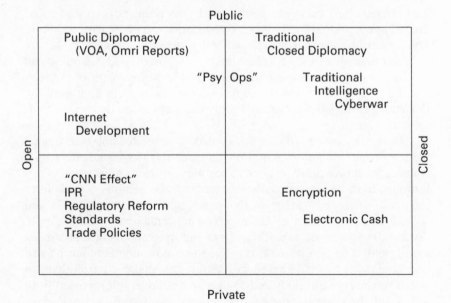

**Fig. 1.  Mapping of the information and communication revolution**

more and more design policies to influence private actors and private markets. As we see in the illustration, this newly salient vertical y-axis encompasses novel decision areas, from private sector competition and antitrust, to encryption efforts by private firms. These changes require the policymaker not only to develop substantively new policies to respond to altered market conditions, but also to be aware of new patterns of issue linkages that may arise between very different areas (i.e., between information security in government and information security in the private sector).

This mapping exercise illustrates the ways that new conditions will create new linkages across issue areas and also suggests that each quadrant may have different internal dynamics of which public officials should be aware. The northeast quadrant will have different interest-group configurations, different regulatory and legislative incentives, and different kinds of politics than the southwest quadrant. Presenting complex information in this easily accessible but powerful form reveals critical cross-issue differences, dynamics, and linkages in ways that might not otherwise be apparent to busy policymakers.

## Conclusion

The relationships between scholars and policymakers are much more multichannel and multidimensional than other accounts care to admit. During periods of rapid change especially, the channels and the dimensions themselves can shift, rendering both scholarly understanding and effective policy actions more problematic. The key element of the relationship, I suggest, is less the supply of interesting ideas and more the demand by officials for material and perspectives needed to do their jobs.

University-based scholars can contribute to better policy through a variety of means. The channels of influence run from graduate school training for future policymakers, to scholars' articles published in policy journals, to short-term consultancies and onetime seminars. Aside from influence channels, I argue in this essay that the relationship is and should be driven mainly by the needs of policymakers, which are quite diverse. They include everything from the need for reconceptualizing world politics to reporting on rural peasant movements in one part of one country. University-based academics can make contributions to broad reconceptualizations and to narrow empirical information. Both are useful; the latter is more needed on a regular basis by more officials. The former, also important in its own right, is illustrated in this essay by the four-cell matrix of the policy implications of the information revolution. An illustration of this type is more likely to be developed by a scholar outside the hurly-burly of internal policy battles than by one of the day-to-day combatants.

This essay has concentrated on the flow of ideas and influence from the academy to the government. I assume that this is a good thing, and that both sides can benefit from such a flow. One could analyze as well the dynamics behind the selection of research topics by scholars, and whether some policy topics are more relevant than others to an academic research program. But that is the topic of another essay.

REFERENCES

Axelrod, Robert. 1984. *The Evolution of Cooperation.* New York: Basic.
Barber, Benjamin. 1995. *Jihad vs. McWorld: How Globalism and Tribalism Are Reshaping the World.* New York: Ballantine.
Choucri, Nazli, ed. 1993. *Global Accord: Environmental Challenges and International Responses.* Cambridge: MIT Press.
Clough, Michael. 1994. "Grass-roots Policy Making," *Foreign Affairs* 73 (1): 2–7.
Destler, I. M., and Daniel Yankelovitch, eds. 1994. *Beyond the Beltway: Engaging the Public in U.S. Foreign Policy.* New York: W.W. Norton.
Drake, William, ed. 1997. *The New National Information Infrastructure.* New York: Twentieth Century Fund.
Fukuyama, Francis. 1992. *The End of History and the Last Man.* New York: Free Press.
George, Alexander. 1993. *Bridging the Gap: Theory and Practice in Foreign Policy.* Washington, D.C.: U.S. Institute of Peace Press.
Goodman, Louis W., Kay King, and Stephen F. Szabo. 1994. *Professional Schools of International Affairs on the Eve of the Twenty-first Century.* Washington, D.C.: Association of Professional Schools of International Affairs.
Huntington, Samuel. 1996. *The Clash of Civilizations and the Remaking of World Order.* New York: Simon and Schuster.
Kaplan, Robert. 1994. "The Coming Anarchy." *Atlantic Monthly,* February, 44–76.
Klare, Michael T., ed. 1994. *Peace and World Security Studies: A Curriculum Guide.* 6th ed. Boulder: Lynne Rienner.
Lindberg, Leon, ed. 1977. *The Energy Syndrome.* Lexington, Mass.: Lexington Books.
National Research Council. 1991. *The Transition to Democracy: Proceedings of a Workshop.* Washington, D.C.: National Academy Press.
Newsom, David. 1996. "Foreign Policy and Academia." *Foreign Policy* 101 (winter): 52–68.
Nincic, Miroslav. "Policy Relevance and Theoretical Development: The Terms of the Tradeoff." In this volume.

Niou, Emerson M. S., Perter C. Ordeshook, and Gregory Rose. 1989. *The Balance of Power: Stability in the International Systems.* New York: Cambridge.

Rutkowski, Anthony M. 1995. "Multilateral Cooperation in Telecommunications: Implications of the Great Transformation." In William Drake, ed., *The New National Information Infrastructure*, 223–50. New York: Twentieth Century Fund.

Schwartzstein, Stuart J. D. 1996. *The Information Revolution and National Security.* Washington, D.C.: Center for Strategic and International Studies.

Snyder, Alvin A. 1995. *Warriors of Disinformation: American Propaganda, Soviet Lies, and the Winning of the Cold War.* New York: Snyder.

Soroos, Marvin. 1986. *Beyond Sovereignty: The Challenge of Global Policy.* Columbia: University of South Carolina Press.

Thompson, W. Scott, and Kenneth Jensen, with Richard N. Smith and Kimber M. Schraub. 1991. *Approaches to Peace: An Intellectual Map.* Washington, D.C.: U.S. Institute of Peace.

Wilson, Ernest J., III. 1987. "World Politics and International Energy Policy." *International Organization* 41 (1): 125–50.

———. 1997. "Introduction: The What, Why, Where, and How of National Information Initiatives." In Brian Kahin and Ernest J. Wilson III, *National Information Infrastructure Initiatives: Vision and Policy Design.* Cambridge: MIT Press.

# In Pursuit of Praxis: Applying International Relations Theory to Foreign Policy-Making

*Bruce W. Jentleson*

> I am not the first, nor will I be the last, intellectual to do
> this. On the contrary, my feeling is that there will be more
> and more of them all the time. If the hope of the world lies
> in human consciousness, then it is obvious that intellectuals
> cannot go on forever avoiding their share of responsibility
> for the world and hiding their distaste for politics under an
> alleged need to be independent. It is easy to have
> independence in your program and then leave others to
> carry that program out. If everyone thought that way,
> pretty soon no one would be independent.
> — Václav Havel, 1989

For many of us the problem is not just the existence of a gap between the scholarly and policy practitioner communities in international relations/foreign policy, but its chasmlike widening in recent years. The limited valuation of "bridging" efforts, as Alexander George terms them, is disturbing even if not surprising.[1] The cross-criticisms that have created this gap are well known: policymakers dismissing the bulk of the scholarly literature as lacking relevance; academics deriding policymakers as more reactive and ad hoc-ish than strategic or systematic in their thinking. Both views, however, suffer from stereotyping and straw-manning. Moreover, they underestimate, if not ignore, that in this era in which debate rages not only over the foreign policy "answers" but even more fundamentally over what the defining "questions" are, the costs and consequences of the gap not being bridged are all the greater, on both sides.

Each of the essays in this volume speaks to this issue in a different way. Most are about policy relevance through various types of and approaches to academic scholarship. Mine is principally about actually being "a professor-in-government" and seeking to apply international relations theory to the making of foreign policy. In 1993–94 I was appointed to the State Department Policy Planning Staff as special assistant to the director.[2] This essay draws on that experience for two mini–case studies of bridging efforts. One involves Clinton administration efforts in the fall of 1993 to orchestrate a series of paradigmatic speeches and articles for defining an overarching post–Cold War framework, and the relationship to such efforts of IR "general" theory. The other involves the Middle East Multilateral Arms Control and Regional Security (ACRS) negotiations, for which I served on the U.S. delegation, and the relative applicability of middle-range IR theory, particularly regime and cooperation theories. Whereas the paradigm–general theory effort largely failed, the ACRS security regime application had at least a degree of success. The argument thus to be made is one of scope and limits, affirming the policy-relevance value of middle-range theory but demonstrating the difficulties in a policy context of more grandiose theorizing and paradigm formulation and articulation.

To be sure, my role was well, well short of that of a Václav Havel. But I cite his statement — and kept it on my bulletin board — for its eloquent expression of the essence of the challenge that IR scholars, and other scholars and intellectuals as well, face. It is not that *all* intellectuals must do stints in government, or even make policy relevance a priority for their research and scholarship. But the reverse is too true: as a discipline we place too little value on these kinds of hands-on experiences and this kind of scholarship, to our own detriment as scholars and teachers — and as a discipline.

The essay is organized in four sections. First is a discussion of the needs of policymakers, and of why middle-range theory serves these much better than general theory. Second is a particular focus on the professor-in-government approach. Third are the two mini–case studies. Then in the last section I come back to the initial arguments and draw lessons and implications from my experience regarding the value as well as the difficulties of professor-in-government–type bridging efforts.

### Theory and the Needs of Policymakers

In recounting interviews with policy professionals for *Bridging the Gap,* Alexander George observes that he quickly learned not to speak of theory when making the case for what academia had to contribute to foreign policy. "The eyes of practitioners often glaze over," George writes, "at the first mention of the word 'theory' in conversations."[3] The very word evoked a sense of limited utility if not irrelevance. But it was the word and its connotations, not the notion of conceptual or generalizing thinking, that was the main problem. When he substituted the term *generic knowledge,* George found his interviewees much more receptive.

> This always met with nods of approval and understanding! I wondered why and finally decided that the explanation was a simple one. Policy-makers know that certain types of problems occur repeatedly in the conduct of foreign policy — for example, deterrence or coercive diplomacy or crisis management. These are "generic problems" with which they are familiar. To speak to policy-makers of the need to develop "generic knowledge" about each of these problems makes perfect sense to them.[4]

George goes on to lay out a useful basic dictum, consistent with what academics have to offer and what policymakers need, that "the most promising way to bridge the gap is to focus on the relationship between knowledge and action in the conduct of foreign policy."[5] This knowledge-action relationship has three key aspects.

First is the *diagnostic* value that theory can have. Policymakers need to be able to assess the nature of the problem they face, the trend they are observing, the incipient warning signs they may be sensing. Often the problem is less a dearth than a glut of information, and the need to discern patterns, establish salience, and trace causal connections. Theory can help both in helping provide general road maps and in conceptualizing more focused solutions to problems, to use two of the categories defined by Judith Goldstein and Robert Keohane.[6] Another way of putting it is that theory provides an "intellectual tool . . . helping to separate the important from the trivial by pointing out what we really wish to look at and what is unimportant enough to ignore."[7] This goes back to the basic framework for any theory of specifying dependent and independent variables, and differentiating them from the general context of any particular policy, crisis, era, and so forth. In this manner what can otherwise be a seemingly overwhelming amount of information and detail can be organized, prioritized, and filtered through the framework that theory provides.

The literature on ethnic conflict provides a good example of the value of this diagnostic function. One of the central arguments advanced in the conflict-prevention literature is for "purposive" over "primordialist" theories of the sources of ethnic conflict.[8] The primordialist view holds post–Cold War ethnic conflicts to be primarily manifestations of fixed, inherited, deeply antagonistic historical identities. The purposive view acknowledges the deep-seated nature of intergroup animosities and unfinished agendas, but takes a much less deterministic view of how, when, and if these identity-rooted tensions become deadly conflicts, in which the calculations made by the involved parties of the purposes to be served by going violent is the dominant dynamic. The policy implications of these contrasting diagnoses are profoundly different — resignation on the one hand and preventive diplomacy on the other.

Second, theory can have some *prescriptive* value in contributing to "the conceptualization of strategies." Such analysis, while abstract and not itself in operational form, "identifies the critical variables of a strategy and the general logic associated with [its] successful use." Theory thus "is not in itself a strategy," but it is a valuable "starting point for constructing a strategy."[9] It must be combined with other types of knowledge, especially specific understanding of the particular situation and actor at hand. Its value often is in providing the framework for putting a particular situation and strategy in the type of broader context that can facilitate the design and implementation of effective strategies.[10]

The economic sanctions literature provides a good example of this function. One of the reasons for the problems sanctions have had in being successful is that, as one recent study puts it, policy decisions "are made on the basis of ill-defined generalizations."[11] While there of course cannot be a single strategy, foolproof and universal, there clearly is a need for better "conceptualization of strategies," identifying "the critical variables" and the "general logic associated with [a strategy's] successful use."[12]

Third, theory can help with *lesson-drawing*. It is bad enough for a policy to fail, but if the wrong lessons are drawn, that failure can have an additive or even multiplicative effect. Similarly, the benefits of a policy success can be countered by lessons poorly drawn, leading to some future misapplication of what worked the first time. Theory deepens our understanding of patterns of causality within any particular case by penetrating beyond the situational and particularistic to identify independent variables of a more fundamental nature. It also helps broaden what we can learn from any particular subject or case.

Here we hark back to the Cold War era deterrence literature in which IR theorists extensively and intensively debated the appropriate lessons to be drawn about the scope, the limits, the conditionalities, and the applications of deterrence strategy.[13] The concerns were over both taking successes too far, leading to indiscriminate pursuit of deterrence, and drawing overly constraining lessons from cases in which deterrence failed but for reasons that were more due to flaws in implementation rather than an inherent inapplicability to the particular type of case.

### Differential Relative Utility of General and Middle-Range Theory

Differentiations among levels or categories of theory vary extensively, as is evident within this volume as well as in the broader literature.[14] My use of the term *general theory* has two principal criteria: the scope of the argument and the extent of conditionality. Theories that purport to explain the general behavior of states (very broad scope) on the basis of minimal variables or qualifications (very few conditionalities) are what I mean by *general theory.* The rough equivalent is paradigmatic theory, although not necessarily in the full macro-Kuhnian sense, but as with the competing theory "debate among the -isms" that occupies much of the academic literature debates that dominate IR journals and graduate school core courses.

In considering why general theory has limited relative utility for policy, it is not even just a question of poor fit with these particular needs. It really starts with two inherent limitations, one or both of which all such efforts encounter.

First is that they fall short of the standard they set for themselves of postulating broadly encompassing "covering" behavioral laws. On the one hand it is useful to differentiate among theories that stress the causal importance of political-military power (realism, neorealism), economic interests (imperialism, versions of liberalism), ideas and perceptions (idealism, constructivism), and other master variables. The problem, though, is that while different theories have different strengths, and arguments can be made about greater *relative* explanatory power, there are too many variables that come into play, on too many distinct issue areas in too many different scenarios involving too many diverse decision makers, for any single IR or foreign policy theory to hold for everything, everyone, and every time.

Consider, for example, realism and its central proposition, as formulated by Hans Morgenthau in his classic 1948 book *Politics among Nations,* that "we assume statesmen think and act in terms of interest defined as power."[15] While Morgenthau claims that "the evidence of history bears this out," it was but three years later that he wrote another book, *In Defense of the National Interest: A Critical Examination of American Foreign Policy,* which lambasted American statesmen for *not* acting in this manner and instead being "guided by moral abstractions without consideration of the national interest."[16] Whether or not Morgenthau was right as to how "politics among nations" should be, his need to write a "critical examination of American foreign policy" was precisely because it wasn't the way things actually were.

Another problem is with those versions of general theory that may achieve broad generalizability but do so at such a vague level of abstraction as to fail to convey insightful explanation of the dynamics of the actual formulation and interactions of foreign policy. This is a major shortcoming of rational choice theories, both those that seek to build abstract models (e.g., game theories) and those based on mathematical formulas (e.g., expected utility theories). These theories express their notion of rationality in terms such as "preference orderings" and "payoff structures." Their central thesis is that foreign policymakers act rationally to maximize their preferences/payoffs, and that thus we can best understand foreign policy by determining which choice was the most rational. However, even if we accept the premise that policymakers seek to be rational maximizers, the key point is that they do so not according to some objective reality but rather within their own particular construing of reality. How preferences are ordered and how payoffs are structured is affected by who is doing the deciding and through what processes it is being done. The problem thus is that while these theories "provide insights into strategic choices that can be expected of individual players once the configurings of all the actor's preferences are fully detailed," as Benjamin Cohen notes for game theory, "there is nothing in the essential logic of game theory that tells us how the configuring of preferences gets to be determined in the first place . . . Preference orderings are simply assumed."[17] We end up with a circularity in the logic of asserting that a particular policy will be followed because it is rational, and affirming that it is rational because it is the one that was followed, without sufficient or genuine explanation of the how and why that are at the heart of understanding foreign policy.[18]

What is most useful is *middle-range theory,* defined as such by two characteristics. First is a more self-consciously limited scope than general theory, seeking to explain, as Kal Holsti puts it, "selected aspects of international politics and foreign policy." Examples include:

How do "images," stereotypes and ideologies affect policy makers' perceptions of reality and, consequently, their choices among alternative courses of action?

Is a strategy of bargaining in which one side threatens to punish more effective than one in which it offers rewards?

What conditions are most conductive to escalation in a crisis situation?

[What are] the consequences of interdependence on national economic policy making?

[What are t]he conditions under which alliances are formed or disintegrate?[19]

All of these questions fit the criterion for theory of seeking to explain a group of phenomena and not just a single incident, yet they are more focused and limited in their scope than "Why do states do what they do?" and other sweeping general theory questions.

The second characteristic of middle-range theory is the contingent nature of the generalizations that are sought (and, again, self-consciously so). There is no purporting to have discovered ironclad laws about international relations or foreign policy, but rather well-specified *conditional generalizations*.[20] By *well-specified* I mean that these are much more than just "maybe" statements, that the key variables that affect whether or not the generalization holds and the causal pattern by which they interact are identified. Middle-range theory thus doesn't tell us with certainty whether a particular foreign policy strategy is going to succeed. But it can tell us factors and conditions (the conditionalities) that are most conducive to policy success.

Thus while less is claimed by middle-range theory, its policy utility is greater. It provides sufficiently strong propositions to have value diagnostically, prescriptively, and for drawing usable lessons. That it also makes for better theory qua theory is a separate point, but an important reminder that the argument for policy-relevant theory is not just a "service" one of how "we" can help "them." It also, albeit somewhat paradoxically, is about benefits for the IR discipline itself/ourselves. This is a central point to many of the essays in this book; I come back to it in the concluding section.

## Being Policy-Relevant: A Professor-in-Government

One of the reasons that I conceived of myself as a "professor-in-government" — as someone whose primary identity remained as an academic and who was on leave from, but not leaving, the university — was that I believe we academics have a number of skills that can make for valuable contributions to foreign policy.

First, of course, is our *substantive expertise.* This is not to say we necessarily have more expertise than policy officials. Indeed many State Department officers are enormously knowledgeable of the countries, regions, policy areas, and so on, that are their domains. There can be a nice complementarity here as well, given the different emphases that tend to characterize academic and policy career tracks in terms of training, regular data sources, analytic foci, and so forth. The one's contribution thus is not more or less than the other's, just different. When viewed like this, the shared substantive interests can be a very valuable basis for collegiality.

Second, and in some respects even more important, are the *tenets of inquiry* in which we are schooled and with which we work. By this I mean a number of things: thinking deductively from general propositions to specific applications; thinking inductively in a manner that gets beyond sui generis and uniqueness to search for insights from more general concepts and middle-range theories; differentiating between necessary and sufficient conditions; rigorous standards of empirical evidence and analytic logic for claiming validity for comparisons, relationships, and other generalizations.

Third, there are our *skills as teachers, writers, and communicators.* The opposite often gets assumed, about pointy-headed intellectualizations and jargon-laden language — as one publisher's representative once put it to me, when inquiring about whether the book I was writing might have a broader market, the tendency of many academics to write in language so abstruse to outsiders as if to be a love letter to colleagues. Like all generalizations, this one is not without some basis. But good teaching and good writing skills are good preparation for policy-world communication, with the numerous audiences and multiple forms that such communication of ideas must take.

In trying to bring such skills to bear and play a meaningful policy role, a number of organizational cultural adjustments need to be made. One is the linguistic one mentioned earlier, of which the "theory"/"generic knowledge" quasi synonyms were indicative. Michael Barnett of the University of Wisconsin, who worked for a year at the U.S. Mission to the United Nations, provides a sense of some of the other organizational culture differences that one also experiences. He writes of how "the foreign policy bureaucracy, like all organizations, has its own culture to the extent that it has its own discourse, symbols and norms of interaction, in both practices and language choice, that mark insiders from outsiders."[21] And while never losing his own identity as a professor-in-government, Barnett stresses the importance for his own effectiveness within the organization of becoming "comfortable with the cultural terrain."[22]

My own experience also had its linguistic and cultural adjustments. There were the organizational structure charts to be mastered of intra–State Department bureaucratic subdivisions, some of which had a logic to their acronyms (e.g., P for Political Affairs, M for Management,

NEA for Near Eastern Affairs), but others for which if there were a logic, it wasn't apparent (H for Legislative Affairs, T for Security Affairs, ARA for Inter-American Affairs—which also, by the way, did not include Canada, which was included with Europe in EUR). There were the memos that had to be completed by COB (close of business), and the ones that may have been quite profound but didn't matter anymore because they took too long and were OBE (overtaken by events).

Ideas could have all the innate merits in the world, but to have impact they needed to be "sold" and "worked." This is true to an extent within academia as well, but there still are differences between intellectual entrepreneurship and policy entrepreneurship. Corresponding adjustments thus need to be made, for example, to roll up one's sleeves and engage in coalition building in support of one's ideas on an intra- and often interdepartmental basis as well as at times with relevant foreign policy constituencies. Among other things this requires writing good "one-pagers"—too long a memo won't be read. The challenge of being simple without being simplistic is easy to underestimate. And it helps to have a catchy title—amidst all the stacks of paper this is a good technique for garnering attention.

No doubt many of us often feel frustrated by just trying to keep up with all the quarterly journals, not to mention the book displays at American Political Science Association (APSA) and International Studies Association (ISA) annual conferences. Managing the daily information overload at state was even more of a challenge. A typical day begins with one's computer full of overnight cables from embassies around the globe, intelligence reports to be read, press clips, memos from other bureaus, periodic reports just issued, summaries of congressional hearings, and must-read articles sent by interest groups, other NGOs, and colleagues. The problem was how on the one hand not to miss key data, yet on the other not to spend one's whole day data gathering. And where might the time be found to read the latest edition of *International Security* or *Foreign Affairs,* let alone *International Organization* or *World Politics?*

This is just the reading. Then there were standard workload items like memos to be written, others to provide input for, yet others to be "cleared." And the meetings—lots of them, too many of them, eating up time for thinking and writing and acting. But the organizational culture stresses being invited to the right ones or risking efficacy-stripping perceptions of being out of the loop.

In sum, as a professor-in-government one enters with some very useful and transportable skills, and also faces major organizational cultural adjustments.

## Applying Theory to Policy: Two Cases

### Case #1: The Clinton Administration's Search for a New Paradigm, 1993–94

The term *post–Cold War era,* used most often to characterize our current period in history, is quite telling. It indicates that we know what this period is not, but are still not sure what it is. We are searching for a new paradigm.

This search has been quite evident in the scholarly literature: consider the end of history, democratic peace, unipolarism, clash of civilizations, global chaos, liberal institutionalism, geo-economics, age of identity, America first. It also occupied a great deal of effort in the first part of the Clinton administration.

During the 1992 presidential campaign candidate Bill Clinton gave foreign policy very limited attention. He gave enough speeches and took the kinds of positions needed to clear the threshold of basic credibility that had been a problem for Michael Dukakis in 1988 and to counter his own very limited foreign policy experience as well as the doubts and aspersions about him personally stemming from the Vietnam War draft issue. He criticized President Bush on issues like China and Bosnia. But mostly he ran on domestic policy ("It's the economy, Stupid!").

Efforts at the beginning of the Clinton administration to articulate a foreign policy vision cum strategy didn't go much further than the "three pillars" formulation (defense, economics, democracy) laid out by secretary of state nominee Warren Christopher at his confirmation hearings. Indeed the prevailing approach was a minimalist one. It wasn't isolationism in the sense of antagonistic and nationalistic "Go it our way," but rather "Don't bother us unless you absolutely have to."

Criticism of this "foreign policy morass," as one newspaper headline put it, was coming not only from partisan Republicans but from the foreign policy community writ large. The October 1993 Somalia crisis brought these criticisms to a head, but the critique ran much deeper and preceded the Mogadishu debacle. Indeed it was earlier in the summer that efforts began to pick up within the State Department for a "big think" piece by Secretary Christopher. The intent was to provide more of a framework for the overall Clinton post–Cold War foreign policy, an overarching sense of strategy based on a clearer and more coherent articulation of the national interest and on a conception of the central dynamics and driving forces of the post–Cold War international system — in effect, a new paradigm. This was important for both policy and political reasons, as it was one thing for specific policies to be criticized, but quite another to have an administration's overall foreign policy competence questioned.

The Policy Planning staff sought to play a major role in these efforts. This seemed logical and appropriate given its history and role. Policy Planning (S/P in its State Department acronym)[23] was set up in the early years of the Cold War, with George Kennan as its first director. The creation of S/P was based on recognition that there needed to be an entity within the State Department that had as its primary mission two functions not provided by either the geographic bureaus (Europe, Asia, Latin America, etc.) or the functional ones (Economic Affairs, Political-Military Affairs, later Human Rights, and others). One was to think integratively, across regions and functional areas; the other was to think a bit longer term, not futuristically but also not so immersed in daily cable traffic and immediate issues as to be strictly in-box, firefighting, crisis managing — that is, to "plan."

S/P is thus somewhat analogous to the strategic planning division of a major corporation. At a Microsoft or a Sony or a Siemens, it is neither the next quarterly returns nor the ten- to twenty-year long-term scenarios that define the portfolio of the vice president for strategic planning and his/her staff. The former is the domain of the other corporate divisions with more immediate time horizons; the latter is left to the think tanks, futuristic prognosticators, Tofflers, and the like. It is the medium-term time frame that corporate strategic planners work on, that which bears upon and is affected by present performance but also which by working on it now helps anticipate and to the extent possible shape the medium-term future environment in ways that can help performance when that point in time is reached.

This is what S/P is supposed to do. Even recognizing that the greater uncertainty of international affairs combined with the less controllable rationality of a political environment make foreign policy strategic planning more difficult than corporate, this should not be taken so far as to say it makes it impossible. However, S/P's strategic-planning successes have been all too rare. Kennan's period is often cited as "the golden age" of policy planning, when S/P "made the major recommendations that led to the Marshall Plan . . . played an important role in the development of U.S. postwar policy in Germany and Japan, as well as predicting the break between Tito and Stalin in 1948 and guiding the subsequent U.S. policy response."[24] Yet Kennan's greatest influence, the "Mr. X" telegram, was done as an embassy official in Moscow and outside of regular channels. Similarly, while S/P under Paul Nitze did the original draft of what would become NSC-68, often cited as one of the most important planning documents in the Cold War era, the influence of this study came despite its never being formally adopted. Indeed, all told, Barry Rubin cites S/P in his study of the State Department as one of the bureaus that "has found it hard to live up to its potential."[25]

In the Clinton post–Cold War paradigm case, the record was no better, although it was hardly just an S/P problem. The process began with S/P working with the secretary's office, the speech-writing office (the vehicle initially was to be a major speech), and other bureaus. In one sense it was an intellectually lively and robust process, with aspects akin to contending theories. There were those who pushed for the prevailing framework to be based on Kantian democratic peace theory; others who pushed for more of a globalization-of-international-society approach; others who harked to Huntington's then just published "clash of civilizations"; some unipolarists; some economistic approaches. Had the process led to a speech that opted for one or another theoretical approach, or even a coherent eclecticism, that would have been one thing. But the end result was largely the absence of choice.

The major speech as delivered in September 1993 became a policy-specific one on the Middle East. This was in part because of the unexpected historic Oslo agreement breakthrough and the signing of the Israeli-Palestinian "Declaration of Principles" (DOP) on the White House lawn on September 13. Secretary Christopher used the speech to hail this major achievement and to announce an immediate follow-on initiative to provide economic assistance to the Palestinians. But the effort at a paradigmatic speech had fallen apart for its own reasons. Moreover, a follow-on effort to write a journal article also resulted in only a scaled-down one that was more a list of priorities for the coming year than a framework to guide policy in a new era — and even that was over a year after the initial effort.[26]

Two main reasons, a mix of generalizable and particularistic, underlay these limited and disappointing results. The first involves domestic political constraints on what Secretary Christopher and his top political advisers were willing to say.[27] The felt political imperative of not offending various groups and interests impeded the making of choices and trade-offs essential both to prioritization among competing interests and values, and to working through tensions and contradictions as needed for policy coherence. Even more, there was the extensive cautiousness, based ostensibly on public opinion, against taking anything resembling a tough position on the use of military force.[28]

Second was a matter of the cognitive worldviews of key policymakers. We know how important belief systems and worldviews are in providing cognitive maps through which key decision makers approach foreign policy.[29] In the case of Warren Christopher, unlike a secretary of state like

Henry Kissinger, he did not think in terms of broad concepts like balance of power and deterrence. It wasn't just that he was a lawyer — Dean Acheson and John Foster Dulles were lawyers as well; it was his particular legalistic approach with its case-based and negotiations-inclined emphasis. Each case or issue was to be taken up on its own, with minimal attention to applying or setting broader precedents and strategies. Success was seen in highly instrumental terms, and largely as a matter of negotiating persistence, figuring out ways to split differences and find common ground (thus, e.g., all those trips to Damascus). Christopher and his principal aides thus had little receptivity to anything akin to broad conceptualizations for thinking about and articulating key issues such as the interrelationship between force and diplomacy.

Interestingly a parallel effort by the NSC staff on a paradigmatic speech for National Security Advisor Anthony Lake actually came to fruition. This was Lake's "enlargement" speech, which drew heavily from democratic peace theory and sought to play its new central term off the old "containment."[30] The speech was highly influential; indeed, President Clinton expressed almost pure Kantianism in his 1994 State of the Union speech, asserting that "democracies do not attack each other," and that therefore "ultimately the best strategy to insure our security and to build a durable peace is to support the advance of democracy elsewhere."

The fact that Lake's speech reached fruition fits with the earlier point about cognitive worldviews. Tony Lake — former policy planning director, former college professor — was much more disposed to thinking conceptually.[31] However, whereas the Christopher effort shows the constraints that make it difficult actually to bring general theory to bear on policy, the Lake effort also shows the problems that come when general theory is taken in too straightforward a manner. Even leaving aside the basic challenge to the validity of democratic peace theory from competing paradigms, the undifferentiated proposition of a core democracy-peace causal relationship has been shown to have contingencies and conditionalities that need specification.[32] There was significant concern that the enlargement strategy was insufficiently attentive to these factors, and so it exemplified the problem of misapplication of general theory to policy, as distinct from nonapplication.

Beyond just the Clinton administration case, it needs to be said that both the value and achievability of "grand strategy" based on general theory often are exaggerated. There is a bit of rose-colored selective recall as to the neatness and validity of the Cold War containment paradigm: we forget too easily how it led us astray (e.g., Vietnam). And there is quite a bit of truth to assessments of the current period that stress its complexity as well as the inherent volatility of periods of historic transition. Nevertheless something more than the what-it-is-not view of "post–Cold War" is achievable, and remains to be achieved.

### Case #2: The Middle East Multilateral Arms Control and Regional Security (ACRS) Negotiations

Coming out of the October 1991 Madrid Middle East peace conference, two sets of negotiations were established. The "bilaterals" were the main talks, with four tracks: Israel-Palestinians, Israel-Jordan, Israel-Syria, Israel-Lebanon. In addition, five tracks of multilateral talks also were set up, involving Israel and Arab states from throughout the region (e.g., Maghreb states such as Morocco and Tunisia, Gulf states such as Saudi Arabia and Oman, as well as Egypt and the bilateral track states and parties).[33] One of these tracks was the Arms Control and Regional Security (ACRS) talks. I served as a member of the U.S. ACRS delegation in 1993–94. Since then I have been involved in a number of "track-two diplomacy" efforts related to ACRS.[34]

At their outset ACRS and other multilaterals were intended more as just context-setters for the bilaterals than as negotiations in their own right. As Secretary of State James Baker stated in his speech at the January 1992 organizational meeting, the main purpose of the multilaterals was to facilitate the work of the bilaterals by sending "a powerful signal that all [regional] parties are unequivocally committed to peace and reconciliation." Yet Baker did also lay out the additional goals: to "address a range of regional problems crying out for resolution" and to "create a basis for stability in the area."[35] For ACRS, in the most fundamental sense, this meant an effort to foster multilateral security cooperation and begin building a regional security regime in the Middle East.

Over time ACRS developed its own agenda, indeed quite an itemized one. The various countries came to the periodic meetings with their respective priorities and positions. Being able to look past this or that issue, and this or that country position, and conceptualize ACRS in terms of an effort to build multilateral security cooperation and initiate a regional security regime provided an invaluable perspective. What do we know from IR theory about the key conditions — conducive, necessary, sufficient — for achieving multilateral security cooperation and creating the structures of a regional security regime? How is the Middle East unique, and how much can we generalize to it from general theoretical propositions and comparative analysis of other regions?

To be sure, remembering Alexander George's caveat about generic knowledge and theory, one had to be discreet about terminology and what was articulated or left implicit. But the theoretical framing had significant policy utility in this case in four respects.

First, consistent with what was delineated earlier as the diagnostic function, was to help overcome the tendency among Middle East specialists and Middle Easterners to overassume the uniqueness of the region by adding to the analytic mix the broad context of systemic dynamics of the post–Cold War era. One of the main overarching patterns of this new era is that whereas during the Cold War sources of conflict and instability tended to be globally transmitted through bipolarity and the superpower rivalry, now conflict and instability are much more rooted in regional rivalries and interests. Indeed, in every region, regional multilateral cooperation has become more important and more developed relative to respective Cold War–era levels: for example, in Europe, the greater institutionalization as reflected in the name change from *Conference on,* to *Organization for,* Security and Cooperation in Europe (CSCE/OSCE); the expanded membership and agenda of the ASEAN (Association of Southeast Asian Nations) Asian Regional Forum; the greater conflict resolution role of the Organization of African Unity (OAU). The Middle East's past as a region in which the very notion of multilateral cooperation was considered an oxymoron at best, if not pure naïveté, does make for some uniqueness. But the systemic framing, in terms of global trends from which no region is immune, checks against taking uniqueness too far, and it establishes the broader diagnostic basis for comparability to other regions.

Second was checking against taking cross-case comparability too far with regard to lesson-drawing. Both Shimon Peres, Israeli foreign minister and then prime minister, and Crown Prince Hassan of Jordan strongly pushed proposals for a Conference on Security and Cooperation in the Middle East (CSCME). As the name and acronym reflect, this was very closely modeled on the European CSCE. While in other ways ACRS did draw usefully on the European case, the CSCME proposals went too far, with too much Europhiliac emulation and too little rigorous adaptation. Yet given its proponents it had strong political momentum, and in mid-1994 there was substantial political-diplomatic pressure on Secretary of State Christopher to endorse a CSCME. It thus was key to be able to make a strong analytic critique to counter this political pull. The memos and discussion again were couched in terminology and tone appropriate to the organizational culture, while I kept to myself the resemblance of the underlying mode of analysis to political science methodological arguments about criteria for establishing cross-case generalizability.

Third was prescriptive utility within the ACRS negotiations regarding the relative balance and sequencing of CBMs (confidence-building measures) and CSBMs (confidence- and security-building measures) and more direct and explicit arms control measures. Israel stressed the need to start with CBMs and CSBMs for trust-building and initial tangible achievements, while Egypt in particular pushed for priority for more extensive arms control measures, particularly on Israel's presumed nuclear weapons. With this in mind one of the early ACRS sessions tried to break out of the political debate and provide some more objective baseline through a seminar-like format with "comparative case" briefings from experts and veterans of U.S.-Soviet and East-West European arms control and regional security negotiations. One of the key lessons stressed was that while some progress was made on arms control while relations were still hostile, and while this progress did in turn contribute to improved political relations, the major arms control agreements were achieved only after the political climate was substantially improved. The discussions that followed were very much about the validity of the cross-case lesson-drawing, and here the analytic basis was objectively much stronger. This was important, albeit not sufficient, for trying to counter the political dynamics.[36]

Fourth, and combining both lesson-drawing and prescriptiveness, was the issue of the "Declaration of Principles on Arms Control and Regional Security in the Middle East," or the "ACRS DOP" as it was known for short. There was a point in early 1994 when these negotiations had gone surprisingly far, and agreement almost was achieved on a document that could have established the kind of norms and procedures crucial to a strong multilateral regime. Yet for a number of reasons drafts of the agreement weakened over time, with even the name of the document being diluted first to "Declaration on Arms Control and Regional Security" and then to just "Statement on Arms Control and Regional Security." One of the key debates here was within the American delegation over how hard we should push for an agreement on the weaker version, more or less as a matter of whether any agreement was better than none. My view that it wasn't was based in part on precautionary lessons from the 1972 U.S.-Soviet Basic Principles Agreement (BPA), when both sides proclaimed the BPA as the charter for détente, but it was so full of ambiguities that each side felt free to interpret it in its own self-serving way. This helped undermine rather than provide a foundation for building security cooperation.[37]

In each of these ways theory had real policy utility. It was middle-range theory, propositions, and formulations, rather than broad paradigmatic abstractions, that were limited in their scope. There was a real value added to the policy process by being able to bring theory to bear.

## Conclusion: The Value of Praxis

In a 1993 symposium at the Mershon Center of Ohio State University, focusing on Alexander George's *Bridging the Gap,* Edward Kolodziej noted that while he found the book "stimulating and provocative," he lamented that it "comes at a time when interest in bridging the gap may well be flagging despite the greater than ever need for cooperation among scholars and policy-makers." Joseph Kruzel, who at the time was on leave from Ohio State and serving in a key Defense Department position, added, "What strikes me in thinking about how to bridge the gap between academics and policymakers [is] how rarely this question is asked anymore."[38]

Why? The academic world and the policy world do have their own distinct principal missions. With these come their own career paths, reward structures, organizational cultures, and other differences. Yet one sees many more bridges in other disciplines. In economics, for example, much of the cutting-edge scholarship exemplifies policy-relevant theory, and many leading academics have served and continue to serve in government (national, international). Moreover, within IR in the early Cold War era, in what many refer to as the "golden age of strategic studies," academics and scholarly theory played crucial roles in the development of foreign policy.[39]

The disillusionment of Vietnam had a great deal to do with the alienation of the academic and policy communities from each other. Feelings of animosity and suspicion abounded. Of course, there was nothing particularly unique about this; the disillusioning effects of the Vietnam era were wide and deep throughout American society. Yet the bridge-building efforts in so many other spheres, and as noted in other academic disciplines, have managed to make their respective headways.

There always will be limits, as seen herein. One of the main conclusions to be drawn from this analysis is that *the policy relevance of IR theory inversely correlates to the level of abstraction.* The effort to bring security cooperation and regime theory to bear on policy was much more successful than an effort with more general theory. A number of factors were at play, but the key one goes back to the theory needs of policymakers and how middle-range theory has greater utility for diagnostic, prescriptive, and lesson-drawing objectives.

In addition to the contribution we can make to policy, there also is much to be gained for us as academics. We can genuinely reality-test our theories, if not under methodologically strict control conditions, at least as plausibility probes. We can do a type of fieldwork empirical data gathering that is less systematic than opportunistic, but quite unique and potentially rich in insights. We can quite simply learn experientially — absorbing, observing, mulling, doing.

We also can gain as teachers, conveying to our students a sense of the synergies that can come from linking theory and practice, not only exposing them to some real-world learning but also reinforcing our argument that theory really is relevant. Ambassador David Newsom is right in his concern that one of the most worrisome consequences of "the growing withdrawal of university scholars behind curtains of theory and modeling" is the effect on our role in "the preparation of new generations."[40] Our teaching often gets underemphasized and underappreciated generally, and to the extent that government or other policy experience enhances our capacities as teachers, this is a further benefit for us and our universities.

Serving in government thus is not just a "service" responsibility. It also is an opportunity to learn, experience, and grow in our capacities as scholars and teachers. It makes possible the overall philosophical and practical benefits of praxis.

NOTES

The author gratefully acknowledges helpful discussions with and comments from Alexander George, Joseph Lepgold, and Miroslav Nincic.

1. Alexander L. George, *Bridging the Gap: Theory and Practice in Foreign Policy* (Washington, D.C.: U.S. Institute of Peace Press, 1993). See also Joseph Lepgold, "Is Anyone Listening? International Relations Theory and Policy Relevance," *Political Science Quarterly* 113 (spring 1998); David D. Newsom, "Foreign Policy and Academia," *Foreign Policy* 101 (winter 1995–96); Joseph Kruzel, "More a Chasm than a Gap, But Do Scholars Want to Bridge It?" *Mershon International Studies Review* 38 (April 1994).

2. I also had previous policy and political experience. In 1987–88 while an International Affairs Fellow (IAF) of the Council on Foreign Relations, I worked in the U.S. Senate as a foreign policy aide to then-Senator Al Gore; Senator Gore also was a candidate for the Democratic presidential nomination then, and thus the position also provided exposure to the politics of foreign policy. The Council's IAF Program is intended as an exchange program of sorts, providing opportunities for young academics to gain policy experience as well as for young policy professionals to research and write at a university or research institute. In addition, I served as a foreign policy adviser to the 1992 Clinton-Gore campaign, and on the foreign policy transition team in 1992–93.

3. George, *Bridging the Gap*, xviii.

4. Alexander George, Ohio University lecture, Oct. 19, 1994.

5. George, *Bridging the Gap*, 16.

6. Judith Goldstein and Robert O. Keohane, "Ideas and Foreign Policy:

An Analytical Framework," in Goldstein and Keohane, eds., *Ideas and Foreign Policy: Beliefs, Institutions and Political Change* (Ithaca: Cornell University Press, 1993), 3–30.

7. Bruce Russett and Harvey Starr, *World Policies: The Menu for Choice,* 5th ed. (New York: W. H. Freeman and Company, 1996), 30.

8. See, for example, Bruce W. Jentleson, ed., *Opportunities Missed, Opportunities Seized: Preventive Diplomacy in the Post–Cold War World* (Lanham, Md.: Rowman and Littlefield, 1999); David A. Lake and Donald Rothchild, eds., *The International Spread of Ethnic Conflict: Fear, Diffusion and Escalation* (Princeton: Princeton University Press, 1998).

9. George, *Bridging the Gap,* 117–18.

10. For another application and discussion see my book *With Friends Like These: Reagan, Bush and Saddam, 1982–1990* (New York: W. W. Norton and Company, 1994).

11. George A. Lopez and David Cortright, "Economic Sanctions in Contemporary Global Relations," in Cortright and Lopez, eds., *Economic Sanctions: Panacea or Peacekeeping in a Post–Cold War World?* (Boulder: Westview, 1995), 4.

12. Bruce W. Jentleson, "Economic Sanctions and Post–Cold War Conflict Resolution: Challenges for Theory and Policy," a study for the Committee on International Conflict Resolution, Commission on Behavioral and Social Sciences, National Research Council, National Academy of Sciences, Occasional Paper, forthcoming fall 1999.

13. See, for example, Alexander George and Richard Smoke, *Deterrence in American Foreign Policy: Theory and Practice* (New York: Columbia University Press, 1974); Richard Ned Lebow and Janice Gross Stein, *When Does Deterrence Succeed and How Do We Know?* (Ottawa: Canadian Institute for International Peace, 1990).

14. In addition to other chapters herein, see Joseph Lepgold, "Is Anyone Listening? International Relations Theory and the Problem of Policy Relevance," *Political Science Quarterly* 113 (spring 1998): 43–62.

15. Hans J. Morgenthau, *Policies among Nations: The Struggle for Power and Peace* (New York: Alfred A. Knopf, 1961; first edition, 1948), 5.

16. Hans J. Morgenthau, *In Defense of the National Interest: A Critical Examination of American Foreign Policy* (New York: Alfred A. Knopf, 1951).

17. Benjamin J. Cohen, "The Political Economy of International Trade," *International Organization* 44 (spring 1990): 276–78.

18. For further discussion and application to decision-making analysis, see Bruce W. Jentleson, "Discrepant Responses to Falling Dictators: Presidential Belief Systems and the Mediating Effects of the Senior Advisory Process," *Political Psychology* 11 (June 1990): 353–84.

19. K. J. Holsti, *International Policies: A Framework for Analysis,* 5th edition (Englewood Cliffs, N.J.: Prentice Hall, 1988), 7–8.

20. Alexander George and Richard Smoke, *Deterrence in American Foreign Policy: Theory and Practice* (New York: Columbia University Press, 1993), chapter 21; George, *Bridging the Gap,* chapter 10.

21. Michael N. Barnett, "The UN Security Council, Indifference, and Genocide in Rwanda," *Cultural Anthropology* 12, 4 (1997): 555. Barnett also did his stint through the Council on Foreign Relations IAF Program.

22. Barnett, "The UN Security Council," 555.

23. The *S* designates that it is in the Office of the Secretary, the *P* stands for Policy.

24. Lucian Pugliaresi and Diane T. Berliner, "Policy Analysis at the Department of State: The Policy Planning Staff," *Journal of Policy Analysis and Management* 8, 3 (1989): 383. See also an excellent paper by James MacDougall, a graduate student at Georgetown University, "The Planner's Dilemma," October 1997 (unpublished).

25. Barry Rubin, *Secrets of State* (New York: Oxford University Press, 1985), 134, cited in MacDougall, "The Planner's Dilemma," 1.

26. Warren Christopher, "America's Leadership, America's Opportunity," *Foreign Policy* 98 (spring 1995): 29–43.

27. A good account of foreign policymaking in the first year of the Clinton administration is Elizabeth Drew, *On the Edge: The Clinton Presidency* (New York: Simon and Schuster, 1994).

28. This was a misreading of trends in public opinion, missing key differentiations; see Bruce W. Jentleson and Rebecca L. Britton, "Still Pretty Prudent: Post–Cold War American Public Opinion on the Use of Military Force," *Journal of Conflict Resolution* 42 (August 1998): 395–417.

29. Ole R. Holsti, "The Belief System and National Images: A Case Study," *Journal of Conflict Resolution* 3 (1962); Martha Cottam, *Foreign Policy Decision-Making: The Influence of Cognition* (Boulder: Westview, 1986); Stephen Walker, "The Motivational Foundations of Political Belief Systems: A Re-Analysis of the Operational Code Construct," *International Studies Quarterly* 27 (1983); Jentleson, "Discrepant Responses to Falling Dictators."

30. Key works on democratic peace theory include Michael Doyle, "Kant, Liberal Legacies and Foreign Affairs, Part I," *Philosophy and Public Affairs* 12 (summer 1983), and "Liberalism and World Policies," *American Political Science Review* 80 (December 1986); Bruce Russett, *Grasping the Democratic Peace: Principles for a Post–Cold War World* (Princeton: Princeton University Press, 1993); John M. Owen, "How Liberalism Produces Democratic Peace," *International Security* 19 (fall 1994).

31. Lake also wrote an article ("Confronting Backlash States," *Foreign Affairs* 73, 2 [March/April 1994]) that, while not broadly paradigmatic, was consistent with motions of middle-level conceptualization with a cross-national focus on rogue regimes.

32. See, for example, Edward D. Mansfield and Jack Snyder, "Democratization and the Danger of War," *International Security* 20 (summer 1995): 5–38. David E. Spiro, "The Insignificance of the Liberal Peace," *International Security* 19 (fall 1994): 50–86.

33. The other multilateral tracks are Regional Economic Development, Water, Environment, and Refugees. See Dalia Dassa Kaye, "Madrid's Forgot-

ten Forum: The Middle East Multilaterals," *Washington Quarterly* 20 (winter 1997), and Joel Peters, *Pathways to Peace: The Multilateral Arab-Israeli Peace Talks* (London: Royal Institute of International Affairs, 1996).

34. For fuller discussion of ACRS, see my monograph *The Middle East Arms Control and Regional Security (ACRS) Talks: Progress, Problems and Prospects,* Policy Paper no. 26, September 1996, University of California Institute on Global Conflict and Cooperation; also Bruce W. Jentleson and Dalia Dassa Kaye, "Securing Status: Explaining Regional Security Cooperation and Its Limits in the Middle East," *Security Studies* 8, 1 (autumn 1998): 204–38. The track twos referenced are one run by the Stockholm International Peace Research Institute (SIPRI) on Middle East regional security and arms control, and one by the University of California Institute on Global Conflict and Cooperation (IGCC) on the military and Middle East arms control.

35. Jentleson, *ACRS: Progress, Problems, Prospects,* 2.

36. Jentleson and Kaye, "Securing Status."

37. Alexander George assesses the BPA as little more than a pseudo-agreement. See "The Basic Principles Agreement of 1972: Origins and Expectations," in his book *Managing U.S.-Soviet Rivalry: Problems of Crisis Prevention* (Boulder: Westview, 1983), 107–18.

38. Edward A. Kolodziej, "What Is the Challenge and Will We Accept It?" *Mershon International Studies Review* 38 (April 1994), 175; Kruzel, "More a Chasm than a Gap." In August 1995, while serving as deputy assistant secretary of defense for European and NATO policy, and playing a major role in the Bosnia peace negotiations, Joe Kruzel was killed on a road in Bosnia when the military vehicle he was traveling in hit a land mine.

39. Lawrence Freedman, "International Security: Changing Targets," *Foreign Policy* (spring 1998); Stephen M. Walt, "The Renaissance of Security Studies," *International Studies Quarterly* 35 (June 1991).

40. Newsom, "Foreign Policy and Academia."

# Part 2
# The Relevance of Theory
A. The Relevance of the Domestic Context

# Domestic Political Consequences of the Cold War's End: The International Impact on America's Foreign Policy Capacity

*Robert J. Lieber*

Since the end of the Cold War and the collapse of the Soviet Union, the United States has found itself the lone superpower. By traditional measurements of state capabilities, in relation to the power and capacity of other states,[1] the relative predominance of the United States has rarely been so pronounced as in this post–Cold War era. Yet the ability of the United States to exercise its power and influence and to achieve its objectives in foreign policy has not matched the predominance of capabilities that it possesses. A closer look, however, at the consequences of the end of the Cold War can provide a policy-relevant understanding of this paradox. In essence, a more careful assessment offers insights that are not, on first examination, self-evident.

While America's capabilities, measured in both absolute and relative terms, remain unparalleled, there is another dimension of state capability that must be accounted for. This is the internal capacity of a political system to formulate, implement, and sustain its foreign policies. By focusing on which instruments of foreign policy are in fact likely to be available, the analysis in this chapter suggests how academic work can help to define the range of feasible foreign policy options. To do so requires an appreciation of the nature of the American political system and the multiple concurrences required for policies to be implemented.

The ability of the United States to sustain its international role remains vital both for a more stable and less dangerous world and for America's own economy and security. Yet changes within the United States itself, triggered by the end of the Cold War, especially the disappearance of the external threat posed by the Soviet Union, make it more difficult for the country to play fully the role its own interests require, as well as to sustain a high level of cooperation with other countries and international institutions.

Emphasis on the way in which changes in the international system impact upon state capabilities is not unprecedented. A number of other theoretical approaches to international relations and foreign policy have previously devoted attention to this linkage. For example, Peter Gourevitch has called attention to this in his work on the second-image reversed, in which he addresses international system effects on the state.[2] In addition, Robert Putnam, in his treatment of two-level games, has developed a metaphor in which statesmen must bargain simultaneously on the two "tables" of international negotiation and domestic policies. In order to be successful, they must reach agreement in both these realms.[3]

There also is an important body of work that addresses the impact of domestic policies on foreign policy. Miroslav Nincic has dealt with the way in which American policy toward the Soviet Union was shaped by "domestic political rhythms" within the United States. As in the present study, moreover, he has noted that this is a level of causality that contemporary international relations thinking has tended to relegate to the sidelines because of its prevailing assumption that foreign policy reflects the structure of the international system. Yet, as Nincic notes, the domestic goals of political leaders have tended to separate foreign policy from the "objective nature of external challenges, thus impairing a nation's ability to deal with its international environment."[4]

Other insightful work on domestic sources of foreign policy includes Mark Lagon's recent study identifying important domestic sources of the Reagan doctrine[5] and Robert Paarlberg's assessment (discussed below) of the way in which U.S. international environmental policy has been determined more by domestic considerations than by international dimensions (such as the character of international interactions, problems of relative and absolute gains, the nature of international institutions and regimes, or even the existence of epistemic communities).[6]

With these previous theoretical efforts in mind, the present study makes clear that analysis of American foreign policy behavior will not be sufficiently nuanced and comprehensive until it integrates the way in which a major change in the international system, in this case the end of the Cold War and a significantly reduced external threat environment, has impacted the domestic political system. This change has shaped the power and preferences of domestic interest groups and actors as well as the role and strength of domestic institutions, and in turn it has had important feedback effects upon the policy process.

It matters a great deal whether and how the United States takes an active role in Bosnia, the Arab-Israeli peace process, the Persian Gulf,

NATO and the G-7, aid to Russia, relations with China and Japan, nuclear proliferation, the Comprehensive Test Ban Treaty, the Chemical Weapons Convention, the World Trade Organization, international peacekeeping, the environment, and Mexican loan guarantees. However, even when these and other issues are discussed, analysis of them largely fails to take into account an underlying shift affecting the ability of the United States to act effectively in foreign policy. The problem goes beyond the widely discussed end of the Cold War, which left policy-makers without the familiar guidelines that shaped policy for a generation, to the profound impact of this event upon the United States itself.

In essence, the disappearance of the Soviet threat has brought to an end an era of more than half a century in which the United States faced grave international challenges to its security. Fascism, World War II, and then the Cold War posed external threats that dominated in calculations of American national interests and foreign policy. These perils, and a domestic consensus — or near consensus — on grand strategy (though not always on specific policies), fostered an unprecedented expansion of the power and scope of the federal government and what Arthur Schlesinger once termed "the Imperial Presidency."[7]

Now, however, the end of more than five decades of world war and Cold War brings fundamental consequences for the American national state and for its ability to sustain an engaged and effective global role. These repercussions include an erosion of presidential and executive power, and a reassertion of the historical Madisonian features of the American political system. The origins of this system lie in the late-eighteenth-century founding of the United States, with its distrust of monarchical absolutism and its preference for a political system that would limit centralized executive authority. Its features, familiar to students of U.S. government, include separation of powers, checks and balances, federalism, and the restraints on executive authority embodied in the role of Congress and the judiciary.[8]

Domestic consequences of the end of the Cold War also include two other elements that have received relatively little attention. One is the increased scope for the personal and idiosyncratic characteristics of an administration, reflecting different generational experiences. In the case of the Clinton administration, these have included the Vietnam era and hesitations about the use of American power. A second consequence is the demise of Cold War liberalism together with the social and economic policies that accompanied it, whose passing may exacerbate social, regional, and class divisions within the country.

Together, these domestic effects are increasingly affecting the capacity of the United States to deal with the outside world. As a result, and in the absence of an unambiguous external threat, the problems the United States has faced in recent years in developing and carrying out a coherent foreign policy are likely to intensify. While political leaders are likely to be aware of these effects, the academic work discussed in this essay has the advantage of making many details about them cohere into intelligible patterns. Knowledge of such patterns may help policymakers in recognizing and coping with situations they confront.

### The Madisonian Resurgence

In practice, much of American constitutional history involves a tension between competing conceptions of governmental power. The American Revolution, the Declaration of Independence, and the Constitution were marked by a revolt against authority.[9] This wariness of government and of majority power is evident in the words of James Madison and in the institutions he helped to create. In Federalist No. 10, published in 1787, Madison writes of the need to control the excesses of faction, the causes of which are "sown in the nature of man."[10] While he deems a large republic more likely to take in a variety of parties and interests than a small one, and thus thinks it is "less probable that a majority of the whole will have a common motive to invade the rights of other citizens," he finds the means to protect the minority in rendering the majority "unable to concert and carry into effect schemes of oppression."[11]

In Federalist No. 51, written in 1788, Madison stresses the need to "contriv[e] the interior structure of the government as that its several constituent parts may, by their mutual relations, be the means of keeping each other in their proper place."[12] To this, Madison adds the classic admonition "Ambition must be made to counteract ambition."[13] He observes, "In republican government, the legislative authority necessarily predominates," and he proposes to remedy the dangers this poses by dividing the legislature into different branches with different modes of election.[14]

In the more than two centuries since publication of those words, much has changed. In the early years of the U.S. Republic, the legislative branch did often predominate. However, during the past century and a half, the presidency and the executive have enhanced their powers in coping with the exigencies of industrialization, urbanization, and the needs of modern society, though this expanded role has been particularly evident in response to domestic crises and foreign threats (the Civil War, World War I, the Depression, World War II, the Cold War). Yet postwar or postcrisis eras, particularly after the Civil War and again after World War I, have seen at least temporary reductions in executive power.[15]

Notwithstanding the Madisonian design of its institutions, the modern U.S. political system has proved itself capable of reacting forcefully to domestic crises and external threats. The mobilization of military capacity and international leadership in the 1990–91 case of Operations Desert Shield and Desert Storm having been the most recent major example. However, in noncrisis situations, and absent the galvanizing effects of a significant external threat, the system becomes unwieldy, and it is often difficult to undertake coherent policy initiatives. The absence of a security imperative reduces the priority and urgency of foreign affairs for most Americans, which makes it significantly more onerous for an administration to gain agreement with Congress and even within the executive branch itself.

In the post–World War II era, the relative deference of Congress to the executive was most marked during the 1950s.[16] This reflected the buildup of the national security state in response to the challenge posed by the Soviet Union, as well as by the need to direct and control the vast defense and foreign policy establishment, including the nuclear arsenal, that had grown up along with it.

If the imperatives of World War II and the Cold War, and the conduct of the presidency in leading the U.S. and international response in reaction to these threats, fostered the growth of greatly expanded presidential and executive powers, the excesses of power in Vietnam and Watergate triggered a reaction and then initial steps toward a reassertion of congressional prerogatives. However, with the end of the Cold War and the collapse of the Soviet Union, the balance of governmental authority has been more profoundly affected. The constraint on resources caused by budget deficits stemming from the Reagan era, as well as the greatly diminished international security imperative after the collapse of the Soviet Union, have led to major reductions in defense and foreign affairs spending. These brought defense outlays down from a peak of 6.5 percent of GDP in 1986 to just 3.2 percent in 1997. In real terms, inflation-adjusted defense budget authority has declined 40 percent since 1985 (though, by some estimates, the United States continues to spend more on defense than all its potential enemies and neutral states combined).[17] Appropriations for the international affairs budget (State Department, AID, ACDA, USIA, UN) have been even harder hit, dropping by some 50 percent in the fiscal years from 1984 through 1996. Accompanying these huge spending cuts, a shift in governmental authority and influence, away from traditional defense and foreign policy priorities, has become much more pronounced.

## The Inattentive Public

Without the widely acknowledged common threat represented by the Cold War, popular interest in foreign policy has plummeted. Although U.S. public opinion after the Cold War has not become isolationist, it does accord a far lower priority to foreign policy than at any time in the past half-century. Only 9 percent of voters in the 1992 presidential election listed foreign policy as among the top two issues influencing their vote.[18] Among those voters, 87 percent supported George Bush over Bill Clinton or Ross Perot.[19] As scholarly work that focuses on domestic-international linkages suggests, the growth of an inattentive public has the effect of increasing the domestic political risks of policies that impose large claims on human and economic resources.

The quadrennial poll taken in October 1994 by the Chicago Council on Foreign Relations showed foreign policy making up the smallest number of overall problems since 1978 for the public and the smallest among leaders since the council began its polling in 1974. While the same survey found 65 percent of the public and 98 percent of the leaders in favor of the United States taking an "active part in world affairs," respondents identified no threat comparable to that of the former Soviet Union.[20]

Voters in the November 1994 elections for the House of Representatives evinced even less interest in foreign policy. Crime, the economy, health care, and education led the list of issues that mattered most in determining how they voted. Only 2 percent of those polled cited foreign trade and NAFTA; no other foreign policy issue elicited even a 1 percent response.[21]

Opinion polls during 1995 continued to show few Americans identifying foreign policy as the most important issue facing the country. A Gallup poll late in the year produced a mere 2 percent response, as contrasted with figures of 20 to 27 percent during the mid-1980s,[22] and data during the 1996 primary and general elections remained consistent with these numbers. According to exit polls, only 4 percent of those voting in the November 1996 presidential election gave priority to foreign policy. The lessening of interest in foreign affairs makes it more difficult for any administration to galvanize support for activist foreign policies, particularly when these require spending money or committing U.S. troops. This does not altogether preclude military intervention, but public support for military intervention has been greater when the main objective has been to coerce foreign policy restraint by an aggressor state, when there has been a clear military strategy, and when the policy has been made a priority by the president and Congress.[23]

The practical effects of a growing inattention to foreign policy are increasingly evident. In the 1994 midterm elections, for example, the celebrated Republican "Contract with America" made only cursory reference to foreign policy. President Clinton's State of the Union speech in January 1996 devoted only five minutes to foreign policy. In the 1996 Republican presidential primaries, one prominent candidate (Pat Buchanan) advocated policies that were starkly isolationist and protectionist, while another (Steve Forbes) campaigned exclusively on the issues of a flat tax and term limits, and distributed a four-page campaign letter containing not a single word about foreign policy.

In the presidential contest itself, candidate Dole attacked President Clinton's leadership, and GOP thinkers set out ambitious designs for a more assertive America with missile defenses and a beefed-up defense budget. For their part, Bill Clinton and his administration claimed foreign policy successes in Bosnia, Haiti, the Middle East, Russia, and Korea. Yet both parties' positions were heavily ritualistic: the Republicans provided little indication of how they would pay for increased defense spending in the prevailing budgetary environment, and a number of the administration's proclaimed successes were fragile and potentially reversible. Overall, partisan differences on foreign policy remained mostly matters of nuance; indeed, Clinton and Dole typically had sharper disagreements with elements of their own parties than with each other. This was evident on issues such as NAFTA, the Mexican bailout, and the commitment of troops to Bosnia, as well as in a shared recognition that only the United States was capable of providing global leadership.

The changed circumstances in which post–Cold War America finds itself also result in more scope for the personal and idiosyncratic characteristics of an administration. In the case of Clinton foreign policy, the fact that external, structural imperatives no longer dominate American grand strategy as they did during the Cold War provides increased latitude for the impact of generational change and individual behavior. For the president and most of his foreign policy team, the more salient foreign policy reference points are not — as they were for the generations of John F. Kennedy, George Bush, and Bob Dole — the role of the United States in using force to defeat Nazi Germany and Japan in World War II, or the postwar success in containing Soviet power and rebuilding Europe and Japan, but instead the trauma of Vietnam and abuses of power abroad and at home. Indeed, a number of the administration's leading officials have been ambivalent about the Cold War itself,[24] and others — including President Clinton — were by no means unambiguous supporters of U.S. (and UN Security Council) policies leading up to the Gulf War.

Absent the necessities imposed by the Cold War and the need to counterbalance Soviet power, these experiences and political socialization tended to leave the president and many of his closest advisers hesitant about the use of military power, even as a companion to successful diplomacy. In the early part of the Clinton administration, the same factors helped to explain a strong preference for multilateralism even at the expense of inaction. Initially, the result was evident in areas as diverse as Somalia, Haiti, Rwanda, and Bosnia.[25]

## The Congressional Resurgence

In this environment, Congress reasserted many of the constitutional prerogatives in foreign policy that it had been less active in pressing during the Cold War, and the administration consequently found it difficult to implement foreign policy commitments. Thus, in its first two years in office, the Clinton administration was unable to deliver on international environmental pledges made during the 1992 presidential campaign. Despite solid Democratic majorities in both houses of Congress, the administration could not gain passage of legislation to meet carbon dioxide emission standards under the Rio Treaty, or win Senate ratification of the Biodiversity Convention.[26] Environmental measures lacked the urgency and consensus that might have enabled the administration to obtain congressional agreement on a proposed energy tax or overcome the problem of gaining a two-thirds majority for Senate ratification.

The administration also encountered delays in obtaining Senate ratification of the START II Treaty and the Chemical Weapons Convention, though both of these had been initiated under Republican presidents and originally enjoyed bipartisan support. The Chemical Weapons Convention first was delayed by the administration and then, after the Republican takeover of the Senate, became temporarily stalled in the Foreign Relations Committee. Ratification of START II eventually was achieved — by an overwhelming 87–4 margin — but the vote did not occur until late January 1996, more than three years into the Clinton administration.

As previously suggested, policies that make large claims on resources become politically risky in such an environment, making it difficult to form and sustain coalitions that will support such measures. Appropriations to fund international affairs activity came under intensified pressure after the Republicans gained control of Congress in the November 1994 midterm elections. Reductions in the international affairs budget led to cuts in requested funds for foreign aid (down by 20 percent since 1991), the United Nations ($1 billion overdue in U.S. payments), and the USIA (which absorbed staff cuts of 25 percent), and to additional personnel reductions at the State Department, AID, and ACDA. The much contested and delayed FY 1996 budget providing $18.44 billion (and approved only after President Clinton had vetoed an earlier version because of its interference with executive prerogatives) represented an 8.4 percent reduction from the previous year's figure of $20.13 billion.[27]

In the face of a Senate Foreign Relations Committee led by Jesse Helms, the administration encountered repeated difficulty in securing timely confirmation of its ambassadorial appointees. In addition, it found itself struggling with Helms over his proposals to eliminate USIA, AID, or ACDA and to transfer their functions to the State Department.

Congress also increasingly asserted its role in the policy arena. In mid-1995, and with veto-proof majorities, the House and Senate passed legislation ending U.S. compliance with the arms embargo against Bosnia. Facing the prospect that this policy reversal would cause a confrontation with the United States' allies, and the likelihood that U.S. troops would have to extricate European forces from their deployments in the former Yugoslavia, the Clinton administration took the initiatives that led to effective NATO air strikes against Bosnian Serb forces and the Dayton agreement among the warring parties. Even then, however, in December 1995, nearly half of the House membership signed a letter opposing deployment of 20,000 American troops in Bosnia,[28] despite the administration's commitment to withdraw U.S. forces within twelve months. Subsequently, with the completion of the Implementation Force (IFOR) mission, the administration gained grudging support for the follow-on Stabilization Force (SFOR) and the commitment of some 10,000 U.S. troops to be withdrawn in eighteen months. The logic of this July 1998 deadline had far less to do with circumstances in the region — where deployment remained essential to deter the resumption of fighting — than it did with the presumed reluctance of Congress and the American public to sustain an open-ended troop commitment.

For the Congress, the lessened urgency of foreign affairs has been evident not only in decreased budgets and the leisurely pace with which ambassadorial appointments and treaty ratifications have been met, but even in the travel schedules of members. Compared with the previous Congress, overseas travel fell by half. Not only did newly elected House members (most of them Republicans) evince little interest in foreign affairs, but congressional visits to the capital of one of America's most important allies, Germany, practically ceased. During the period from January 1995 to the spring of 1996, when Senator Richard Lugar of the

Senate Foreign Relations Committee paid a visit, not a single member of the House or Senate made an official trip to Bonn.[29] Notwithstanding the fact that more than half the members of Congress had been elected since the fall of the Berlin Wall, the lack of interest was remarkable.

This selective attention to foreign affairs was also evident within the administration. For example, according to figures provided by the State Department in May 1996, Secretary of State Warren Christopher had made at least 26 trips to Israel, 24 to Syria, and 13 to Egypt. There is no doubt that the Middle East was worthy of high-level attention, but the secretary's visits to Syria alone far outnumbered those he made to four of the most important countries in the world combined: Russia (6), Japan (4), Germany (4), and China (1).[30]

## The Demise of Cold War Liberalism

The passing of the Cold War era and the disappearance of the global threat to the United States represented by the Soviet Union has had yet another unanticipated consequence, albeit one that fits the larger pattern of second-image reversed effects discussed earlier. That is the demise of Cold War liberalism. For the United States, competition with the Soviet Union on a worldwide basis entailed not only the military component of containment, but economic, social, and ideological dimensions as well. The need to assure broad and sustained popular support at home, as well as to strengthen the attractiveness of the American model in foreign eyes, provided a powerful stimulus to expansion of the welfare state, educational opportunity, trade union activity, civil rights, and progressive taxation.

These measures, together with those initiated during and after World War II, had a broad impact upon American society. They fostered social mobility, democratization, and a national commitment to sharing the benefits of American prosperity, however imperfectly, across the boundaries of region, class, and race. With the end of the Cold War, however, many of these social impulses are weakening. In some cases this is due to disillusion with particular programs (as in the case of welfare) as well as with the role of government itself. At the same time, and more to the point in this chapter, the external impetus for such programs has been reduced. The importance of this impetus can be inferred from the fact that just as the rise of Cold War liberalism occurred under the presidencies of both Democrats (Truman, Kennedy, Johnson) and Republicans (Eisenhower, Nixon), its demise has taken place under similarly bipartisan auspices (Bush, Clinton).

A widening income gap and growing economic polarization within the United States may thus be due not only to the forces of global competition and the increased importance of educational and technical skills in a modern postindustrial economy, but also to a reduction in governmental efforts that had been put in place during the previous half-century.[31]

World War II and the Cold War had progressive effects within the United States, but with these conflicts now receding into history, it remains to be seen whether the country could again face sharper domestic divisions comparable to those of the 1920s and 1930s. If the domestic climate were to become more conflictual, the capacity of the United States to act effectively in foreign security and economic policy realms could be further diminished.

## Domestic Politics and Foreign Policy

Even during the height of the Cold War, American foreign policy was never made without some reference to domestic concerns. There were sometimes bitter differences over policy in the early years of the Cold War (1946–49), the Korean War (1950–53), and Vietnam (1965–73), and in the contrasting approaches of the Carter and Reagan administrations during the last decade of the Cold War (1977–88).

Moreover, there were occasions when domestic political considerations prevailed over foreign policy, albeit mostly on secondary issues. One such case in 1962 involved a proposed sale of U.S. aircraft to Yugoslavia. Despite the backing of President Kennedy, anti-Tito émigrés gained support for their opposition among congressional critics and within the Pentagon. Not only did the sale by the administration fail, but against the vociferous objections of Ambassador George Kennan, Congress also adopted punitive economic restrictions on Yugoslavia. The pained reaction of Kennan was evident when he wrote in his memoirs, "I have had some thirty-five years of experience with the affairs of Eastern Europe, [and Wilbur Mills, then House Ways and Means Committee chairman,] so far as I know had never been outside the United States. Yet on an important matter of foreign policy, affecting most intimately not only the East European post at which I was stationed but also the attitudes of surrounding countries, the elected representatives of my own country had supported his judgment over my own."[32]

Despite such incidents, the president and executive branch continued to predominate in the foreign policy realm. However, their role came under increasing challenge from the early 1970s onward as a result of Vietnam, Watergate, and the increased importance of international economic issues. These events tended to enhance the role of Congress and afford more access for domestic interest groups.

Taken together, the effects of reduced foreign threat amplify the weight of domestic priorities in the shaping of foreign policy, and these can affect not only the outcome of budgetary decisions, but also ambassadorial approvals, treaty ratifications, and broad lines of policy toward specific countries and regions.

When domestic and foreign priorities correspond, the result can be strong public and congressional support for administration policy. This is evident, for example, in the Middle East and Persian Gulf, where domestic public and interest-group sympathies have been broadly congruent with U.S. national interests. The Department of Defense posture statement for the Middle East sets out three criteria for determining whether a threat affects vital U.S. interests: if it threatens the survival of the United States or its key allies; if it threatens critical U.S. economic interests; and if it poses the danger of a future nuclear threat. "Nowhere," the report observes, "are these criteria met more clearly than in the Middle East."[33]

The Middle East is the one area in which threats to U.S. vital interests have been the most unambiguous and widely recognized. Elsewhere, there are few instances where this is the case. In the absence of an overarching foreign threat, policy across a broad array of issues is much more heavily affected by domestic factors. Many of these make it harder to shape coherent policies and to achieve cooperation with allies or even former adversaries.

At the same time, countries with which the United States has had long-standing relationships are also affected because the end of the Cold War has taken away the underlying motivation to limit differences over economic and security issues in the face of the Soviet threat.[34] Although the internal circumstances of America's allies and trading partners differ, domestic priorities take on greater weight as they calculate their own international relationships. Here too, the end of the Cold War may well prove to make the extension of cooperation more difficult than originally imagined.

**In Search of a New "Bear in the Woods"**

During the 1984 presidential election, a Reagan television commercial suggested there probably was a dangerous Russian "bear in the woods" and that it was prudent for the United States to craft its foreign policies accordingly. With the metaphorical bear having come in from the cold, however, is there any prospect that some new peril may take its place as the focus of U.S. grand strategy?

This is more than an academic question. The Madisonian elements of the American political system have admirable virtues, and they have served the country well for more than two centuries. Yet the world of 1787 is an era apart from that at the end of the second millennium, particularly when its political legacy is an executive branch with diminished capacity to respond effectively to the foreign policy tasks facing the United States. A plethora of global problems and dangers does exist, and the world is likely to be a less peaceful, less ordered, and more chaotic place if the United States finds itself unable to sustain its global role.

Both the Clinton administration and Republican strategists recognize that only the United States has the capacity for global leadership. The administration, after an initial exploration of multilateral alternatives followed by a declaratory policy of "engagement and enlargement" of the sphere of democracies and market economies, gravitated to a more activist style. This became evident in Haiti, Bosnia, North Korea, and the Middle East, as well as in negotiations over the comprehensive nuclear test ban treaty, the GATT, aid to Russia, counterterrorism initiatives, and conflict resolution in Northern Ireland and between Turkey and Greece. These actions reflected practical experience, bluntly summed up by the administration's Bosnia negotiator, Richard Holbrooke, in words directed at Europe but applicable across the board: "Unless the United States is prepared to put its political and military muscle behind the quest for solutions to European instability, nothing really gets done."[35]

In turn, the 1996 GOP platform called for "restoring America's world leadership" and endorsed Senator Dole's proposal for deployment of a national missile defense system to defend all 50 states by the year 2003.[36] In his speech accepting the party's presidential nomination, Dole criticized the Clinton administration's "massive cuts in funding for our national security."[37] In a similar spirit, other mainstream Republicans urged what William Kristol and Robert Kagan described as a "neo-Reaganite policy of military supremacy and moral confidence."[38] Their grand strategy called for preserving and enhancing an American "benevolent global hegemony" as the only reliable defense against a breakdown of peace and international order. The proposal was based on three imperatives: a defense budget with $60 to $80 billion in additional spending per year; citizen involvement to reduce the growing gap between the professional military and a civilian population indifferent to the importance of military efforts abroad; and moral clarity through active promotion of democracy, free markets, and respect for liberty.[39]

These Republican proposals failed to elicit broad public or elite backing. The lack of response was characteristic of a post–Cold War era in which foreign policy concerns had greatly diminished salience and there was little domestic support for the financial, political, and military commitments that more ambitious measures would have required. By contrast, reductions in defense spending by the Clinton administration followed a trajectory established by the Bush administration in seeking to adapt to the post–Cold War world, and funding for international affairs declined under both Democratic and Republican auspices. It was only with the onset of the second Clinton term that some effort to redress this decline began. In recognition of President Clinton's belated description of America as the "indispensable nation," his newly appointed secretary of state, Madeleine Albright, called for a foreign affairs budget increase of more than $1 billion and efforts to pay America's overdue UN assessment.

Historically, it has taken dramatic threats to provide the impetus for broad, sustained American engagement and resources. German submarine warfare in 1916–17, Pearl Harbor, the Soviet takeover of Eastern Europe, Soviet deployment of atomic and hydrogen bombs, the Korean War, Sputnik, Afghanistan, and Iraq's invasion of Kuwait are among the most important examples. By comparison, the emergence of a comparable challenge in the short run seems highly problematic. Moreover, even a relatively direct and unambiguous threat may not elicit universal domestic reaction. It is sobering to recall that in response to the principal post–Cold War challenge presented by Saddam Hussein, the January 1991 resolution authorizing use of force on the eve of the Gulf War passed the Senate by a narrow 52–47 margin.

Among possible future threats would be a resurgent and belligerent Russia under an intensely nationalist and xenophobic leadership, perhaps as the result of a dramatic economic crisis. However, the Yeltsin presidency made this unlikely for a period of at least several years, and it is not at all evident that the desires of Russia's people, let alone its economy, would sustain such a renewed threat to Europe and the United States. Russian economic restructuring requires a stable and cooperative relationship with Western countries and with international financial institutions. In addition, neither Yeltsin nor those who might succeed him in the immediate future seem to represent a serious threat, and the Russian defense minister General Rodionov even announced in 1966 that he did "not see any direct external threat to Russia."[40] In addition, according to CIA estimates, defense spending has plummeted some 80 percent from the Soviet figure in 1988, and among voters in

the 1996 Russian presidential elections, only 2 percent identified foreign policy as their primary concern.[41]

China is another candidate for the role of global threat, and the
longer-term course of that country is not at all clear. Predictions that
economic transformation will ineluctably lead to a more democratic and
internationally cooperative China rest on economic determinist models
that are simplistic and ahistorical. While the desired benign evolution
deserves wide support, the late-nineteenth- and twentieth-century case
of Germany from Bismarck to Hitler and that of Japan in the 1930s and
early 1940s provide sobering reminders of potential alternatives.[42] For
the medium term, however, even a more nationalistic and aggressive
China would be primarily a regional threat and not yet a global chal-
lenger to the United States.

A third possibility identifies a Middle Eastern rogue state, such as
Iran, in collusion with militant and anti-Western Islamic groups. Terrorist attacks, such as the bombing of Pan Am flight 103 in December 1988,
car bomb and truck bomb attacks on American forces in Saudi Arabia in
November 1995 and June 1996, and the World Trade Center bombing in
New York, are cases in point. Threats to American allies (Israel, Egypt,
Jordan, Saudi Arabia), actions in Europe (Iranian-sponsored terrorist
activity, as evident in a large mortar discovered in a shipment of cucum-
bers on an Iranian freighter docked in Antwerp in March 1977), and
more ominous covert efforts (e.g., to enhance missile and chemical
weapon capabilities and to acquire nuclear weapons) make this a threat
to be taken seriously. However, Iran suffers from severe economic problems that are likely to constrain the threat it may pose to its neighbors
and the outside world. Absent a massive upsurge in the number and
intensity of terrorist attacks, the threat does not appear sufficient to
replace the major ones the United States has previously faced in this
century.

Finally, there remains a loose collection of nontraditional threats.
These new global dangers include disease, famine, ethnic conflicts, refu-
gee flows, environmental pollution, and even economic upheaval. In
addition, more specific and readily identifiable threats may be posed by
weapons of mass destruction (chemical, biological, and nuclear), especially if married to missile delivery systems. Of these, perhaps the single
greatest and most realistic threat to the United States comes from nuclear proliferation. Successive American administrations have given this
increasing attention, though without a specific and deadly challenge, this
has not engaged the intense concern of Congress or the media.

Indeed, whether or not the threat of missile or nuclear attack should now be a priority concern, it has not caught the public's attention. Recent polling data finds 57 percent of the American public viewing a nuclear missile attack as "very unlikely" in the next five years, with only 15 percent describing this as "likely." By contrast, 55 percent find it likely that the United States will be attacked by terrorists who bring bombs or bomb-making equipment into the country.[43]

In all, there exists no shortage of potential threats. However, none has yet presented the kind of overriding, unambiguous danger that forces Americans, their institutions, and their elected leaders to reorient their attentions and priorities. In the absence of such a confrontation, the Madisonian reassertion is likely to persist or even intensify, and with it the shifting balance toward Congress and the states, along with a diminished capacity and effectiveness of presidential and executive authority.

In this evolving domestic political environment, there are several possible options for those concerned with foreign policy and who believe that the subject deserves continued priority. One such measure is the ritual call for bipartisanship in foreign policy. This has the sanctity of motherhood and apple pie, and during war and Cold War, bipartisanship has often been a fact of life. However, in the absence of crisis it is not now likely to become a priority.

A second option is deliberately to amplify the threat, that is, to alarm the public. While the Soviet danger to American national interests was indeed very real, the Truman administration found it necessary to package aid to Greece and Turkey in 1947 (the Truman Doctrine) in grandiose terms in order to gain public and congressional support for passage. The North Korean invasion of South Korea in June 1950 and the Soviet launching of Sputnik in October 1957 occasioned comparable warnings that America and the West faced dire peril. In the current circumstances, however, absent a dramatic change in the external world, exhortation and the invocation of some new threat is not likely to gain renewed national attention and resources for America's world role.

In an environment of diminished threat, with fewer clear and compelling imperatives for a specific course of action, an individual president and his administration have considerable latitude in the choices they make. The renewed emphasis on foreign policy by President Clinton and Secretary of State Albright in the Clinton second term thus appears to reflect an appreciation not only of the importance of U.S. leadership, but of the need for political leaders to galvanize domestic support. Nonetheless, the lesser priority accorded to foreign policy by Congress and the public continues to make it more difficult for an administration to secure political and material support for the foreign policies it does seek to implement.

Administrations of either party thus face the need to adapt to the changed domestic climate and to work effectively within it. Paradoxically, to the extent that this environment hampers the ability of the United States to sustain an engaged and effective global role — and one in which it might act to anticipate or ward off foreign perils — the result may make more likely the reemergence of a bona fide external threat that ultimately leads, once again, to the reappearance of the imperial presidency and national security state.

## Implications

Analyses of foreign policy behavior and of cooperation problems have typically emphasized international dimensions such as the character of international interactions, problems of relative and absolute gains, the nature of international institutions and regimes, or even the existence of epistemic communities. As Robert Paarlberg has observed in assessing international environmental policy, even the work on "two-level games," which does incorporate a domestic dimension, is inclined to treat domestic obstacles as more likely to be dealt with effectively following the preemptive achievement of international agreement.[44] On the other hand, the Madisonian resurgence described here can also be understood as effectively diminishing in size and number the "win-sets" (i.e., the set of potential agreements that the domestic polity would ratify).[45] As a result, it has become harder to secure domestic approval for agreements and actions at the international level. This point, and the related one that international circumstances condition the size and nature of domestic institutions and their key functions, may be clarified by theories that focus on domestic-international linkages.

Analysis of American foreign policy behavior thus will be incomplete unless it now takes significantly into account the impact of the end of the Cold War, a greatly diminished international threat environment, and the domestic consequences of these for the United States as they feed back into the policy process.

Together with sharply reduced public and congressional attention and priority for foreign affairs, these changes in the domestic political environment make it more difficult for any administration to frame and implement coherent foreign policies. As a consequence, the ability of the United States to cooperate internationally, with allies, with former adversaries, or with regional and multilateral bodies, is constrained. To some degree this constraint can be mitigated by the choices and behavior of particular administrations. Moreover, the United States remains capable of acting decisively in crisis situations – as in the case of the 1990–91 Gulf crisis and war. Nonetheless, the policy-relevant insights provided by this study help us to understand how the consequences of the absence of major external threat have fed back into the American domestic realm in fundamental ways and in turn have impacted on the ability of the United States to act in the global arena.

NOTES

For comments on earlier versions of this essay, I wish to thank Joseph Lepgold, Miroslav Nincic, Robert Paarlberg, Victor Cha, Keir Lieber, George Downs, Charles Lipson, Robert Art, Bruce Jentleson, Benjamin J. Cohen, and participants in seminars at the Woodrow Wilson School at Princeton and the PIPES (Program in International Politics, Economics and Security) Seminar at the University of Chicago. Portions of this essay develop and expand upon material in "Eagle without a Cause: Making Foreign Policy without the Soviet Threat," in Lieber, ed., *Eagle Adrift: American Foreign Policy at the End of the Century* (New York: Longman, 1997), 3–25.

1. On relative gains, see especially Joseph Grieco, "Anarchy and the Limits of Cooperation: A Realist Critique of the Newest Liberal Institutionalism," *International Organization* 42, no. 3 (summer 1988): 485–508; Grieco, *Cooperation among Nations: Europe, America, and Non-Tariff Barriers to Trade* (Ithaca: Cornell University Press, 1990); Robert Jervis, "International Primacy: Is the Game Worth the Candle?" *International Security* 17, no. 4 (spring 1993): 52–67; and Robert Powell, "Absolute and Relative Gains in International Relations Theory," *American Political Science Review* 85, no. 4 (December 1991): 1303–20.

2. See Peter Gourevitch, "The Second Image Reversed," *International Organization* 32, no. 4 (autumn 1978): 881–912; also *Politics in Hard Times: Comparative Responses to International Economic Crises* (Ithaca: Cornell University Press, 1986).

3. Robert D. Putnam, "Diplomacy and Domestic Politics: The Logic of Two-Level Games," *International Organization* 42, no. 3 (summer 1988): 427–60 (also in Peter B. Evans, Harold K. Jacobson, and Robert D. Putnam, eds., *Double-Edged Diplomacy: International Bargaining and Domestic Politics* [Berkeley: University of California Press, 1993], 4, 431–68).

4. Miroslav Nincic, "U.S. Soviet Policy and the Electoral Connection," *World Politics* 42, no. 3 (April 1990): 370–96, at 370.

5. Mark P. Lagon, *The Reagan Doctrine: Sources of American Conduct in the Cold War's Last Chapter* (Westport, Conn.: Praeger, 1994), especially the preface and pages 1–3.

6. Robert Paarlberg makes this point lucidly in demonstrating the broader implications for understanding the U.S. role in international environmental cooperation. See "Earth in Abeyance: Explaining Weak Leadership in U.S. International Environmental Policy," in Lieber, ed., *Eagle Adrift*, 149–54.

7. Arthur M. Schlesinger Jr., *The Imperial Presidency* (New York: Houghton Mifflin, 1973).

8. Clinton Rossiter discusses James Madison as an exponent of limited government in the introduction to *The Federalist Papers,* by Alexander Hamilton, James Madison, and John Jay (New York: Mentor/New American Library, 1961), xv. See especially Federalist No. 10. Also see George W. Carey, *The Federalist: Design for a Constitutional Republic* (Urbana: University of Illinois Press, 1989).

9. Seymour Martin Lipset discusses this in *American Exceptionalism: A Double-Edged Sword* (New York: Norton, 1996).

10. Alexander Hamilton, John Jay, and James Madison, *The Federalist: A Commentary on the Constitution of the United States, Being a Collection of Essays written in Support of the Constitution agreed upon September 17, 1787, by the Federal Convention,* with an introduction by Edward Mead Earle (New York: Modern Library, n.d.), 55.

11. *The Federalist: A Commentary,* 61.

12. *The Federalist: A Commentary,* 336.

13. *The Federalist: A Commentary,* 337.

14. *The Federalist: A Commentary,* 338.

15. This includes a struggle between what Bruce W. Jentleson has referred to as presidentialists and congressionalists. See "Who, Why, What and How: Debates over post–Cold War Military Intervention," in Lieber, ed., *Eagle Adrift* 41–42.

16. James M. Lindsay, *Congress and the Politics of U.S. Foreign Policy* (Baltimore: Johns Hopkins University Press, 1994).

17. E.g., Lawrence J. Korb, "Our Overstuffed Armed Forces," *Foreign Affairs* 74, no. 6 (November/December 1995), 23.

18. Voter Research and Surveys, election day poll conducted by a consortium of CBS, NBC, ABC, and CNN, November 3, 1992.

19. Voter Research and Surveys, election day poll conducted by a consortium of CBS, NBC, ABC, and CNN, November 3, 1992.

20. Chicago Council on Foreign Relations, *American Public Opinion and U.S. Foreign Policy, 1995* (Chicago, 1995), 6, 21. Concern about unfriendly countries becoming nuclear powers led the list of "critical threats" (cited by 72 percent of the public and 61 percent of leaders), followed by immigration (public 72 percent, leaders 31 percent), and international terrorism (public 69 percent, leaders 33 percent).

21. Data from Mitofsky International of New York, *Washington Post,* November 10, 1993, A33.

22. Steven Kull, "What the Public Knows that Washington Doesn't," *Foreign Policy* 101 (winter 1995–96), 124.

23. Jentleson, "Who, Why, What and How"; also see Jentleson, "The Pretty Prudent Public: Post-Vietnam American Opinion on the Use of Military Force," *International Studies Quarterly* 36, no. 1 (March 1992): 49–73.

24. Henry Kissinger has criticized Deputy Secretary of State Strobe Talbott

for writing in *Time* magazine in 1990 that the Cold War had been unnecessary and that a more conciliatory Western policy would have ended it decades earlier. See Henry Kissinger, "It's an Alliance, Not a Relic," *Washington Post,* August 16, 1994, A19; also Kissinger, "For U.S. Leadership, a Moment Missed," *Washington Post,* May 12, 1995, A25.

25. Elsewhere, Michael Mandelbaum has described events in Somalia, Bosnia, and Haiti during the first nine months of the Clinton administration as "failed military interventions" that "set the tone and established much of the agenda of the foreign policy of the United States from 1993 through 1995." See "Foreign Policy as Social Work," *Foreign Affairs* 75, no. 1 (January/February 1996): 26–33, at 26.

26. The convention was signed by a U.S. representative on June 4, 1993, and sent to the Senate five months later. It was never submitted to a floor vote because thirty-five Republican Senators, one more than needed to defeat the treaty, had decided to oppose it. Robert Paarlberg, "Earth in Abeyance: Explaining Weak Leadership in U.S. International Environmental Policy," in Lieber, ed., *Eagle Adrift,* 138–39. The case also illustrates Putnam's observation that the requirement to secure domestic approval is "a crucial theoretical link" between the two levels of international and domestic bargaining. See Robert D. Putnam, "Diplomacy and Domestic Politics: The Logic of Two-Level Games," *International Organization* 42, no. 3 (summer 1988): 427–60, at 436.

27. *Washington Post,* April 29, July 28, 1996.

28. *New York Times,* December 8, 1995, A-18.

29. In that period, a few congressmen and senators did travel to meetings in Munich, Dresden, and Berlin (German Embassy, Washington, D.C., author interview, March 18, 1998). Information on the overall reduction in congressional travel was provided to the author by the State Department.

30. *Economist,* June 8, 1996, 28. Indeed, due to criteria used by the State Department, the published data may actually undercount the number of times the secretary landed in Damascus.

31. For insightful treatments of this phenomenon, see John B. Judis, "The Contract with K Street," *New Republic,* December 4, 1995, 18–25; and Daniel Deudney and G. John Ikenberry, "America after the Long War," *Current History* 95, no. 595 (November 1995): 364–69.

32. George F. Kennan, *Memoirs, 1950–1963* (Boston, 1970), quoted in the lucid account provided by Dusko Doder in *The Yugoslavs* (New York: Random, 1978), 148–49.

33. Department of Defense, Office of International Security Affairs, "United States Security Strategy for the Middle East," Washington, D.C., May 1995, 5.

34. See Benjamin J. Cohen, " 'Return to Normalcy'?: Global Economic Policy at the End of the Century," in Lieber, ed., *Eagle Adrift,* 74.

35. Quoted in the *Washington Post,* February 8, 1996, A-17.

36. *New York Times,* August 13, 1996, A12.

37. *New York Times,* August 16, 1996, A27.

38. William Kristol and Robert Kagan, "Toward a Neo-Reaganite Foreign Policy," *Foreign Affairs* 75, no. 4 (July/August 1996): 18–32, at 23.

39. Kristol and Kagan, "Neo-Reaganite Foreign Policy," 20, 23–27.

40. Quoted in David Hoffman, "Lebed Choice Gets Defense Post," *Washington Post,* July 18, 1996.

41. Data cited by Robert Kagan, *Weekly Standard,* July 1, 1996.

42. Edward Friedman provides a thoughtful treatment of the German parallel; see "The Challenge of a Rising China: Another Germany?" in Lieber, ed., *Eagle Adrift,* 215–45. In a subsequent paper, he assesses a growing tendency toward xenophobia in China, in "Avoiding War with China — Containment, Appeasement or Engagement?" paper presented to the July 1996 Conference on Taiwan-Mainland Relations Entering the Twenty-first Century, sponsored by the *China Times,* Taipei.

43. Survey of 1,012 people, conducted May 3–5, 1966, by the Mellman Group, as reported in John V. Parachini, "Public Not Fearful of Nuclear Missile Attack," *Polling Report* 12, no. 12 (June 17, 1996) (the margin of error was plus or minus 3.1 percent).

44. Robert Paarlberg makes this point lucidly in demonstrating the broader implications for understanding the U.S. role in international environmental cooperation. See "Earth in Abeyance: Explaining Weak Leadership in U.S. International Environmental Policy," in Lieber, ed., *Eagle Adrift,* 149–54.

45. For a discussion of "win-sets," see Evans, Jacobson, and Putnam, eds., *Double-Edged Diplomacy,* 23, 439–40.

# Putting Theory to Work: Diagnosing Public Opinion on the U.S. Intervention in Bosnia

*Eric V. Larson*

## Introduction

This essay elaborates on and applies theoretically based models that have successfully been used to understand the dynamics of public support for past U.S. wars and military operations.[1] Its narrow aim is to apply theory in a policy-relevant way to understand the underlying dynamics of public support for the U.S. peacekeeping operation in Bosnia. In so doing, it offers a very different perspective from that taken by most scholarly research in the area, and it represents a challenge to the scholarly community to develop theories that are more useful.[2]

The chapter has three sections. In the first, policy-relevant theory is embedded in simple policy models that can be used to diagnose support for a military operation, and the robustness or sensitivity of that support to various outcomes. These models are then used in the second section to diagnose data on presidential and congressional leadership, the changing tempo of events in Bosnia, and media reporting, to describe and better understand the antecedents and dynamics of public attitudes toward the U.S. peacekeeping operation in Bosnia. The third section completes the essay with a discussion of some implications for policy and for improving the policy relevance of theory in this area.

Although this contribution relies upon many of the same sorts of tools and data sources that are used in theory building and testing, it presents an analysis that is unabashedly oriented toward informing policy rather than theory development. It accordingly emphasizes two of the forms of policy relevance that were described in the introduction to this volume: the identification of patterns and regularities to shed light on the limits of the possible where changes are desired, and the illumination of potential domestic costs of various policies and outcomes. It also focuses on one too-often neglected way that theory can profitably be used in a policy setting — as a diagnostic tool for illuminating the opportunities and constraints that inhere in a specific case, in this instance, the U.S. peacekeeping operation in Bosnia that began in December 1995.

**I**

> In contemporary usage the term "model" is, I think, simply
> a synonym for "theory." I am to speak, then, on "Theories:
> Their Uses and Limitations." This is a topic I can handle
> very briefly: the uses of theories are obvious, and their only
> limitations are that they are often bad theories.
> — Herbert A. Simon

The aim of policy analysis is to understand the impact of alternative policies under a range of possible conditions: in this way, robust policies — policies that do acceptably well under a range of possible conditions — can be chosen. By integrating policy and contextual variables in a way that allows contingent predictions of outcomes to be made, theory can contribute in an important way to the construction of models that can assist in evaluating the consequences of policy alternatives.

In policy analysis, the focus is typically problem-oriented, catholic in the tools it uses, and heavily reliant upon the maturity of the preexisting empirical knowledge base. As a consequence, policy modelers frequently have to draw from a number of disciplines and integrate a mix of deductive theory, isolated empirical generalizations, or single-variable models that have not yet been embedded in fully developed empirically based theory:[3]

> Deductive theory can often provide the first-order logic for establishing relationships between variables and can compensate for unavailable data;[4]
> Empirical generalizations and single-variable models can provide insights into the nature of the relationships between pairs of variables;
> Fully developed empirically based theory can reduce uncertainty about these relationships or better delineate the circumstances under which these relationships hold, as well as specifying the relative importance of variables in determining outcomes.

Because the emphasis is on capturing the essential characteristics of the policy problem, policy analysts generally tend to prefer simple, aggregate-level models — or even several such models — to larger, more detailed ones that may do more to obscure than illuminate. The reason is that policy modeling focuses on understanding the larger context of the policy problem, and capturing its most salient dimensions, while remaining willing to sacrifice either parsimony or precision in favor of robustness.[5] Accordingly, I will first propose a model that can be used to understand public support for military operations and then describe another that captures the essential features of the broader domestic environment for military operations.

## A Simple Model of the Public's Ends-Means Calculus

While much of the research on public opinion toward military operations has focused on "rally effects" or average levels of support, less work has been oriented toward general models that can explain the observed patterns in support for a particular military operation over time.[6] A few scholars have in fact recognized the policy relevance of two core phenomena — declines in support over the course of an operation, and diverging preferences regarding the level of commitment.[7] Beyond these authors, however, little additional research has been undertaken to place these recurring phenomena into a broader theoretical framework.

The model that will next be described is a deductive model that provides a cogent explanation for two distinct aspects of support for military operations: (1) the factors associated with increasing and decreasing support for military operations, and (2) the factors associated with diverging preferences regarding strategy and the level of commitment.

### The Deductive Model

At the most fundamental level, members of the public attempt to weigh ends, ways, and means in deciding whether to support a military operation. A simple model has been shown to assist in thinking about support for military operations by characterizing support as the result of a series of tests or questions that need to be answered collectively by political leaders and the public:[8]

Do the benefits seem to be high enough?
Are the prospects for success high enough?
Are the expected or actual costs low enough?
Taken together, does the probable outcome seem (or seem still)
    to be worth the costs?

The nature of the relationships can be encapsulated in a simple mathematical expression. Let each individual *i*'s utility be defined by the following function, which relates the three variables in an intuitively logical way.[9]

$$U_i = (p_i \cdot b_i)/c_i$$

where:

$U_i$ = the utility that individual *i* has for the military operation

$p_i$ = the subjective estimate of the probability of success for the operation

$b_i$ = the perceived benefits of the operation for individual *i*

$c_i$ = the anticipated or actual costs in blood and treasure

This expression tells us that an individual's utility from a military operation will depend on the ratio between the expected benefits and the costs. Now, let

$U\text{min}_i$ = the minimal acceptable utility for individual *i* to remain a supporter of the operation; in the vernacular of microeconomics, this can be thought of as the level of utility at which an individual is just indifferent between support and opposition.

Put another way, the individual will be a supporter of the operation so long as his subjective expected utility ($U_i$) is greater than or equal to the minimal threshold for continued support ($U\text{min}_i$), and where each of the three parameters ($p_i$, $b_i$, and $c_i$) and $U\text{min}_i$ are greatly influenced by the positions of political leaders and experts, to the extent that individuals are aware of them (discussed below). If an individual's utility falls below this threshold, he will oppose the operation, and if the utility climbs above this threshold, he will support it.

*Benefits.*    Approaches have varied in characterizing the perceived benefits of military operations.[10] In order to simplify analysis, we can evaluate the benefits of a military operation in terms of two dimensions:[11] the first is the importance of the interests that are directly engaged in a situation (the litmus test for the Realist), and the second is the importance of the normative or moral principles, values, or goals being promoted (the litmus test for the Idealist).[12] All else equal, the greater the importance of the interests and principles that are engaged, the higher the level of utility, although departures from strict rationality may lead to inconsistent evaluations of utility.[13] On the basis of simple microeconomic theory, one would expect that individuals will be willing to trade off across the two dimensions at an increasing marginal rate — somewhat low interests in a situation may be compensated for by particularly important principles that are engaged, and vice versa.[14] The benefits will be highest for military operations that are seen to engage U.S. vital interests and for operations whose political objectives promote foreign policy goals or principles that are deemed to be quite important.[15]

*The probability of success.*   In addition to being animated by principles and interests, public attitudes toward the use of force are suffused with a strong component of pragmatism that tempers unquestioning support for pursuit of these abstractions.[16] Therefore, the second parameter of the simple model of ends and means has to do with the prospects for a successful outcome. Because the deductive model of ends and means incorporates the probability of success in the numerator, the probability of success operates in the same fashion as the level of benefits: as the probability of a successful outcome declines, the expected benefits to be achieved by the operation also decline. Put another way, operations that are clearly failing to achieve their objectives will tend to lose support.[17]

*Costs.*   The third parameter of the simple model has to do with the expected or actual costs of the military operation, including blood and treasure, and any opportunity costs. The deductive model predicts that as the costs increase, any individual's estimate of utility will decline, and these declines in individuals' utilities will result in lower aggregate levels of public support for the military operation, as the weakest supporters pass their minimal utilities for supporting the operation.

The role of casualties in support for a military operation is far more complex and sensible than most realize.[18] The record reveals two important lessons: (1) support generally declines as casualties increase, but (2) the sensitivity to casualties (i.e., the rate at which support declines as a simple function of casualties) varies greatly across past wars and military operations. The simple algebraic model explains why this should be so: there is an interaction between casualties and other factors such that sensitivity to casualties is regulated by beliefs about the importance of the benefits and evaluations of the prospects for success.[19] In World War II, the stakes were judged to be vitally important, and there was generally continued optimism about the outcome of the war; the result was continued high support for the war in the face of horrific casualties and changing fortunes on the battlefield. In the limited wars in Korea and Vietnam, both the benefits and the prospects for success came into question even as casualties mounted, resulting in much greater sensitivity to casualties than in World War II. In the Gulf War, the important benefits and high prospects for success led to relatively high *prospective* tolerance for casualties, but not quite the tolerance for casualties as in Korea or Vietnam. And following the change of U.S. objectives in Somalia in May 1993 (from providing a secure environment for humanitarian relief operations to engaging in nation building) and the subsequent deterioration in the situation, the importance of the objectives and the prospects for success declined for most, even as the costs increased. The result was very high sensitivity to costs in Somalia.[20]

*The minimal acceptable utility ($U\min_i$).* Finally, there is the parameter $U\min_i$ — the individual's minimal acceptable utility to be a supporter of the military operation. This parameter suggests that at some level of utility — whether as a result of changed benefits, prospects for success, or costs — every individual will be indifferent between supporting and opposing the military operation; any additional costs or a decline in benefits or prospects will push the individual into opposition.[21]

*The key role of leadership.* For any individual, the values of all of these parameters will be influenced by media reporting on the positions taken by trusted political leaders and experts, as well as those taken by friends, coworkers, or other opinion leaders that are known personally to the individual.[22] We can now explore the implications of this model in more detail.

### Predictions of the Model

The simple model of ends and means makes predictions about two distinct phenomena:[23] (1) the level of support or opposition for a military operation, and (2) the changing level of commitment to a military operation, that is, preferences regarding an increased or decreased level of commitment.[24]

*Predictions regarding the level of support or opposition.* When individuals are aggregated, the ceteris paribus predictions of this model are as follows.

Because the political objectives of a war or military operation provide the basis for assessing the possible benefits of the operation, a change in objective or mission ("mission change" or "mission creep") can entail a change in the perceived benefits of the operation for any individual. In response to a change in objectives, the benefits may either increase or decrease, depending on the individual's value structure and the particular configuration of variables in the case at hand. When there is a net increase in the number of individuals who believe benefits have declined, this will result in a decline in the percentage supporting the operation; net increases in the number of individuals believing that the benefits have increased will result in sustained — or increased — levels of support.

Net increases in the number of individuals believing that the probability of success has declined will also occasion a loss of support, while net increases in the percentage believing the probability of success has increased will lead to gains in support. Similarly, quicker than expected success may lead to higher support, while uneven or slower than expected success will lead to lower support.

Higher (or higher than expected) costs will lead to lower support, while lower (or lower than expected) costs may lead to higher support.

The sensitivity to costs will be highest when the benefits and/or prospects for success are declining.

*Predictions regarding the level of commitment.* The individual's support or opposition is not the end of the story, nor does it adequately address what is perhaps the key dimension in understanding public attitudes toward military operations: the individual's diagnosis and preferred prescription for successful conclusion of a military operation.

As seen in Korea and Vietnam, domestic support for limited wars can be difficult to sustain, and presidents almost certainly understand that either defeat or high war costs can erode their political standing. Although a cheap victory is rationally preferred to a costly defeat, leaders — and members of the public — may disagree about whether a costly victory is preferred to a cheap defeat.[25] And when political leaders and members of the public come to oppose a limited war or military operation, they can arrive at opposition via two very different diagnoses.

As the costs increase — and especially as judgments about the benefits or prospects for success diverge — leaders have tended to become polarized as some advocate escalation or an increased commitment, while others advocate withdrawing or otherwise reducing the level of commitment. As Presidents Truman and Johnson found, presidents can thus come to be criticized by both those who would increase the level of commitment and those who would decrease or terminate it.[26] Importantly, there is a logic to each position, keyed to the set of beliefs about the operation that influence diagnosis and prescription.

*The logic of an increased commitment.* Support for an increased commitment arises from beliefs that extremely important (or vital) interests and/or principles are engaged, including crucial matters of credibility or national pride, and that the losses already incurred must be redeemed through a successful outcome. In this analysis, not enough effort is being made to assure a successful outcome:[27] forces are fighting "with one hand tied behind their backs," and victory is not only possible but could possibly even come cheaply (e.g., through strategic bombing).[28] The prescription is escalation and elimination of restrictions on combat operations.

*The logic of a decreased commitment.* The second diagnosis is that the war or military operation is simply not worth the costs in blood and treasure, that there is little relationship between losses and actual progress on the battlefield, and that in any case the operation is unlikely to yield success at an acceptable cost. The prescription that emerges from this analysis is that the best course of action is to reduce the level of commitment and to withdraw once U.S. prisoners of war are returned.

When the stakes are important enough (e.g., in Korea and Vietnam), there may be a plurality or majority supporting a third (middle) course: simply concluding the war on acceptable terms (e.g., a "peace with honor"). This course of action is politically costly to presidents, as Presidents Truman and Johnson discovered, because in pursuing a middle course, a president is subject to criticism from both those who would escalate and those who would reduce the level of commitment and withdraw. By way of contrast, in cases where most view the stakes as not very important (e.g., in Lebanon or Somalia), an orderly withdrawal following recovery of U.S. servicemen held hostage is typically preferred — the stakes are simply not important enough to most members of the public to justify any greater commitment than ensuring the safe recovery of U.S. servicemen.[29]

This divergence between a president's sustained level of commitment to war or military operation and the lower level of commitment evidenced by political opponents and many members of the public has found expression in a small body of scholarly work. Milstein (1974) described the phenomenon in terms of differences in the willingness of policymakers and members of the public to trade off costs and benefits. Since most of the benefits (e.g., a reputation for successfully wielding the military instrument) would accrue to policymakers, they were posited to be willing to accept higher costs to achieve political objectives than are members of the public. Perhaps a better metaphor is that provided by Nincic and Nincic (1995) — that policymakers (and by extension, one might conclude, their key supporters) tend to treat costs that are incurred as part of an investment function, while members of the public treat it as a demand function.[30] Both views offer promise in that they are fully extensible to include differences among partisan or ideologically based subpopulations.[31]

## A Social Process Model

Consider the following simple social process model of the president's decision to use force and the broader political and social environment:[32]

Based upon an assessment of the situation and the broader strategic and domestic environment, the president decides whether to use force, what political objectives are to be achieved, and what (if any) constraints are to be imposed on the military operation.[33]

The president makes his case to his audiences (other political leaders, experts, and the public) that the principles and interests that are engaged are important enough to make the military operation worth doing, and that it is likely to achieve its objectives at acceptable cost.[34]

Other political and opinion leaders decide whether or not they agree that the operation is worthwhile and doable and, if not, make their case that the intervention is not worth doing, or that it is unlikely to achieve its objectives at an acceptable cost.[35]

Editorial decisions regarding newsworthiness determine the level of media reporting given to the military operation, while the tone of media reporting — the balance of pro and con positions in the media — is roughly indexed to the tone of the debate among political leaders.[36] The initial deployment and any subsequent combat — whether military action on the ground or political debate in Washington — will cue higher levels of media reporting because they are inherently newsworthy (i.e., members of the public are interested in, and concerned about, combat and political dissension). The probability that members of the public will be aware of events or exposed to political messages, and that the issue will be considered more salient or important at the time of polling, is associated with media reporting levels.[37]

Members of the public, who vary in their level of attention to political issues, develop opinions on the military operation based upon selective attention to pro and con arguments in the elite discourse

reported by the media, or on political conversations.[38] This includes not only the interpretation of objective events and conditions that are offered by political leaders and experts, but also the
normative judgments they offer.[39] As Zaller and Feldman (1992)
have suggested, the rate at which members of the public *receive*
these messages is a function of media reporting levels (as just
described) and individual-level news-gathering habits, political interest, and sophistication (the extent to which a respondent pays
attention to politics and understands what has been encountered).
The rate at which messages in the media-reported elite discourse
are *accepted or rejected* is determined by political predispositions
(more stable, individual-level traits that regulate the acceptance or
rejection of the persuasive communications that are received).[40]

We can now apply these simple policy models to evaluate the nature of
the challenge President Clinton faced in attempting to mobilize support
for a U.S. peacekeeping operation in Bosnia.

## II

> The aim of formal theories is to give us an understanding of
> a relational structure that exists somewhere in the world.
> Once this aim has been achieved by developing an
> adequate, well-interpreted, and well-analyzed model, the
> model can be used in various ways.
> —Diesing 1971, 108

### Diagnosis

Consider now the contributions that might have been made in December 1995 by a net assessment of domestic support for U.S. participation
in a peacekeeping operation in the Balkans and how such an assessment
might have informed policy development on the U.S. intervention in
Bosnia. Assume the availability of the models developed in the last
section, the relevant public opinion and other data available in December 1995, and a general mistrust of public opinion data that has led to a
desire to understand the robustness of support for a Bosnia operation
and its sensitivity to potential adverse developments. I will begin by
identifying the president's objectives in Bosnia, turn to a description of

the broader domestic environment, and then examine the public opinion data on support for Bosnia.

## The President's Objectives in Bosnia

I begin with the president's objectives in Bosnia. Like the Bush administration before it, the Clinton administration sought to contain the conflict in the Balkans and foster its resolution. Although the Clinton administration was criticized for the zigzag course of its diplomacy on Bosnia, it had at least one strand of continuity in its policy toward Bosnia: while it was willing to introduce ground troops as peacekeepers once the combatants had agreed to peace, it remained unwilling to introduce ground forces to actually halt the fighting, instead focusing on containing the violence and scope of the conflict and providing humanitarian relief.[41] As the president put it during his November 27, 1995, address to the nation announcing U.S. participation in implementing the peace agreement in Bosnia-Herzegovina:

> When I took office, some were urging immediate intervention in the conflict. I decided that American ground troops should not fight a war in Bosnia because the United States could not force peace on Bosnia's warring ethnic groups, the Serbs, Croats, and Muslims. Instead, America has worked with our European allies in searching for peace, stopping the war from spreading, and easing the suffering of the Bosnian people . . . I refuse to send American troops to fight a war in Bosnia, but I believe we must help to secure the Bosnian peace.[42]

In pursuing this middle course in Bosnia, President Clinton was caught between those who supported an intervention with ground troops to halt the fighting and those who opposed virtually any form of U.S. involvement in Bosnia beyond air strikes and arming the Bosnian Muslims.[43] As a consequence, the Clinton administration pursued a presidential leadership strategy that navigated a turbulent course between these two camps, while seeking to retain a permissive public opinion environment for the eventuality of a peace agreement in Bosnia and the introduction of U.S. peacekeepers to underwrite that agreement.

## The Domestic Environment

The social process model described earlier suggests that media reporting levels follow objective events and conditions on the ground in

Bosnia and in Washington, including interpretations of events by political leaders and experts of various political stripes and the articulation of policy alternatives for dealing with the situation. The model also suggests that the salience of Bosnia to members of the public is closely associated with media reporting levels on Bosnia. I now turn to a test of these propositions.

*Media Reporting as a Function of Objective Events and Conditions*
We first want to understand the sources of influence on public attitudes, starting with objective events and conditions. There is no altogether satisfactory way to measure the changing tempo of an ongoing military conflict that does not rely upon the media as a source for the data.[44] Because it relies upon unfiltered wire-service reporting on diplomatic and military activity, however, the data from the Kansas Events Data System (KEDS) appears to come about as close to measuring the changing level of events in Bosnia as is possible.[45] Monthly totals of the KEDS data on activity in Bosnia from April 1992 through December 1995 were used as a crude measure of the political and military activity of the various actors, including Bosnians, Serbs, Croats, European nations, and the United States. To measure the tempo of public presidential and congressional attention to Bosnia in Washington, we used the monthly count of documents in the *Public Papers of the President* and *Congressional Record* that mentioned Bosnia.

The correlations between the monthly count of events in Bosnia (proxied by the KEDS data) and the two variables describing political activity in Washington were positive, ranging from 0.26 to 0.55. The highest correlations were between presidential activity and events in Bosnia (0.546) and between presidential and congressional activity (0.541); by comparison, the relationship between congressional activity and events on the ground in Bosnia was only 0.26.[46] The implication seems to be that the White House was reacting to developments, increasing or decreasing its attention to Bosnia (and probably its diplomatic activity as well) in response to events on the ground. It also suggests that the Congress was cuing not on the tempo of activity in Bosnia, but on the level of presidential activity in Bosnia. One reasonable interpretation is that Congress tended to become more active on Bosnia when it appeared that the Clinton administration might be moving toward deeper involvement.[47]

We next need to understand the relationship between the objective events and conditions in Bosnia and Washington that would have been newsworthy and the actual media reporting levels on Bosnia.[48] To better understand this relationship, the monthly count of *New York Times* news

Dependent variable is:     Z-NYT
$R^2 = 73.8\%$     $R^2$ (adjusted) $= 71.1\%$
$s = 0.5372$ with $45 - 5 = 40$ degrees of freedom

| Source | Sum of Squares | df | Mean Square | F-ratio |
|---|---|---|---|---|
| Regression | 32.4578 | 4 | 8.114 | 28.1 |
| Residual | 11.5422 | 40 | 0.288554 | |

| Variable | Coefficient | S.E. of Coefficient | t-ratio |
|---|---|---|---|
| Constant | 0.352572 | 0.1762 | 2.00 |
| MONTHNUM | −0.015329 | 0.0068 | −2.25 |
| Z-LKEDS | 0.568517 | 0.1038 | 5.48 |
| Z-PRES | 0.289686 | 0.1112 | 2.60 |
| Z-CR | 0.273566 | 0.0978 | 2.80 |

**Fig. 1.   Diagnostics for regression of *New York Times* reporting on objective events and conditions**

articles on Bosnia between April 1992 and December 1995 were regressed on four variables: (1) the monthly count of events in Bosnia as operationalized in the KEDS data, (2) monthly presidential and (3) congressional activity levels, and (4) a variable that measures the passage of time.[49] Figure 1 reports the results.

The four variables accounted for more than two-thirds of the variance in *New York Times* reporting levels, and each is statistically significant. It appears from the standardized coefficients, furthermore, that objective events and conditions (Z-LKEDS, the standardized score for the log of monthly KEDS events) were the most important determinant of *New York Times* reporting, followed by presidential activity (Z-PRES) and, finally, congressional activity (Z-CR). Put another way, the predominant driver of news reporting on Bosnia appears to have been the changing level of diplomatic and military activity in Bosnia and political activity in Washington.[50] Also of interest, however, is the fact that the coefficient for the passage of time was negative and statistically significant. Whether this is because the editors — or their audiences — became inured to or fatigued by the incessant daily reports of tragedy we cannot say, but it is clear that media reporting levels generally declined over time.[51]

The findings reported here are entirely consistent with the social process model of the individual's environment, which posits that media reporting on a foreign policy situation like Bosnia responds both to objective events and conditions and to political activity in Washington. We can now turn to the relationship between media reporting and the salience of Bosnia to members of the public.

### Salience to the Public as a Function of Media Reporting Levels

There is strong reason to believe that public awareness and salience of policy issues are associated with the changing level of media news reporting, and in the case of Bosnia, this appears to be no different. Sobel (1996) provides the results of 29 polls in which members of the public were asked how closely they were following news of Bosnia, and the question was subsequently asked several additional times.[52] On average, during this period about one in six (16 percent) typically said they were following Bosnia "very closely," and a little over half (53 percent) said they were following news on Bosnia "very" or "somewhat" closely.[53]

When the relationship between media reporting and the public's level of attention to Bosnia is assessed empirically, the evidence suggests that public interest in and attention to Bosnia were closely associated with news reporting levels for the preceding three weeks:[54] simple regression analysis revealed that *New York Times* reporting on Bosnia in the preceding three weeks explained 52.5 percent of the variance among those who said they were watching the civil war in Bosnia very or fairly closely, and both the constant and slope coefficient were statistically significant.[55] The fact that media reporting levels had clear antecedents in both the objective events and conditions and the political activity related to Bosnia provides strong evidence against the argument that the media were the motive force behind either leadership actions or public attitudes — they were fundamentally responding to events.[56] In short, all relationships are as predicted by the social process model. We can now turn to a diagnosis of the public opinion data to see how attitudes toward Bosnia had crystallized by the time of the intervention.

### Public Support for Bosnia

To illustrate the power of the simple model of ends and means in predicting support for a prospective military operation, I will now examine two separate forecasts regarding the level of support for a U.S. operation in Bosnia. The first was made prior to the U.S. deployment by the Program on International Policy Attitudes (PIPA) of the University of Maryland. The second is based upon the model of ends and means, informed by the social process model described earlier; it also is based upon data available at the time of deployment.

The following prediction regarding support for Bosnia was made by PIPA in late November 1995:

A new poll conducted Nov. 22–25 by the University of Maryland's Program on International Policy Attitudes (PIPA) finds that contrary to widely held assumptions, the public is not opposed to sending U.S. troops to enforce a peace agreement. If the parties to the peace agreement insist on U.S. participation, a strong majority would then support contributing U.S. troops . . . Fifty percent of those polled favor contributing U.S. troops to a Bosnian peacekeeping operation, and 47 percent oppose the idea. Support jumps to 66 percent, however, if the parties to the agreement insist on U.S. involvement in the enforcement operation as a condition for going forward with the agreement.[57]

This forecast was based upon the public opinion questions reported in table 1.

PIPA was not the only organization that sought to gauge public opinion on Bosnia, however, and a good policy analyst would want to understand whether PIPA's prediction of 50 percent (66 percent, if the

**TABLE 1.   PIPA Forecast of Support for a U.S. Operation in Bosnia**

As you may know, in Dayton, Ohio, the leaders of the conflict in Bosnia have come to a peace agreement. In addition to ending the fighting, the peace agreement includes provisions for redistributing land, stopping ethnic cleansing and holding elections. The agreement is to be enforced by 60,000 well-armed troops under an American commander and with UN approval. The U.S. has committed to contribute one-third of these troops, with the other two-thirds to come from other countries, mostly European. Some members of Congress, though, are against contributing U.S. troops. Do you favor or oppose contributing U.S. troops to this operation?

50%     Favor
47       Oppose
4        Don't know/Refused

(*For those who say oppose or don't know in last question*): What if the parties to the conflict will only go forward with the peace agreement if the U.S. contributes troops to the enforcement operation? Would you then favor or oppose contributing U.S. troops?

31%     Favor (16 percent of total sample)
60       Oppose (30 percent)
8        Don't know/Refused (4 percent)

*Source:* Program for International Policy Attitudes, University of Maryland, news release of 11/22–25/95.

*Note:* Numbers in parentheses are the percentage of the total sample.

follow-up question is included) was a good predictor of the actual level of support for a peacekeeping venture in Bosnia, so as to gauge the robustness of that support in the face of a potentially deteriorated situation, including significant casualties.

One approach to diagnosing the available public opinion on Bosnia is to organize the public opinion data around the key parameters of the simple model of ends and means described earlier—beliefs about the benefits, the prospects for success, and the expected costs—and examine the relationship between beliefs about these variables and support. When this is done, the evidence suggests not only that public support would be much lower than PIPA's result implies, but that it was closely tied to beliefs about the benefits that would accrue from a U.S. peacekeeping operation, the prospects for its success, and the likely costs, beliefs entirely consistent with respondents' natural opinion leaders in Washington.[58] For each of the parameters—benefits, prospects, and costs—I will next examine polling on Bosnia before the president's speech, leadership cuing in the form of the presidential and congressional arguments that were made, and polling done after the president's speech.

*Perceived Benefits*
*Polling before the speech.*    The first parameter of the simple model of ends and means is the perceived benefits of a U.S. peacekeeping operation in Bosnia. Polling before the president's speech suggests that fewer than half thought the United States had a vital interest in Bosnia. For example, according to the 1994 quadrennial survey by the Chicago Council on Foreign Relations (CCFR), only 45 percent of those polled in the fall of 1994 said that they believed that the United States had a vital interest in Bosnia.[59] Furthermore, only about three in ten respondents indicated that they felt that the United States had a responsibility to do something about the fighting in Bosnia.[60]

As table 2 shows, as early as February 1994—following a mortar attack on a market square in Sarajevo that killed or wounded several hundred civilians—there was a statistically significant relationship between beliefs in the benefits of military action and support for that option; it shows that three out of four of those who perceived a moral obligation or a need to protect U.S. interests supported air strikes; by contrast, those who failed to perceive these imperatives opposed air strikes by a large margin.

By October 1995, the relationship between perceived benefits and support for military action still held, as can be seen in table 3. The table cross-tabulates the level of importance with support of a U.S.

**TABLE 2. Cross-Tabulation of Support for Air Strikes and Two Conceptions of Benefits, February 1994**

Currently there is some discussion that President Clinton should order U.S. military planes to conduct air strikes against Serbian military positions in Bosnia, along with planes from some Western European countries. Would you favor or oppose such air strikes?

Do you think the United States has a moral obligation to stop the Serbian attacks on Sarajevo, or don't you think so?

| *Favor* | *Oppose* | |
|---|---|---|
| 74% | 26% | Yes (47 percent) |
| 28 | 72 | No (45 percent) |
| 41 | 59 | No opinion (8 percent) |

($p < .001$ in chi-square test of independence)

Do you think the United States needs to be involved in Bosnia in order to protect its own interests, or don't you think so?

| *Favor* | *Oppose* | |
|---|---|---|
| 76% | 24% | Yes (32 percent) |
| 39 | 61 | No (59 percent) |
| 43 | 57 | No opinion (9 percent) |

($p < .001$ in chi-square test of independence)

*Source:* Gallup, 2/7/94.

*Note:* Numbers in parentheses are marginal percentages of total sample.

**TABLE 3. Cross-Tabulation of Support and Importance of a Peaceful Solution to Bosnia, October 1995**

Now that a peace agreement has been reached by all the groups currently fighting in Bosnia, the Clinton administration plans to contribute U.S. troops to an international peacekeeping force. Do you favor or oppose that?

As far as you are concerned, should the development of a peaceful solution to the situation in Bosnia be a very important foreign policy goal of the United States, a somewhat important goal, not too important, or not an important goal at all?

| *Favor* | *Oppose* | |
|---|---|---|
| 94% | 6% | Very important (30 percent) |
| 66 | 34 | Somewhat important (48 percent) |
| 22 | 78 | Not too important (11 percent) |
| 11 | 89 | Not important at all (8 percent) |
| 33 | 67 | Don't know/Refused (3 percent) |

*Source:* Gallup, 10/95.

*Note:* $p < .001$ using chi-square test for independence. Numbers in parentheses are marginal percentages of total sample.

contribution to an international peacekeeping force. Again, the chi-square test showed a strong relationship between beliefs in the importance of developing a peaceful solution to the situation in Bosnia and support for a U.S. peacekeeping contribution.

*Leadership cuing.* In his November 25 radio address and his November 27 address to the nation, President Clinton sought to build support by emphasizing three main themes. First, he sought to appeal to those who would be moved by arguments that emphasized core American values. Second, he sought support from those who would be moved by references to national interests. Finally, he hoped to move those who would respond to claims that U.S. leadership was at stake in Bosnia.

The president's was not the only voice on Bosnia, however, and members of Congress had much to say about a U.S. peacekeeping operation in Bosnia. During the congressional debates leading up to December 13, 1995, votes on Bosnia, congressional Democrats generally saw more important U.S. stakes in Bosnia than Republicans, but each group used very different language to express the presence or absence of U.S. equities.

Among the congressional Democrats who supported the president's line, Senator Bob Kerry (D-Neb.) argued that vital interests were in fact involved, Senator Edward M. Kennedy (D-Mass.) focused on the humanitarian dimension, and Senator Daniel Patrick Moynihan (D-N.Y.) expressed his approval for the president's emphasis on the centrality of the rule of law. By comparison, Republican congressional leaders generally tended to diminish the importance of the U.S. moral and strategic interests in Bosnia, and the consequences of a U.S. demurral on sending forces to Bosnia.[61] In the final analysis, then, the peacekeeping mission to Bosnia sparked a lively, highly partisan debate, and a joint resolution that was far from supportive of the intervention.[62]

*Polling after the speech.* Table 4 shows that although a majority following the president's speech said the United States had a moral obligation "to help keep the peace in Bosnia,"[63] only 36 percent believed that the United States needed to be involved in Bosnia to protect its own interests — not terribly different from the 32 percent who had indicated such a belief in February 1994. The table also shows that the relationship between support and beliefs about the benefits of a U.S. peacekeeping operation — the strength of the moral obligation or need to protect U.S. interests — was statistically significant.

Table 5 shows that the president failed to persuade many that the United States' leadership position hung in the balance — only about four in ten believed that the United States needed to send troops to maintain the U.S. leadership position in world affairs. It also shows, however,

**TABLE 4.  Cross-Tabulation of Support and Two Indicators of Perceived Benefits, November 27, 1995**

Now that a peace agreement has been reached by all the groups currently fighting in Bosnia, the Clinton administration plans to contribute U.S. troops to an international peacekeeping force. Do you favor or oppose that?

**Moral Obligation**

Do you think the United States has a moral obligation to help keep the peace in Bosnia, or not?

| *Favor* | *Oppose* | |
|---------|----------|---|
| 78% | 22% | Yes, does have moral obligation (53 percent) |
| 24 | 76 | No, does not (40 percent) |
| 44 | 56 | Don't know/Refused (3 percent) |

($p < .001$ using chi-square test for independence)

**Interests**

Do you think the United States needs to be involved in Bosnia in order to protect its own interests, or don't you think so?

| *Favor* | *Oppose* | |
|---------|----------|---|
| 87% | 13% | Yes, needs to be involved (36 percent) |
| 28 | 72 | Don't think so (52 percent) |
| 91 | 9 | Don't know/Refused (12 percent) |

($p < .001$ using chi-square test for independence)

*Source:* Gallup, 11/27/95.
*Note:* Numbers in parentheses are marginal percentages of total sample.

**TABLE 5.  Cross-Tabulation of Support and Importance to U.S. World Leadership, November 27, 1995**

Now that a peace agreement has been reached by all the groups currently fighting in Bosnia, the Clinton administration plans to contribute U.S. troops to an international peacekeeping force. Do you favor or oppose that?

Do you think the United States needs to send troops to Bosnia in order to maintain its leadership position in world affairs, or not?

| *Favor* | *Oppose* | |
|---------|----------|---|
| 84% | 16% | Yes, needs to send troops (41 percent) |
| 29 | 71 | No, does not (52 percent) |
| 69 | 31 | Don't know/Refused (7 percent) |

*Source:* Gallup, 11/27/95.
*Note:* $p < .001$ using chi-square test for independence. Numbers in parentheses are marginal percentages of total sample.

that support was again tied to beliefs about the importance of the benefits—four out of five of those who thought the U.S. leadership position was at stake supported sending troops, while only about three in ten of those who did not supported the action.

*Prospects for Success*
*Polling before the speech.*   The second parameter in the simple model of ends and means is the subjective estimate of the probability of successfully accomplishing the objectives. The public opinion data suggest that few in fact believed that an increased U.S. commitment to Bosnia would yield a favorable outcome.

For example, table 6 shows that only 42 percent in February 1994 believed that air strikes in Sarajevo would be effective in stopping Serbian attacks, but that seven in ten of those who believed that air strikes would be effective supported such attacks, compared to only about one in four of those who did not.

By October 1995, the relationship between estimates of the prospects for success and support for a U.S. operation in Bosnia continued to hold, as can be seen in table 7. The table shows that only 28 percent in October 1995 were very or somewhat confident that U.S. troops would be withdrawn from Bosnia in a year as planned, and that confidence in the United States' ability to accomplish its objectives and withdraw within one year were closely associated with support; nearly eight in ten of those who were very or somewhat confident supported the operation, and smaller percentages of those who were less confident supported it.

**TABLE 6.   Cross-Tabulation of Support for Air Strikes and Their Expected Effectiveness, February 1994**

Currently there is some discussion that President Clinton should order U.S. military planes to conduct air strikes against Serbian military positions in Bosnia, along with planes from some Western European countries. Would you favor or oppose such air strikes?

In your view, would air strikes against Serbian forces be effective in stopping the Serbian attacks on Sarajevo, or not?

| Favor | Oppose | No opinion | |
|-------|--------|------------|---|
| 71% | 22% | 6% | Effective (42 percent) |
| 26 | 68 | 7 | Not effective (47 percent) |
| 38 | 28 | 34 | No opinion (11 percent) |

*Source:* Gallup, 2/7/94.
*Note:* $p < .001$ in chi-square test for independence. Numbers in parentheses are marginal percentages of total sample.

And in both of the cross-tabulations presented in table 6 and 7, the relationship between support and beliefs about prospects was statistically significant.

*Leadership cuing.* In his November 27 address, President Clinton argued that the prospects for success were quite good as a consequence of the high level of planning that had gone into the operation:

> First, the mission will be precisely defined with clear, realistic goals that can be achieved in a definite period of time . . . Our Joint Chiefs of Staff have concluded that this mission should and will take about one year . . . In Bosnia we can and will succeed because our mission is clear and limited, and our troops are strong and very well-prepared.

In sharp contrast, during congressional debates, great concern was expressed that the operation was unlikely to succeed in separating the combatants. As Senator Phil Gramm (R-Tex.) argued:

> It seems to me the second question we have to ask ourselves is: Will our intervention be decisive in promoting the objectives we seek? It's one thing to have good intentions. It's one thing to have pure motives. It is another thing to have a plan that would allow you to put those good intentions into force. I see no evidence whatsoever to substantiate any claim that our intervention as a buffer force

**TABLE 7.   Cross-Tabulation of Support and Prospects for Success, October 1995**

There is a chance a peace agreement could be reached by all the groups currently fighting in Bosnia. If so, the Clinton administration is considering contributing U.S. troops to an international peacekeeping force. Would you favor or oppose that?

The Clinton administration has stated that if the United States were to send U.S. troops to Bosnia, they would be withdrawn within one year. How confident are you that U.S. troops would be withdrawn within one year as planned: very confident, somewhat confident, not too confident, or not at all confident?

| Favor | Oppose | No Opinion | |
|-------|--------|-----------|---|
| 78% | 16% | 6% | Very confident (7 percent) |
| 78 | 17 | 5 | Somewhat confident (21 percent) |
| 50 | 44 | 6 | Not too confident (34 percent) |
| 26 | 69 | 5 | Not at all confident (36 percent) |

*Source:* Gallup, 10/19–22/95.
*Note:* $p < .001$ using chi-square test for independence. $N = 1228$.

between warring factions in Bosnia is going to be decisive in promoting the objectives we seek.

*Polling after the speech.* Notwithstanding the president's argument, according to polling by Gallup, 53 percent of those polled immediately after the president's speech thought that if the United States sent troops as part of a peacekeeping mission, it was likely to lead to a long-term commitment in Bosnia involving many casualties; only 35 percent thought this unlikely.[64] As table 8 shows, the president's speech did little to allay the concerns that the U.S. involvement in Bosnia would turn out badly — more than half thought it was "likely to lead to a long-term commitment involving many casualties." Put another way, the president failed to overcome deep skepticism about the prospects for the operation, and this had important consequences for the resulting level of support.

Table 8 shows that support in December continued to be associated with the expectations regarding the prospects for success. By December, 44 percent said they expected the U.S. effort to establish peace in Bosnia to succeed.[65] In fact, there is evidence that one of the predictions of the simple model of ends and means — that better-than-expected performance should result in higher support — was fulfilled: by mid-January, there was growing evidence that U.S. forces might not become engaged in combat operations, and only about four in ten of those polled at that time felt that the United States would become involved in a major shooting war.[66] Put another way, by avoiding a breakdown of the peace, Bosnia turned out better than expected, and this may have resulted in a slight increase in support for the operation.[67]

**TABLE 8. Cross-Tabulation of Support and Confidence in Success, December 1995**

Do you approve or disapprove the presence of U.S. troops in Bosnia?

Regarding the situation in Bosnia, how confident are you that each of the following will happen? . . . The U.S. effort to establish peace in Bosnia will succeed.

| *Favor* | *Oppose* | |
|---|---|---|
| 80% | 20% | Very confident (13 percent) |
| 64 | 36 | Somewhat confident (31 percent) |
| 33 | 67 | Not too confident (27 percent) |
| 10 | 90 | Not at all confident (24 percent) |
| 32 | 68 | Don't know/Refused (5 percent) |

*Source:* Gallup, 12/15–18/95.

*Note:* $p < .001$ in chi-square test for independence.

*Expected Costs*
*Polling before the speech.*    The third parameter in the simple model is the expected costs of achieving the objectives. Most of the polling that touched on the issue of possible casualties in Bosnia was done in 1993, two and a half years before the United States introduced ground troops. These questions asked respondents whether they thought U.S. involvement in the war in Bosnia would be quick and successful, like the Gulf War, or long and costly, like Vietnam. According to this polling, the percentages expecting a Vietnam-like involvement averaged about 42 percent, while an average of 47 percent expected a Gulf War–like involvement.[68] Nevertheless, there is strong reason to believe that members of the public became increasingly sensitive to casualties as a consequence of congressional cuing — congressional arguments opposing ground troops in Bosnia on the basis of the potential casualties.

Table 9 shows that only 35 percent believed a long-term commitment in Bosnia involving many casualties was *unlikely,* and that again support was closely associated with the belief that the intervention was not likely to lead to a long and costly commitment; 65 percent of those who expected a long and costly commitment opposed the operation, while 81 percent who thought it unlikely supported the operation. And again, the relationship between support and beliefs about a long and costly commitment was statistically significant.

One of the best possible tests of the relationship between casualties and support can be provided by natural experiments; in fact, a natural experiment on the relationship between casualties and support was performed by Gallup in their poll of October 22–24, 1995, the results of which are reported in table 10.[69] Gallup experimentally varied the hy-

**TABLE 9.   Cross-Tabulation of Support and Prospects for Success, November 27, 1995**

Now that a peace agreement has been reached by all the groups currently fighting in Bosnia, the Clinton administration plans to contribute U.S. troops to an international peacekeeping force. Do you favor or oppose that?

If the United States sends troops as part of a peacekeeping mission, do you think that it is likely to lead to a long-term commitment in Bosnia involving many casualties, or not?

| *Favor* | *Oppose* | |
|---|---|---|
| 35% | 65% | Yes, likely to lead to long-term commitment (53 percent) |
| 81 | 19 | No, not likely (35 percent) |
| 60 | 40 | Don't know/Refused (12 percent) |

*Source:* Gallup, 11/27/95.
*Note: p* < .001 using chi-square test for independence.

pothesized number of casualties in questions that asked about support for sending a U.S. peacekeeping force to Bosnia. The experiment confirms the prediction of the simple model of ends and means: as the prospective level of casualties was increased, prospective support declined.

*Leadership cuing.* Returning now to the president's appeal for support, the president argued in his November 27 address,

> [T]he risks to our troops will be minimized. American troops will take their orders from the American general who commands NATO. They will be heavily armed and thoroughly trained . . . But my fellow Americans, no deployment of American troops is risk-free, and this one may well involve casualties. There may be accidents in the field or incidents with people who have not given up their hatred. I will take every measure possible to minimize these risks, but we must be prepared for that possibility.

Congressional discussion of casualties in fact was a staple in the debates about Bosnia, primarily among those who most opposed an increased level of commitment to Bosnia — congressional Republicans. Arguments about Bosnia frequently turned upon the rather emotional issue of potential casualties that might be incurred, and the belief that the stakes were not worth the loss of American lives.

**TABLE 10. Natural Experiment: Support and Hypothesized Costs, October 1995**

Suppose you knew that if the United States sent U.S. troops to Bosnia as part of an international peacekeeping force that X American soldiers would be killed. With this in mind, would you favor or oppose sending U.S. troops to Bosnia?

. . . that no American soldiers would be killed. (Asked of 298 respondents, $+/- 6\%$)

. . . that 25 American soldiers would be killed. (Asked of 332 respondents, $+/- 6\%$)

. . . that 100 American soldiers would be killed. (Asked of 293 respondents, $+/- 6\%$)

. . . that 400 American soldiers would be killed. (Asked of 306 respondents, $+/- 6\%$)

| Hypothesized Casualties | Favor | Oppose | No Opinion |
|---|---|---|---|
| None | 69% | 29% | 4% |
| 25 | 31 | 64 | 5 |
| 100 | 29 | 65 | 6 |
| 400 | 21 | 72 | 7 |

*Source:* Gallup/CNN/*USA Today,* 10/22–24/95.
*Note: N* = 1229.

A query was constructed to explore the frequency with which American casualties were mentioned in the *Congressional Record* in the context of a prospective intervention in Bosnia during the period from January 1991 through May 1996.[70] The frequency increased at the time of discussions of a possible U.S. intervention in the early fall of 1993, in the summer of 1994, and in the fall of 1995. Congressional debate over the issue of whether what might be accomplished in Bosnia was worth the potential loss of life appears not to have peaked, however, until President Clinton's announcement to actually introduce U.S. forces to underwrite the Dayton agreement in November 1995, and the actual deployment in December.

Furthermore, this congressional attention appears to have led to media reporting on the issue of potential casualties in Bosnia — the correlation between monthly mentions of casualties in the *Congressional Record* and mentions in the *New York Times* was about 0.3.[71] In short, in addition to establishing that there was a relationship between congressional activity and media reporting, there is at least some empirical evidence that the *content* of this congressional activity was carried by mainstream media and almost certainly reached many members of the public. More will be said of this shortly.

In terms of the content of congressional commentary, I now consider the following two statements on the question of casualties in the debates prior to the congressional voting in December 1995. Senator Edward M. Kennedy (D-Mass.) stated that the peacekeeping operation in Bosnia would prevent a larger number of casualties that would result from a wider war: "[T]his mission is the only chance to achieve peace in Bosnia. That peace is essential to prevent a wider war in Europe; a wider war would inevitably involve the United States, with vastly greater risk of casualties." Meanwhile, Senator Jesse Helms (R-N.C.) made the more traditional oppositional argument that Bosnia was not sufficiently important to warrant the risk of casualties:

> Now the American people should be prepared for the possibility that American lives will be lost any time our national interest is at stake. And I'm certain that if asked to go to war our brave men and women in uniform would, without hesitation, heed any President's call . . . I cannot and will not support President Clinton's decision to ask them to make this sacrifice. The risk to the lives of our troops far exceeds any national interest the United States could possibly have . . . in the Balkans . . . Americans do not deserve to die in support of a policy that will not bring peace to the Bosnians.

*Polling after the speech.* Polling following the president's speech suggests that, depending on wording, an average of about 42 percent believed that the U.S. intervention in Bosnia would entail few or no American casualties, while an average of 52 percent expected somewhat or much higher casualties.[72] Differences in expectations about casualties, furthermore, were systematically associated with support or opposition. Table 11 shows that as confidence declined regarding the United States' ability to accomplish its goals with very few or no American casualties, support also declined, and this relationship was statistically significant.

## Presidential Leadership and Its Discontents

The social process model and the analysis of the relationship between objective events and conditions, media reporting, and salience of Bosnia to the public explained the process by which the Bosnia issue became salient to members of the public. Similarly, the diagnosis of public opinion using the simple model of ends and means helped to explain in an aggregate way why a majority failed to support the U.S. intervention in Bosnia. Although the statements of supporters and opponents of a Bosnia operation offer clues, they do not provide an adequate explanation of the intermediate steps by which segments of the public — ultimately constituting a majority — came to their pessimistic views about benefits, prospects, and costs. Nor is there an explanation of how majorities judged that the combination of benefits, prospects for success, and

**TABLE 11. Cross-Tabulation of Support and Confidence in Low to No Casualties, December 1995**

Do you approve or disapprove the presence of U.S. troops in Bosnia?

Regarding the situation in Bosnia, how confident are you that each of the following will happen? . . . The U.S. will be able to accomplish its goals with very few or no American casualties.

| Favor | Oppose | |
|-------|--------|---|
| 66% | 34% | Very confident (12 percent of sample) |
| 67 | 33 | Somewhat confident (28 percent) |
| 38 | 62 | Not too confident (29 percent) |
| 14 | 86 | Not at all confident (28 percent) |
| 48 | 52 | Don't know/Refused (3 percent) |

*Source:* Gallup, 12/15–18/95.
*Note:* $p < .001$ in chi-square test for independence.

costs were unacceptable, that is, insufficiently compelling to warrant support for a U.S. peacekeeping operation in Bosnia.

## Leadership and Public Support

It is sometimes argued that failures to rally public support for a military operation are due to the lack of clarity in a president's argument or in his articulation of the objectives that are to be achieved. In this line of thinking, if only the president had done a better job of communicating his reasons, a majority would clearly have supported his use of force. The case of Bosnia suggests that this view is both simplistic and wrong— 51 percent of those polled by CBS News/*New York Times* in early December said that the president had explained the situation in Bosnia well enough so they understood why the United States was sending troops; however, only 36 percent said that they thought that it was the "right thing" to do. As was seen, the president's contentions about the benefits, prospects for success, and acceptable costs were found lacking by large segments of the public.

The argument presented in this chapter is that the simple model of ends and means is informed by the social process model, and that individuals' beliefs about benefits, prospects, and costs are informed by the public positions taken by trusted political leaders and experts, which are disseminated by the media. It also relies on the proposition that to a large extent, individuals sort through the cacophony of voices by attempting to identify trusted leaders on the basis of partisan or ideological cues. To test this proposition, we require a better understanding of the partisan differences, if any, among political leaders and their natural constituencies. As will be seen next, the data suggest that the fault lines within the public mirrored and followed from partisan or ideological divisions among political leaders.

This suggests the importance of the *credibility* of the president's argument, which not only is absolutely essential but, as will be shown next, appears to be established by the extent to which the president's arguments are echoed by political leaders, experts, and other commentators who are not necessarily the president's natural allies and supporters. Put another way, the credibility of the president's argument is established to a great extent by the Greek chorus of members of Congress, experts, and other pundits who either support or refute the president's position. We will now examine divisions among national leaders and within the public to ascertain the extent to which they exhibited the same fault lines.

*Partisan divisions among leaders.* Although criticism of the Clinton administration's Bosnia policy in the spring of 1993 cut across parti-

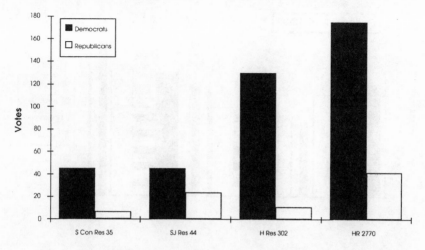

**Fig. 2.    Congressional support for the Clinton administration on Bosnia**

san lines, policy preferences regarding Bosnia became an increasingly partisan affair over time, and by November 1995, the leadership divisions were almost entirely partisan in nature, with the president's partisan allies in Congress generally more optimistic about and favorably disposed toward a peacekeeping operation in Bosnia. Figure 2 shows the importance of partisanship in four congressional votes on Bosnia.[73]

The figure shows that the strongest support for the Clinton administration's position was from Democrats and the highest levels of opposition from Republicans. Nevertheless, while congressional Democrats were generally more inclined to support the president's deployment of troops to Bosnia, congressional Republicans were divided: some opposed the deployment outright, while some advocated a very carefully qualified form of support — they supported the operation because of the president's constitutional prerogatives as commander in chief even though they were generally opposed to U.S. troops in Bosnia.

*Leadership divisions were mirrored in the public.*    The public opinion data that were presented earlier showed that the president's efforts to persuade the public of the benefits, prospects, and costs of an operation in Bosnia were found to be compelling by only about four in ten, but little was said about the underlying partisan or ideological orientations of supporters and opponents. Because the simple model of ends and means is premised upon the notion that members of the public are most influenced by the political leaders they find most credible, and that they use partisan or ideological cues to this end, this suggests that public opinion

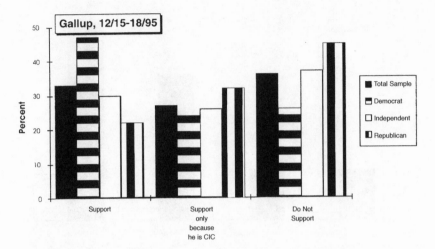

**Fig. 3.   The partisan nature of support for an intervention in Bosnia**

on Bosnia should flow somewhat predictably from individual-level differences in partisanship or ideology. In fact, the public opinion data suggest that beliefs about benefits, prospects, and costs within the public were closely tied to partisanship (see fig. 3).[74]

As shown in the figure, not only were Democrats most likely to support the president's peacekeeping venture in Bosnia and Republicans least likely, but the data also provide some clear evidence of a more subtle form of Republican followership.[75] Importantly, the category receiving the second highest level of support from Republicans was for those who did not think the United States should send troops, but supported the president's decision because he was commander in chief—precisely the argument that some Republican congressional leaders had made.

This analysis provides strong evidence that the willingness to support a U.S. peacekeeping venture in Bosnia was related to key underlying beliefs about the benefits, prospects for success, and costs, and that these beliefs—and ultimately support or opposition—emerged from partisan followership.

Net Assessment

Pulling the pieces together:

> three in ten thought a peaceful solution in Bosnia should be a very important foreign policy goal;[76]

fewer than four in ten thought the United States had to be in Bosnia
to protect its vital interests;

four in ten thought the United States needed to send troops to
Bosnia to maintain its leadership position;

perhaps four in ten thought the operation was likely to succeed;

four in ten thought the operation was likely to involve few to no
casualties;

all of the critical beliefs — about benefits, prospects for success, and
costs — were associated with partisanship, and divisions in the
public over Bosnia appear to have followed from divisions among
national political leaders.

Taken together, this would lead us to believe that support for the operation would be limited to about four in ten and that support and opposition
would be quite partisan in nature and somewhat sensitive to casualties
and changing prospects on the battlefield. The clear implication is that
military planning for the intervention in Bosnia would need to devote a
great deal of attention on force protection issues, coercive quick strike
capabilities, and other related issues, to better provide means for hedging
against a breakdown of the peace and quickly restoring peace if it should
break down. The reason is that a breakdown of the peace, particularly if it
was accompanied by combat and U.S. casualties, would upset the permissive environment that was granted by the Congress and the public. As in
Lebanon and Somalia, the president would have been forced to spend
scarce political capital defending an operation that was widely perceived
to be failing, and at too high a cost.

Also of great interest to policymakers would have been an understanding of how support for Bosnia compared with other recent cases,
particularly where support was judged to be low or highly conditional
(e.g., on low casualties). As table 12 shows, the level of support for
Bosnia was modest even by the rather tepid standard set by Haiti.[77] In
part, these differences can be attributed to differences in perceptions

**TABLE 12.   Comparison of Support for Bosnia, Somalia, and Haiti**

Do you approve or disapprove of the presence of U.S. troops in . . .

| Approve | Disapprove | No Opinion | |
| --- | --- | --- | --- |
| 41% | 54% | 5% | Bosnia (12/15–18/95) |
| 46 | 50 | 4 | Haiti (9/19/94) |
| 79 | 17 | 4 | Somalia (1/93) |
| 43 | 46 | 11 | Somalia (9/93) |

*Source:* Gallup. See Newport 1995.

regarding the benefits — although few saw vital interests in any of these cases, in Somalia there was a broad feeling of U.S. responsibility that was less apparent in Haiti and Bosnia (see table 13). But this tepid support also can be attributed to differences in the expectations regarding the other underlying parameters of support, as can be seen in table 14: members of the public were less confident about the costs, duration, and prospects for success in Bosnia than in these other cases.

**TABLE 13.   Comparison of Support and Perceived Benefits in Bosnia, Somalia, and Haiti**

**Vital Interests**

Do you think America's vital interests are at stake in [the situation involving] _____, or not?

| | |
|---|---|
| 39% | Bosnia (ABC News/*Washington Post,* 11/27/95) |
| 21 | Somalia (ABC News, 10/5/93) |
| 31 | Haiti (ABC News, 9/15/94) |

**U.S. Responsibility**

Do you think the United States has a responsibility to enforce the peace agreement in Bosnia, or doesn't the United States have this responsibility? (CBS News, 11/27/95)

| | |
|---|---|
| 33% | Has responsibility |
| 59 | Doesn't have responsibility |
| 8 | Don't know/No answer |

Do you think the United States has a responsibility to help every country that needs the kind of assistance U.S. troops are providing in Somalia, or do you think Somalia is a special case? (*Time*/CNN, 1/13–14/93)

| | |
|---|---|
| 27% | Help every country |
| 67 | Somalia a special case |
| 6 | Not sure |

Do you think the United States has a responsibility to do something to restore democracy in Haiti, or doesn't the United States have this responsibility? (CBS News/*New York Times,* 9/19/94)

| | |
|---|---|
| 41% | Has responsibility |
| 53 | Doesn't have this responsibility |
| 6 | Don't know/No answer |

*Source:* Bosnia data from Gallup, 12/15–18/95; Somalia data from Gallup, 9/19/94; and Haiti data from Gallup, 9/19/94. See Newport 1995.

*Note:* Until October 1993, no questions were asked about whether vital interests were engaged in Somalia.

Finally, we can compare the prospective sensitivity to casualties in Bosnia with that in the Gulf War and with observed support in a number of other wars and military operations. Figure 4 shows that, as might be expected, prospective casualty tolerance for the operation in Bosnia is well below the observed tolerance for casualties in World War II and the Korean and Vietnam Wars; well below the tolerance suggested by similar questions about hypothetical support in the Gulf War; and somewhere between the observed sensitivity to casualties in Somalia, Lebanon, and the Dominican intervention of 1965, three interventions that were characterized by congressional and domestic discord.

To put a finer point on it, prospective casualty tolerance in Bosnia lay between Lebanon and Somalia — two operations that most ultimately have judged as failures on the basis of their inability to achieve objectives and the high casualties that were incurred.[78] In the end, support for Bosnia was not only low, but also quite brittle and conditional. This

---

**TABLE 14. Comparison of Expectations regarding Prospects for Success and Costs in Bosnia, Somalia, and Haiti**

Regarding the situation in Bosnia, how confident are you that each of the following will happen? Are you very confident, somewhat confident, not too confident, or not at all confident that: the United States will be able to accomplish its goals with very few or no American casualties; most U.S. troops will be able to withdraw within a year, as planned; the U.S. effort to establish peace in Bosnia will succeed. (Random order)

Percentage very/somewhat confident in . . .

Meeting goals

| | |
|---|---|
| 44% | Bosnia |
| 49 | Somalia |
| 52 | Haiti |

Timetable for withdrawal

| | |
|---|---|
| 46% | Bosnia |
| 52 | Somalia |
| 50 | Haiti |

Few or no casualties

| | |
|---|---|
| 40% | Bosnia (12/95) |
| 64 | Somalia (12/92) |
| 61 | Haiti (9/94) |

*Source:* Newport 1995, 32.

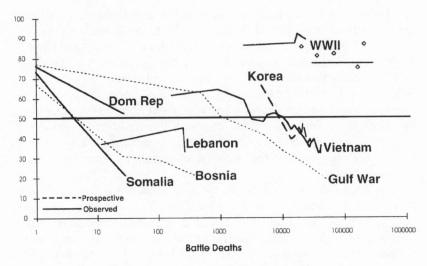

**Fig. 4.   Support as a function of casualties**

public opinion environment required a creative response from the Clinton administration, a response that was forthcoming.

Implications for Bosnia Policy

In the face of the weak and highly conditional support for a U.S. intervention in Bosnia suggested by this diagnosis, the Clinton administration was faced with the challenge of squaring a circle: intervening in a way that would create good prospects for a successful outcome at low cost, while creating for the operation a generally permissive domestic environment that might be sustained until the operation could be successfully concluded. The approach that the administration took met these basic requirements:

> By hewing to his commitment to introduce peacekeepers if a peace agreement was signed, the president left most members of Congress with only one alternative that was unpalatable to most — undercutting the president and U.S. credibility abroad.
> By gaining grudging congressional acquiescence, President Clinton — like President Reagan on Lebanon — gained breathing room that was unlikely to be undercut by partisan attacks, so long as the situation didn't deteriorate into open warfare involving U.S. troops.

To minimize the possibility of a congressional revolt, as in the operation in Somalia, the intervention in Bosnia was designed to stay within fairly stringent political constraints, especially on the hot-button issues of mission, casualties, timeline, and U.S. command.[79]

By introducing overwhelming force and threatening a disproportionate response to any attacks on U.S. peacekeepers, the president effectively deterred any such attacks.

In short, the Clinton administration's intervention policy in Bosnia was a creative response to the domestic constraints it faced, and it created an opportunity to prove that administration objectives in Bosnia could successfully be achieved at an acceptable cost, while hedging against the downside risks of a deteriorated situation.

### Which Forecast Was More Accurate?

We can now step back from the policy domain to the question of forecasting support for the intervention in Bosnia. I have examined two separate forecasts regarding the level of support for a U.S. operation in Bosnia — the PIPA forecast of 50 percent supporting (66 percent, if the follow-up question is included), and one based upon an analysis of the dynamics of the environment and of the underlying parameters of support, which suggested that only about four in ten should have been expected to support a U.S. peacekeeping operation in Bosnia. We can now turn to polling taken after the president's speech to see which forecast was more accurate.

When questions were posed that asked members of the public explicitly to weigh ends and means in Bosnia, *fewer* than four in ten ultimately believed that sending troops to Bosnia was worth incurring *any* loss of American lives — for most, the operation was simply not worth it.[80] Nevertheless, judged from the results of the 24 separate public opinion questions between late November 1995 and late June 1996 that asked somewhat more straightforward questions about support, an average of only 41 percent of the public have supported the U.S. intervention in Bosnia (the percent varied from 29 to 51, depending on wording).[81]

For whatever reasons — wording, order, context, house effects, or other potential — the November 1995 PIPA survey appears to have overestimated by nearly 10 points the level of support that actually obtained,[82] a fact that should make us very wary of accepting these results as a good index of public support for the U.S. peacekeeping mission in

Bosnia.[83] To be fair, PIPA was not alone in misgauging the level of support that would obtain — other polling questions also either over- or underestimated support, a fact that should make us wary of accepting *any* single polling result or source.[84] By comparison, however, the assessment of the data organized around the underlying parameters of support in the simple model of ends and means — the perceived benefits, the prospects for a successful outcome, expected costs, and the crucial role of leadership cuing — provided a reasonably accurate basis for bounding the actual level of support that would obtain in a U.S. peacekeeping operation in Bosnia, as well as revealing the origin of key beliefs that regulated the level of support.

## The Importance of Assessing the Robustness of Support

The foregoing analysis has suggested that, despite the importance of the policy question, some estimates of public support for military operations may not be very robust and may accordingly mislead policymakers as to the level and depth of support for a military operation. Stepping back to gain some perspective, it seems clear that there are at least three conceptions of robustness in public opinion that must be addressed by public opinion analysts to assure policymakers that their analyses are sufficiently robust to be used in a policy setting.

*Robustness as Sensitivity to Cues in Question Wording*
One conception of robustness in public opinion analysis focuses on the level of stability or crystallization in public opinion, judged in part by the sensitivity of polling results to wording differences and other ephemera.[85] Robust support for a military operation is support that remains relatively stable across, or insensitive to, public opinion questions with wide differences in question wordings. Returning to the illustrative November 1995 PIPA result of 50 percent supporting a U.S. operation in Bosnia, it is clear that policymakers who relied upon PIPA's polling to gauge the likely level of support would have been quite surprised and disappointed with the actual level of support for the operation that obtained: the PIPA result was simply not a very robust predictor of actual support, which appears to have been about 10 percentage points lower, or about four in ten supporting the operation.

*Robustness as Sensitivity to Adverse Developments*
Closely related to the last point is that robustness is also related to the extent to which respondents have actually worked through the sometimes difficult trade-offs and costs of particular choices,[86] so that their

support is likely to remain reasonably solid in the face of setbacks, higher-than-expected costs, or other factors.[87] As we have seen, support for Bosnia was not very robust in the face of potential adverse developments: it was quite sensitive both to expectations about the prospects for success and to the costs that might be incurred in Bosnia.

*Robustness as Measured by the Alignment of Preferences*
Yet another way to think about robustness is in terms of the alignment of opinion toward support or opposition, and the degree of polarization in this alignment. The reason this is important is inertia in public opinion: support that is polarized along partisan lines will be more sensitive to emergent leadership divisions than will unimodal distributions where supporters are drawn equally from different partisan or ideological camps.

As was seen earlier, public support mirrored divisions in the leadership along essentially partisan lines; figure 5 presents additional data showing that the strength of support and approval for U.S. action also was highly polarized.[88] In the case of all of the polling questions — except the PIPA result — the alignment of preferences was toward disapproval, although each of the different polling results shared a relatively high degree of polarization, with sizable percentages at the extremes. When the results of the five polls are compared, once again the PIPA result stands out: where PIPA finds 51 percent strongly or weakly approving, the other polls find 38, 41, 42, and 43 percent supporting — PIPA's result is 8 percentage points higher than the next highest result and the overall average of 43 percent approving. PIPA also finds the highest percentage strongly approving (24 percent, shared by Gallup's mid-December result) and the lowest percentage strongly disapproving (13 percent).[89] In short, as with their November polling on Bosnia, PIPA's result is not replicated by other polling — it is not a very robust finding.

Policymakers who relied solely upon PIPA's polling would not have understood just how polarized and brittle support was. The sort of polarized support illustrated by figure 5 would be expected to be among the least robust types of support for military interventions for one simple reason: support from the weakly committed would quickly evaporate if setbacks led to divisions among political leaders.[90] As in Korea, Vietnam, Lebanon, and Somalia, criticism probably would have been led by disaffected members of Congress, and the Clinton administration would have been caught between the great majority who would advocate a reduction in the level of commitment, and a smaller percentage who would advocate increasing the commitment to whatever level was necessary to achieve a successful outcome.[91] Because the U.S. equities were so small, the foregone conclusion is that preferences regarding Bosnia would in all

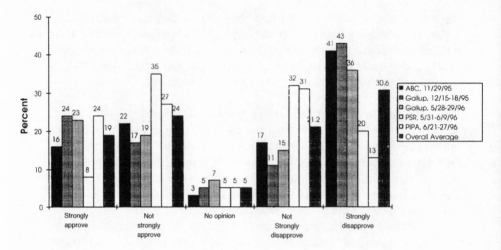

**Fig. 5.  Polarized alignment of support for Bosnia**

likelihood resemble those in Lebanon or Somalia — favoring withdrawal following the recovery of prisoners of war.[92]

   This treatment of polling results on Bosnia is a cautionary tale to those who consume public opinion results without understanding whether those results are particularly robust, that is, representative of the overall pool of available public opinion data. In this case, both PIPA's 50 percent approving from November 1995 polling and its finding of 51 percent approving in June 1996 are properly viewed as chimerical; they are not representative of the available public opinion polling, and they overestimated support by nearly 10 points. The lesson is that the results of one-time surveys should only be used cautiously, with full awareness of their limitations and the broader distribution of public opinion results.

**III**

> Much additional scholarly research in academic centers and
> within government is needed to improve the knowledge
> base for foreign policy.
> — Alexander George, introduction to *Bridging the Gap*

This essay has shown how theory can profitably be used to diagnose public opinion toward military operations and to provide results that are policy-relevant. By illuminating the sorts of constraints that inhered in the U.S. intervention in Bosnia, this essay has illustrated how theory and models can inform policy-relevant diagnoses of public opinion toward U.S. military operations. The analysis provided a robust net estimate of support, identified the underlying premises of that support, and described how support might be sensitive to plausible variations in key variables: information essential to understanding the possibilities and limits of presidential efforts to mobilize support; the sorts of constraints that would need to be imposed on the operation to create a permissive public opinion environment; and other actions (e.g., threats of punishment) that might be taken to create a reasonably secure environment for U.S. forces in Bosnia — the sine qua non for the continuation of a permissive, if pessimistic, public opinion environment.

The analysis suggested that weak support for the U.S. peacekeeping operation in Bosnia was the result of neither isolationism, media effects, nor presidential failure to clearly articulate objectives. Instead, low support for Bosnia was the consequence of rational beliefs about the specific merits of the operation that arose from selective attention to leadership debates over the credibility of the president's case for Bosnia. Bosnia provides a good example of the difficulties a president can face in mobilizing support for a military operation in a situation where Congress is divided and few in the public accordingly see important enough benefits or a high enough probability of success to readily accept the likely costs. Viewed this way, it is little surprise that the Clinton administration was less than successful in gaining very strong congressional or public support: when leaders are divided over the wisdom of a military operation, we should expect those divisions to be mirrored in the public.

While the resulting congressional and public environment for U.S. peacekeeping in Bosnia was not supportive, it was permissive so long as things went well; a reading of the congressional environment and the public opinion data suggests that if the situation devolved from peacekeeping to combat operations, leadership and public divisions probably would have emerged. In this scenario, the president would have been caught between administration desires to redeem the situation through an increased commitment, and broad congressional and public opposition to escalation or deeper involvement. Like Haiti, the Bosnia operation benefited from careful planning and execution, a good understanding of the limits of domestic support, and not a little luck.

By providing robust estimates of support and its sensitivity to possible adverse developments, a better and more policy-relevant theory on public opinion and policy can serve the important normative end of improving both policy and democratic control of policy. For in the end, presidents are accountable for the success or failure of their policies, and in as important and sensitive a policy area as that of military operations, the chief executive should have the most accurate diagnosis of the constraints and possibilities in the domestic environment they face. While presidents should always make decisions about the employment of U.S. troops on the basis of their conceptions of U.S. national interests and values, they also would be well advised to eschew wishful thinking and overly optimistic polling results in favor of a sober and clear-eyed view of the political landscape they face, and to assure that intervention policies are designed in ways that will help to hedge against adverse developments and the emergence of domestic opposition.

There also are implications for scholarly research. Although this community has made many important contributions to our understanding of U.S. public opinion on military operations,[93] much of the literature appears still to be at a somewhat pretheoretic stage. Evidence of this can be found in the penchant for regression analyses that seek to understand the predictors of *average* levels of support for a large number of very different operations, even though in many cases support changed dramatically over the course of the operation in response to factors that are not captured in the regression models.[94] It also can be found in the competition between dominant single-variable theories of support, all apparently motivated by a fixation on parsimony, rather than within- and across-case explanatory power and robustness.[95] Theories that are modified by somewhat ad hoc exceptions for specific conditions [96] and theories built upon small numbers of cases where data are rich but generalizability is questionable also provide evidence of the pretheoretic state of the literature. Finally, there continues to be a fixation on public opinion data from Korea and Vietnam — two cases that have much in common and where the data are rather rich — but it is far from clear that models fitted to these data are of much help in explaining the patterns in other cases.[97]

Additional evidence can be found in researchers' inexplicable inattention to the complex relationship between support and policy preferences over the level of commitment (e.g., escalation or withdrawal). This suggests that few have considered fully this fundamental dimension of support in their theories of public opinion on military operations. Nor have scholars sought to explore the variables that regulate sensitivity to casualties (i.e., the relationship between support and casualties), which (see fig. 4) has varied widely across wars and military operations, apparently, as has been argued in this essay and elsewhere,[98] as a result of changing perceptions of the benefits and prospects for success.

Until the scholarly community addresses policy-relevant questions such as these, its theories may continue to occasion heated debate in its own journals, but they seem unlikely to foster the cumulation of reliable and useful scientific knowledge that might actually inform policy development. By comparison, the development of theories that can demonstrate robustness, not only in diagnosing the likely path of support over a broad range of conditions in any particular case at hand, but also by explaining support in a wide range of cases, offers great promise; in short, there remain ample opportunities for scholars both to improve theory in this area and to improve theory's relevance to policy.

## Postscript

The foregoing analysis made predictions on the level of public support based upon public opinion data available at the time of the intervention. Data on key beliefs were used to bound a prediction of the approval for the operation that would actually obtain, and these predictions favorably compared with the average level of support exhibited in 24 public opinion questions on approval for the operation through June 1996.[99] The prediction of about four in ten supporting was found to be a highly reliable basis for predicting the actual level of support for the Bosnia operation. In July 1998, a search for additional public opinion questions on support for Bosnia was performed to update this essay. The nine questions that were asked since June 1996 suggest that public support for the Bosnia operation has continued to hover around four in ten, with an ephemeral but discernible rally in support for the venture around the time of President Clinton's visit to Bosnia in December 1997, probably accounted for by two factors: that the president was accompanied by congressional leaders, and that the trip generally received favorable leadership and press commentary.[100]

APPENDIX

**TABLE A1. Questions on Support for the U.S. Intervention in Bosnia, 11/95–6/96 (in percentages)**

| Poll Dates | Approve | Disapprove | No Opinion | Source |
|---|---|---|---|---|
| 11/22–25/95 | 50 | 47 | 4 | PIPA #1 |
| 11/27/95 | 39 | 57 | 4 | ABC News |
| 11/27/95 | 33 | 58 | 9 | CBS News #1 |
| 11/27/95 | 46 | 40 | 14 | Gallup/CNN/*USA Today* |
| 11/29/95 | 38 | 58 | 3 | ABC News #1 |
| 11/29–12/3/95 | 30 | 58 | 12 | Associated Press |
| 11/30–12/3/95 | 29 | 67 | 4 | Harris #1 |
| 12/1–3/95 | 40 | 56 | 5 | ABC News #1 |
| 12/6–7/95 | 36 | 57 | 7 | Time/CNN/Yankelovich #1 |
| 12/6–7/95 | 38 | 55 | 7 | *Time*/CNN/Yankelovich #2 |
| 12/9–11/95 | 40 | 55 | 5 | CBS/*New York Times* #1 |
| 12/9–11/95 | 36 | 58 | 6 | CBS/*New York Times* #2 |
| 12/15–18/95 | 41 | 54 | 6 | Gallup |
| 1/2–3/96 | 43 | 50 | 8 | CBS News #1 |
| 1/2/–3/96 | 41 | 54 | 6 | CBS News #2 |
| 1/5–7/96 | 36 | 58 | 6 | Gallup |
| 1/10–11/96 | 41 | 50 | 9 | *Time*/CNN/Yankelovich #1 |
| 1/11–14/96 | 48 | 49 | 3 | PSRA #1 |
| 1/13–16/96 | 38 | 54 | 8 | NBC/*Wall Street Journal* |
| 1/18–22/96 | 46 | 51 | 4 | ABC/*Washington Post* #1 |
| 1/18–22/96 | 50 | 47 | 3 | Harris, question wording #2 |
| 5/28–29/96 | 42 | 51 | 7 | Gallup |
| 5/31–6/9/96 | 43 | 52 | 5 | PSRA #2 |
| 6/21–27/96 | 51 | 44 | 5 | PIPA #2 |

*Note:* Precise wording of questions available through the Roper Center.

**TABLE A2. Questions on Support for the U.S. Intervention in Bosnia, 7/96–1/98 (in percentages)**

| Poll Dates | Approve | Disapprove | No Opinion | Source |
|---|---|---|---|---|
| 2/5–6/97 | 40 | 54 | 6 | *Time*/CNN/Yankelovich |
| 6/26–29/97 | 39 | 53 | 8 | Gallup/CNN/*USA Today* |
| 10/15–16/97 | 40 | 53 | 7 | Harris |
| 11/12–16/97 | 50 | 42 | 8 | Pew Research Center |
| 12/18–21/97 | 43 | 50 | 7 | Gallup |
| 12/18–21/97 | 49 | 43 | 8 | Gallup |
| 1/98 | 53 | 43 | 5 | Gallup |
| 1/14–18/98 | 43 | 50 | 7 | Pew Research Center |
| 1/14–18/98 | 43 | 50 | 7 | Pew Research Center |

*Note:* Precise wording of questions available through the Roper Center.

NOTES

The author is a policy analyst at RAND, Santa Monica, California. The views expressed here are the author's alone and do not reflect the positions of RAND or its sponsors. The author would like to thank Arthur Brooks, John Mueller, Miroslav Nincic, John Peters, and Richard Sobel for comments on earlier versions of this essay. Any errors of commission or omission are solely the author's responsibility.

1. See Larson 1996a, 1996b, for application to a wide range of cases including World War II, Korea, Vietnam, the Gulf War, Panama, and Somalia.

2. This piece is in the spirit of Sobel's (1993, 2) observation that "[t]ogether the insights of . . . policy analysts and the perspectives of policymakers provide both provocative support and pointed challenges to the existing common wisdom and theories."

3. The mix of deductive theory, empirical generalizations, and inductive theory will typically depend on the state of knowledge for that problem area. Generally speaking, however, scientific theories require both abstract concepts and concrete implications that are logically connected. See Costner 1971, 299.

4. As Paul Diesing (1971, 63) has suggested, "The first stage in the development of a mathematical model, constructing a skeleton or first approximation model, is one in which formal clarity is more important than empirical adequacy. Consequently refined empirical data are not really necessary, and the model-builder can rely on common sense observation and introspection as a source of his initial postulates." Fiorina 1975 is one of the earlier works in political science that seems to have appreciated this school of modeling. Fiorina recounts that "although [Anthony] Downs took pains to explain his intent [in *An Economic Theory of Democracy*], the idea of constructing and applying a model was discomforting to many political scientists."

5. The aim in policy modeling is generally "to be roughly right rather than precisely wrong." Put another way, while all models are generally evaluated on the basis of how well they accomplish their specific purposes, robust models that can make predictions under a wide range of circumstances are generally preferred to those that can make accurate predictions in only a very narrow set of circumstances.

6. On the rally effect, see Mueller 1973, Brody 1991, and Burbach 1994.

7. See Converse and Schuman 1970, Modigliani 1972, and Mueller 1973.

8. See Larson 1996a, 1996b.

9. A comparable formulation of this pseudocardinal utility measure can be found in Churchman and Ackoff 1954. Other, more elaborate formulations are also possible.

10. Some of this work has identified differences based upon the objectives being pursued. For example, Mueller (1977), Russett (1990–91), and Jentleson (1992) report that U.S. military responses to external aggressions typically received higher levels of support than strictly internal conflicts; Jentleson and Britton (1998) believe that humanitarian objectives typically receive more support than internal change objectives, but less than external restraint objectives.

Richman (1994, 1995) provided a broader list of factors that could be used to impute importance. Finally, Wittkopf (1990) associated willingness to use force with the extent it comports with broader value structures. What has been lacking is a broader structure for integrating these empirical findings with the other factors that are associated with support. See the appendix in Larson 1996b for a complete discussion in simple microeconomic terms, animated by public opinion data.

11. By virtue of semantics, efforts by individuals to achieve cognitive consistency, and other factors, these two dimensions are most likely not entirely independent for most individuals or necessarily all-inclusive. For example, the promotion of an important principle could easily be viewed by some individuals as an important interest. The benefits dimension is not very well understood at present and is deserving of more serious empirical research. See Wittkopf 1990 for a related discussion.

12. The two dimensions described here aim to tap the impulses that animate two competing normative views of foreign policy — idealism and realism. For the idealist, the aim of foreign policy is world order through promotion of important principles as embodied in international law, multilateral organization, and promotion of democracy and human rights. For the realist, the aim is world order through a strong defense, the preservation of vital interests, and responses to changing power calculations. For a recent effort to classify U.S. interests in terms of their importance, see Commission on America's National Interests 1996. They also provide a framework for mapping political or policy objectives. For example, humanitarian operations promote humanitarian goals.

13. See Kahneman, Tversky, and Slovic 1982 and Nincic 1996.

14. The rate at which individuals are willing to trade off interests and benefits may vary, however. For example, those who place the greatest importance on principles in the use of force may only support a use of force when absolutely vital (e.g., existential) interests are at stake.

15. In fact, there is strong evidence that the aggregate public displays a somewhat differentiated but consistent view about where U.S. interests lie abroad and what foreign policy goals are most important, and, as will be seen in the case study, this hierarchy can be used to assist in the diagnosis of the perceived benefits in actual military operations. The quadrennial surveys by the Chicago Council on Foreign Relations (CCFR) show a high degree of year-to-year consistency in the ranking of nations on the basis of whether the U.S. has a vital interest there and the ranking of various foreign policy goals. See the appendix of Larson 1996b.

16. For example, Schuman (1972) found that opponents of the Vietnam War opposed the war for at least two distinct reasons. One group opposed the war for moral reasons, the belief that Vietnam was not a just war. The second group opposed the war for pragmatic reasons, the belief that the costs that were being incurred were in vain, and that there was no relationship between inputs and outputs.

17. There are numerous examples where declining belief in success has led to declining support for a policy option. For example, in the fall of 1990, as belief

in the efficacy of sanctions against Iraq declined, so too did support for reliance upon that policy.

18. Larson 1996a, 1996b.

19. Put another way, when the expected benefits are low, an individual's utility from an operation will be low, and when casualties are increasing, an individual's utility will fall at a much faster rate when the numerator (the expected benefits) is declining.

20. Few are aware, however, that support for Somalia in fact had declined to about four in ten even *before* the deaths in Mogadishu.

21. This parameter is included simply to be complete — the model is entirely agnostic as to whether an individual establishes a priori a threshold below which he will withdraw his support; it simply represents the observed level at which the individual withdraws his support.

22. Zaller (1992), for example, is somewhat agnostic as to whether the media or personal networks are in fact more important in the diffusion of mass attitudes.

23. The point of view taken here is consistent with Milton Friedman's (1953) "as if" argument — that people behave *as if* the model underlies their behavior.

24. See Converse and Schuman 1970 and Mueller 1973 for the seminal discussions of the differences between the two.

25. See Bueno de Mesquita and Siverson 1995. The absence of a total victory may be viewed by many as defeat.

26. See Hamilton 1968, Converse and Schuman 1970, and Mueller 1973 for what appear to be the first analyses of this phenomenon.

27. This was basically the analysis of those who wanted to escalate in the Korean and Vietnam Wars.

28. Advocates of this position either would tend to discount the possibility of a widened war and the costs attendant with such an outcome, or would in any case not be deterred by that prospect.

29. Contrary to the conventional wisdom, support for *immediate* withdrawal from military operations has typically not been supported by a majority of the public — even in low-stakes cases such as Somalia. See Larson 1996a, 1996b.

30. This can lead to distortions in decision making as leaders become increasingly willing to accept risks in a "bargain for resurrection" that might yield a successful outcome. See Downs and Rocke 1994.

31. That is, some members of the public may most closely identify themselves with the president's position and view casualties as an investment to be redeemed, some with those leaders and experts who would increase the level of commitment, and still others with leaders and experts who would decrease or terminate the commitment. See Modigliani's (1972, 972) discussion of how some groups may be more oriented toward costs, while others are more oriented toward achievement of the objectives.

32. Lasswell (1971, 15–26) posited the "social process model" as describing the context in which and with which the policymaker interacts. In the context of

a military operation, the president (and executive branch) interacts with external actors, including allies, neutrals, adversaries, and international organizations, and with such internal actors as the Congress, the media, and the public.

33. The literature on presidential leadership strategies is somewhat limited. The best works include Neustadt 1990, Skowronek 1993, Zaller 1994b, Kernell 1993, and Pfiffner 1996. A great deal of scholarly research on presidential decision making with regard to the use of force is, to this author's mind, somewhat problematic from a policy perspective. However, a well-balanced analysis can be found in Meernik 1994.

34. See Kernell 1993 for a discussion of the strategy of going public, and how it differs from Neustadt's (1990) classic conception of presidential strategies that rely upon bargaining with Congress.

35. See Brody 1991 and Zaller 1984, 1992, for discussions of the role of debates among political leaders in establishing frames of reference on policy issues.

36. A classic in this area is Cohen 1963. For recent scholarly work on the media, see Iyengar 1991 and Bennett 1996. A number of perspectives on media reporting on the Gulf War can be found in Bennett and Paletz 1994 and Jeffords and Rabinovitz 1994. Neuman 1996 places current ruminations on the media and foreign policy in historical perspective. Bennett 1990 showed that the media tended to "index" the slant of their coverage to the range of opinions prevailing in the elite discourse.

37. MacKuen and Coombs 1981, MacKuen 1984a and 1984b, and Behr and Iyengar 1985. Zaller 1994a, 201, ff. 15, 16, provides a cogent discussion of the difficulties of determining the relative importance of political leadership and media effects.

38. Zaller's (1992) three-stage Reception-Acceptance-Sampling (RAS) model provides a recent discussion of the process by which mass attitudes become diffused that seems likely to become the standard analysis. Downs 1957, Converse 1964, McCloskey 1964, Gamson and Modigliani 1966, Hastie 1986, Newman 1986, Ferejohn and Kuklinski 1990, and Popkin 1994 offer views that share much with Zaller's, while Downs and Popkin also offer credible discussions of the political reasoning processes used by members of the public.

39. Zaller 1992, 16–28.

40. This observation seems to be amply supported by psychological research on persuasion. See, for example, Petty and Cacioppo 1981, 1986. Ajzen and Fishbein (1980, 219–21) provide a good review of the relevant literature.

41. For example, on May 23, 1995, President Clinton said, "[F]rom the beginning of my campaign for president, I said that the one thing we should not do is to send American troops into combat into Bosnia." On June 7, 1995, Secretary of Defense Perry supported this view: "I do not believe—that while this war is in our interest, it is not in our vital interest. And therefore, it does not pose a sufficiently great risk to U.S. interests to warrant the risk of the lives of thousands of troops."

42. "Address to the Nation on Implementation of the Peace Agreement in Bosnia-Herzegovina," November 17, 1995.

43. Air strikes and arming the Muslims was a policy preferred by many Republican congressional leaders, although some others opposed any sort of deeper involvement.

44. See MacKuen's (1981, 1984) somewhat unsuccessful effort to separate the effects of objective events and conditions and media effects on the salience of the Vietnam War.

45. The KEDS data code diplomatic and military interactions as events between actors, e.g., "Bosnian Serbs attacked Bosnian Croats" or "the U.S. threatened Bosnian Serbs." See Gerner, Schrodt, Francisco, and Weddle 1994.

46. In fact, the correlations between the measures of political activity are both in the predicted positive direction and rather healthy: the correlation between presidential papers and the *Congressional Record* is 0.54.

47. A reading of the *Congressional Quarterly Almanac* supports this view.

48. The importance of this step lies in establishing the degree to which so-called media effects were at work — we would hope to understand what proportion of media reporting might be attributed to objective events and conditions in Bosnia and the changing level, volume, or tone of the leadership debate on Bosnia; the remaining variance might be thought of as the residual attributable to media effects.

49. Standardized scores were used for all four variables to better interpret the relative importance of the explanatory variables.

50. These results were confirmed by stepwise regression models using both forward and backward elimination — none of the explanatory variables could be dropped without a significant loss of explanatory power.

51. A brief comment is necessary to explain the use of standard multiple regression techniques for this part of the analysis. Methodological purists might argue that because of the intercorrelations among the independent variables, and possible feedback loops between the dependent and independent variables, standard regression modeling may be inadequate. Although the intercorrelations among the independent variables are somewhat high (potentially leading to overly high standard errors and unstable estimates for the coefficients), the robust statistical significance of each of the coefficients suggests that this is not a major problem in the present case. Second, it might be argued that multiple regression is likely to be inferior to other econometric techniques that are designed to handle feedbacks or simultaneity. Five justifications, two substantive and three practical, are offered for relying upon multiple regression. First, as with Occam's razor, the argument that media reporting has antecedents in real-world events and conditions is the most parsimonious and intuitively obvious explanation that accounts for the result, and inclusion of feedbacks is unlikely to change this. Second, the feedback loops are in any case far less interesting for policy purposes than the main directional effects described by the regression model just presented, all of which were statistically significant. Third, multiple regression appears to be the standard tool used in other research in this area (e.g., MacKuen 1984b), and the present work in fact expands and enriches somewhat this other work. Fourth, the data used in the present research are aggregated counts by month, too gross to understand well

any feedbacks. And fifth, as a practical matter there are no available data to create instrumental variables for better estimation models, so the issue is in any case a moot point. Put another way, in spite of its limitations, the multiple regression model is judged both to be adequate to establish empirically a clear relationship between real-world events and conditions and media reporting, and to be all that is technically feasible at present. With more and better data, of course, these issues could be explored, but that is well beyond the scope of the present work.

52. Sobel 1996, 162. The general question was "Tell me if you happened to follow this news story very closely, fairly closely, not too closely, or not at all closely . . . the civil war in Bosnia." The question was asked by Princeton Survey Research Associates (PSRA), NBC, CBS, and Gallup. PSRA also asked the question in polling done 3/28–31/96, 4/19–25/96, and 7/25–28/96. For a more recent compilation, see Sobel 1998.

53. The percentage of those following very closely ranged from 8 to 37 percent; those following very or somewhat closely ranged from 37 to 82 percent. By comparison, the percentage following Somalia very closely appears to have ranged between 7 and 34 percent, and those following very or somewhat closely ranged between 46 and 75 percent.

54. The level of media reporting on Bosnia was operationalized by counting the total number of stories in the *New York Times* that mentioned Bosnia in the 21 days preceding each of the polls that asked how closely respondents were following Bosnia; previous unpublished work by the author suggested that the correlation between awareness variables and media reporting fell off with much more or less than 21 days of aggregation.

55. The $t$-ratio for the constant was $-3.16$, and that for the percentage who were following very or fairly closely was 6.04. The $F$-ratio for the regression was 36.4.

56. It would be desirable to control for the potential interactions between the explanatory variables—the KEDS measure of activity in Bosnia, the *Presidential Papers,* and the *Congressional Record*—e.g., through two-stage least squares. This requires the use of instrumental variables, however, that are simply unavailable.

57. University of Maryland at College Park news release, November 27, 1995.

58. Throughout this analysis, efforts will be made to present data that are broadly representative of the available data.

59. The question the CCFR asked was "Many people believe that the United States has a vital interest in certain areas of the world and not in other areas. That is, certain countries of the world are important to the U.S. for political, economic or security reasons. I am going to read a list of countries. For each, tell me whether you feel the U.S. does not have a vital interest in that country." See Rielly 1995.

60. A typical result was the response to the question "Do you think the United States has a responsibility to do something about the fighting between Serbs and Bosnians in what used to be Yugoslavia, or doesn't the United States

have this responsibility?" The percentage believing the U.S. had a responsibility never got above four out of ten, and occasionally dipped as low as one in four, while more than half thought that the United Nations had a responsibility to do something about the fighting. See Sobel 1996, 165, table 6.4. By contrast, three out of four or more thought the U.S. should insist that other European countries help before taking military action (ibid., table 6.3).

61. According to Seelye 1995: "Those who supported the Hutchinson resolution [supporting the troops but opposing President Clinton's decision to send them] generally said that the United States had no vital strategic interest in Bosnia, that the mission was ill-defined, with no clear objective, and that Washington could not be the world's policeman." For example, Senator Phil Gramm (R-Tex.) stated that the United States had no vital national security interest in Bosnia, and Senator Arlen Spector (R-Pa.) argued that the Congress should support the troops without endorsing the president's policy, because U.S. national security was not imminently threatened and the United States was not "the world's policeman."

62. According to *Congressional Quarterly*, SJ RES 44 on the Bosnia troop deployment expressed support for U.S. troops in Bosnia but expressed reservations about the deployment of the troops. The measure also limited the deployment to "approximately" one year and required the president to limit the use of U.S. troops in Bosnia to the enforcement of the military provisions of the peace agreement and to provide for an exit strategy from Bosnia that would include an international effort to achieve a military balance in Bosnia by arming the federation of Bosnia. Republican senators voted 29 to 24 against the measure, while Democratic senators voted 45 to 1 in favor. In the House, H Res 302 declared that the House had serious concerns and opposed the president's policy to deploy U.S. ground troops to Bosnia. The resolution also declared that the House was confident that the members of the U.S. armed forces will perform their responsibilities with excellence; that the president and defense secretary should rely on the judgment of the commander of the U.S. Armed Forces in Bosnia in all matters affecting the safety, support, and well-being of the troops and that the commander should be furnished with the resources necessary to ensure troop safety; and that the U.S. government should be impartial and evenhanded with all parties in the Bosnian conflict as necessary to ensure the safety of U.S. troops. Republican members voted 221 to 11 in favor, while Democrats voted 130 to 65 against the measure.

63. The data are far from unequivocal regarding the United States' responsibilities in Bosnia. A representative result was the response to the question "Do you think the U.S. has a responsibility to enforce the peace agreement in Bosnia, or doesn't the U.S. have this responsibility?" following the president's speech; only 33 percent thought the United States had the responsibility, while 59 percent said that it did not, and 8 percent had no opinion. And by mid-December, 37 percent thought the U.S. had the responsibility, 56 percent said it did not, and 7 percent had no opinion (CBS/*New York Times,* 11/27/95 and 12/9–11/95).

64. The question asked by Gallup/CNN/*USA Today* on 11/27/95 was "If the United States sends troops as part of a peacekeeping mission, do you think

that is likely to lead to a long-term commitment in Bosnia involving many casualties, or not?" Fifty-three percent expected a long-term commitment, while 35 percent thought that was not likely, and 12 percent had no opinion. A majority of both those who saw the speech and those who didn't expected a long-term commitment. *Gallup Poll Monthly,* November 1995, 47.

65. The question asked by Gallup was "Are you very confident, somewhat confident, not too confident, or not at all confident that: the U.S. effort to establish peace in Bosnia will succeed?" (Gallup, 12/15–18/95) Twenty-seven percent of those polled by Time/CNN/Yankelovich in their 12/6–7/95 poll responded affirmatively to the question "In your view, will the NATO peacekeeping force — which includes 20,000 U.S. troops — be successful in establishing a long-lasting peace, or don't you feel that way?" Sixty percent did not feel that way.

66. Princeton Survey Research Associates (PSRA) asked: "Do you think that U.S. forces will become involved in a major shooting war in Bosnia, or do you think the peace will hold in Bosnia?" A slender majority of 52 percent thought that peace would hold, while 38 percent expected a major shooting war, and 10 percent had no opinion.

67. ABC News asked the same question about support for a U.S. operation in Bosnia on three different occasions: on November 29, 1995, 38 percent supported "sending 20,000 U.S. troops there as part of an international peacekeeping force"; by December 1–3, the percentage had increased almost imperceptibly, to 40 percent; and by January 18–22, 1996, 46 percent indicated their support. While this is only one series, it provides reasonably strong evidence of one of the less obvious forecasts of the simple model of ends and means.

68. *Time*/CNN/Yankelovich, 4/28–29/93 and Gallup, 1/24–26/93; Gallup/ CNN/*USA Today,* 5/6/93.

69. See Mueller 1994 and Larson 1996b for analyses of questions on casualties and support in the Gulf War.

70. The query that was used in the *Congressional Record* database in LEXIS/NEXIS was "Bosnia and (American casualties or American lives)"; because of its narrow formulation, this logic would be expected to underestimate the actual number of times the topic was raised; i.e., the actual frequency would be expected to be somewhat higher.

71. Generally speaking, there has historically been a high correlation between discussions of casualties in Congress and the prominence of the casualties issue in the media. See Larson 1996b.

72. Based on three polling results with different question wording, including Gallup/CNN/*USA Today,* 11/27/95; Harris, 11/30–12/3/95; and Gallup, 12/ 15–18/95. Forty percent of those polled by Gallup in mid-December were very or somewhat confident that the U.S. would be able to accomplish its goals with very few or no American casualties when asked: "Regarding the situation in Bosnia, how confident are you that each of the following will happen? Are you very confident, somewhat confident, not too confident, or not at all confident that: . . . The U.S. will be able to accomplish its goals with very few or no American casualties?"

The smaller percentage in the second question may be due to the fact that it asks the respondent if he feels the United States would be able to accomplish its goals with very few or no casualties; i.e., it asks about the joint probability of success and success at few or no casualties (*Gallup Poll Monthly,* December 1995, 32). By way of comparison, the public was more optimistic about casualties in Haiti and Somalia (where more than six in ten expected few or no casualties).

73. These are votes in support of the Clinton administration position. See the votes on S Con Res 35, SJ Res 44, H Res 302, HR 2770. In the Senate, Senate Continuing Resolution 35, which opposed President Clinton's decision to deploy U.S. troops while expressing congressional support for the U.S. troops, was narrowly defeated in a highly partisan vote with 45 Democrats and 7 Republicans (94 percent of the Democrats and 7 percent of the Republicans) supporting the president's position. Senate Joint Resolution 44, which expressed support for U.S. troops in Bosnia but expressed reservations about the deployment of the troops, was also partisan: 45 of the Democrats and 24 of the Republicans (94 percent of the Democratic senators and 46 percent of the Republicans) supported the measure. In the House, 130 Democrats and 11 Republicans (64 percent of the Democratic House members and 5 percent of the Republicans) opposed House Resolution 302, which declared that the House had serious concerns and opposed the president's policy to deploy U.S. ground troops to Bosnia. The voting on House Resolution 2770, which prohibited the use of federal funds for the deployment of U.S. ground troops to Bosnia, was similarly partisan: 175 Democrats and 42 Republicans (86 percent of the Democrats, 18 percent of the Republicans) opposed the measure (*Congressional Quarterly,* December 16, 1995, 3817–18, 3842–43, and 3846–47).

74. In fact, clear statistical associations were found between partisanship and selected measures of the evaluation of benefits, prospects for success, and expected costs. Benefits were measured by the rating given President Clinton's negotiation of a peace settlement. Harris, 11/30–12/3/95, was statistically significant at the .001 level in chi-square test of independence. Prospects for success were measured by the confidence that the U.S. effort to establish peace in Bosnia would succeed. Gallup, 12/15–18/95, was statistically significant at the .001 level in chi-square test of independence. Expected costs were measured by the confidence that the United States will be able to accomplish its goals with very few or no American casualties. Gallup, 12/15–18/95, was statistically significant at the .001 level in chi-square test of independence. There were also differences in tolerance for casualties that appear to have been associated with partisan beliefs. When the data in figure 3 are broken out by ideology (Liberal, Moderate, Conservative) or party (Democrat, Independent, Republican), support from Liberals and Democrats was generally higher and less sensitive to casualties than that from Conservatives and Republicans. This provides strong circumstantial evidence that divisions in the public mirrored and followed those among political leaders.

75. Figure 3 is based on the following question asked by Gallup in mid-December 1995: "Which of the following statements comes closer to your view about the President's decision to send U.S. troops to Bosnia as part of an

international peace-keeping force: You think the United States should not send troops to Bosnia and you oppose the President's decision, or, you think the U.S. should not send troops to Bosnia, but because the President is Commander-in-Chief, you support his decision, or, you think the United States should send troops to Bosnia and you support the President's decision."

76. As shown earlier, another 48 percent believed the goal should be "somewhat important."

77. The table also shows that even before the firefight in Mogadishu in October 1993, support for Somalia had collapsed to about four in ten.

78. See Larson 1996a, 1996b.

79. Nevertheless, the troops have remained well beyond the one-year deadline that the president announced, and the current position of the administration is that U.S. forces will not leave until the summer of 1998.

80. For example, only 30 percent agreed that "it will be worth the loss of some American lives if sending U.S. troops brings peace to Bosnia" (ABC News, 11/27/95); 28 percent thought that sending U.S. troops was "worth the possible loss of American lives" (CBS News, 11/27/95); and 37 percent thought that saving the lives of civilians in Bosnia was worth putting U.S. soldiers at risk (Associated Press, 11/29–12/3/95).

81. PIPA was, however, consistent — their June 1996 polling returned the highest percentage supporting a U.S. peacekeeping operation in Bosnia — 51 percent. Interestingly, Harris was responsible for both a rather high result (50 percent) and a low one (29 percent). See table A.1 in the appendix for the data.

82. The probability of such a difference occurring by chance (i.e., that the PIPA results even come from the same distribution as the other polls) is quite small. Sobel (1996, 159) offers two possible explanations for the inflated support: "In part, because the introductions to the questions provide significant background and the respondents tend toward those with more education, the Program in International Policy Attitudes (PIPA) polls typically find higher support for U.S. intervention than do other surveys." Mueller's (1973, 1994) approach to public opinion analysis — an approach that is also favored here — is to compare differences in wording to better understand what cues are associated with higher or lower levels of support. Five good sources that explore wording and other reasons for differences in polling results are Smith 1978, Taylor 1984, Brady and Orren 1992, Kagay 1992, and Zaller and Feldman 1992.

83. In fact, when the 191 questions on support that Sobel provides are regressed on wording cues and a dummy variable for questions that are asked by PIPA, the mere fact that PIPA asked the question raised the level of support by 18.3 points; the $t$-ratio on the coefficient was 5.11, connoting a very low probability of this result being by chance.

84. Others who appear to be proponents of a higher level of commitment also overestimated public support for becoming engaged in Bosnia. For example, Brown 1995 estimated that 500 to 1,000 deaths to Western soldiers would result from an intervention in Bosnia and then asserted: "[t]he American people will support military actions that are morally and strategically compelling, as they showed in the Gulf. The American people are willing to pay a high price to

safeguard the country's interests—interests that are clearly on the line in Bosnia." As seen in this essay, a sizable percentage of American leaders and a majority of the American public did not share Brown's enthusiasm for an intervention in Bosnia.

85. The literature on wording effects, context effects, and other sources of poll-to-poll variation are quite plentiful. See Sudman 1982, Taylor 1984, and Clogg 1984.

86. Yankelovich 1994 offers suggestions on measuring the level of crystallization, but the idea has not been applied.

87. For example, polling before the Gulf War suggests that the public was initially willing to accept much higher casualties than most pundits and many policymakers realized. See Larson 1996a, 1996b. For a somewhat less optimistic perspective, see Mueller 1994.

88. The figure presents data on public attitudes toward support or opposition for a U.S. operation in Bosnia from five separate public opinion questions asked between December 1995 and June 1996, including a polling question asked by PIPA in June 1996. Each question asked the respondent whether he approved or disapproved, and then to rate the strength of that approval or disapproval.

89. One of the reasons that PIPA researchers argue that their questions receive higher levels of support than other questions that are asked is that their questions frequently solicit information about the *strength* of public attitudes. However, as figure 5 shows, even when using questions with a similar structure that ask about the strength of support, the other questions suggest that only about four in ten of those polled have ever supported the operation; when compared to the other questions (if slightly different wording), the June 1996 PIPA result still appears to be at least 7 points higher than the others. Even the two June 1996 results are strikingly different, with the PIPA result showing nearly one in four strongly approving, but the Pew/PSRA result showing fewer than one in twelve strongly approving.

90. The evidence generally supports Sobel's (1996) assessment that public support for deploying U.S. peacekeepers after a settlement never reached a majority (151). Sobel also seems to suggest, however, that majority support might have resulted if a quick and successful operation had taken place. Such an operation was never in the cards, however, and the result has been a prolonged peace operation. Nevertheless, the evidence does support Sobel's statement that "if costs and casualties rose, leadership weakened, intervention dragged on, and a way out became elusive, support would have dropped and opposition would have increased in both public opinion and the now more partisan Congress" (150).

91. There is surprisingly little good work that seeks to provide the connective tissue between public opinion and the rather rich literature of social choice theory. See Ordeshook 1986, 192, and Brady and Ansolabehere 1989 for two such efforts. Modigliani (1972, 969–72) found that preference orderings regarding escalation, continuation of the current policy, or withdrawal were associated with belief systems.

92. See Larson 1996a, 1996b, for a close analysis of attitudes toward escala-

tion and withdrawal options in Somalia — the reality is much more complex than the conventional wisdom on the matter, and Larson comes to somewhat different conclusions from PIPA's analysis. See Kull and Ramsay 1993.

93. I would count among relevant works those by Richard Brody, Ole Holsti, Bruce Jentleson and his colleagues, Lou Klarevas and Dan O'Connor, Jeffrey Milstein, John Mueller, Miroslav Nincic and his colleagues, Eugene Wittkopf, and John Zaller.

94. This would seem to represent a misspecification, either in logic or in modeling. A good example is Somalia, which began with support from eight out of ten and ended up with support from fewer than four in ten; an average support level would not be a very good measure of support for Somalia in such a case and might in fact be biased, since polling was not conducted with a great deal of regularity over the course of the operation. See Larson 1996a for an analysis of the date on Somalia.

95. For example, Jentleson and colleagues (1992, 1998) focus on principal policy objective, while Klarevas and O'Connor (1994) focus on costs, and Gartner and Segura (1998) claim "a generalizable theory of casualties and opinion," not a generalizable theory of support for wars and other military operations.

96. Jentleson's (1992, 1998) "halo effect" for quick-and-decisive outcomes is such an ad hoc exception to his more general theory of support as a function of principal policy objective. In the present work, the rather obvious prediction of higher support for faster- and cheaper-than-expected success is an explicit prediction of the model, and no ad hoc exceptions are necessary.

97. Gartner and Segura (1998) seek to explain support for Vietnam and Korea as a function of marginal casualties in those wars, but appear to have developed a theory of questionable value for making predictions outside the cases they used. For example, their theory does not help to explain how it is that support remained both high and relatively constant both in the case of Panama, where there were roughly as many casualties as in Somalia, and over the course of World War II, where the casualties were horrific. Nor does the theory explain why most of the decline in support for Somalia might have occurred between January and September 1993, when casualties increased only modestly. Put another way, their theory inadequately addresses the factors that regulate the rate at which support declines as a function of casualties, despite clear evidence that this rate of decline varies widely across cases.

98. See Larson 1996a, 1996b, and this essay, for one pretheoretic conjecture on why this should be.

99. See table A1, in the appendix.

100. See table A2, in the appendix.

REFERENCES

Ajzen, Icek, and Martin Fishbein. 1980. *Understanding Attitudes and Predicting Social Behavior.* Englewood Cliffs, N.J.: Prentice-Hall.

Almond, Gabriel. 1950. *The American People and Foreign Policy.* New Haven: Yale University Press.

Ayres, Robert U. 1969. *Technological Forecasting and Long-Range Planning.* New York: McGraw-Hill.

Behr, R. L., and Shanto Iyengar. 1985. "Television News, Real-World Cues, and Changes in the Public Agenda." *Public Opinion Quarterly* 49:38–57.

Belknap, George, and Angus Campbell. 1951–52. "Political Party Identification and Attitudes Toward Foreign Policy." *Public Opinion Quarterly* 15, no. 4 (winter): 601–23.

Bennett, Lance W. 1990. "Toward a Theory of Press-State Relations in the United States." *Journal of Communication* 40 (spring): 103–25.

———. 1996. *News: The Politics of Illusion,* 3d ed. White Plains, N.Y.: Longman.

Bennett, Lance W., and David L. Paletz. 1994. *Taken By Storm: The Media, Public Opinion, and U.S. Foreign Policy in the Gulf War.* Chicago: University of Chicago.

Betts, Richard K. 1995–96. "What Will It Take to Deter the United States." *Parameters* (winter): 70–79.

Blalock, Hubert M. 1963. "Correlated Independent Variables: The Problem of Multicollinearity." *Social Forces* 62 (December): 233–38.

Brady, Henry E., and Stephen Ansolabehere. 1989. "The Nature of Utility Functions in Mass Publics." *American Political Science Review* 83, no. 1 (March): 143–63.

Brady, Henry E., and Gary R. Orren. 1992. "Polling Pitfalls: Sources of Error in Public Opinion Surveys." In *Media Polls in American Politics,* ed. Thomas E. Mann and Gary Orren, 55–94. Washington, D.C.: Brookings.

Brown, Michael. 1995. "Operation Balkan Storm." *Washington Post* (July 25): 15.

Bueno de Mesquita, Bruce. 1983. "The Costs of War: A Rational Expectations Approach." *American Political Science Review* 77:347–57.

Bueno de Mesquita, Bruce, and Randolph M. Siverson. 1995. "War and the Survival of Political Leaders: A Comparative Study on Regime Types and Political Accountability." *American Political Science Review* 89:841–55.

Burbach, David T. 1994. "Presidential Approval and the Use of Force." DACS working paper, Defense and Arms Control Studies Program, MIT Center for International Affairs (May).

Cantril, Hadley. 1947. *Gauging Public Opinion.* Princeton: Princeton University Press.

Churchman, C.W., and R.L. Ackoff. 1954. "An Approximate Measure of Value." *Journal of Operations Research Society of America* 2, no. 2 (May).

Clogg, Clifford C. 1984. "Some Statistical Models for Analyzing Why Surveys Disagree." In *Surveying Subjective Phenomena,* ed. Charles F. Turner and Elizabeth Martin, 2:319–66. New York: Russell Sage Foundation.

Cohen, Bernard C. 1963. *The Press and Foreign Policy.* Princeton: Princeton University Press.

Commission on America's National Interests. 1996. *America's National Interests* (July).

Converse, Philip. 1964. "The Nature of Belief Systems among Mass Publics." In *Ideology and Discontent,* ed. D. Apter, 206–61. New York: Free Press.

Converse, Philip, and Howard Schuman. 1970. " 'Silent Majorities' and the Vietnam War." *Scientific American* (June): 17–25.

Costner, Herbert L. 1971. "Theory, Deduction, and Rules of Correspondence." In *Causal Models in the Social Sciences,* ed. Hubert M. Blalock, Jr., 299–319. Chicago: Aldine Publishing.

Diesing, Paul. 1971. *Patterns of Discovery in the Social Sciences.* Chicago: Aldine-Atherton.

Downs, Anthony. 1957. *An Economic Theory of Democracy.* New York: Harper and Row.

Downs, George W., and David M. Rocke. 1994. "Conflict, Agency, and Gambling for Resurrection: The Principal-Agent Problem Goes to War." *American Journal of Political Science* 38 (May): 362–80.

Dror, Yehezkel. 1969. *The Prediction of Political Feasibility.* Santa Monica: RAND, P-4044 (April).

Easton, David. 1953. *The Political System.* New York: Alfred A. Knopf.

———. 1965. *A Framework for Political Analysis.* Englewood Cliffs, N.J.: Prentice-Hall.

Ferejohn, John A., and James H. Kuklinski. 1990. *Information and Democratic Processes.* Urbana: University of Illinois Press.

Fiorina, Morris P. 1975. "Formal Models in Political Science." *American Journal of Political Science* 19, no. 1 (February): 133–59.

Friedman, Milton. 1953. "The Methodology of Positive Economics." In *Essays in Positive Economics,* 3–43. Chicago: University of Chicago Press.

Gamson, William, and Andre Modigliani. 1966. "Knowledge and Foreign Policy Opinion." *Public Opinion Quarterly* 30:187–99.

George, Alexander L. 1980. "Policy-Relevant Theory." In *Presidential Decisionmaking in Foreign Policy: The Effective Use of Information and Advice,* 239–62. Boulder, Colo.: Westview.

———. 1989. "Domestic Constraints on Regime Change in U.S. Foreign Policy: The Need for Policy Legitimacy." In *American Foreign Policy: Theoretical Essays,* ed. G. John Ikenberry, 583–608. New York: HarperCollins.

George, Alexander L., and Richard Smoke. 1974. "The Role of Theory in Situational Analysis." In *Deterrence in American Foreign Policy: Theory and Practice,* 509–15. New York: Columbia University Press.

Gerner, Deborah J., Philip A. Schrodt, Ronald A. Francisco, and Judith L. Weddle. 1994. "Machine Coding of Event Data Using Regional and International Sources." *International Studies Quarterly* 38:91–119.

Habermas, Jürgen. 1996. *Contributions to a Discourse Theory of Law and Democracy.* Cambridge: MIT Press.

Hamilton, Richard F. 1968. "A Research Note on the Mass Support for 'Tough' Military Initiatives." *American Sociological Review* 33, no. 3 (June): 439–45.

Hastie, Reid. 1986. "A Primer of Information-Processing Theory for the Political Scientist." In *Political Cognition,* ed. Richard R. Lau and David O. Sears, 11–39. Hillsdale, N.J.: Lawrence Erlbaum Associates, Publishers.

Hodges, James. 1991. *Six (or So) Things You Can Do with a Bad Model.* Santa Monica: RAND, N-3381-RC.

Hodges, James, and James Dewar. 1992. *Is It You or Your Model Talking? A Framework for Model Validation.* Santa Monica: RAND, R-4114-AF/A/OSD.

Holsti, Ole R., and James N. Rosenau. 1990a. "The Emerging U.S. Consensus on Foreign Policy." *Orbis* (Fall): 579–95.

———. 1990b. "The Structure of Foreign Policy Attitudes among American Leaders." *Journal of Politics* 52, no. 1 (February).

Hsüntze. 1928. *The Collected Works.* London.

Iyengar, Shanto. 1991. *Is Anyone Responsible?* Chicago: University of Chicago.

Janis, Irving L., and Leon Mann. 1977. *Decision Making: A Psychological Analysis of Conflict, Choice, and Commitment.* New York: Free Press.

Jeffords, Susan, and Lauren Rabinovitz. 1994. *Seeing through the Media.* New Brunswick: Rutgers University Press.

Jentleson, Bruce. 1992. "The Pretty Prudent Public: Post Post-Vietnam American Opinion on the Use of Military Force." *International Quarterly* 36:49–74.

Jentleson, Bruce, and Rebecca Britton. 1998. "Still Pretty Prudent: Post–Cold War American Public Opinion on the Use of Military Force." *Journal of Conflict Resolution* 42, no. 4 (August): 395–417.

Kagay, Michael R. 1992. "Variability without Fault: Why Even Well-Designed Polls Can Disagree." In *Media Polls in American Politics,* ed. Thomas E. Mann and Gary Orren, 95–124. Washington, D.C.: Brookings.

Kernell, Samuel. 1993. *Going Public: New Strategies of Presidential Leadership.* 2d ed. Washington, D.C.: Congressional Quarterly.

Klarevas, Louis, and Daniel O'Connor. 1994. *At What Cost? American Mass Public Opinion and the Use of Force Abroad.* Photocopy.

Krone, Robert M. 1981. "Political Feasibility and Military Decisionmaking." *Journal of Political and Military Sociology* 9 (spring): 49–60.

Kull, Steven, and Clay Ramsay. 1993. *U.S. Public Attitudes on Involvement in Somalia.* Program on International Policy Attitudes, School of Public Affairs. College Park: University of Maryland (October 26).

———. 1994. *U.S. Public Attitudes on U.S. Involvement in Haiti.* Program on International Policy Attitudes, School of Public Affairs. College Park: University of Maryland (August 22).

Larson, Eric V. 1996a. *Casualties and Consensus: The Historical Role of Casualties in Domestic Support for U.S. Military Operations.* Santa Monica: RAND, MR-726-RC.

———. 1996b. *Ends and Means in the Democratic Conversation: The Historical Role of Casualties in Domestic Support for U.S. Wars and Military Operations.* Ph.D. diss., Santa Monica: RGSD-124.

Lasswell, Harold. 1971. *A Pre-View of the Policy Sciences.* New York: American Elsevier.

Lippmann, Walter. 1922. *Public Opinion.* New York: Macmillan.

———. 1925. *The Phantom Public.* New York: Harcourt, Brace.

———. 1955. *Essays in the Public Philosophy.* Boston: Little, Brown.

Lunch, William L., and Peter W. Sperlich. 1979. "American Public Opinion and the War in Vietnam." *Western Political Quarterly* 32, no. 1: 21–44.

Luttwak, Edward. 1994. "Where are the Great Powers?" *Foreign Affairs* (July/August).

MacKuen, Michael B. 1984a. "Exposure to Information, Belief Integration, and Individual Responsiveness to Agenda Change." *American Political Science Review* 78:372–91.

———. 1984b. "Reality, the Press, and Citizens' Political Agendas." In *Surveying Subjective Phenomena,* ed. Charles F. Turner and Elizabeth Martin, 443–73. New York: Russell Sage Foundation.

MacKuen, Michael B., and Steven L. Coombs. 1981. *More than News: Media Power in Public Affairs.* Beverly Hills: Sage Publications.

Majone, Giandomenico. 1975a. "The Feasibility of Social Policies." *Policy Sciences* 6:49–69.

———. 1975b. "On the Notion of Political Feasibility." *European Journal of Political Research* 3:259–74.

McClosky, Herbert. 1964. "Consensus and Ideology in American Politics." *American Political Science Review* 58:361–82.

Meernik, James. 1994. "Presidential Decision Making and the Political Use of Military Force." *International Studies Quarterly* 38:121–38.

Meltsner, Arnold. 1972. "Political Feasibility and Policy Analysis." *Public Administration Review* 32:859–67.

Miller, James G. 1978. *Living Systems.* New York: McGraw-Hill.

Milstein, Jeffrey S. 1974. *Dynamics of the Vietnam War.* Columbus: Ohio State University.

Modigliani, Andre. 1972. "Hawks and Doves, Isolationism and Political Distrust: An Analysis of Public Opinion on Military Policy." *American Political Science Review* 66:960–78.

Mueller, John E. 1973. *War, Presidents, and Public Opinion.* New York: John Wiley.

———. 1977. "Changes in American Public Attitudes toward International Involvement." In *The Limits of Military Intervention,* ed. Ellen Stern. Beverly Hills: Sage Publications.

———. 1994. *Policy and Opinion in the Gulf War.* Chicago: University of Chicago Press.

Neustadt, Richard E. 1990. *Presidential Power and the Modern Presidents.* New York: Free Press.

Neuman, Johanna. 1996. *Lights, Camera, War: Is Media Technology Driving International Politics?* New York: St. Martin's Press.

Newman, W. Russell. 1986. *The Paradox of Mass Politics: Knowledge and Opinion in the American Electorate.* Cambridge: Harvard University Press.

Newport, Frank. 1995. "Americans Still Cautious about U.S. Involvement in Bosnia." *Gallup Poll Monthly* (December): 31–33.

Nincic, Donna J., and Miroslav Nincic. 1995b. "Commitment to Military Intervention: The Democratic Government as Economic Investor." *Journal of Peace Research* 32 (November): 413–26.

Nincic, Miroslav. 1992a. *Democracy and Foreign Policy: The Fallacy of Political Realism.* New York: Columbia University Press.

————. 1992b. "A Sensible Public: New Perspectives on Popular Opinion and Foreign Policy." *Journal of Conflict Resolution* 36 (December): 772–89.

Ordeshook, Peter C. 1986. *Game Theory and Political Theory.* Cambridge: Cambridge University Press.

Page, Benjamin I., and Robert Y. Shapiro. 1992. *The Rational Public.* Chicago: University of Chicago Press.

Petty, R.E., and J.T. Cacioppo. 1981. *Attitudes and Persuasion: Classic and Contemporary Approaches.* Dubuque, Iowa: William C. Brown Company, Publishers.

————. 1986. *Communication and Persuasion: Central and Peripheral Routes to Attitude Change.* New York: Springer-Verlag.

Pfiffner, James P. 1996. *The Strategic Presidency.* 2d ed. Leavenworth: University of Kansas Press.

Popkin, Samuel L. 1994. *The Reasoning Voter.* Chicago: Chicago University Press.

Richman, Alvin. 1994. "The American Public's 'Rules of Military Engagement' in the Post Cold War Era." Paper presented at the annual meeting of the American Political Science Association.

————. 1995. "When Should We Be Prepared to Fight?" *Public Perspective* (April/May): 44–49.

Rielly, John E., ed. 1995. *American Public Opinion and U.S. Foreign Policy, 1995.* Chicago: Chicago Council on Foreign Relations.

Rosen, Steven. 1970. "Cost Limits for Preferences in Foreign Policy Issue-Areas." *Peace Research Society, Papers,* XVII, Philadelphia Conference: 61–73.

————. 1972. "War Power and the Willingness to Suffer." In *Peace, War, and Numbers,* ed. Bruce Russett, 167–83. Beverly Hills: Sage Publications.

Rosenau, James N., and Ole R. Holsti. 1989. "U.S. Leadership in a Shrinking World: The Breakdown of Consensus and the Emergency of Conflicting Belief Systems." In *American Foreign Policy: Theoretical Essays,* ed. G. John Ikenberry, 561–82. New York: HarperCollins.

Russett, Bruce. 1990–91. "Doves, Hawks, and U.S. Public Opinion." *Political Science Quarterly* 105, no. 4: 515–38.

Russett, Bruce, and Miroslav Nincic. 1976. "American Opinion on the Use of Military Force Abroad." *Political Science Quarterly* 91, no. 3 (fall): 411–31.

Schaar, J. 1970. "Legitimacy in the Modern State." In *Power and Community,* ed. P. Green and S. Levinson, 276–327. New York: Pantheon. Cited in Trout 1975.

Schuman, Howard. 1972. "Two Sources of Antiwar Sentiment in America." *American Journal of Sociology* 78, no. 3: 513–36.

Simon, Herbert, and Allen Newell. 1956. "Models: Their Uses and Limitations." In *The State of the Social Sciences,* ed. Leonard D. White, 66–83. Chicago: University of Chicago Press.

Seelye, Katherine Q. 1995. "Balkan Accord: In Congress; Anguished, Senators Vote to Support Bosnia Mission; Clinton Off to Paris Signing." *New York Times* (December 14): 1.

Skowronek, Stephen. 1993. *The Politics Presidents Make: Leadership from John Adams to George Bush.* Cambridge, Mass.: Belknap Press.

Sloan, Stanley R. 1994. *The United States and the Use of Force in the Post–Cold War World: Toward Self-Deterrence?* Report prepared for the Committee on Foreign Affairs, House of Representatives, by the Congressional Research Service, Library of Congress (August).

Smith, Tom W. 1978. "In Search of House Effects: A Comparison of Responses to Various Questions by Different Survey Organizations." *Public Opinion Quarterly* 42 (winter): 443–63.

Smoke, Ricard. 1976. "Theory for and about Policy." In *In Search of Global Patterns,* ed. James N. Rosenau, 185–91. New York: Free Press.

———. 1994. "On the Importance of Policy Legitimacy." *Political Psychology* 15, no. 1: 97–110.

Smoke Richard, and Alexander George. 1973. "Theory for Policy in International Affairs." *Policy Sciences* 4:387–413.

Sobel, Richard. 1993. "Public Opinion in U.S. Foreign Policy: The Controversy over Contra Aid." In *Public Opinion in U.S. Foreign Policy: The Controversy over Contra Aid,* 1–18. Lanham, MD: Rowman Littlefield Publishers.

———. 1996. "U.S. and European Attitudes toward Intervention in the Former Yugoslavia: Mourir pour la Bosnie?" In *The World and Yugoslavia's Wars,* ed. Richard Ullmann, 145–81. New York: Council on Foreign Relations.

———. 1998. "The Polls—Trends: United States Intervention in Bosnia." *Public Opinion Quarterly* 62:250–78.

Stanton, Frank. 1978. *Public Policy and Public Assent.* Santa Monica: RAND, P-6320 (May).

Sudman, Seymour. 1982. "The President and the Polls." *Public Opinion Quarterly* 46 (fall): 301–10.

Sunstein, Cass R. 1996. "Democracy Isn't What You Think." Review of Jürgen Habermas' *Between Facts and Norms: Contributions to a Discourse Theory of Law and Democracy. New York Times Book Review* (August 18): 29.

Taylor, Charles F. 1984. "Why Do Surveys Disagree? Some Preliminary Hypotheses and Some Disagreeable Answers." In *Surveying Subjective Phenomena,* ed. Charles F. Turner and Elizabeth Martin, 159–214. New York: Russell Sage Foundation.

Trout, B. Thomas. 1975. "Rhetoric Revisited: Political Legitimation and the Cold War." *International Studies Quarterly* 19, no. 3 (September): 251–84.

University of Maryland at College Park. 1995. "New Poll Finds Public Divided on Sending Troops to Bosnia but Majority in Favor if U.S. Participation Essential to Peace." News release (November 27).

Wittkopf, Eugene. 1990. *The Faces of Internationalism: Public Opinion and American Foreign Policy.* Durham, N.C.: Duke University Press.

———. 1994. "Faces of Internationalism in a Transitional Environment." *Journal of Conflict Resolution* 38, no. 3 (September): 376–401.

———. 1996. "What Americans Really Think about Foreign Policy." *Washington Quarterly* 19, no. 3 (summer): 91–106.

Yankelovich, Daniel. 1991. *Coming to Public Judgment: Making Democracy Work in a Complex World.* Syracuse, N.Y.: Syracuse University Press.

Zaller, John R. 1984. *The Role of Elites in Shaping Public Opinion.* Ph.D. diss., University Microfilms.

———. 1992. *The Nature and Origins of Mass Opinion.* Cambridge: Cambridge University Press.

———. 1993. "The Converse-McGuire Model of Attitude Change and the Gulf War Opinion Rally." *Political Communication* 10:369–88.

———. 1994a. "Elite Leadership of Mass Opinion: New Evidence from the Gulf War." In *Taken by Storm: The Media, Public Opinion, and U.S. Foreign Policy in the Gulf War,* ed. Lance W. Bennett and David L. Paretz, 186–209. Chicago: University of Chicago Press.

———. 1994b. "Strategic Politicians, Public Opinion, and the Gulf Crisis." In *Taken by Storm: The Media, Public Opinion, and U.S. Foreign Policy in the Gulf War,* ed. Lance W. Bennett and David L. Paretz, 250–74. Chicago: University of Chicago Press.

Zaller, John R., and Stanley Feldman. 1992. "A Simple Theory of the Survey Response: Answering Questions versus Revealing Preferences." *American Journal of Political Science* 36, no. 3 (August): 579–616.

# B. The Relevance of Related Approaches

# Ethnic Fears and Security Dilemmas: Managing Uncertainty in Africa

*Donald Rothchild*

The purpose of this essay is to draw certain parallels between domestic and international strife and, thus, shed light on the manner of control by the latter. Specific implications for U.S. foreign policy may follow from a contribution to relevant knowledge that, like this essay, focuses on both the contextual and instrumental dimensions of actions. A policy view on ethnic relations cast in instrumental and contextual terms raises hopes among many observers that intergroup cooperation can be facilitated through the adoption of appropriate policies. For the primordialist school, ethnic groups are characterized as natural units with firmly engraved characteristics; the effect of this primordialist mindset is to make conflict well-nigh inevitable and to complicate reciprocity and political bargaining. Instrumental and contextual approaches considerably widen the scope for political exchange relations, enlarging the possibilities for policy to play a key role in facilitating peace negotiations and to encourage the adoption of moderate politics. This essay begins by recognizing the chance that ethnic conflicts, like conflicts between states, can spiral out of control and create a security dilemma; it then goes on to probe the instrumental relations between various domestic and international policies and the desired outcome of peace.

Africa's ethnic relations vary according to the situation on the ground, ranging from the stable and predictable to the highly threatening. In best-case circumstances (such as Botswana and Mauritius), where groups have felt secure in their relationship with the state and with each other, they have been able to work out regularized rules of relations. By the way that these rules structure interactions, they can help to *prevent* intense conflicts from arising and from developing a dynamic and possibly destructive life of their own. The ethnic leaders' sense of uncertainty about the intentions of an ethnic-dominated state have therefore declined noticeably, and they have come to perceive a situation of increasing interdependence. To be sure, intergroup conflicts over resources, positions, and power continue to manifest themselves; however, such conflicts can be managed within the broadly accepted norms of the political system.

These norms generally include the participation of all main ethnic interests in the decision-making and administrative processes. The main ethnic and state actors come as a result to recognize the possibility of achieving beneficial outcomes in accordance with accepted regime rules. Such a realization of possible benefit from working within the system over time contributes in turn to moderate, centrist politics and to the stability of the political system. The security that evolves from such encounters represents a constructive form of social learning, important "because it gives people an opportunity to relax enough in a risk-free environment so that they stop seeing strangeness and difference as a threat."[1]

Contrary to the impressions of Western observers, many of Africa's ethnic groups have in fact lived comfortably side by side for a considerable time, emphasizing other lines of cleavage and adopting pragmatic perceptions about each other's purposes. Ethnic elites have generally made reasonable demands on governing authorities and displayed a preparedness to include elite representatives from other ethnic groups within the government's decision-making arena.[2] Those observers of the African political scene who overstate the enduring antipathies of ethnic groups or who minimize the opportunities for constructive interethnic relations are not only ill-informed but also perpetuating cultural myths that may result in very harmful outcomes.

However, what about the less common (but potentially dangerous) circumstances where the rules of the game are unclear or unenforceable, and where misperceptions about an opponent's aims can lead to a narrow calculation of elite and group interests? The kinds of intense conflicts that will be discussed in this essay arise in large part both from the political elite's disregard of the political rules of encounter and from the decline of the state capacity. The appearance of a repressive, authoritarian state, which often covers over the reality of weakness at the political center, and the decline (even collapse) of the state itself create the conditions for an emerging anarchy in which intense conflicts among ethnic groups are most likely to emerge. Uncertainty about the state and its capabilities already is evident. As the state enforcer weakens and leaves groups to their own devices, a spiraling competition and conflict can emerge, causing a firming-up of ethnic group loyalties and a cycle of interethnic violence.

In a context of state weakening, limited information, hostile historical memories, competitive arming, and spiraling individual and group insecurity, it would be wishful thinking to anticipate that all group leaders would be able to negotiate their differences within the political system. Driven by intense emotions of fear and hostility and by a strong desire to be included in their group, members also come at times to view their self-interest in terms of nonnegotiable demands for power and autonomy. In civil war encounters, for example, hard-line perceptions are evident in currently available data that indicate that intrastate struggles in the twentieth century have ended in military victory or capitulation in some 75 percent of the cases.[3] With memories of peaceful coexistence obscured by new uncertainties and antipathies in the contemporary context, the incentive structure makes negotiation or renegotiation of a contract among ethnic leaders difficult. Leaders cannot make the kinds of credible commitments necessary for a binding contract that will stand the test of time.[4] In the absence of such believable commitments, the circumstances are set in place that will lead to increasing group anxieties and interethnic violence. Commenting on the evolution of intense ethnic conflict, Russell Hardin notes the possibility of "a step-wise progression from identification with a group, to mobilization of still stronger identification, to implicit conflict with another group, and finally to violence, particularly when both the group and other group are faced with increasing incentives for preemptive action."[5]

Hardin's point regarding preemptive action touches on important theoretical insights. Fearing that their opponent will gain control of the state and its distributive processes, the main ethnic actors, lacking reliable information about an adversary's intentions, can move from moderate to extremist politics — and, in unique circumstances, launch a preemptive military strike. Both sides are not likely to take preventive action at the same time, giving rise to what international relations theorists call a *security dilemma*, where unilateral action based on the calculations of group self-interest and security become paramount. It is a relatively unique but fearsome possibility.

The setting conducive to these military-type actions within the state is critical. Where ambitious ethnic elites mobilize their supporters to protect or advance group interests, old patterns of social cleavage frequently recede and enable ethnicity to "emerge as the only relevant defining characteristi[c] of group identities."[6] Such ethnic polarization may be a very modern phenomenon, but the strong desire of ethnic constituents to have their representatives included and the perception of common purpose that members associate with the group can prove mighty catalysts for collective action.

In those special situations where high-stakes struggles for scarce resources, the safeguarding of identities, and physical survival have occurred (often in a context of weak states), political competition and conflict among political elites can act as a magnifier of a people's uncertainty about its own fate.[7] Individuals in developing countries understandably fear an uncertain political and economic future as well as the less tangible, but psychologically quite real, needs for massive readjustments in terms of new values, outlooks, and orientations. Moreover, leaders and group members dread the prospect of permanent minority status and the insecurity this can entail, especially where ethnic polarization and lack of reliable information about the intentions of rivals weaken ties of reciprocity and contribute to zero-sum assessments of adversary intentions. Under such circumstances, ethnic elites can manipulate stereotypic perceptions of adversary groups and evoke extreme fears based on past myths (whether real or imagined), causing an increase in social distance and an undermining of orderly coexistence between ethnic peoples.

These belligerent stereotypes, made acutely threatening through the diffusion of ideas by the mass media, may be directed by majorities against minorities, by minorities against majorities, and by subethnic elements against one another. In both Rwanda and Serbia, the radio proved a particularly powerful weapon in the hands of determined elites. Serbian president Slobodan Milosevic used state radio to mobilize support for aggressive action and subsequent war. In Rwanda, Hutu ideologues used the privately owned Radio Mille Collines to fan the frenzied flames of genocide among people harboring memories of past oppression and violence.[8] Thus, even though grossly exaggerated in relation to empirically verifiable phenomena, this media-directed ethnic stereotyping gravely broadened and intensified conflict between neighboring ethnic peoples.[9]

In this essay I examine worst-case scenarios to gain insight into the opportunities to develop what Miroslav Nincic describes in the introduction as "policy-relevant" approaches to contain the spread of ethnic fear. I emphasize the importance of understanding the factors that give rise to group uncertainties, and I stress the role that confidence-building measures can play. This leads me to conclude that confidence-building measures are very useful in promoting cooperation where relatively stable relations persist; however, they are not likely to be sufficient where a security dilemma prevails and elite suspicions give rise to escalating threats and actions. In today's world, the breakdown of states and the occurrence of genocidal practices can make hitherto unacceptable scenarios seem more palatable. Such alternatives as population exchanges, ethnic regroupment, partition, and secession become logical in this changed environment, because they appear to offer reduced "incentives and opportunities for further combat."[10] But in the end, when threatening perceptions are accepted as reality, no individual or group feels secure, and there are no dependable protections against state or ethnic groups determined on a destructive course.

Because an increasing number of wars are intrastate, a focus on the ethnic and intrastate dimensions seems warranted in post–Cold War times. However, my findings, which are drawn from Africa's contemporary experiences, have generalizable implications of interest to international relations theorists who concentrate on other kinds of issues. For example, the difficulties in securing reliable information and communicating among ethnic elites who are engaged in conflict are analogous to the situation of severe security dilemmas among states: the dilemma exists because intentions are not transparent, and communication and reliable information are most needed when they are most difficult to secure. Similarly, confidence-building mechanisms and humanitarian interventions are necessary but, in some instances, insufficient safeguards against abusive and damaging behavior. Rwanda and Bosnia should alert us to the fact that firebreaks are essential to prevent belligerence from spiraling out of control.

## Possible Entrapment in a "Security Dilemma"

How can one explain that a people's need for identification can lead to terrible acts of organized destruction, including the planned and systematic murder of the members of another community? To understand this, it is first necessary to stress the potential costs of membership in a group. As ethnic leaders pursue their separate interests and play "the ethnic card" among peoples conscious of their ethnic identities, they may, in emotionally charged situations, find themselves and their constituents entrapped in a deadly encounter from which there may be no escape.[11]

Such a fatal outcome seems paradoxical. In theory, all would benefit from mutual cooperation; yet the defection of group leaders and their ethnic constituents, explained in part by their ambitions and their fears of being "violated" (possibly annihilated), may preclude joint problem-solving outcomes.[12] The result is to be ensnared in a "security dilemma."[13] If an anarchic world order requires self-help to reassure states against extreme vulnerability, the African ethnic counterpart is their residence in a "soft" state that is unable to impose its regulations throughout the territory regarded as being under its control. Such a soft state cannot (and may not want to) guarantee the safety of its ethnic minorities, who must then fend for themselves, providing for their own well-being and preservation.[14] The political context within such countries as Liberia, Somalia, and Rwanda can therefore come to resemble the lack of central control that marks the international realm.[15]

In such a situation, one group's efforts to obtain its own security (gaining extraproportional allocations or positions, arming, seizing territory) may be threatening to another. Aggression leads to countermeasures, lessening the safety of all. As Hans Morgenthau noted about relations among states at the time of World War I:

> In the end, the general conflagration in 1914 was made inevitable by the fear that the other side would change the power relations decisively in its favor if not forestalled by such a change in one's own favor. In the two antagonistic blocs, Russia and Austria especially were animated by fear. The fear of the other's suspected imperialism bred imperialism in reaction, which, in turn, gave substance to the original fear.[16]

Robert Jervis observes (when writing about interstate relations) that "because offensive and defensive postures are the same, status-quo states acquire the same kind of arms that are sought by aggressors. And because the offense has the advantage over the defense, attacking is the best route to protecting what you have; status-quo states will therefore behave like aggressors."[17] The logic at work here is that of a process culminating in a preventive strike: "the party that is likely to become weaker may choose to fight now rather than later."[18] Under these circumstances, the element of surprise is viewed as shifting the cost ratio in favor of a first strike.[19]

When leaders and constituents perceive their goals to be incompatible with those of their adversary and when they become entrapped in a situation where intergroup perceptions are menacing and the norms of managing conflict ineffective, strife can escalate dangerously. Each side searches for security and rules out compromise; each fears treachery and a loss of face and remains anxious that any concessions on its part will be perceived as a sign of weakness by its state or ethnic opponent.

In the most constructive scenarios in intensely conflictive situations, people on both sides of the ethnic divide, believing that neither party can prevail in a war, may pull back from the brink and recognize the existence of a mutually hurting stalemate. In this Chicken-type game, leaders may conclude that a peace agreement is preferable to no agreement at all and consequently retreat from the prospect of an extended military encounter. Such a swerving to avoid the consequences of a deadly struggle may lead the representatives of both contending groups to negotiate their differences and therefore to prevent the slide down a slippery slope to combat. In highly charged situations, leaders may not always have the maneuverability to compromise with their rivals, but the chances for some type of conflict avoidance increase where rival leaders are careful to save face for their opponent at critical junctures.

However, when ethnic leaders (including those controlling the state and its institutions) pursue their interests to the logical end, irrespective of the consequences to their constituents and the society at large, the breaking of connections may seem preferable to political negotiations or concessions. Fear on the part of ethnic elites that their opponents will take advantage of cooperative moves to engage in cheating leads communal leaders to justify an airing of past grievances in the mass media and possibly to take military action.[20] Such moves may assume the form of a preventive strike intended to ensure a group's domination or separation. Ethnic leaders can attempt to justify such resorts to forceful measures by contending that they provide for the group's safety and survival. As Arnold Wolfers observes, high levels of enmity increase "the likelihood that Machiavellian practices will become necessary and morally justified."[21]

The dilemma is manifest: Efforts to promote the security of one actor leave all actors with a heightened sense of insecurity. In the process of enhancing the safety of one group, interelite linkages become gravely weakened, leading to societal incoherence and state collapse. When the logic of the security dilemma is pursued to its ultimate end, everyone may be snared in a destructive relationship yet remain unwilling on their own to risk the cooperative intergroup initiatives needed to overcome their fears. As the actors retreat to their ethnic containers, the trap is sprung, leaving everyone enmeshed in a Hobbesian world of group against group. At this point, the initial tactical moves intended to promote group security can give way to a *system* of genocide.[22] In René Lemarchand's words, "As much as the appalling scale of the massacre, it is the element of planned annihilation that gives the Rwanda killings their genocidal quality."[23]

Once such frenzied ethnic killings take place, political memory sets in; at this point, it becomes extremely difficult to pick up the pieces and return to normal patterns of relationship. Thus one Tutsi survivor declared in Rwanda, "How can we talk about reconciliation with people who killed your family? I think the only solution is to kill the killers."[24] The continuing sense of threat becomes an incentive for an ongoing process of strikes and counterstrikes. In principle, preventive measures represent the best possible escape from the prospect of continuing war, because they structure ethnic group relations in such a way as to promote an iterated bargaining scenario that leads over time to the development of trust.[25] But once the norms of reciprocity break down and the containment of conflict seems increasingly doubtful, what courses of internal or external action offer practical possibilities for managing this deteriorating cycle of encounters between the ethnically controlled state and other ethnic groups? To begin to answer this question, we turn to a discussion of the policy-relevant options for escaping from an insecure future.

### Policy Relevance: Internal Options for Coping with Uncertainty

Once one recognizes that severe limits exist on choice, it is important to ask what scope remains for promoting trust and restructuring payoffs after an ethnic-based crisis has burst upon the scene. At the outset, it is important to start by stressing the limited scope for interethnic bargaining within the state and then turn to the role of institutions in channeling conflict along constructive lines and thereby reducing fear and ill will.

Efforts to negotiate agreements between competing ethnic interests can take place over a variety of issues: the allocation of state resources, recruitment policies, political autonomy, the location of industries, university scholarships, election procedures, cabinet positions, territory, minority rights and protections, and even issues affecting group identity. These negotiations can be direct or indirect, bilateral or trilateral. In normal times, when groups feel relatively secure in their relations and make modest demands upon state elites for tangible resources, ethnic groups act in a manner similar to other interest groups, and the bargaining process can lead to mutually acceptable outcomes.

However, because of the intensity of ethnic loyalties and commitments, ethnic-related bargains can also be difficult to achieve, even where a mediator is prepared to step into the intrastate conflict to facilitate a peaceful resolution of differences. In these cases, rivals' aggrieved memories and deep distrust of each other's intentions can lead to a severe credibility problem: their sense of uncertainty that their opponent will actually deliver on its bargain causes one if not both of them to be more vulnerable than if no agreement had been reached at all. Moreover, negotiated agreements can result in terms that are perceived to be disadvantageous. Thus, the concessions to ethnic minorities imposed by colonial outsiders as a condition for granting independence often lacked legitimacy in African eyes; in Ghana, Kenya, Zimbabwe, and elsewhere, the new leaders therefore moved quickly after independence to amend the most irksome provisions of their settlements. Later, when African states had consolidated their control, this distrust took other forms of expression. For example, Hutu hard-liners in Rwanda exhibited marked fears regarding the consequences of the power-sharing arrangement agreed to at Arusha in 1993 under extensive pressure from a coalition of external mediators; in their view, the Arusha accords threatened both their material ambitions and their desire to maintain their current dominance in Rwandan affairs.[26] This sense of menace is explained partly by the Tutsi mystique of great prowess and partly by the effects of the October 1993 Burundi coup where the Tutsi army launched a counterstrike four months after Melchior Ndadaye, a Hutu, emerged victorious in the country's first multiparty presidential election. These ambitions and fears combined into a destructive fury following the Arusha settlement, leading the Hutu hard-liners to deal with their perceived predicament by launching a preemptive strike.

In situations where the political rules of the game remain fluid and the negotiating parties continue to be distrustful of one another's intentions, to what extent can agreements on elite pacts help them to cope with the problem of commitment? Such pacts are relatively easy to put into place, because they involve "mutual security agreements in which parties forswear the use of violence to achieve their aims in exchange for protection under agreed-upon rules of the political game."[27] Participation in the pact is essentially limited to the elites who negotiated this security arrangement, and it lasts only so long as it fulfills the limited but important security needs of the signers. The pact as such tends to be a very personal and fragile form of agreement that survives only so long as a balance of military power persists and the rival elites are unable to create or restore regularized interethnic relations after civil wars. Thus, in Angola, when National Union for the Total Independence of Angola (UNITA) president Jonas Savimbi defected from the Bicesse peace process following the first round of the 1992 elections, deep distrust had carried over between adversaries into the postagreement period. Later, following renewed fighting and considerable destruction of life and property, the balance of forces tilted decisively in favor of government forces. This left Savimbi with little option but to agree to the UN-brokered Lusaka Protocol of 1994. Savimbi's reluctant compromise represented a coerced submission rather than a straightforward commitment to abide by the political rules of the game. As of 1998, peace in Angola still appears to be shaky, and a resumption of war remains quite conceivable. Nevertheless, there is still a possibility that over time trust could develop between the Angolan parties provided their behavior becomes routinized and confidence grows that the former adversaries are prepared to make a sustained commitment. In that event, it is the ongoing bargaining process that will establish the credibility of the new arrangement, a reflection of a learned relationship among formerly hostile elites that cannot be taken for granted.

Negotiated solutions are more likely to reduce uncertainty and the costs of encounter in more secure polyarchical circumstances, where agreements are genuinely acceptable to the authentic representatives of both sides. If the parties to an agreement have a stake in their rival's future cooperation, then they may be more prepared to negotiate in good faith; they have less need to keep up their guard, because a measure of interdependence has become an accepted fact. The processes of interelite negotiations leading up to independence or to a change of regimes after independence are more important guarantees of future security than are the provisions of the peace agreements themselves. The Kenyan and Zimbabwean independence negotiations brought together peoples who viewed one another in adversarial terms; through an ongoing bargaining relationship, they engaged in a learning process regarding each other's aspirations, fears, and shortcomings.[28]

People's attitudes and preferences have certainly undergone change during negotiations. Perhaps the most dramatic of these shifts in perception emerged in the Sudan during the 1971–72 peace negotiations in Addis Ababa. A northern general reportedly cried along with Canon Burgess Carr, who was leading a prayer at the end of the talks; the general was apparently remorseful over the large number of southerners killed during the war.[29] South Africa's African National Congress (ANC), despite the intensity of its struggle to overcome the apartheid regime, nevertheless continues to pursue a policy of reconciliation with the country's white community, even after winning decisively at the polls; ANC leaders are motivated largely by a desire to build a sense of confidence among the still economically powerful whites and to make the country appear an attractive place to foreign investors.[30] Thus, when negotiators become sensitized to their opponents' feelings of insecurity, they are often more prepared to create institutions aimed at moderating minority group fears and ending their sense of collective alienation. Such concessions make it possible for political minorities to begin to overcome their estrangement and to perceive a sense of common fate with the larger community. As René Lemarchand wisely notes regarding South Africa following the transition, "Because both whites and blacks have a stake in the economy a compromise on the economic front could be negotiated as part of a larger package proposal on the distribution of power."[31]

## Institutionalized Limitations within the State

Not only do political elites bargain over the nature of political institutions and over such contending issues as the allocation of resources and political positions, but they can also attempt to use institutions to reassure ethnic minorities about their future security in the country. In doing this, they use confidence-building measures to seek to create an institutional framework that reassures minority ethnic peoples about their future. As Howard Adelman writes, "Confidence building is not about the subjective feeling of trust but about the objective conditions that engender trust, that is, controlling the factors which produce legitimate fear, both the underlying unchanging realities and the rules or norms according to which conflict is waged."[32] In order to prevent ethnic interactions of a destructive type, then, it is important to focus on institutions within the state that engender trust between rival interests. This is a difficult but not impossible task.

Confidence-building measures are concessions by the state to societal elements anxious about their future. Such reassurance encourages their commitment to the new political order. It can involve an extension of material or psychological benefits, or a combination of these, in order to promote a sense of trust and well-being among political minorities or marginalized peoples.[33] Through packages of incentives, combining demonstrations of goodwill with rewards and punishments to promote cooperation, it may be possible to get recalcitrant elites to rethink their belligerent behavior and to cooperate in achieving common purposes. The context in which these confidence-building measures are employed is critical. The policy measures must be appropriate to satisfy the needs of the disaffected; otherwise they are likely to do little to overcome minority feelings of uncertainty and exposure.

Confidence-building measures designed to help adversaries cope with their feelings of insecurity are exemplified by establishing rules encouraging the formation of inclusive coalitions, organizing the rules on elections to promote wide participation and minority representation, and providing for the decentralization of political power to assure minority influence over local cultural and social affairs. Not only do institutional forms have an important, short-term impact on group autonomy, participation, and political influence, but by moderating ethnic fears, they can contribute to the development of democratic regimes (where losers can afford to lose because their ability to compete in the future is assured).[34] Instituting confidence-building rules can also help to constrain negative behavior, such as the generation of excessive demands by ethnic interests and the attempt by extremist politicians to outbid moderate leaders within their own community.

*First,* instituting rules promoting inclusive coalitions engenders trust among the affected ethnic elites, and to some extent among their followers, because participation in the cabinet, administration, or legislature involves an active role in setting policies that affect their interests. Inclusion is a concession made by a strong party to promote confidence on the part of minority ethnic interests; in making these concessions, governments assume that if minority organizations will participate in state affairs, they will have an incentive to act cooperatively. Exclusion has indeed resulted in destructive behavior: politicians who see no opportunity of playing a significant role in election processes may at times act as spoilers and may even mount violent opposition against state authority.[35] However, inclusion may not be the whole solution for antisocial behavior: in some cases, as Stephen Stedman asserts, "A leader's paranoia can render it impossible to assuage his fears of a negotiated settlement."[36] Ultimately, then, inclusiveness is likely to promote trust where the parties have pragmatic perceptions of their opponent's intentions and are prepared to respond reciprocally and enter into bargaining relationships.

Formal constitutional provisions promoting wide-ranging coalitions appeared in such polyarchical or elite power-sharing regimes as Mauritius, Nigeria (1979), and South Africa. Mauritius's "best loser" formula assured the inclusion of underrepresented communities in the legislature; and Nigeria's constitutional provisions on "federal character" provided that representatives from all states be appointed to the cabinet and other decision-making bodies.[37] As part of the negotiated compromise over pacted democracy in South Africa, the interim constitution stated that any party winning over 5 percent of the seats in the National Assembly was to be included in the cabinet on a proportional basis.[38] After the 1994 general election, this provision led to the establishment of a cabinet coalition composed of 18 members from the ANC, 6 from the National Party (NP), and 3 from the Inkatha Freedom Party (IFP). Such an incorporative strategy, as against that of a winner-take-all one, no doubt sacrificed some measure of equity and ANC party control over policy but was pursued to reassure minorities that they had a reserved place in the new South Africa.[39]

These elite power-sharing arrangements often leave certain groups disadvantaged (such as the Oromo Liberation Front and the All Amhara Peoples' Organization in Ethiopia) and are of very brief duration. In South Africa, the African community, with 75 percent of the vote, had no long-term incentive to concede formal power-sharing at the political center and therefore pushed for majoritarian features in the follow-up constitution of 1996. Even so, as in Kenya and Zimbabwe following decolonization, a process of informal political exchanges can be expected to survive in South Africa between an economically influential white community and a politically powerful ANC. The ANC would seem to have little choice but to negotiate informally with an Afrikaner-led bureaucracy, army, and business community, granting them security of tenure to gain regime stability.

Putting minorities in situations of power can certainly represent a means of reassuring these interests about their security. However, because such arrangements are often transitional in nature, these insurance incentives are at best limited protections. Moreover, as Robert Mattes contends, elite power-sharing can result in proportionally representative outcomes while still not ensuring proportional influence.[40] Numbers are not in themselves a protection of group interests, especially where the representatives of minority parties are assigned less important portfolios or where they lack access to key government officials. In fact, both majority and minority parties have at times rejected power-sharing arrangements, seeing these measures as coopting them into a system they oppose, or as inimical to their interests. Sri Lanka is a case of the former, for the rebel Liberation Tigers of Tamil Eelam rejected President Chandrika Kumaratunga's conciliatory proposal in 1995 for a new power-sharing arrangement, under which the Tamils would gain control of a semiautonomous region in the north; in part, the Tigers's decision is explained by the government's unwillingness to lift the siege of Jaffna before peace negotiations begin, uncertain whether the Tigers would use the cease-fire to prepare for future warfare.[41] The latter case of perceived disadvantage following from an agreement on power-sharing is exemplified by Rwanda. The signing of the Arusha Accords would have brought the Tutsi-led insurgents into the government and army on a favorable basis, but the accords triggered deep resentment among hard-line Hutu elites, who planned and subsequently carried out genocidal actions against both the Tutsi and the Hutu moderates. Thus inclusive policies can backfire and, if they are not handled with great sensitivity, can lead to unintended consequences.

*Second,* institutional rules can have a significant impact on the way that competitive elections are organized and administered, engendering minority confidence if the rules are respected. When party leaders agree to compete according to the political rules, there is the possibility of maintaining civility, encouraging openness, and providing for broad political participation. Under these circumstances, elections can have stabilizing implications and lead to long-term expectations of future electoral

competitions. Particularly in polyarchies, elections can open up the system to innovation and change, thus building confidence and preempting
more destructive forms of conflict. Elections can also legitimate the right
to rule, something that may be reassuring to highly exposed minorities
fearful of possible turbulence. Thus in Namibia, the UN-supervised voting for the constituent assembly in November 1989 followed by the
election of South West Africa People's Organization leader Sam Nujoma
as president in February 1990 had a calming effect on ethnic minorities,
because SWAPO leaders immediately set about supporting a mixed economy and adopting reconciliatory political policies. These liberal gestures
proved critical in reassuring most elements of civil society about their
roles during the postagreement implementation phase.

Elections can also be catalysts for contention and strife, however.
Particularly when politicians attempt to enlist the support of their ethnic
kinsmen by outflanking moderate political leaders through the use of
exclusivist and uncompromising appeals, they can undermine the networks of reciprocity so critical to stable intergroup relationships.[42] Ethnic outbidding can also endanger the position of minorities, especially
where values and identities remain unsettled and poverty makes the
struggle for state-controlled resources intense. These outbidding appeals
unleash passions that might remain latent under the prevailing centrist
politics. Moreover, the results of elections can be threatening to the
status of minority groups. Recognizing that the ethnic voter casts his or
her ballot in terms of a predetermined script, minority groups can come
to feel permanently excluded from power. The long-term prospect of
being overlooked in terms of political appointments contributes to their
feelings of alienation and to their fears about the future. Finally, if an
election victory should lead to a one-party dominant system, then minorities must rely on the vagaries of informal, face-to-face contacts rather
than institutionalized constraints to protect themselves.

There are several ways of organizing election rules to promote the
objective of inclusiveness. Election rules can be designed to ensure that
the president has the support of a broad-based constituency. In an effort
to break down parochialism by forcing candidates to appeal to a wide
cross-section of the community, Nigerians provided in the abortive 1993
Constitution that a winning candidate would have been deemed to be
elected when that person secured a simple majority of the total number
of votes cast as well as one-third of the votes cast in each of at least two-
thirds of the states. The regime of President Daniel arap Moi in Kenya
enacted similar provisions, requiring that the winning presidential candidate secure a plurality of the national vote as well as 25 percent of the
votes in at least five of the eight provinces. The impact of these rules is

to advantage a candidate with a national appeal, thus ensuring that the winning candidate had diverse, multiethnic support.[43] As the rising ethnic tensions of Kenya indicate, however, such electoral provisions do not always encourage moderate politics.

Elections can also make use of some type of proportional representation (PR) system, seeking to encourage minority representation in the party lists as well as in the coalitions at the political center. In South Africa, the ANC, which regarded PR as a second-best method, nonetheless supported its use during the transitional period, because it provided ethnic and racial minorities with a sense of security at a moment of great emotional stress.[44] PR did prove a worthwhile experiment in South Africa, for racial flanking remained minimal during the first free, postapartheid election, and the polling facilitated the adoption of a coalition government at the political center. Subsequently, South Africans have revised the electoral system, combining PR with a single-member, plurality system. In doing so, they have attempted to blend the representativeness of PR with the accountability and close links that a representative has with constituents under a plurality voting system. The effect is to give this institutional mechanism a stability that should engender trust in the country's various minority communities.

*Third,* in an attempt to reassure minorities, some African leaders have reconstituted their state designs, creating new political systems based on regional autonomy and federalism. They seek both to empower local elites and to place structural limitations on excessive political centralization. Thus Ethiopia's constitutional provisions on national federalism, the ruling Ethiopian People's Revolutionary Democratic Front (EPRDF) contends, is a reaction to the abuses of the past. Asserting that the "previous [repressive, assimilationist, and centralizing] attempts to [unify Ethiopia] have led to wars," President Meles Zenawi decided to reverse past practices and to institute a national-based federal system.[45] He seeks to allay minority feelings of insecurity by creating another level of power and accountability. Even so, the potential for the emergence of new conflicts combined with the possible frustration arising from the subregions' limited capacity to develop their areas makes the outcome of this experiment far from clear at this time.

Such federal-type experiments are suggestive of "tensional" (rather than "cooperative") federalism.[46] Ethnoregional minorities, who are anxious about their identity and survival in a hostile political environment, have gained significant functions at the regional level. The resulting federalism takes account of minority uncertainties and suspicions by establishing institutional protections that partially insulate these local elites from central state control. Under Ethiopia's 1994 Constitution, the so-called nation is given a wide responsibility over internal affairs, including the right to levy and collect taxes. The Constitution also provides that "every nation, nationality and people in Ethiopia has an unconditional right to self-determination, including the right to secession."[47] The danger arising from this combination of separate identities and extensive substate powers is its potential to fragment Ethiopia, protecting group interests against the whole at a possible cost in terms of economic development and future intrastate conflicts.

Practical applications of tensional federalism have generally proven difficult in African circumstances. The Sudan witnessed growing co-operation in the 1990s among opposition elements in the north and south regarding a loose confederal arrangement as an interim solution to the north-south conflict, but little accommodation by governmental authorities on the issue of meaningful southern self-determination.[48] And in South Africa, the tensional dynamic appears to be at the heart of IFP president Chief Mangosuthu Buthelezi's efforts to use federalism to create a fiefdom for himself in the KwaZulu/Natal area.[49] However, Buthelezi's demand that the final constitution accord the provincial government significant powers received little support from the largely dominant ANC government.[50]

More commonplace (and probably more enduring), however, are limited institutional adjustments, in the form of experiments with administrative decentralization. Nigerian federalism has secured broad acceptance as a political necessity in a complex multiethnic environment, even from a series of military rulers who have kept the country under tight control.[51] And even though South Africa's ANC specifically rejects any suggestions of ethnically inspired federalism, the existence of relatively autonomous provinces nonetheless acts to reassure ethnic minorities regarding their ability to participate in various local matters that have a direct bearing on their lives.

In brief, Africa's state authorities have at times accepted cooperative federal-type institutions to reduce minority uncertainty about their future; however, they remain anxious about the possible divisive political effects they associate with these institutions. Critics charge that federal systems will provide a thin wedge in the door, possibly leading over time to the fragmentation of the state. This general critique remains unproven. Nevertheless, it is evident that, where federalism has been put into effect in Africa, it has been beset by some of the following problems. For one thing, there have been difficulties containing an energetic center. In the Sudan, where negotiators hammered out an autonomy agreement for the south in 1972, an overweening political center nonetheless intervened in regional elections, changed regional boundaries, redivided the southern region, applied *Sharia* (Islamic) law, and, ultimately, terminated the agreement itself. In the opinion of the *Sudan Democratic Gazette,* "the subsequent unilateral abrogation of that agreement by the North illustrated that such agreements were ultimately worthless to the South," leading, in turn, to new tensions and insecurities.[52] For another thing, the dominant fiscal position of the political center means that the subregions in South Africa and Ethiopia are heavily dependent on central government transfers. Such dependence enables the center to set terms and apply administrative regulations in fields assigned to subregional decision makers in the constitution. And for still another thing, there are difficulties in delineating boundaries to the satisfaction of all subregional interests, a point already noted with respect to Sudanese politics. In Ethiopia, moreover, the subregional boundaries set by the EPRDF leadership appear to favor Tigray and the Afars, at the expense of the Amhara and the Somali Isaks in the Awash Valleyland. The effect is to create suspicions that might become the source of new conflicts in the future.[53]

Clearly, institutions can be put in place that will encourage ethnic minority inclusion, participation, and autonomy, thereby building minority confidence in the majority community or communities' goodwill. A government's recognition of ethnic fears and preparedness to address these legitimate concerns is evidence of its commitment to developing constructive intergroup relations in its society. The effect of these government-inspired confidence-building initiatives can be most constructive in terms of mitigating the security dilemma. Enlightened central authorities, through evidence of sensitivity regarding the feelings and aspirations of their ethnically vulnerable peoples and through repeated political initiatives (without necessarily expecting reciprocity in the short run — the so-called Graduated and Reciprocated Initiatives in Tension Reduction [GRIT] strategy), can attempt to engender an element of trust across groups. Such assurances by the state can help to prevent conflict from occurring and can possibly set the basis for a confident and secure societal pluralism.

Despite this political logic, however, ethnic conflicts are likely to remain as a serious (and sometimes dangerous) problem. The state, in the real world, may not act creatively and may not respect the institutions it establishes. Parochially minded politicians will continue to emerge and continue to use the ethnic issue as a means of mobilizing their constituents for action. And Africa's weak states will also remain fertile grounds for ambitious forays by ethnic champions. In sum, ethnic fears are containable, but the actions of state and ethnic leaders can be expected to keep the fears of future security dilemmas from disappearing.

## Policy Relevance: External Intervention
and "Guarantees"

Normally the main responsibility for maintaining political order and ensuring the rights of ethnic minorities resides with the state. Hence, when interethnic conflicts occur within their borders, it is central state authorities who are expected to intervene as intermediaries between contending groups. The state, paradoxically, has itself all too often been the violator of ethnic rights; nevertheless, at times, it has also played the role of an indispensable buffer between groups. For example, the Ghana government interceded on several occasions in the mid-1990s to halt interethnic fighting and to mediate between the warring groups in the country's north. Moreover, in the East Rand townships of Tokoza, Katlehong, Vosloorus, and Phola Park near Johannesburg in South Africa, local mediators, backed by the army, have engaged in a process they describe as "enforced stability," preventing violent conflict between ANC and IFP members. Depending on the situation, then, states can either be third parties interceding between disputant ethnic groups or, as in the Sudan or Rwanda, acting themselves to repress the fundamental rights of ethnic peoples, and thereby to provoke deadly encounters with societal groups.

When Africa's states act irresponsibly and fail to assure minority rights, where else can ethnic minority groups go to ensure their survival? More specifically, when a security dilemma materializes, as in Rwanda and Burundi, can the international community be expected to intervene and prevent genocidal actions from occurring? The international community is the logical safety net of final resort, and this is where observers look to hold down the spiraling conflict before it escalates out of hand. Thus, René Lemarchand looks outward to the United Nations and the Organization of African Unity in 1996 and asserts:

> Given the pathological fear of genocide among Tutsi (which more often than not provides justification for pre-emptive strikes against Hutu civilians) it is essential that the Tutsi minority be given proper security guarantees. Unless such guarantees have a measure of credibility there is no way one can expect the army to return to its barracks or lay down its arms. On the other hand, if the army does not go back to its barracks, the Hutu 'armed bands' will not shrink from further acts of terrorism. Nor of course will they accept to be retooled into a police force. What is needed is a highly trained, rapid deployment force under joint UN/OAU control to prevent future outbreaks of violence in the provinces.[54]

In addition to such humanitarian interventions, international action takes various forms, including conciliation, mediation, arbitration, verification, trusteeship, peacekeeping, peace enforcement, and guaranteeing postconflict accords. All of the forms of international action mentioned above can promote regular relationships between state and ethnic elites, and I will examine three of these briefly — the enforcement of peace agreements, election monitoring, and humanitarian interventions — to see whether such international action can fill the void left by state irresponsibility or ethnic recklessness.

The extension of *credible external protections* and their subsequent enforcement have proven important during and after the negotiation process to ensure the future place of ethnic minorities in their society. For example, international assurances played a role in the Rhodesian independence settlement, the Mozambican peace agreement, and the Lusaka Protocol on Angola. In facilitating such agreements, powerful states and international organization provide insurance against future risks, thereby encouraging an insecure party to commit itself to a peace accord. Such actions are by their nature intrusive and potentially expensive. The external actors are promising that they will intercede if one of the parties to an agreement violates the accord. This type of preventive action is not something that external third-party actors do lightly, because their domestic publics are likely to recoil from the long and costly police actions that might follow from such promises;[55] also, the guarantor power may not be able to deliver on its pledges of protection, as seen in Iraq and Bosnia, where safe areas were overrun and many of the local people killed. Even so, credible protections may make a contract possible. Hence, the negotiation and survival of a peace accord and the creation or return to stable norms of relations may be dependent on the willingness of an international third party or parties to take on this critically important assignment.

Less dramatic (but nonetheless important) forms of international intervention involve the roles of regional and global organizations in the *postconflict peace-building* process. In the implementation stage, international mediators can reduce the signers' sense of uncertainty by undertaking the tasks of verification, thereby providing the negotiating parties with information about the intentions and actions of their adversaries. External verification gives the parties a reason to assume that the terms of the agreement will be put into effect. The disarming and demobilization of armies during the implementation of a peace accord is inevitably a frightening prospect for both state and insurgent forces, who fear a preemptive attack and are encouraged by the presence of an intervening external force.[56] An external presence can make defection from an agreement costly; a third party can exert pressure on the parties involved in implementation of agreements by informing them that their reputations will come into question if they renege on their accords. Clearly, ambiguity is needed during the negotiation stage to encourage the parties to reach a compromise, but this ambiguity may lead to credibility problems when these accords must be put into effect. An active international third-party role in overseeing the cease-fire, the demobilization of contending forces, and the transition to elections can contribute in important ways to a successful outcome, by stabilizing a fragile agreement during the difficult transition period.

No aspect of the postconflict peace-building is more significant than the holding of free and fair elections. When administered fairly, as in Zimbabwe, Namibia, and Mozambique, such elections can legitimate the transition to new regimes in both the society and the international community. In the way they have helped to oversee the election process, international organizations have made a major contribution to reassuring political minorities about their future security. The UN, involved in promoting free and fair elections since 1945, has helped third world states through training and other forms of capacity building. The United Nations Operation in Mozambique (ONUMOZ) trained 32,000 party election observers and sent 2,215 international observers to monitor the Mozambican election. This initiative contributed to the credibility of the electoral process, alleviating suspicions that the smaller parties had about dishonest practices. Although always limited to an outsider's role in Africa's electoral processes, a UN presence can nonetheless contribute to a successful outcome by validating the right of the opposition to participate, informing the parties as to alternative procedures, sanctioning the results, and helping in any follow-up referenda or state-creations (as in the case of Eritrea). The effect is to give the UN a highly significant role as a go-between in the ethnic struggles taking place in the affected African countries.

The extension of external protections and postconflict peace-building activities help the local parties to cope with two important elements that contribute to the emergence of a security dilemma, the lack of reliable information and the difficulty of making commitments. As the external third party communicates between the adversaries and makes a commitment to enforce the peace, it facilitates the process of consolidation — despite the distrust that both antagonists continue to display. But if none of these initiatives proves sufficient to promote stable relations and fighting erupts, then it becomes necessary to go beyond prevention, guarantees, and mediatory actions to what we will characterize broadly as *humanitarian intervention.*

Increasingly, enlightened statesmen in Africa are justifying humanitarian intervention and questioning the principle of noninterference when rulers blatantly abuse the basic rights of their citizens. With the decline of traditional notions of sovereignty, third world countries are now more prepared than before to accept the idea that if sovereign states do not act in a responsible manner toward their minority peoples and a security dilemma becomes manifest, then individual states and subregional, regional, and international organization can have legitimate cause to intervene in intrastate disputes.[57] Organization of African Unity (OAU) secretary-general Dr. Salim Ahmed Salim has contended that a balance must be maintained between national sovereignty and international responsibility; this search for balance leads him to call for a redefining of national sovereignty to take account of "the need for [the] accountability of governments and of their national and international responsibilities."[58]

To be sure, states and international organization are still loath to intercede in internal conflicts and to violate the norms of sovereignty; however, in worst-case scenarios, where ethnic tensions within a state seem likely to bring on the collapse of a state or to spread and become the source of severe international tensions (as was the case in Liberia), then these external actors may feel that international norms justify some form of intervention. As Ibrahim Gambari, Nigeria's ambassador to the United Nations, put it:

> Presently, . . . with the breakdown of law and order in several African states that has led to interventions by multilateral military and humanitarian forces, "the cruel calculus of sovereignty versus misery has changed the way the international community thinks about foreign intervention and the rights of states." . . . It is doubtful that these interventions [in Liberia and Somalia] would have received international support without the change in African policy, which now seems ready to make some qualifications to the principle of the sovereign right of nations.[59]

Humanitarian intervention can take noncoercive forms (financial support for one or more actors, confidence-building measures, or the recognition of [or refusal to give recognition to] a government or state) or coercive initiatives, such as the supply of arms, training, advisers, and intelligence information, and active military operations. Dramatic examples of external intervention in Africa's internal wars include the Intergovernmental Authority on Development's (IGAD's) efforts to mediate the civil war in the neighboring Sudan and the Economic Community of

West African States' (ECOWAS's) military intervention in the Liberian civil war. The OAU's 1993 enactment and subsequent implementation of a Mechanism on Conflict Prevention, Management, and Resolution, which represents a cautious movement toward regional and continental responsibility for dealing with Africa's internal conflicts (for example, in Burundi and Western Sahara), will have to be buttressed by adequate financial resources and by the development of supporting norms in order to become an important element in Africa's conflict-management process.[60] It will take time to clarify the conditionalities and contingencies under which future OAU humanitarian interventions can be expected to occur. The OAU is constrained militarily, argues Ademola Adeleke, because "none of its members is a continental power, and none has that hegemonic interest and capability to move the organisation towards intervention, as Nigeria has done with ECOWAS and the United States with the UN."[61]

UN-mandated intervention forces have been dispatched to the Congo, Somalia, and Rwanda. UN observers, mediators, and peacekeepers have played active roles in Angola, Mozambique, and South Africa. Such UN-military initiatives are defined and approved by the Security Council, which legitimizes the intervention, pays the costs of the action, and provides needed equipment and logistical support. However, Security Council approval politicizes the process and results in possible vetoes by the permanent members (who may object to the command structure or the costs involved in the undertaking). Such efforts represent early forms of external insurance against human rights abuses by African governments. Should these international protections become more predictable, they could help allay minority fears about their future safety.

The uncertainties felt by local parties seem likely to persist, however. The industrialized states currently exhibit commitment fatigue and are reluctant to obligate themselves because of a combination of domestic pressures, economic constraints, and the desire to get on to other, immediately pressing problems. As a consequence, a gap exists between what member states expect of international organizations in terms of solving the world's intrastate conflicts and the unwillingness of wealthy member states to provide the financial and logistical resources necessary to accomplish the task. As UN secretary-general Boutros-Ghali stated:

> As regards the availability of troops and equipment, problems have become steadily more serious. . . . A considerable effort has been made to expand and refine stand-by arrangements, but these provide no guarantee that troops will be provided for a specific opera-

tion. For example, when in May 1994 the Security Council decided to expand the United Nations Assistance Mission for Rwanda (UNAMIR), not one of the 19 Governments that at that time had undertaken to have troops on stand-by agreed to contribute.[62]

In light of this discrepancy, calls by U.S. diplomats for the use of a permanent African Crisis Response Force (ACRF) involving 10,000 African troops and costing an estimated $40 million a year seemed sensible in principle; it could have provided training and logistical support to African countries for future peacekeeping operations. Yet, the problems with the ACRF seemed substantial. Not only could difficulties be anticipated regarding the selection of commanding officers and the participating African contingents, but there were also complications regarding the external actors' direct interests in the outcomes of interventions. Certainly, unless the revamped African Crisis Response Initiative is backed generously over time by the major powers, it will likely prove a hollow shell, lacking in the capabilities necessary to cope with future violent flare-ups.

Perhaps of more significance in dealing with future security dilemmas will be ad hoc groupings of African states, formed in response to particular crises and sanctioned by the UN or other multilateral organizations. These interventions often involve neighboring countries that are familiar with one another, know the terrain, and can be deployed quickly in the face of a crisis. The intervention by ECOWAS in the Liberian conflict in the 1990s, backed financially and logistically by the Western powers, showed the ability of an African-led force to contain a spreading conflict, although not without some criticism of its use of tough military tactics against an African opponent. In addition, the limited leverage of these regional peacekeeping efforts becomes apparent when the experience of IGAD in northeast Africa is examined. Although a predecessor body did facilitate talks between Somalia and Ethiopia in the 1980s, its current efforts to mediate the emotionally charged and brutal internal conflict in the Sudan's south have provided few notable successes.

Another type of African-inspired, collective action is the 1996 initiative by neighboring states to apply an economic embargo against Major Pierre Buyoya's Tutsi-dominated regime in Burundi. Led by former president Julius Nyerere of Tanzania, the eastern African neighbor countries have pressed the Buyoya regime to respect human rights and negotiate an end to the ethnic confrontation in that country. The Tutsi-led regime, fearing the logic of a return to majoritarian principles, has so far resisted these external pressures, but not without enormous costs in terms of goodwill and economic well-being.[63] Paradoxically, just as the West has begun to disengage from African involvements in a serious way, African heads of state, after reexamining their earlier positions on intervention and sovereignty, have taken up some of the slack and demanded movement toward peace within conflict-ridden states. A failure on the part of the world community to adopt a supportive stance toward these efforts might have serious unintended consequences: an elite planning to launch a preventive strike might conclude that it is dealing with a paper tiger, leaving the door open to further security dilemmas in Africa.

## Conclusion

The idea of the ethnic security dilemma, combined with the real-world experiences of Rwanda and Bosnia, is a useful warning to international relations theorists and others: in our anarchic world order, terrible outrages are still possible, and there are practical limits to the reliability of state or international preventive actions and, in the event of a breakdown, to external humanitarian interventions.

In many instances, leaders have designed institutions that play a constructive role in reassuring ethnic minorities about their future security and well-being. Thus, confidence-building incentives of various types have proved useful in promoting cooperation; they tend to work where moderate politics prevail and the rules of relations are predictable and widely acknowledged and accepted.

Ethnic minority uncertainty declines as these groups come to recognize that institutions are in place that can promote positive-sum outcomes. As shown above, a recognition of mutual benefits is facilitated through learned experiences in the negotiating processes and through developing an awareness of the functional interdependence that follows. Moreover, the resulting linkages that crosscut the ethnic fault lines represent stabilizing influences that promote cooperation between groups and hence counteract uncertainty.

Whenever African leaders have successfully nurtured confidence through their informal practices and constitutional arrangements (such as inclusive coalitions, balanced recruitment into high government and party offices, proportional allocations, electoral procedures that encourage representativeness and discourage ethnic outbidding, and decentralized decision making), they have encouraged minorities to commit themselves to common purposes. Realizing that they can anticipate a secure future and a fair share of resources within the established order, ethnic minority interests may be prepared to live with a limited amount of uncertainty and, in Adam Przeworski's words, "continue to submit their interests and values to the uncertain interplay of the institutions."[64] This was once the case in Rwanda, where, tragically in terms of expectations of democratic governance, multiparty elections took place and prospects of peaceful intergroup competition seemed encouraging.

However, these institutions are not likely to prove sufficient in worst-case encounters, because state elites may not uphold their contractual obligations and ambitious ethnic politicians may take advantage of state weakness to outbid the moderate coalition at the political center. Where ethnic leaders (some of whom control the state) are prepared to paly the ethnic card and plan communal murder, as in Rwanda and Bosnia, the international relations notion of self-help prevails, resulting all too frequently in a preventive first strike and insecurity for all. In these circumstances, international action in the form of protections, third-party enforcement, or humanitarian intervention becomes an urgent matter. When the state represses its citizenry or cannot regulate or buffer intense state/ethnic or interethnic conflicts on its own, active regional and global intervention may become necessary to make sovereign powers act responsibly.

Under such circumstances, a problem that the international community must deal with is building the capacity for legitimate and necessary interventions before future crises become apparent. Both international prevention and effective crisis response require enormous leverage at the disposal of diplomats. The third party must combine commitment to a peaceful outcome with the ability to influence the local actors to reconsider their preferences by means of diplomatic pressure or incentives.[65] In this respect, the West African initiative in 1996 to mediate Sierra Leone's internal conflict was a heartening event, because neighboring countries with a legitimate stake in the outcome skillfully united in a diplomatic initiative. The Nyerere-led peace effort in Burundi also represented an important African peace undertaking; however, in contrast to Sierra Leone, it involved a more forceful intercession into an internal ethnic crisis and sought, through an embargo, to induce the adversaries to reexamine their preferences.

Africa is compensating as best it can for the lack of capabilities at the disposal of third parties; however, it is not able to do this task of peacemaking on its own. The international community cannot afford to remain aloof from internal security crises such as Rwanda, standing on the sidelines while these confrontations burn themselves out. If not attended to, some of these crises may spread with disastrous consequences for all. Consequently, international organizations must be reformed and strengthened to enable them to plan in advance to ensure the safety of ethnic peoples at risk; this involves the provision, as the need arises, of early warning signals, mediators, peacekeeping units, monitoring teams, and military contingents that are ready to intercede at short notice. Also, an increased organizational capacity to extend combinations of pressures and incentives to the rival parties might contribute to averting a potential security dilemma situation, enabling beleaguered leaders to save face and explore alternative options before a crisis point is reached. In Burundi, Rwanda, and Yugoslavia, a failure to act decisively in the early stages of the crisis sent a bad message and heightened minority uncertainty. Effective international planning and global preparedness to intercede are therefore essential to overcome other such security dilemmas that may be waiting in the wings.

NOTES

I wish to express my appreciation to Miroslav Nincic, Joseph Lepgold, Edmond J. Keller, Bruce Jentleson, and Matthew Hoddie for helpful suggestions on the first draft of this essay.

1. Stephen Ryan, "Peacebuilding Strategies and Intercommunal Conflict: Transforming Divided Societies," paper presented at the International Political Science Association Research Committee on Politics and Ethnicity Conference, Witwatersrand University, South Africa, July 1995.

2. David A. Lake and Donald Rothchild, "Containing Fear: The Origins and Management of Ethnic Conflict," *International Security* 21, 2 (fall 1996): 43; and James D. Fearon and David D. Laitin, "Explaining Interethnic Cooperation," *American Political Science Review* 90, 4 (December 1996): 717.

3. Roy Licklider, "The Consequences of Negotiated Settlements in Civil Wars, 1945–1993," *American Political Science Review* 89, 3 (September 1995): 684; Stephen J. Stedman, *Peacemaking in Civil Wars: International Mediation in Zimbabwe, 1974–1980* (Boulder: Lynne Rienner, 1991), 5–7; Paul R. Pillar, *Negotiating Peace: War Termination as a Bargaining Process* (Princeton: Princeton University Press, 1993), 25.

4. James D. Fearon, "Commitment Problems and the Spread of Ethnic Conflict," in David A. Lake and Donald Rothchild, eds., *Ethnic Fears and Global Engagement: The International Spread and Management of Ethnic Conflict* (Princeton: Princeton University Press, 1998), 107–26. See also Barbara F. Walter, *Designing Transitions from Violent Civil War,* Policy Paper no. 31 (San Diego: University of California Institute for Global Conflict and Cooperation, 1997).

5. Russell Hardin, *One for All: The Logic of Group Conflict* (Princeton: Princeton University Press, 1995), 23.

6. René Lemarchand, *Burundi: Ethnocide as Discourse and Practice* (Cambridge, England, and New York: Cambridge University Press and Woodrow Wilson Center Press, 1994), 14.

7. Rui J. P. De Figueiredo Jr. and Barry R. Weingast, "The Rationality of Fear: Political Oportunism and Ethnic Conflict," in Jack Snyder and Barbara F.

Walter, eds., *Civil War, Insecurity, and Intervention* (New York: Columbia University Press, 1999).

8. Leonard J. Cohen, *Broken Bonds: The Disintegration of Yugoslavia* (Boulder: Westview Press, 1993), 52; and René Lemarchand, "The Apocalypse in Rwanda," *Cultural Survival Quarterly* 18, 2/3 (summer/fall 1994): 30.

9. On the diffusion of ideas through the mass media and its effect on contemporary ethnic relations, see Stuart Hill and Donald Rothchild, "The Contagion of Political Conflict in Africa and the World," *Journal of Conflict Resolution* 30 (December 1986): 716–22.

10. Chaim Kaufmann, "Possible and Impossible Solutions to Ethnic Civil Wars," *International Security* 20, 4 (spring 1996): 137; and John J. Mearsheimer, "The Only Exit from Bosnia," *New York Times,* October 7, 1997, A21.

11. Of course, the notion of playing the ethnic card need not imply only a negative action. Ethnic leaders could also play the ethnic card in a legitimate manner, seeking to gain the economic rights of their ethnic constituents.

12. Emma Rothschild, "What Is Security?" *Daedalus* 124, 3 (summer 1995): 62.

13. See Robert Jervis, "Cooperation under the Security Dilemma," *World Politics* 30, 2 (January 1978): 172; and Barry R. Posen, "The Security Dilemma and Ethnic Conflict," in Michael E. Brown, ed., *Ethnic Conflict and International Security* (Princeton: Princeton University Press, 1993), 104.

14. John Stremlau, "Antidote to Anarchy," *Washington Quarterly* 18, 1 (winter 1995): 34.

15. Stephen M. Saideman, "Is Pandora's Box Half-Empty or Half-Full? The Limited Virulence of Secessionism and the Domestic Sources of Disintegration," in Lake and Rothchild, eds., *Ethnic Fears and Global Engagement,* chap. 6.

16. Hans Morgenthau, *Politics among Nations,* 1st ed. (New York: Alfred A. Knopf, 1948), 46. I am grateful to Thomas J. Johnson for bringing this quotation to my attention.

17. Jervis, "Cooperation under the Security Dilemma," 211.

18. David Lake, "Ethnic Conflict and International Intervention," *IGCC Policy Brief* 3 (March 1995): 1.

19. Stephen Van Evera, "Offense, Defense, and the Causes of War," *International Security* 22, 4 (spring 1998): 9; and Charles L. Glaser and Chaim Kaufmann, "What Is the Offense-Defense Balance and How Can We Measure It?" *International Security* 22, 4 (spring 1998): 49.

20. On the logic of fear in interethnic relations, see Figueiredo and Weingast, "Rationality of Fear."

21. Arnold Wolfers, "Statesmanship and Moral Choice," *World Politics* 1, 1 (October 1948): 182.

22. David Rieff, *Slaughterhouse: Bosnia and the Failure of the West* (New York: Simon and Schuster, 1995), 112.

23. Lemarchand, "The Apocalypse in Rwanda," 29.

24. Donatella Lorch, "As Rwanda Trials Open, a Nation Struggles," *New York Times,* April 7, 1995, A1.

25. Carnegie Commission on Preventing Deadly Conflict, *Preventing Deadly Conflict: Final Report* (Washington, D.C.: Carnegie Commission on Preventing Deadly Conflict, 1977), 41.

26. On the predatory motivations of the *genocidaires,* see Bruce D. Jones, "Keeping the Peace, Losing the War: Military Intervention in Rwanda's 'Two Wars,' " in Jack Snyder and Barbara F. Walter, eds., *Civil Wars, Insecurity, and Intervention* (New York: Columbia University Press, 1999).

27. Timothy D. Sisk, *Power Sharing and International Mediation in Ethnic Conflicts* (Washington, D.C.: U.S. Institute of Peace Press, 1996), 81.

28. Donald Rothchild, *Racial Bargaining in Independent Kenya* (London: Oxford University Press, 1973), chap. 7.

29. Hizkias Assefa, *Mediation of Civil Wars: Approaches and Strategies — The Sudan Conflict* (Boulder: Westview Press, 1987), 142.

30. Interviews with Steven Friedman and Lloyd Vogelman, Johannesburg, South Africa, July 10, 1995.

31. René Lemarchand, "Managing Transition Anarchy: Rwanda, Burundi, and South Africa in Comparative Perspective," *Journal of Modern African Studies* 32, 4 (December 1994): 586–87.

32. Howard Adelman, "Towards a Confidence Transformational Dynamic," in Gabriel Ben-Dor and David B. Dewitt, eds. *Confidence Building Measures in the Middle East* (Boulder: Westview Press, 1994), 317.

33. Saadia Touval, "Managing the Risks of Accommodation," in Nissan Oren, ed., *Termination of Wars* (Jerusalem: Magnes Press, 1982), 19.

34. Adam Przeworski, *Democracy and the Market* (Cambridge, England: Cambridge University Press, 1991), 33.

35. Stephen John Stedman, "Spoiler Problems in Peace Processes," *International Security* 22, 2 (fall 1997): 5–53.

36. Stephen John Stedman, "Negotiation and Mediation in Internal Conflict," in Michael E. Brown, ed., *The International Dimensions of Internal Conflict* (Cambridge: MIT Press, 1996), 347. See also Donald Rothchild and Alexander J. Groth, "Pathological Dimensions of Domestic and International Ethnicity," *Political Science Quarterly* 110, 1 (spring 1995): 69–82.

37. See Eghosa E. Osaghae, "The Federal Cabinet, 1951–1984," in Peter P. Ekeh and Eghosa E. Osaghae, eds., *Federal Character and Federalism in Nigeria* (Ibadan: Heinemann, 1989), 150–51.

38. See Timothy D. Sisk, *Democratization in South Africa: The Elusive Social Contract* (Princeton: Princeton University Press, 1995).

39. See *Foreign Broadcast Information Service* 93, 029 (February 16, 1993): 15.

40. Robert B. Mattes, "Beyond 'Government and Opposition': An Independent South African Legislature," *Politikon* 20, 2 (December 1993): 76.

41. John F. Burns, "Rebel Attack Ends a Cease-Fire in Sri Lanka," *New York Times,* April 20, 1995, A8.

42. On ethnic outbidding, see Donald L. Horowitz, *Ethnic Groups in Conflict* (Berkeley: University of California Press, 1985), 410–16.

43. Donald L. Horowitz, "Making Moderation Pay: The Comparative Poli-

tics of Ethnic Conflict Management," in Joseph V. Montville, ed., *Conflict and Peacemaking in Multiethnic Societies* (Lexington, Mass.: Lexington Books, D.C. Heath, 1990), 471.

44. Timothy D. Sisk, "South Africa Seeks New Ground Rules," *Journal of Democracy* 4, 1 (January 1993): 87.

45. Cameron McWhirter and Gur Melamede, "Ethiopia: The Ethnicity Factor," *Africa Report* 37, 5 (September/October 1992): 33.

46. On the distinction between tensional and cooperative federalism, see Donald Rothchild, *Toward Unity in Africa: A Study of Federalism in British Africa* (Washington, D.C.: Public Affairs Press, 1960), 191–93.

47. Constitution of Ethiopia, Art. 39 (1).

48. "Can the NDA Sustain the Momentum against the Khartoum Regime?" *Sudan Democratic Gazette* 62 (July 1995): 2.

49. Interview with Steven Friedman, Johannesburg, July 10, 1995.

50. "South Africa: ANC-IFP at Loggerheads," *Africa Research Bulletin, Political, Social and Cultural Series* 35, 4 (April 1–30, 1995): 11822.

51. Federal Republic of Nigeria, *Report of the Political Bureau* (Lagos: Federal Government Printer, 1987), 80; and *The Republic* (Lagos), January 19, 1993, 1.

52. *Sudan Democratic Gazette* 53 (October 1994): 3.

53. Marina Ottaway, "Nationalism Unbound: The Horn of Africa Revisited," *SAIS Review* 12, 2 (summer/fall 1992): 123.

54. René Lemarchand, "Policy Options on Local-Level Reconstruction," paper presented at the U.S. Institute of Peace Conference on Burundi, Washington, D.C., December 8, 1996, 5.

55. John Chipman, "Managing the Politics of Parochialism," in Brown, ed., *Ethnic Conflict and International Security,* 252–53.

56. Stephen John Stedman and Donald Rothchild, "Peace Operations: From Short-Term to Long-Term Commitment," *International Peacekeeping* 3, 2 (summer 1996): 17–35.

57. Francis M. Deng, Terrence Lyons, Sadikiel Kimaro, Donald Rothchild, and I. William Zartman, *Sovereignty as Responsibility: Conflict Management in Africa* (Washington, D.C.: Brookings, 1996).

58. Quoted in Solomon Gomes, "The OAU, State Sovereignty, and Regional Security," in Edmond J. Keller and Donald Rothchild, eds., *Africa in the New International Order: Rethinking State Sovereignty and Regional Security* (Boulder: Lynne Rienner, 1996), 41.

59. Ibrahim A. Gambari, "The Role of Regional and Global Organizations in Addressing Africa's Security Issues," in Keller and Rothchild, eds., *Africa and the New International Order,* 31.

60. Edmond J. Keller, "Transitional Ethnic Conflict in Africa," in Lake and Rothchild, eds., *Ethnic Fears and Global Engagement,* chap. 12.

61. Ademola Adeleke, "The Politics and Diplomacy of Peacekeeping in West Africa: The ECOWAS Operation in Liberia," *Journal of Modern African Studies* 33, 4 (December 1995): 592.

62. "Supplement to an Agenda for Peace: Position Paper of the Secretary-

General on the Occasion of the Fiftieth Anniversary of the United Nations," United Nations, General Assembly, 50th sess. (January 3, 1995), A/50/60, 11.

63. "Burundi: Arusha Summit Decides to Maintain Embargo," *Africa Research Bulletin,* Political, Social and Cultural Series 33, 10 (November 28, 1996): 12438; and Frederick Ehrenreich, "Burundi: The Current Political Dynamic," paper presented at the U.S. Institute of Peace Conference on Burundi, Washington, D.C., December 8, 1996.

64. Przeworski, *Democracy and the Market,* 26.

65. See Donald Rothchild, *The Management of Ethnic Conflict in Africa: Pressures and Incentives for Cooperation* (Washington, D.C.: Brookings, 1997).

# Military Diffusion, the Information Revolution, and U.S. Power

*Emily O. Goldman*

## The Issue for the Policy Community

Scholars and policymakers are currently debating the exact dimensions of an impending information "revolution in military affairs" (RMA). RMA advocates contend advanced technologies such as microelectronics, computers and software, and precision-guided munitions promise to shift the technological basis of military power, affect the means of military competition and advantage, and alter the essence of world power (Krepinevich 1994; Toffler and Toffler 1993; Cohen 1996; Nye and Owens 1996). Moreover, they argue, the United States is poised to make a successful transition through the information revolution. Policymakers determined to accelerate the RMA believe it can be leveraged to shape a new world order and further solidify U.S. military preeminence in the aftermath of the Cold War. Critics deny the information revolution can be so leveraged and counter that driving such a revolution will only encourage competitors to arise, accelerating the pace at which others will close the gap on U.S. dominance (Bacevich 1994). For proponents and critics alike, how other military organizations are likely to adapt to the information revolution and to a U.S. military substantially transformed to exploit the power of information are topics of considerable importance.

There is little consensus about how to define a military revolution or a revolution in military affairs, whether these are conceptually the same, and whether we are currently passing through either one. Nor is there much rigorous analysis on how the information-based military revolution will affect U.S. power and position over the long term. Those effects will be determined to a large extent by how the innovations associated with the information RMA diffuse through the international system and are adopted by other military organizations. The aim of this essay is to help policymakers anticipate some of these consequences by using insights from organization theory's research on diffusion of innovations. From a contemporary U.S. defense policy perspective, the diffusion of military innovations is a key issue, whether or not we are in a period of revolutionary military transformation. Much of U.S. foreign and security policy counts on a large and long-lasting U.S. conventional superiority over most possible challengers, in most types of warfare. Is this a reasonable expectation? Advocates of the RMA seem to believe that whatever the current situation, if the United States could somehow achieve this "new way of war," then current apparent U.S. military superiority could be sustained for a very long time. There are implicit assumptions about diffusion that underlay this larger belief, and these assumptions need to be subjected to intensive scrutiny.

Like previous military revolutions, this one promises to have a variety of consequences for U.S. foreign and national security policy. It will reshape the way military forces are organized, equipped, and trained. Proponents argue as casualties of combat decline with greater reliance on unmanned vehicles, standoff precision munitions, and exploitation of information asymmetries, costs associated with the use of military force will fall, possibly strengthening U.S. resolve and enhancing domestic political support for foreign military endeavors. Information warfare challenges many conceptual premises that underlay the theory and practice of deterrence (Harknett 1996; Feaver 1997a). Information technologies also render much of America's traditional arms control agenda problematic (Goldman 1997a).

This analysis focuses on the systemic consequences likely to result from diffusion of technologies[1] and behavioral practices through the international system in order to understand the impact of the military revolution on the international distribution of capabilities, and on the likelihood that peer competitors will arise to erode America's relative power position. Conventional wisdom holds that competition drives the diffusion of pioneering military methods through the international system and innovations spread quickly and uniformly among states. The competitive logic governing the international system also tends to produce similarity in military formats[2] as states strive to emulate the successful practices of other states. As one leading scholar puts it, "The possibility that conflict will be conducted by force leads to competition in the arts and the instruments of force. Competition produces a tendency toward the sameness of the competitors" (Waltz 1979, 128).

Historical analysis of military diffusion suggests the process may not be so rapid and uniform. While innovations in hardware often play an important role in realizing large gains in military effectiveness, they are rarely sufficient. Doctrinal, organizational, and tactical adaptations are also necessary, and societal transformations are as likely to spawn revolutionary changes as are technological innovations. New hardware usually must be coupled with innovations in operational concepts, doctrine, and organization — with new ideas and new processes — to realize a radical increase in military effectiveness. These distinctions are important because to the extent a military innovation requires significant changes in sociocultural values and behavioral patterns to exploit, as most do,[3] it will face greater obstacles to adoption and will spread less uniformly. If militaries and societies are unable or unwilling to make the necessary changes to fully emulate innovative military practices, diffusion will not necessarily produce sameness across national military organizations. The assumption that competition produces military convergence rests on a host of auxiliary assumptions that need to be scrutinized — assumptions about type of threat environment, nature and extent of military contact, resources at the nation's disposal, geographic situation, and political, social, economic, and cultural characteristics of the state. When we unpack these assumptions, we discover diffusion is as likely to spawn partial emulation, reinvention (change or modification of the innovation in the process of its adoption and implementation),[4] offsets (employment of methods to counter the innovation), or no response. When we do see convergence across military establishments, organization theory posits it need not be the result of competition. Noncompetitive processes can produce convergence in organizational fields and professions across different social and political systems.

Organization theory has developed a rich body of knowledge about the diffusion of ideas, forms, and practices. For policymakers interested in determining how other states and military organizations will respond to an American-led military revolution, organization theory offers insights not suggested by dominant paradigms of international relations. Competitive pressures exist today, but for reasons having to do with the nature of information technologies that will be discussed, they are more likely to produce offsets rather than emulation of superior military forms and practices. Where there is convergence in military forms and practices, it is not likely to be the result of competitive processes. Thus, where competition with the United States exists, we are less likely to see military convergence. Where there is military convergence, it is not likely to result from competition with the United States.

## International Relations Theory: Insights and Limitations

The dominant theoretical approach in international relations research, neorealism, provides a useful starting point for assessing the international consequences of the information military revolution. Neorealism makes assumptions about the causes and consequences of diffusion. The theory has come under fire from a host of quarters, but its logic remains entrenched in scholarly and policy circles.[5] Neorealism assumes the competitive logic governing the international system will cause pioneering military methods to diffuse quickly and uniformly among states.[6] Military historians note the power of competition as a factor in the convergence of military forms. John Lynn (1996, 509) writes, "More than any other institution, militaries tend to copy one another across state borders, and with good reason. War is a matter of Darwinian dominance or survival for states, and of life or death for individuals. When an army confronts new or different weaponry or practices on the battlefield, it must adapt to them, and often adaptation takes the form of imitation." The consequence of competition is the emergence of similarity in military forms as states conform to survive.

Neorealists assume competition drives diffusion and will produce convergence in organizational forms and practices. If we inspect the theory's conclusions closely, we see they rest on questionable assumptions that render predictions of convergence in military form and practice problematic. First, neorealism is a theory of great power politics, specifically great power politics in the European heartland. Neorealists assume away variation in political, social, economic, and cultural characteristics. This follows from the logic of the theory, but is also an artifact of the theory's empirical base. Building a theory around interaction patterns in the European state system brings basic similarities to the fore, while allowing differences to recede. Yet within Europe, differences have been important and have influenced rates and patterns of diffusion. Nationalism allowed the French to transform their military in a way the Prussians and British could not for risk of undermining monarchical power and privileges of the nobility (Lynn 1996, 511). Neorealism, by assuming either similarity or nonimportance of domestic contextual factors, does not consider how varying social characteristics can produce diversity in organizational forms. These characteristics take on greater import with the passage of the European state system to a Cold War system dominated by two nonheartland powers, and with the rise of post–Cold War regional subsystems.

Second, competition is neorealism's primary conduit for diffusion, and there need not be direct confrontation to stimulate emulation. Even geographically remote small states have expended tremendous effort to emulate the successful practices of major European military powers, sometimes spurred by local competition (Resende-Santos 1996). Still, highly specialized local military environments, or the need to develop frontier practices, could logically generate unique standards and regional paradigms (Lynn 1996, 511–12). Not only the intensity but the nature of the threat environment will influence how military diffusion affects military form and practice.[7]

Neorealism also assumes peer competition. Absence of competition among core industrialized powers is one of the hallmarks of the post–Cold War era. The dominant axis of military rivalry is no longer between peer competitors. Lacking money, population, and size relative to the United States, inferior powers do not command the resources to emulate U.S. innovations. Asymmetric rivalry predicts offsets, rather than emulation, as a response to superior capabilities.

Finally, neorealism assumes away diversity in the way technology affects military form and practice (Sagan and Waltz 1995, 2–8). Technology rarely dictates one path, but presents a menu from which to choose. Factors such as resource capacity and threat environment will influence choices and results. Neorealism can incorporate these. But the theory has more difficulty acknowledging internal characteristics, such as sociocultural values, that will affect the speed and uniformity with which innovations will be adopted (Mansfield 1968, 123). Technological innovations have been associated in the past with dramatic increases in military effectiveness, but increases in lethality (e.g., rifled artillery, machine guns, nuclear weapons, advanced conventional munitions), range (e.g., steam power, railroads, internal combustion engine, aircraft), and defense (e.g., barbed wire, mines) were alone insufficient to constitute a revolution. They often required doctrinal, tactical, and organizational innovations (e.g., Swiss pike square, ship-of-the-line tactics, drill, Napoleon's general staff system, blitzkrieg, carrier task force). The most far-reaching military revolutions incorporated macrosocial, political, and economic innovations (e.g., professionalization of armed forces, centralization of political authority, marketization, nationalism) that caused tremendous disruption in adopting societies (Ralston 1990).

History shows how dramatic increases in military effectiveness rest not on adoption of a single technology or practice, but on multiple components interacting. The infantry revolution (ca. 1300) depended on use of the pike and longbow, and the rise of professional forces. The revolution in drill (ca. 1600) made linear warfare possible, but the establishment of classical drill and discipline was effective only due to radical improvements in military administration and the key role played by the absolutist state. The Napoleonic revolution (ca. 1790) built on institutional and motivational changes, injection of nationalism, and universal conscription. The industrial warfare revolution (ca. 1840) depended not only upon industrial weaponry but also the full mobilization of societies for war and the rise of popular states.[8] By overlooking this complexity, neorealism overestimates the degree to which states and military organizations can exploit military innovations and the likelihood emulation will result. Neorealism is a poor guide for policymakers because it presumes a functional logic of the international system that subsumes important variation.

Another type of functional logic with bearing on the question of military diffusion operates at the level of the organization. Based on assumptions of bureaucratic organization theory, militaries adopt innovations that enhance their resources, autonomy, and essence (Allison 1971, 67–100). Technologies that serve these functional needs for survival in competitive resource and bureaucratic environments are likely to be adopted. We should again expect convergence in organizational forms because military organizations have an institutional interest in adopting offensive technologies and strategies that increase the organization's resources and control over its environment (Posen 1984; Snyder 1984a, 1984b; Van Evera 1984).

This functional bureaucratic logic is well entrenched in scholarly, if not policy, circles and is an equally poor guide for policymakers because it also subsumes important variation. Historians and social scientists have long noted the conservative biases in military organizations (Posen 1984; Katzenbach 1958), but the bureaucratic characterization has not gone unchallenged. The classic statement of the professional military views the services as rational in striving to efficiently attain their goal of securing the state (Huntington 1957). Military organizations respond to the dictates of strategic geography, technological developments, and enemy behavior in rational pursuit of their goals (Rosen 1988, 1991; Zisk 1993; Goldman 1997b). The bureaucratic approach has also come under assault from societal and cultural perspectives, which focus on the complex interdependent relationship between organizations and their environments (Legro 1995; Kier 1995; Rosen 1996).

Military organizations can be viewed as rational systems seeking to improve the efficiency with which they pursue their goals, as natural systems driven by the need to survive and protect their self-interests in response to a hostile budgetary environment and interservice rivalry, or as open systems embedded in and constituted by their environments (Scott 1992; Farrell 1996). Neorealism's rational systems view and the bureaucratic perspective's natural systems view share an understanding of innovation as driven by a competitive logic, be it of the international system or of the organization's domestic bureaucratic and budgetary environments.

Organization theory, particularly research from sociology on the diffusion of innovations, can be of immense use to policymakers. It seeks to explain variation in rates and speed of adoption that the neorealist and bureaucratic approaches assume away. It draws attention to frequently overlooked noncompetitive processes that stimulate diffusion. It highlights consequences of diffusion other than emulation and military convergence. Organization theory provides fertile ground for policymakers interested in understanding the causes, process, and consequences of military diffusion.

## Insights from Organization Theory

Organization theory opens up a line of questioning for policymakers that for neorealist and bureaucratic approaches are nonissues. Can the organization and society adopt the innovation in question? Are they likely to incorporate the new practice in the same way as the innovating organization, or is adaptation likely to produce new hybrid forms? If hurdles to emulation are high, what are the likely consequences of diffusion? Finally, is emulation always driven by competitive pressures, or are there other processes fueling diffusion that policymakers must take into account? These questions are important for policymakers trying to map the contours of the new strategic environment.

The spread of information technologies is probably inevitable. Knowledge-intensive technologies are pouring into the marketplace and spreading across national borders exceedingly rapidly, fed by the globalization of finance and trade. Knowledge-intensive goods can be converted for military use and acquired or developed relatively easily and quickly (Davis 1996, 47). Revolutionary dual-use technologies, like computer and software capabilities, are not capital intensive and do not require a huge industrial capacity to exploit. India, Israel, South Korea, and Taiwan already possess significant computer software capabilities. Moreover, information technologies are driven as much by the civilian commercial economy as by government-sponsored military research and development. They are critical for success and competitive advantage in the global economy. The ability to monitor and control their dissemination, let alone develop a normative consensus on the desirability of control, is highly questionable. The nations of the south view with suspicion efforts of the industrialized north to limit technology transfers because of the discriminatory implications that extend well beyond the military realm to affect modernization and the eradication of sources of social unrest in civil society (Nolan 1991, 6; Moodie 1995, 190–95).

Though we can expect the hardware associated with the information revolution to diffuse widely, will this produce convergence in military form and practice across different societies? Exploiting the information revolution in military affairs is not just a question of acquiring new hardware like precision-guided munitions. To realize the full potential of information technologies, armed forces must be highly educated, trained, and skilled. Lynn (1996, 523) associates this with the rise of the volunteer-technical army, which developed in response to post-1945 technological advances: "Conventional weapons became more lethal and complex; but their use demanded greater expertise and co-ordination which, in turn, demanded improved education, doctrine, and training." Stephen Biddle (1996) argues the true impact of late-twentieth-century technology is to magnify the skill differential on the battlefield. Skilled organizations, not technology alone, are critical to the revolution.

The ability to fully exploit the information revolution in warfare also requires that information be distributed across the chain of command to improve the situational awareness of leaders all along the hierarchy. The information revolution will increase the number of people who have a "complete" picture of the battlefield. Peter Feaver (1997b, 22–23) argues that these "trends support the American way in war which has tended to reward low-level initiative at the expense of elaborately detailed war plans imposed from above," and that "U.S. tactical commanders currently enjoy a fairly high degree of delegated authority, certainly more than their peers in most rival military organizations." So the U.S. military is well positioned to adjust to the new command realities necessary to exploit the revolution, while others may not be.

Alvin and Heidi Toffler (1993) point out that the way a society makes war reflects how it makes wealth. The information revolution in warfare is a logical outgrowth of the knowledge-based economies and the computer-related technologies upon which modern society now rests. A society must permit the free flow of information to take advantage of the revolution. One can imagine social, political, and cultural resistance in many states to the free flow of information. These types of obstacles are not without precedent. Asian regimes lagged significantly behind their European counterparts in making the market-oriented transformation crucial to industrial expansion that underwrote development of highly effective armed forces in Europe (McNeill 1982, 49). Chinese market behavior and private pursuit of wealth could only function within limits defined by political authorities, educated in Confucian traditions hostile to the ethos of the marketplace (McNeill 1982, 40, 69). Gustavian tactical systems spread relatively quickly across Europe and into Russia, but faced tremendous resistance among the Turks, who came to see innovations from the West as posing a threat to the existing Islamic sociopolitical order (Ralston 1990, 48). It took nearly a century of military disaster before the sultan adopted modern European training methods, and even then they were adopted superficially so as not to undermine the existing medieval social order (McNeill 1982, 135).

So while the diffusion of information technology products is probably inevitable, this says nothing about whether and how those products will be used or incorporated into national (or subnational) military organizations, and if they can be leveraged to take advantage of the information revolution in warfare. Organization research provides some insights into these prospects. From organization research, we learn that ideas not compatible with the prevalent values, norms, and institutional infrastructure of a social system will not be adopted as rapidly and emulated as completely as innovations that are compatible (Rogers 1983, 14–16).[9] Different rates of adoption can be traced, in part, to the degree to which the innovation is perceived to be consistent — or compatible — with the existing values and past experiences, in addition to the needs, of potential adopters. Barbara Levitt and James G. March (1988, 330) concur that "diffusion through imitation is less significant than is variation in the match between the technology and the organization, especially as that match is discovered and molded through learning."

Similarly, Quincy Wright (1955, 375–76) argues, technologies, defined broadly to include both the material and nonmaterial, are not "superficial devices from which all cultures can benefit and which may originate anywhere and diffuse easily and rapidly. On the contrary, technologies are related to the culture as a whole and the origin, diffusion, and influence of a particular invention cannot be understood except in terms of the total culture which originated or utilizes it." Logically, according to D. Eleanor Westney (1987, 6), "since the environment in which the organizational model was anchored in its original setting will inevitably differ from one to which it is transplanted, even the most assiduous emulation will result in alterations of the original patterns to adjust them to their new context, and changes in the environment to make it a more favorable setting for the emerging organization." Incompatibility between local values and imported practices may produce delayed emulation, superficial adoption, or, in the extreme, failure. Capacity to adopt a new model will be influenced by the social, cultural, organizational, and political context of the adopters. A military organization may acquire a new technology, but face obstacles to developing the organizational structure or doctrine needed to realize its potential on the battlefield. This may be because the new practice conflicts with valued local patterns; the organizational set — necessary supporting organizations and institutions, for example, schools — is inadequately developed to facilitate full cross-societal emulation; or reformers lack authority in the face of pressures to conform to existing social institutions (Westney 1987, 28–31). Organization theory predicts potential departure from original patterns as they are imported into different societies, particularly when values and expectations in the importing society diverge from those of the exporting societies. Organization theory suggests predictions of emulation as a response to demonstration of superior U.S. military capabilities may be overblown.

What consequences should we expect when hurdles to emulation are high? Given the absence of competition among core industrialized powers, policymakers are turning their attention to the strategies of smaller powers — such as Iraq, Iran, and North Korea — lacking the capacity to fully emulate the capabilities of a superior power, to what in policy circles are called "asymmetric threats." Moreover, because of the nature of the information revolution, these states do not need to fully emulate U.S. capabilities. Weaker powers only need to offset those capabilities to deter the United States from intervening or deny it the ability to exploit its superior capability. Inferior powers have always sought ways to degrade the capabilities of their superiors. Consider the strategic influence exerted by inferior naval powers that employed a fleet-in-being strategy to maximize the influence of their inferior assets, and by the French navy's *Jeune École,* which relied on the torpedo boat and subsequently the submarine as a way to offset the capabilities of superior maritime powers (Corbett 1918, 191–99; Goldman 1994, 91–93). Today, the relative cheapness and accessibility of new technologies, many of which do not require the infrastructure needed for developing and operating more complicated systems,[10] mean more technologically advanced societies do not command the advantage they once might have. Small powers have increasing access to the capabilities to offset superior capabilities, and there are good reasons to believe they will have an incentive to exploit them.

Diffusion of information technology products promises to empower traditionally weak states and nonstate actors in unprecedented ways. Cruise missiles, mines, diesel-electric submarines, and unmanned aerial vehicles can be coupled with improved civilian $C^3I$ capabilities and navigational enhancements like GPS-based guidance systems and commercial space assets (Mahnken 1991). With differential GPS products that increase the accuracy of long-range standoff munitions, older, less capable platforms can deliver high-tech smart firepower. Weaker states can then project power more accurately, offset superior conventional forces, and deter intervention by militarily superior states (Gregorian 1993).[11]

The spread of information warfare capabilities also poses new types of threats for the most technologically advanced military forces and societies. Richard Harknett (1996, 23) argues that the information age is distinguished by the network and that the strength of the network rests on its degree of "connectivity," be it on the battlefield or in society at large. Connectivity can dramatically enhance the lethality of military forces, but it also increases their vulnerability to cyberwar attacks: electronic warfare tactics (jamming, deception, disinformation, destruction) that deny and disrupt information flows; use of software viruses to destroy, degrade, exploit, or compromise information systems; and destruction of sensing equipment (Harknett 1996, 32–34; Arquilla and Ronfeldt 1993). Preemptive information warfare attacks, like covert sabotage of computer systems, can also be employed by state and nonstate actors against high-tech forces that rely on information dominance (Cohen 1996, 45–46; Schwartau 1996). Information-intensive military organizations are more vulnerable to information warfare simply because they are more information-dependent, while an adversary need not be information-dependent to disrupt the information lifeline of high-tech forces (Ryan 1994–95, 115).

What is true for the networked military is true for the networked society. Information-dependent societies are vulnerable to the infiltration of computer networks, databases, and the media for the purposes of deception, subversion, and promotion of dissident and opposition movements (Arquilla and Ronfeldt 1993, 144–46). Attacks on societal connectivity — netwar — target the very linkages upon which modern societies rely to function: communication, financial transaction, transportation, and energy resource networks. Loss of connectivity is not likely to be as prohibitive for a low-tech society as it is for a state like the United States. Nor is it necessary to be a high-tech networked society to have access to information warfare capabilities.[12] Terrorist organizations and organized crime groups can launch netwar attacks. Information technologies are available to developing states in ways cutting-edge capabilities were not in the past. They can be used to interrupt vital lines of connectivity upon which technologically advanced military organizations and societies depend.

Organization theory suggests policymakers need to be cognizant of the multiple paths along which any military revolution will unfold. Technological change has been broadening and accelerating, giving competitors a rich menu of military innovations to choose from. From the seventeenth to the mid–twentieth centuries, military innovations tended to increase the power differential between great and lesser powers. This is no longer the case. Weapons of mass destruction can function as equalizers. Advanced conventional capabilities exist side by side with weapons of mass destruction and the panoply of low-tech capabilities like guerrilla warfare and terrorism. Advanced information-based societies and high-tech national military establishments are increasingly capable, but also increasingly vulnerable. The spread of information technologies is likely to produce greater diversity in military format than at any time in the recent past, and today it is producing a shift from symmetric peer rivalry to asymmetric rivalry among states at different tiers of military capability.

Where obstacles to emulation are not significant, organization theory alerts policymakers to noncompetitive processes that can result in convergence of military form. Innovative technologies and behavioral practices spread through a variety of transmission belts, to enemies and allies. The tendency is to focus on competitive diffusion, but collaborative processes are equally important and particularly relevant today. Ongoing efforts to socialize foreign military officers into professional modes of conduct associated with Western models of objective civilian control by enrolling them in elite war colleges in the United States, or by developing educational programs abroad for officers from the former Soviet Union and Warsaw Pact states, diffuse organizational practices. Similar implications follow from efforts to train together with allies and new entrants to NATO. Policies valuable for instituting stable civil-military relations, or for cementing relations with new alliance partners, may have unintended consequences for the diffusion not of technologies (because the feasibility of stemming the spread of many information-based ones is slim) but of the innovative operational concepts, doctrine, and organizational forms needed to employ new hardware in a way that dramatically increases military effectiveness. An equally important issue for U.S. planners today is to develop interface standards with NATO allies so that as the U.S. military transitions through the information RMA, allied forces remain interoperable.

Organization theory draws attention to the noncompetitive or normative and legitimating bases for diffusion of ideas, practices, and organizational forms. Sociology's new institutionalism emphasizes noncompetitive processes that stimulate diffusion of forms and practices among organizations in the same line of business or profession. Emulation cannot automatically be attributed to competition and pressures for increased organizational efficiency.[13] Organizations have been known to emulate to attain legitimacy within a social system. Through socialization processes, generally accepted practices also spread within a profession. Paul J. DiMaggio and Walter W. Powell (1983, 149) argue, in their classic article on homogenization in organizational fields, that isomorphism, "a constraining process that forces one unit in a population to resemble other units that face the same set of environmental conditions," has institutional as well as competitive sources. Competitive isomorphism assumes market competition like neorealism, while institutional iso-morphism "can be expected to proceed in the absence of evidence that [the innovation] increase[s] internal organizational efficiency" (DiMaggio and Powell 1983, 153). Dana P. Eyre and Mark C. Suchman (1996, 96) elaborate, "later adoption (after the 'institutionalization' of the innovation) will no longer be predicted by technical characteristics and should be predicted by variables reflecting the *degree to which the adopter is connected to the social system within which the innovation is institutionalized*" (emphasis added).

From a neoinstitutionalist perspective, organizations "compete not just for resources and customers, but for political power and institutional legitimacy, for social as well as economic fitness," both within their own society and in the world system (DiMaggio and Powell 1983, 148–50). The legitimacy a particular practice receives in the world system may be greater than its legitimacy within the adopting society, though the fact that a form or practice is normatively sanctioned abroad increases the likelihood of its diffusion.

Three noncompetitive processes can produce similarity in a profession or field: coercive, mimetic, and normative.[14] Coercive isomorphism is tied to political influence and the problem of legitimacy. Organizational structures and behaviors over time come to conform to wider societal institutions and reflect practices institutionalized by the state. Coercive processes include "formal and informal pressures on organizations by other organizations upon which they are dependent and by cultural expectations in the society within which organizations function" (DiMaggio and Powell 1983, 150). Coercive processes can operate between states and within them. Military formats can be imposed by one state on another. Imperial powers may export their practices and impose them on colonial societies or client states. Within a state, cultural and societal expectations can force an organization to conform to wider institutions in society.

Through mimetic processes, organizations model themselves after other organizations perceived to be highly legitimate or successful. Particularly "when organizational technologies are poorly understood, when goals are ambiguous, or when the environment creates symbolic uncertainty, organizations may model themselves on other organizations" (DiMaggio and Powell 1983, 151). Lynn (1996, 510) notes in his study of the evolution of army style, "from time to time, a particular army became a model for its age; it provided the paradigm for other armies and, thus defined the core characteristics for a stage of military evolution. Until the mid–twentieth century, an army won the role of paradigm on the battlefield; in other words, victory chose the paradigm."[15] Modeling is an easy way to adopt a successful practice without investing resources in a search for alternative options. Modeling can also enhance the legitimacy of the organization to key external audiences.

Finally, normative pressures operate through professionalization (formal educational and professional networks). DiMaggio and Powell (1983, 155) hypothesize that the more professionalized a field, the greater the convergence in organizational form as members come to share norms of appropriate behavior (regulative norms) and identity (constitutive norms). Reliance on professional standards makes normative pressures high for military organizations. Professional networks are very important vehicles for the diffusion of new models. They "create a pool of almost interchangeable individuals who occupy similar positions across a range of organizations and possess a similarity of orientation and disposition that may override variations in tradition and control that might otherwise shape organizational behavior" (DiMaggio and Powell 1983, 152). Networks are also key avenues for transfer of information; accessibility of information about new models is important for explaining which models are adopted.[16] The interesting finding for a research program on military diffusion is that isomorphic processes "can be expected to proceed in the absence of evidence that they increase internal organizational efficiency" (DiMaggio and Powell 1983, 153). From an organization theory perspective, socialization processes are an equally important driver of military diffusion.

These findings suggest neorealist and bureaucratic perspectives on diffusion are incomplete because they focus only on competitive motives for diffusion and because they neglect the important question of *capacity* to emulate, beyond gross resources and organizational inertia. Theorists and practitioners need a usable theory of military diffusion that explains the balance between desire and capacity in determining state behavior. Organization theory's assumptions about compatibility provide a useful starting point for building a more complete theory of diffusion and military change. Given high incentives to emulate, whether motivated by strategic necessity or a quest for legitimacy and identity, one must assess the level of compatibility between local values and imported models, as well as the capacity of reformers to establish the legitimacy of new models and co-opt old traditions into new institutions. Extent of emulation will be driven by the amount of coercive capacity of reformers relative to local opposition, given a particular level of compatibility. Regardless of the level of competition, when social and cultural obstacles to importation of new models are great — or when compatibility is low — emulation is difficult. Under these conditions, coercive authority of reformers must be high for emulation to occur. High compatibility between local values and imported models creates a permissive environment for emulation to proceed, whether motivated by strategic necessity or legitimacy (Goldman 2000).

Organization theory, by embracing competitive and noncompetitive roots of emulation, helps account for emulation among nonadversaries as well as adversaries. Its attention to capacity and compatibility integrates systemic pressures for change with local requirements for change, pointing to a more complete and practically useful theory of military diffusion and its consequences.

### Research Program Challenge I: Definitional Fault Lines

Despite the relevance and intrinsic interest of questions related to the RMA, we have cumulated little theoretical knowledge on the subject. Two factors have contributed to this shortfall. First, the questions scholars pursue often reflect real-world policy problems. Interest in examining military revolutions follows in the wake of decisive events. The nuclear revolution stimulated tremendous debate on how mass destruction weapons had altered the nature of warfare.[17] U.S. performance in the Gulf War has likewise engendered debate in both scholarly and policy circles on the impact of information technologies and advanced conventional munitions on the future of war. Military historians have been engaged in a longer-running dialogue among themselves on the nature of military revolutions with a strategic purview spanning hundreds of years (Rogers 1995). They have just recently entered current policy debates, weighing in as skeptics that information technologies herald dramatic enough changes to be considered revolutionary.

A second reason for the lack of cumulative theoretical knowledge stems from the absence of a consensus on key definitions. To build upon analytical case studies and historical interpretations, one must surmount disagreements over what constitutes a revolution in military affairs. This is not merely a question of semantic difference or of individual preference. The consequences for theory development are far-reaching because a lack of *durability* in the theoretical variables and process events being studied will tend to produce *instability* in research results. Scholars will keep getting different answers to the same question. Lawrence Mohr (1982, 9–18) defines durability as "the extent to which the variable as a theoretical element has constant meaning across actors and is relevant and significant to the human condition in all places and at all times." If the meaning of the concept to actors changes over time or place, the factors deemed to influence it will also change.

The debate over what constitutes a revolution in military affairs is particularly contentious because it pits future-oriented policymakers, who emphasize how technology is altering the basis of military power, against the grand historical perspective of historians, who emphasize the social and cultural prerequisites of transformation. In policy circles, various terms are used interchangeably as a lexicon for future war. Military historians distinguish military-technical revolutions (MTR) from revolutions in military affairs (RMA), yet actually prefer a third term — *military revolution* — as coined by the British scholar Michael Roberts (1956) in reference to the changes in European warfare associated with the military reforms of Maurice of Nassau and Gustav Adolf II of Sweden. While Roberts recognized the importance of new technologies in transforming warfare in sixteenth- and seventeenth-century Europe, he relegated them to a secondary role, arguing that the more critical forces that set in motion the military revolution were nontechnological.[18] Following Roberts's lead, in the historical debate, the term *military revolution* has come to embrace a full range of political, social, economic, and cultural factors. Modern political and social innovations like seventeenth-century statism, eighteenth- and nineteenth-century democratic revolutions, and twentieth-century ideologically based people's war, are as important as developments in metallurgy, cavalry, gunpowder, transport, and communications. The military revolution, for historians, is as much an intellectual as a material event (Sullivan 1996, 3).

The concept of a military-technical revolution is associated with the writings of Soviet General Nikolai Ogarkov, who suggested in the early 1970s that emerging conventional (e.g., chemical, nonnuclear) explosives, coupled with the accuracy of precision weapons, were on the verge of becoming as decisive in warfare as nuclear weapons and would soon render the latter redundant and unnecessary. The U.S. defense establishment adopted the term *RMA* to describe the advanced technologies — microelectronics, computers, precision-guided munitions, sensors, stealth, the panoply of capabilities promised by the information age — that seemed to be rendering traditional approaches to warfare obsolete. An RMA was seen as a logical outgrowth of an MTR, but included as well innovations in operational concepts, doctrine, and organization needed to employ new technologies in order to realize a dramatic increase in military effectiveness.

The definitional debate may seem overly pedantic at first blush. It is important, however, because it bears directly on how one establishes empirical referents — the relevant universe of events — and on how one develops theory. How we choose empirical referents says a great deal about what we believe to be the most critical aspects of the phenomenon under examination. Andrew F. Krepinevich (1994) identifies ten military revolutions spanning the fourteenth century to the present (infantry, artillery, sail and shot, fortress, gunpowder, Napoleonic, land warfare, naval, interwar [including mechanization, aviation, and information], and, finally, nuclear). Alex Roland (1996) also identifies ten, but they are a different set (weapons technology, professionalization, mounted warfare, command of the sea, gunpowder, quantity-of-stuff, quality-of-stuff, air warfare, nuclear war, and guerrilla war). The Tofflers (1993) identify only three revolutions, one each associated with the agricultural, industrial, and knowledge revolutions.

Military revolutions are complex processes, which may explain in part why it is so difficult to build consensus among scholars on their fundamental attributes. The RMA debate labors under a false dichotomy: the technological/material versus sociopolitical/intellectual foundations of military revolutions.[19] Those who emphasize the technological and material foundations of dramatic increases in military effectiveness champion the nuclear revolution (ca. 1943) as evidence to support their model of military revolution, with its reliance on nuclear weapons, jet propulsion, and electronics. Those inclined to focus on the sociopolitical and intellectual foundations of military advantage tout the Napoleonic revolution (ca. 1790) to support their model, dependent as it was upon motivational changes like the injection of nationalism, mobilization of society for war, and universal conscription. The virtue of juxtaposing these two revolutions is that whenever scholars are asked to generate a list of RMAs, they invariably generate different laundry lists. However, the Napoleonic and nuclear revolutions almost always appear; so implicitly there is a recognition that the material-ideational distinction is a false one, and that an RMA must be defined by the result it produces rather than the forces that generate it. Historically, the nuclear and Napoleonic revolutions appear more the exceptions than the rule. Material and sociopolitical developments are interrelated and together produce the kinds of changes we associate with military revolutions. The industrial warfare revolution (ca. 1840) depended as much upon the rise of nationalistic and popular states that could fully mobilize their societies for war as it did upon the advent of industrial weaponry, steam transport, and the dread-nought battleship.

Casting the theoretical puzzle in terms of false dichotomies leads to unresolvable academic debate and hinders cumulation of knowledge, progress in the research program, and generation of policy-relevant insights. As scholars interested in developing theory and as policy-makers interested in operating in an informed manner, we would be better off eschewing debates about the essential causal importance of material versus ideational forces, and focusing instead on the processes of innovation and diffusion associated with them. A productive avenue of attack for examining complex political and social phenomena is to adopt a process perspective, as distinct from a causal perspective, and to focus on the processes associated with military revolutions.

### Research Program Challenge II: Methodological Fault Lines

When scholars cannot agree on definitions of key concepts, like military revolutions, the development of theory and its attendant policy-relevant implications may proceed in an ad hoc manner, and cumulation of knowledge is likely to suffer. A methodological fault line has equally important implications for hindering the advancement of knowledge about complex events. Given that there are likely to be multiple paths along which any military revolution unfolds, policymakers need an appreciation for these various paths and where they might be able to intervene to influence the process. Understanding the consequences of military diffusion involves understanding a policy process, a series of complex event sequences. Theories need to explain not only the policy outcome, but also the process of transformation, or the mechanisms that constitute the event sequence. Understanding the mechanisms by which causes lead to observed reactions, or how inputs are transformed into actions and then effects, is critical for the explanatory enterprise.

The problem is that the types of theories dominating social science thinking do not lend themselves to an understanding of process. Mohr (1982, 35–70) distinguishes the dominant variance-type theory from process theory. Variance theories often take the form of regression models.[20] The social scientist focuses on abstract variables and attempts to establish causal relations among them. Each cause is *efficient* in the sense that it is assumed to have a separable impact on the outcome. Intervening mechanisms may exist, but they need not be specified, because the social scientist is concerned with the independent effect of each variable in order to establish general explanations for an occurrence, not with understanding how causes are intertwined and connected. Causal effects are deemed superior to causal mechanisms as a basis for causal inference. Moreover, because each cause has an independent effect, time ordering among the independent variables is presumed immaterial to the outcome. In Mohr's (1982, 43) words, variance theories deal in snapshots rather than movies. They address the question "Why did the observed effect happen?" and rely on correlation between inputs and outputs to imply causation. As such, variance theories can achieve great parsimony and simplicity, but cannot address agency, action, or complex event sequences (Abbott 1992).

A variance theory must be strictly causal in the sense that the end result is foreordained when the first event occurs. This type of strict causality, however, is rare when explaining complex social phenomena. Depending on the issue area and context, intervening mechanisms or processes may introduce high levels of contingency, affecting the outcome and undermining the notion of efficient causality.[21] Military diffusion is precisely such an issue area and context. Process theories apply in areas where efficient causes are absent or presumed irrelevant. Process theory eschews efficient causality as explanation, focusing instead on how specified conditions combine to produce the outcome. Causal mechanisms serve as the basis for causal inference. Process theories deal with series of occurrences rather than sets of relations among variables. They address the question "How did the observed effect happen?" and present sequences of events over time as explanation. If the end result is not foreordained, a process theory approach is a more appropriate line of theoretical investigation.

Mohr (1982, 45) identifies three critical components of a process theory, which can be used to explain the paths leading to convergence and divergence in military forms: necessary conditions, necessary probabilistic processes, and external directional forces that move the focal unit — the receiving state — and conditions about in a characteristic way, usually by bringing them together. In a research program on military diffusion, necessary conditions include the existence of other military organizations that possess the information associated with the innovation. External directional forces include the pressures of competition and socialization that motivate states to respond to the emergence of superior military practices. Necessary probabilistic processes include the avenues that bring the organizations into contact and facilitate transfer of the new idea (e.g., confrontation, collaboration) and the factors influencing retention of the new idea by the receiving organization (e.g., compatibility, reformer capacity).

Precursor conditions are necessary, but not sufficient as in variance theory. Precursor conditions are only ingredients. They alone do not convey explanation because there is no inherent force that makes them inevitably combine to produce the outcome. Any one input is theoretically capable of leading to more than one outcome. Because the joining of elements does not follow inevitably from any set of antecedent conditions, how elements are combined (the intervening mechanisms or probabilistic processes) is of paramount importance to process theory and must be specified in order to produce explanation. In this sense, process theory resembles a recipe, comprising ingredients and how the ingredients are combined. Time ordering among contributory events becomes critical for explaining outcomes since it is rare for two events to have the type of independent connection with the outcome one sees in variance theory. While intervening mechanisms can remain unspecified in variance theory (since efficient causality ensures the outcome, regardless of the mechanism), in process theory, intervening mechanisms cannot be omitted without loss of vital information. Focusing only on outcomes and ignoring event sequences can lead one to dismiss important information, attribute causality incorrectly, and arrive at erroneous interpretations of what causes the observed behavior. [22]

Social science training is dominated by the variance approach. Process models receive less attention and are valued less by scholars. From the policymaker's perspective, the dominant mode in political science today produces overly broad generalizations, rather than insights based on detailed historical studies and analyses of process, which might truly be helpful. There is also a tendency, as Mohr (1982, 56–58) points out, to force process theory into the variance-theory mold, and this prevents scholars and practitioners from deriving the distinctive benefits of process models. [23] For example, explanations of the process of diffusion, or of how military practices are acquired, are explanations of dynamic processes. This differs from explaining which practice or form was adopted. The latter is an explanation of why one practice or form was adopted over another (Mohr 1982, 13). It is not an explanation of diffusion or innovation per se. Advances in understanding require both models of explanation to be pursued; and because the events of process theory make poor independent variables, and the predictors of variance theory make poor events for process models, the two types of explanation should be pursued separately (Mohr 1982, 66). Both types of theories have policy relevance. Mohr (1982, 70) argues, "From the perspective of the change agent or policy maker, both types of theory . . . can indicate factors that enhance or depress the probability or level of some occurrence. . . . Although each theory must be an integral, inviolate whole as theory, splintering and recombining is eminently possible and desirable in application."

Research on innovation and diffusion in organizations has been characterized by movement from variance to process theory research. Rogers (1983, 356) notes that by the 1970s, diffusion research began to look within organizations to understand the innovation process: "Instead of determining the variables related to more innovative and less innovative organizations, we began to trace the process of innovation within an organization." The process research sought to determine the time-ordered sequence of events, in contrast to earlier variance research, which consisted of determining covariation among sets of variables. Rogers (1983, 357) even goes so far as to argue that the early organizational innovativeness studies "could not have been designed more appropriately to *preclude* understanding the innovation process in organizations."

Process theories by necessity demand in-depth analysis, implying that only a smaller sample can be studied. There will be less basis for generalizations of research results. But, as Rogers (1983, 358) points out, "in return such an in-depth approach provides more reliable data and permits greater insight in tracing the nature of the innovation process in each organization. . . . The researcher learns more about less, rather than less about more." Yet given an area where current understanding is limited, "the in-depth approach of process research is more appropriate."

## Conclusion

Organization theory reveals the complexity of military diffusion that remains concealed by the assumptions of neorealism and the bureaucratic approach to organizational behavior. Since any particular U.S. action designed to forestall diffusion is likely to have only a transient impact, policymakers need a better understanding of the consequences of diffusion. Policymakers must examine a series of questions. What is the scope of diffusion, and is diffusion a uniform and even process? Or, like globalization, do military innovations spread and penetrate into various areas of the world unevenly? Neorealism predicts global diffusion; organization theory reveals obstacles to global diffusion. It compels policymakers to consider more closely factors influencing rates of adoption, such as characteristics of the adopting state (e.g., local threat environment; social, cultural, political, and organizational context; level of integration in the global military system); characteristics of the innovation (e.g., level of compatibility between the innovation and local values and practices); and relationship between the adopting state and the originating state(s). By what paths and what processes do innovations diffuse? Through competition, according to neorealism. This slights alternative noncompetitive transmission paths that should be of interest to policymakers, particularly as they consider the way the former Warsaw Pact and Russian militaries will develop. Finally, what are the likely consequences of diffusion? Emulation, according to neorealism and the bureaucratic model. By contrast, organization theory predicts reinvention, offset, and even no response, and it compels scholars to investigate under what conditions we should expect each of these consequences.

Policymakers require a clear analytical framework for assessing how the impact of new technologies and new ways of thinking may or may not be easily accommodated within existing institutional and organizational structures, processes, and behavior, and thus how likely others will be to assimilate and exploit the technology and organizational skills that embody the ongoing RMA. Organization theory provides such a framework and is the first step toward developing a methodology to assist the military planner in determining the ability of nations to implement new military ideas and practices. The academic community can serve the policy community's need for understanding military diffusion, and can advance academic knowledge in the process, by developing process theories of military diffusion and its consequences.

NOTES

1. A great deal of conceptual ambiguity surrounds the notion of technology. For a good overview of the definitional debate, see Ross 1993, 107–11. Military technology cannot be reduced to artifacts or physical instruments of warfare, to what Ross calls "hardware." Technology also includes "software," the information base for the tool, or "the means by which [the instruments] are designed, developed, tested, produced, and supplied—as well as the organizational capabilities and processes by which hardware is absorbed and employed" (111).

2. Military format refers to the totality of components of combat power, which includes doctrine, technology, recruitment, training, armament, and organization. See Posen 1994, 62–71.

3. Perhaps the one exception is the nuclear revolution, which was primarily technological.

4. Reinvention is defined as "the degree to which an innovation is changed or modified . . . in the process of its adoption and implementation." An innovation is "not necessarily invariant during the process of diffusion. And adopting an innovation is not necessarily a passive role of just implementing a standard template of the new idea." See Rogers 1983, 16–17. "Re-invention

represents changes in an innovation that are made by its adopters in order to fit the technology to their specific conditions" (146).

5. In one telling example, at a workshop on the "Revolution in Military Affairs," held in Washington, D.C., on July 1, 1996, sponsored by the Joint Center for International and Security Studies, a scholar/political consultant off-handedly remarked that there has never been an example where hegemony lasted for a very long time, and that others will balance against the United States, the assumption being that peer competitors will arise to challenge U.S. superiority.

6. Neorealism does not always predict emulation in specific cases. Resource endowments may make a new practice unaffordable. Geography may make it strategically unnecessary. Local threat environment may make it strategically unwise. Nevertheless, if effective offsets are unavailable, neorealism predicts innovative practices will tend to spread, a systemic outcome.

7. Neorealism emphasizes strategic necessity as the chief motive for emulation, but this could logically accommodate responses to highly specialized local military environments. Nevertheless, the theory emphasizes systemic regularities, so a state that neglected to adopt superior practices would eventually pay the price for its neglect, if only because the local adversary might adopt the innovation first.

8. I am grateful to John Lynn for discussion and correspondence on these points.

9. Along with compatibility, Rogers identifies other characteristics of innovations that explain their different rates of adoption. These include relative advantage (the degree to which an innovation is perceived as better than the idea it supersedes), complexity (the degree to which an innovation is perceived as difficult to understand and use), trialability (the degree to which an innovation may be experimented with on a limited basis), and observability (the degree to which the results of an innovation are observable to others). Most of these other factors relate to qualities of the innovation rather than of the adopting organization or society.

10. For example, not only are missiles less expensive than manned aircraft; they require less infrastructure to develop, and less training to operate and maintain. The question becomes whether they can be integrated into existing doctrine and organizations and, if not, how much adaptation is required.

11. Gregorian (1993, 142–47) argues that third world countries have a strong incentive to introduce new innovative systems, like GPS, that will significantly enhance their military capabilities. Moreover, GPS eliminates two major obstacles third world countries have faced: incompatibility with existing systems and dependence on suppliers. GPS is easy to integrate into current systems and can be bought commercially, eliminating any major obstacle to technology acquisition. Finally, targeting for GPS-guided munitions through satellite reconnaissance is an avenue now open to many developing states.

12. Harknett (1996, 37) notes that while "the United States may have required an advanced technological infrastructure to produce the global position-

ing satellite system . . . now all one has to do is go down to Radio Shack to purchase a GPS monitor to access the system."

13. This argument can be traced to Max Weber's contention that homogenization in organizational structures is a function of formal rationality. Rational adaptation results from the values and needs of modern society.

14. The typology is an analytic one, and the types are not always empirically distinct.

15. Following World War II, armies gained paradigm positions for reasons like ideology and arms sales.

16. Information also matters to neorealism. Assuming free information, neorealism predicts perfect adaptation. Assuming expensive information, neorealism predicts satisficing, or adopting the best model one can find out about. Neoinstitutionalism predicts choice of the most familiar model that is also domestically acceptable. The theories' predictions are not identical.

17. In the fall of 1945, T. R. Fox and Bernard Brodie gathered a small group of academics together to address basic questions about the nature of nuclear war. Their efforts led to the publication of *The Absolute Weapon* (New York: Harcourt Brace, 1946), the pathbreaking edited volume on the emerging nuclear age. Debate on the impact of the nuclear revolution continued throughout the succeeding half century.

18. Use of the term *technology* here is intended to distinguish the tools of warfare, like muskets, artillery, fortifications, and cartography, from broader social and cultural developments, such as the creation of the state, that influence military capacity and effectiveness.

19. My thinking on this topic has benefited greatly from conversations and correspondences with John Lynn.

20. Regression models can be structured to reveal a sequenced process as long as the sequence can be represented in the form of a diachronic linear equation. This is not usually done.

21. Mohr (1982, 42) argues the notion of efficient causality is metaphysical, or at least mysterious: "Since causality is an abstraction and cannot be directly observed, it must be an article of faith, but it is logically indispensable to the acceptance of explanatory theory based on necessary and sufficient conditions."

22. For example, the prevailing interpretation of the failure of the U.S. Army to mechanize after World War I focuses on the parochial interests of the Infantry. This turf-protecting argument supports the standard bureaucratic process model. A close tracing of event sequences, however, reveals that it was wartime experience that shaped interpretations of the role of the tank among key leaders like General Pershing. His views, in turn, influenced congressional decisions that only then resulted in increased Infantry control over mechanization. A focus on outcome alone leads proponents of bureaucratic interpretations to elevate a secondary level factor (Infantry parochialism) to a primary level cause. See Goldman 1997b, 48–52.

23. Mohr argues the true way to frame process theory is to state both the necessary conditions and the processes by which they are combined to produce

the outcome. The temptation, however, is to specify only the results of the processes and posit the whole chain as being a necessary and sufficient condition for the outcome. In this way, process theory becomes degenerative variance theory. A rich precursor is reduced to one dichotomy.

REFERENCES

Abbott, Andrew. 1992. "What Do Cases Do? Some Notes on Activity in Sociological Analysis." In Charles C. Ragin and Howard S. Becker, eds., *What Is
a Case? Exploring the Foundations of Social Inquiry.* Cambridge: Cambridge University Press.

Allison, Graham. 1971. *Essence of Decision: Explaining the Cuban Missile Crisis.* Boston: Little, Brown.

Arquilla, John, and David Ronfeldt. 1993. "Cyberwar Is Coming!" *Comparative
Strategy* 12 (April–June): 141–65.

Bacevich, A. J. 1994. "Preserving the Well-Bred Horse." *National Interest* (fall):
43–49.

Biddle, Stephen. 1996. "Victory Misunderstood: What the Gulf War Tells Us
about the Future of Conflict." *International Security* 21 (fall): 139–79.

Brodie, Bernard. 1946. *The Absolute Weapon.* New York: Harcourt Brace.

Cohen, Eliot. 1996. "A Revolution in Warfare." *Foreign Affairs* 75 (March/
April): 37–54.

Corbett, Julian S. 1918. *Some Principles of Maritime Strategy.* 2d ed. London:
Longmans.

Davis, Maj. Norman C., USMC. 1996. "An Information-Based Revolution in
Military Affairs." *Strategic Review* 24 (winter): 43–53.

DiMaggio, Paul J., and Walter W. Powell. 1983. "The Iron Cage Revisited:
Institutional Isomorphism and Collective Rationality in Organizational
Fields." *American Sociological Review* 48 (April): 147–60.

Eyre, Dana P., and Mark C. Suchman. 1996. "Status, Norms, and the Prolifera-
tion of Conventional Weapons: An Institutional Theory Approach." In
Peter J. Katzenstein, ed., *The Culture of National Security: Norms and
Identity in World Politics.* New York: Columbia University Press.

Farrell, Theo. 1996. "Figuring Out Fighting Organizations: The New Organisa-
tional Analysis in Strategic Studies." *Journal of Strategic Studies* 19 (March):
122–35.

Feaver, Peter D. 1997a. "Deterrence in the Information Age." Paper prepared
for the annual meeting of the International Studies Association, Toronto,
Ontario, March 18–22.

———. 1997b. "Information Warfare and the Political Control of Coercion."
Paper prepared for "Les Problèmes Militaires en Europe," conference spon-
sored by the Observatoire du Changement Social en Europe Occidentale,
April 3–7.

Goldman, Emily O. 1994. *Sunken Treaties: Naval Arms Control between the
Wars.* University Park: Pennsylvania State University Press.

————. 1997a. "Arms Control in the Information Age." *Contemporary Security Policy* 18 (August): 25–50.

————. 1997b. "The U.S. Military in Uncertain Times: Organizations, Ambiguity, and Strategic Adjustment." *Journal of Strategic Studies* 20 (June): 41–74.

————. 2000. "The Spread of Western Military Models to Ottoman Turkey and Meiji Japan." In Theo Farrell and Terry Terriff, eds., *The Sources of Military Change*. Boulder: Lynne Rienner.

Gregorian, Raffi. 1993. "Global Positioning Systems: A Military Revolution for the Third World?" *SAIS Review* 13 (winter–spring): 133–48.

Harknett, Richard J. 1996. "The Information Technology Network and the Ability to Deter: The Impact of Organizational Change on Twenty-first Century Conflict." Paper presented at The Revolution in Military Affairs Conference, sponsored by the Joint Center for International and Security Studies and *Security Studies,* Monterey, California, August 26–29.

Huntington, Samuel P. 1957. *The Soldier and the State.* Cambridge: Harvard University Press.

Katzenbach, Edward L., Jr. 1958. "The Horse Cavalry in the Twentieth Century." *Public Policy.* Reprinted in Robert J. Art and Kenneth N. Waltz, eds., *The Use of Force: Military Power and International Politics,* 4th ed. (Lanham, Md.: University Press of America, 1993).

Kier, Elizabeth. 1995. "Culture and Military Doctrine: France between the Wars." *International Security* 19 (spring): 65–93.

Krepinevich, Andrew F. 1994. "Cavalry to Computer: The Pattern of Military Revolutions." *National Interest* (fall): 30–42.

Legro, Jeffrey W. 1995. *Cooperation under Fire: Anglo-German Restraint during World War II.* Ithaca: Cornell University Press.

Levitt, Barbara, and James G. March. 1988. "Organizational Learning." *Annual Review of Sociology* 14:319–40.

Lynn, John A. 1996. "The Evolution of Army Style in the Modern West, 800–2000." *International History Review* 18 (August): 505–45.

Mahnken, Thomas G. 1991. "Why Third World Space Systems Matter." *Orbis* (fall): 563–79.

Mansfield, Edwin. 1968. *The Economics of Technological Change.* New York: W. W. Norton.

McNeill, William H. 1982. *The Pursuit of Power: Technology, Armed Force, and Society since A.D. 1000.* Chicago: University of Chicago Press.

Mohr, Lawrence B. 1982. *Explaining Organizational Behavior: The Limits and Possibilities of Theory and Research.* San Francisco: Jossey-Bass.

Moodie, Michael. 1995. "Beyond Proliferation: The Challenge of Technology Diffusion." *Washington Quarterly* 18 (spring): 183–202.

Nolan, Janne. 1991. *Trappings of Power: Ballistic Missiles in the Third World.* Washington, D.C.: Brookings Institution.

Nye, Joseph S., and William A. Owens. 1996. "America's Information Edge." *Foreign Affairs* 75 (March/April): 21–36.

Posen, Barry. 1984. *The Sources of Military Doctrine*. Ithaca: Cornell University Press.

———. 1994. "Military Lessons of the Gulf War — Implications for Middle East Arms Control." In Shai Feldman and Ariel Levite, eds., *Arms Control and the New Middle East Security Environment*. Boulder: Westview Press.

Ralston, David B. 1990. *Importing the European Army: The Introduction of European Military Techniques and Institutions into the Extra-European World, 1600–1914*. Chicago: University of Chicago Press.

Resende-Santos, Joao. 1996. "Anarchy and the Emulation of Military Systems: Military Organization and Technology in South America, 1870–1930." *Security Studies* 5 (spring): 193–260.

Roberts, Michael. 1956. "The Military Revolution, 1560–1660." Rev. 1967. Reprinted in Clifford J. Rogers, ed., *The Military Revolution Debate: Readings on the Military Transformation of Early Modern Europe*. Boulder: Westview Press, 1995.

Rogers, Clifford J., ed. 1995. *The Military Revolution Debate: Readings on the Military Transformation of Early Modern Europe*. Boulder: Westview Press.

Rogers, Everett M. 1983. *Diffusion of Innovations*. 3d ed. New York: Free Press.

Roland, Alex. 1996. "Comparing Military Revolutions." Paper The Revolutions in Military Affairs Conference, sponsored by the Joint Center for International and Security Studies and *Security Studies*, Monterey, Calif., August 26–29.

Rosen, Stephen Peter. 1988. "New Ways of War: Understanding Military Innovation." *International Security* 13 (summer): 134–68.

———. 1991. *Winning the Next War: Innovation and the Modern Military*. Ithaca: Cornell University Press.

———. 1996. *Societies and Military Power: India and Its Armies*. Ithaca: Cornell University Press.

Ross, Andrew L. 1993. "The Dynamics of Military Technology." In David Dewitt, David Haglund, and John Kirton, eds., *Building a New Global Order: Emerging Trends in International Security*. New York: Oxford University Press.

Ryan, Donald E., Jr. 1994–95. "Implications of Information-Based Warfare." *Joint Forces Quarterly* (autumn/winter): 114–16.

Sagan, Scott D., and Kenneth N. Waltz. 1995. *The Spread of Nuclear Weapons: A Debate*. New York: W. W. Norton and Co.

Schwartau, Winn. 1996. *Information Warfare*. 2d ed. New York: Thunder's Mouth Press.

Scott, W. Richard. 1992. *Organizations: Rational, Natural and Open Systems*. 3d ed. Englewood Cliffs, N.J.: Prentice-Hall.

Snyder, Jack. 1984a. "Civil-Military Relations and the Cult of the Offensive, 1914 and 1984." *International Security* 9 (summer): 108–46.

———. 1984b. *Ideology of the Offensive: Military Decision Making and the Disasters of 1914*. Ithaca: Cornell University Press.

Sullivan, Brian R. 1996. "What Distinguishes a Revolution in Military Affairs from a Military Technical Revolution?" Paper prepared for The Revolutions in Military Affairs Conference, sponsored by the Joint Center for International and Security Studies and *Security Studies,* Monterey, Calif., August 26–29.

Toffler, Alvin, and Heidi Toffler. 1993. *War and Anti-War: Survival at the Dawn of the Twenty-first Century.* Boston: Little, Brown.

Van Evera, Stephen. 1984. "The Cult of the Offensive and the Origins of the First World War." *International Security* 9 (summer): 58–107.

Waltz, Kenneth. 1979. *Theory of International Politics.* Reading, Mass.: Addison-Wesley.

Westney, D. Eleanor. 1987. *Imitation and Innovation: The Transfer of Western Organizational Patterns to Meiji Japan.* Cambridge: Harvard University Press.

Wright, Quincy. 1955. *The Study of International Relations.* New York: Appleton-Century-Crofts.

Zisk, Kimberly Martin. 1993. *Engaging the Enemy: Organization Theory and Soviet Military Innovation, 1955–1991.* Princeton: Princeton University Press.

# From Sea-Lanes to Global Cities: The Policy Relevance of Political Geography

*Donna J. Nincic*

## Introduction

This essay attempts to shed light on the developing context within which the United States will conduct its foreign policy. It points to trends in the global political economy whose implications have largely escaped the notice of political scientists, although they have caught the attention of policymakers. It asks how international relations theory might respond to these developments. Thus, this essay seeks to be relevant in a contextual manner.

One of the major criticisms of post–Cold War U.S. foreign policy has been its lack of identifiable focus. However, these criticisms miss the fact that recent U.S. foreign policy has been grounded in the idea that the world should be conceived in economic, rather than strategic, terms. George Bush, the first post–Cold War president, arguably fought the Gulf War for the economic security of global oil supplies. The Clinton administration has made the economic focus more explicit. "My first foreign policy priority," said president-elect Bill Clinton, "will be to restore America's economic vitality" (Garten 1992/93, 16). The economic focus has continued throughout his second term. Madeleine Albright, accepting the secretary of state nomination, said that a goal of her foreign policy would be to "insure for the American people a future of steadily increasing prosperity" (Excerpts 1996, A14). U.S. policies toward China, and Washington's responses to the Asian financial crisis in general and the Japanese economic crisis in particular, only underscore the primacy of economic well-being as a guiding tenet of U.S. foreign policy. For the first time since the early decades of this century, the United States has a foreign policy that is motivated *primarily* by economic, rather than security, concerns.

The extent of the criticisms about the lack of a coherent post–Cold War foreign policy, coupled with the fact that so many have missed the economic focus of the foreign policy, is, in part, the fault of those who provide the general theoretical framework for understanding foreign policy: the academic community. International relations (IR) and international political economy (IPE) theories provide little help to policymakers in understanding a world that is now primarily oriented toward economic bases of power rather than toward security objectives and "high" politics. IR has focused its attention since the end of World War II on the Cold War and issues of security and hard military power, and has been rudderless since the end of the Cold War. IPE has devoted its attention largely to the north-south divide and to "hard" aspects of economic power such as sanctions and coercive economic instruments. While regime theories and theories of complex interdependence take more cognizance of the economic nature of world affairs, with few exceptions they tend to treat the global political economy *apart* from the policy of states; their approach tends to focus on the systemic level of analysis. When they do deal with international political economy in the context of specific actions of states, they tend to do so either from a hard approach (how economic policy can strengthen the military power or coercive options of states) or from a secondary approach, focusing, for example, on trade negotiations, the bureaucratic politics of foreign economic policy-making, or prescriptions for U.S. economic renewal. This latter approach still treats matters of international economic policy apart from, or secondary to, higher affairs of state — those dealing with traditional national security. Few authors have opted for a more inclusive approach, such as that of Nye (1990) and Gilpin (1975), who recognize that, often, economic power *is* power, quite independent of its coercive potential.

There has been very little attempt in IR generally, or IPE specifically, to move away from the secondary focus of foreign economic policy, and toward a universal informing theory of the general nature of the new global economy and its implications for U.S. foreign policy. Few approaches treat issues of international economic policy as equal to, let alone superior to, national security policy. Additionally, the IPE literature fails to understand that, in the absence of a clear military threat, foreign policy becomes economic policy, and national security becomes economic security. Consequently, with the end of the Cold War and the increasing (and increasingly willing) integration of the south into the north, IR and IPE are to a large extent theoretically rudderless.

Yet, a number of changes have taken place in the international economy over the last decade and a half with serious implications for the

United States. The world has moved toward a truly *global* economy, with more economic linkages between *all* nations of the world than ever before: the "dominant effective boundaries of the capitalist world-economy have expanded steadily from its origins in the sixteenth century such that today it encompasses the earth" (Wallerstein 1984, 2). This has led to two important, and related, structural shifts in U.S. trade with the rest of the world.

First, the United States is more engaged with the *global* economy than it ever has been in this century. With manufacturing accounting for only 17.3 percent of the U.S. economy in 1996 (*Statistical Abstract* 1997, 448), down from 28 percent in 1965 (Hughes 1994, 383) and 21.7 percent in 1980 (*Statistical Abstract* 1995, 452), and trade accounting for 25 percent of the U.S. economy in 1997 (Bureau of Economic Analysis 1998a) — an all-time high — the United States is now importing more of its material goods (producer and consumer) from abroad than ever before. This has specific *policy* implications for the United States that scholars have largely ignored: the increasing U.S. reliance on international trade implies the increased importance of the security of trade transportation, specifically that of global shipping routes. With more trade volume than ever before moving by ship throughout the world's oceans, the United States is finding that the security of the world's sea-lanes of communication (SLOCs) acquires increased importance. At the same time, the security of a number of the more important SLOCs may face significant threats from potentially hostile regional powers.

Second, the U.S. economy is now primarily service-driven; many workers once engaged in manufactured-goods production for the domestic market have now moved into the service sector. This is reflected in U.S. exports as well: services — especially producer services — are becoming a more important component of total U.S. exports, and the United States has been the world's leader in the export of producer services since the 1980s (Price and Blair 1989, 177). As was the case with the increased U.S. reliance on goods trade, the rise of the United States as a global services provider has profound implications for U.S. foreign policy. In a world where international services — especially financial services — are increasingly independent of state control, Washington is no longer able to shape and guide the global economy in ways it used to be able to do in earlier years.

Political science has tended to neglect the globalization phenomenon in a way that has relevance for traditional IR concerns: there is a discipline-wide neglect both of the increased importance of trade routes to the United States and of the importance of the global service economy to the *power of the state*. For example, since 1980, *International*

*Organization* (a leading IPE journal) published only 17 articles on global services (out of a total 295), and most of these dealt with specific aspects of the service economy, such as regulatory issues under GATT, the computer industry, or capital markets. Two articles dealt with trade transportation (Juda 1981; Cafruny 1985), but neither dealt with the integrity of global trade routes. None of these articles addresses issues such as the internationalization of the producer services sector, the increasing importance of services in general to advanced industrial economies, the rise of the "global" or "world" city, or the political impact of financial and technological deregulations in the early 1980s on modern economies.[1] For example, as pointed out by one writer: "The mainstream of political science research on international relations has almost totally ignored cities" (Alger 1990, 100).

Thus, the policy implications of increased U.S. reliance on goods trade, the integrity of global sea-lanes of communication by which this trade is conducted, and the importance of these sea-lanes to U.S. economic strength and security have yet to be explored. Similarly, the international service sector (the most rapidly growing sector of U.S. foreign trade) and the blurring of domestic and foreign financial policies cannot be placed in any solid theoretical context. In either case, the implications for U.S. power are not fully understood.

## Looking Back to the Future: A Reexamination of Political Geography

IR and IPE theories need to redress the intellectual omissions that allow such gaps to persist. To do so, scholars might ask whether a revival of the earlier disciplinary focus on *political geography* might be useful; for, "in a period of accelerated technological and social changes, a re-evaluation of established hypotheses, in light of these changes, can be as useful to the development of theory as a search for novel hypotheses" (Zoppo 1985, 1). Returning to its roots in political geography might help IR become more policy-relevant. As observed by Harold and Margaret Sprout, two of the last political scientists fully to appreciate the importance of geography to political science:

> Without knowledge *both* of man's physical habitat, the earth, *and* of his ever-changing adjustment and relationship to that habitat, there can be no real understanding of the rise and decline of nations, of national aims and policies, of the causes of international strife, or of man's repeated attempts to establish a more stable political order upon the earth. (Sprout and Sprout 1951, 79)

Political geography is concerned both with the impact of geography on a state's power and security and with how states manage their relationship to geography in light of constantly changing technological advances and policy preferences. Traditionally, it has described *static conflict relationships,* since physical geography does not change and conflict is a defining feature of the system (Fox 1985, 31). More recently, however, it has focused on *dynamic "nondeterministic" relationships,* as technology and policy allow for the possibility of a state's relationship to geography to change, but in ways that are not always predictable.

An illustration is in order. According to traditional geopolitical theories, the United States — a physically large, agriculturally productive country, endowed with a population base sufficient to support significant economies of scale in manufacturing — historically has not depended on the world economy for its economic growth. Additionally, as an "island nation," the United States was not presented with easy trade with the economically advanced nations of Europe. Thus, the country developed and thrived in semi–isolation. More recently, however, technology and policy have changed the relationship of the United States to its own geography. The rise of the service sector has lessened U.S. dependence on its *own* physical geography for goods production, but has increased its dependence on the *world* physical geography, due to Washington's greater reliance on foreign trade. While technology has allowed the service sector to thrive, policy has promoted a free-trade orientation that allows the United States to depend on the world economy for increasing amounts of its manufactured goods. Thus, "[g]eography, technology and the power politics of major powers in the modern system of nations continue to be intrinsically related" (Zoppo 1985, 2), but technological innovation fundamentally changes our relationship to our geography by "alter[ing] the role of geographical factors and their comparative importance, without eradicating them" (Kinnas 1985, 255).

Therefore, political geography has two important implications for IR and IPE: (1) it deals with the continued impact of physical circumstances on a nation's possibilities for action; and (2) it addresses the *management* of the changing relationship to these physical realities. Although related, these two components are distinct. The first is rooted in traditional political geography, dealing with the political impact of the hard geographical realities nations face. The second acknowledges that while physical realities are immutable, a nation's relationship to them will change, given technological advances. Nuclear weapons and advanced telecommunications, for example, will necessarily change the relationship between a state's power, its own geography, and the world geography. Political geography, as a discipline, merely recognizes this as fact, and it focuses as much on the study of how nations *control* geographical space (their own physical geography or that of others—their sphere of influence), given those technological advances that have collapsed (but not erased) space and time. At the same time, as a discipline, it continues to focus on the implications of those physical realities that technology has not yet overcome.

I will explore two largely neglected issues that illustrate the policy relevance of political geography. The relevance of traditional political geography will be illustrated by the increasing importance of sea-lanes of communication (SLOCs—the world's shipping routes) to the United States and by the ways in which their security could be threatened. The second aspect of political geography I will discuss concerns the world city and the U.S. position as global leader in international producer services, with the implications this has for U.S. policy.

## Geography, Maritime Trade, and Sea-Lanes of Communication

The United States is the world's largest economy and has dominated the global economic system since the end of World War II. It is the world's largest financial power, and the U.S. dollar is still the international transaction currency of choice. The United States is the world's largest agricultural exporter and the world's largest user of international shipping services (Office of the Federal Register 1996, p. 1942). Trade as a percentage of U.S. GDP (while still not at the levels of the other advanced industrialized economies) is at an all-time high, reaching 23.6 percent in 1995, more than double the figure of 10.8 percent in 1970. At no previous point in its history has the United States been so dependent on the global economy. Three aspects of this dependence are worth considering. First, the United States is importing increasing amounts of industrially significant goods from abroad, as well as greater percentages of consumer goods than ever before. Second, U.S. exports are supporting increasing numbers of U.S. jobs. Third, in spite of great technological advances, the United States remains as dependent as ever on foreign supplies of many raw materials, including oil. Rarely addressed is the fact that the vast majority of these goods and commodities are traded by sea.

*Reliance on goods imports.* U.S. total trade in goods has remained steady since the 1970s, comprising from three-quarters to four-fifths of all U.S. foreign trade; in 1996 merchandise trade was 79 percent of total trade (U.S. Census Bureau 1997b). The import side of the equation, however, reflects an increasing dependence on the import of goods from abroad. In the 1970s, goods imports comprised approximately 73 percent of all U.S. imports; by 1996 that figure had jumped to over 84 percent (U.S. Census Bureau, 1997b).

Looking only at imports of manufactured goods (table 1), we see that capital goods, industrial supplies, materials, and consumer goods account for the bulk of U.S. manufactured imports. Consumer goods alone account for nearly one-fifth of all U.S. merchandise imports, meaning that the United States is relying on the import of less-expensive consumer goods to help maintain its high standard of living. When we consider that many automotive imports are destined for consumer use, and that much of industrial production in the United States (supported by the import of capital goods and industrial supplies and materials) consists of consumer goods, it is clear that a good portion of U.S. imports do, indeed, help support the high U.S. standard of living.

*Jobs, economic growth, and exports.* The export side of U.S. trade paints a similar picture. Exports have accounted for most of U.S. GDP growth in recent years. Some 14 million workers owe their jobs to exports, and since 1984 "virtually all the increase in the U.S. manufacturing sector can be attributed to sales abroad" (Garten 1992/93, 23), helping to resuscitate many manufacturing sectors that had been considered noncompetitive in the global economy. U.S. car exports are up, and U.S. workers have again been declared the most productive in the world—a position lost for many years during the 1980s when the United States was pursuing more protectionist policies toward the rest of the world. In fact, the foreign dimension of the U.S. economy is so integral that "it is misleading to label it 'foreign' " (Garten 1992/93, 19).

*Import dependence on raw materials.* What was true in the early decades of this century still largely obtains today: "[E]conomically, the Western Hemisphere is dependent on the products of the Old World for the strategic raw materials for its war industries, and the same applies to

**TABLE 1. U.S. Merchandise Trade: Percentage of Total Merchandise Imports, 1993–97**

|  | 1993 | 1994 | 1995 | 1996 | 1997 |
|---|---|---|---|---|---|
| Foods, feeds, beverages | 4.7 | 4.6 | 4.5 | 4.5 | 4.6 |
| Industrial supplies and materials | 25.9 | 24.6 | 24.5 | 25.7 | 24.5 |
| Capital goods | 25.9 | 27.6 | 29.8 | 28.8 | 29.1 |
| Automotive | 17.4 | 17.7 | 16.6 | 16.2 | 16.2 |
| Consumer goods | 22.7 | 21.9 | 21.5 | 21.5 | 22.2 |

*Source:* U.S. Census Bureau 1994, 1997a.

many of the articles necessary to preserve its standard of living" (Spyk-man 1942, 451). Now, at the end of the twentieth century, the United States still has a net dependence on many strategic raw materials such as chromium, manganese, and platinum (table 2). Chromium and manganese are vital to the steel and aerospace industries. Chromium is required to augment the hardness of steel and to enhance its resistance to corrosion. It has no known substitute in its antioxidation function and is, therefore, critical to industrial and military applications. Manganese is also a hardener and has the added attraction of being nonmagnetic, making it very useful for navigation systems. The platinum-group metals are essential to the production of automobile emission-control systems.

U.S. reliance on oil imports is also notable (table 3), as Washington currently imports nearly half of its total oil needs (a figure that will rise to over one-half of U.S. consumption early in the next century, according to current projections). While the security of Middle Eastern supplies typically receives the most attention, the United States actually depends on its closer neighbors for the largest share of its oil import needs, meaning that political stability and security of its oil supply are foreign policy issues spanning all continents. Where oil cannot be transported, or transported securely, by pipeline, rail, or truck, it must be transported by ship.

### Geographical Considerations

The *geographical* implications of the current U.S. trade expansion are rarely considered. The United States trades actively with every region of the world. Approximately 31 percent of U.S. trade is with Asia, compared to 38 percent within North America and 19 percent with Europe

**TABLE 2.   U.S. Net Import Reliance on Various Strategic and Critical Materials, 1994**

| Raw Material | Percent Net Reliance | Primary Supplier and Percent Supplied |
| --- | --- | --- |
| Manganese | 100 | South Africa (24) |
| Chromium | 75 | South Africa (43) |
| Platinum | 91 | South Africa (47) |
| Tin | 84 | Brazil (25) |
| Cobalt | 79 | Zambia (26) |
| Bauxite | 99 | Australia (36) |
| Tungsten | 94 | China (45) |

*Source: Statistical Abstract 1995, 715.*

(Bureau of Economic Analysis 1998b). While Canada and Mexico—the largest and third largest U.S. trading partners—are contiguous countries, trade with all other countries must be done by ship or air. Even in the cases of Canada and Mexico, much of this trade is done by these means as well. The importance of maritime shipping to U.S. foreign trade must not be underestimated. For example, while 30 to 50 percent of the dollar value of U.S. trade involves airfreight, over 90 percent of the tonnage of goods traded internationally still moves by ship (*Statistical Abstract* 1995). It is also noteworthy that nearly 68 percent of U.S. shipping imports (by weight) in 1994 consisted of petroleum and petroleum products (Water Resources Support Center 1995).

### Protecting Trade: The Vital Role of the SLOCs

While the world's oceans seem to be a vast open plain, the global seas are actually more similar to a modern superhighway than to the unbroken prairies of former times. Ships can *in theory* go anywhere, but the most efficient means of getting from point A to point B have remained quite constant for more than a century. In spite of technological advances in transportation systems, prevailing winds, as well as ocean currents and predominant weather patterns, determine the safest and most efficient routes and have done so for years. A chart of shipping routes in 1911 shows them as remarkably similar to those used by the United States today.[2]

The United States currently depends on some 20 shipping routes for all of its merchandise and raw materials trade (table 4). While many of these trade routes are on the open ocean, nearly all traverse a narrow

**TABLE 3. U.S. Petroleum Imports and Top Suppliers**

|  | 1993 | 1994 | 1995 | 2000 | 2005 | 2010 | 2015 |
|---|---|---|---|---|---|---|---|
| Imports as percentage of total consumption | 43.6 | 44.4 | 46.8 | 53.3 | 54.0 | 51.7 | 50.1 |
| Top five suppliers: Percentage of total imports |  |  |  |  |  |  |  |
| Venezuela | 14.9 | 14.6 | 15.9 |  |  |  |  |
| Canada | 13.3 | 13.9 | 14.4 |  |  |  |  |
| Saudi Arabia | 18.9 | 18.3 | 17.4 |  |  |  |  |
| Mexico | 12.7 | 13.3 | 14.2 |  |  |  |  |
| Nigeria | 10.7 | 8.8 | 8.6 |  |  |  |  |

*Source: Statistical Abstract 1997, 582, 591.*

area in the territorial seas of another state at one point or another. These are known as *chokepoints* — usually a narrow strait or passage through an isthmus (the Panama Canal), through a group of islands (the Strait of Malacca), or between two continental shores (the Strait of Hormuz). Choke points are vulnerable due to natural hazards (shallow depth, for example, or dangerous shoals), because of greater danger of collision due to increased congestion, and/or because they could be closed by an unfriendly state. While all choke points are vulnerable to oil spills or collisions — merchant shipping tonnage, for example, has doubled in the Western Pacific in recent years, greatly increasing the risk of collision (Anderson 1996) — two are of specific concern due to existing or potential regional instability: the Strait of Malacca connecting the Northern Indian Ocean with the increasingly contentious South China Sea, and the Strait of Hormuz in the Persian Gulf.

### The South China Sea and the Strait of Malacca

Approximately 38 percent of total U.S. trade is conducted with Asia, more than with any other region. U.S. shipping trade routes numbers 12, 17, 22, and 29 connect ports in the United States to ports in the Far East, Malaysia, Indonesia, and Singapore (Maritime Administration 1992, 29, 31). Numbers 12, 22, and 29 serve ports in the South China Sea as well as Pacific Russia, Korea, and Japan. U.S. trade route number 17 goes through the Strait of Malacca to Malaysia, Indonesia, and Singapore. While U.S. trade figures are not broken down for each of the trade routes, in 1990 (the last year for which figures are available), trade routes numbers 22 and 29 alone carried 17 percent (by tonnage) of all U.S. shipping imports and 33 percent (by tonnage) of all U.S. shipping exports (Maritime Administration 1992, 113). As the route through the Straits of Malacca and Singapore is the shortest sea route between

TABLE 4.  **Most Frequently Used U.S. Shipping Routes**

| Trade Routes | Destination |
| --- | --- |
| 10, 13, 65 | Mediterranean, Black Sea, Portugal, Southern Spain, Morocco, Azores |
| 17 | Indonesia, Malaysia, Singapore |
| 18, 28 | India, Persian Gulf, Red Sea, Pakistan, Burma |
| 4, 19, 23, 77, 78 | Caribbean, East Central Mexico, Panama Canal Zone |
| 12, 22, 29 | Far East |
| Remainder | Europe |

*Source:* Maritime Administration 1992.

East and West, it is the most cost-efficient and preferred route. The shortest alternative route would involve at least another three days of sea voyage, making it in the interest of the global community that freedom of passage through the Straits of Malacca and Singapore is assured. At the same time, the Strait is one of the major transit points for Middle Eastern oil destined for such U.S. allies as Japan and South Korea (Department of Energy 1996).

While no direct threat currently confronts U.S. shipping interests in the South China Sea or the Strait of Malacca, these are areas of concern to the United States, largely because of China's 1992 claim to 95 percent of the South China Sea as its territorial waters (Anderson 1996). During the 1980s, China adopted a new "green-water" maritime strategy that was defined to extend its naval reach from Vladivostok in the north to the Strait of Malacca in the south by the year 2000, and a blue-water capacity is expected by the year 2020 (Downing 1996, 130). This area extends up to 1,000 miles from the Chinese mainland, and includes Japan and the Philippines within Beijing's security range. This area also includes the Spratly, Paracel, and Senkaku island chains, which China claims as its own and which are contested in varying degrees by six other states: Taiwan, the Philippines, Indonesia, Vietnam, Brunei, and Malaysia.

Behind China's motivation lies a growing reliance on foreign trade to meet the basic food and resource needs of its population: by the year 2020, it is projected that Beijing will have to import some 285 million tons of grain and some 210 million tons of oil (Downing 1996, 130), which would arrive from the Middle East through the Strait of Malacca; ensuring confidence in its ability to protect its supply lines throughout the South China Sea is a major Chinese priority.

While insisting that its policy is a peaceful one, and that it supports the principle of freedom of navigation in the South China Sea, China has, nevertheless, backed its claims with armed force on more than one occasion (a recent example is its brief military standoff with the Philippines in 1995 over Mischief Reef in the Spratlys). China has also engaged in a number of large and sometimes bellicose military exercises, such as those that coincided with the presidential elections in Taiwan in March 1996, when Beijing engaged in live-fire war games, involving more than 10 warships and as many aircraft dropping bombs, off the southeast coast near the Taiwan Strait.

China's dispute with Indonesia — the world's largest natural gas exporter — over the Natunas Islands is particularly troubling to the United States. In dispute since 1993, when China published a map showing "historic claims" to the islands, the Natunas are rich in oil and natural gas. In the summer of 1996 Mobil Oil purchased a 26 percent stake in a project to develop one of the world's largest natural gas fields in the Natunas; Esso Natuna, a division of Exxon, owns an additional 50 percent of the project (Mobil Takes 1996). In September 1996 the Indonesian military conducted its most extensive war games in four years on the islands; the location was chosen to carry the message that "the Natunas belong to Indonesia" (Ressa 1996).

The United States has expressed repeated concern over China's ambitions in the South China Sea, and it has maintained a highly visible naval presence in the area. In 1994 the USS *Kittyhawk,* en route to South Korea, observed the largest Chinese naval exercise to date and was briefly subject to deliberate tracking by a Chinese submarine (Downing 1996, 132). During the Taiwanese presidential elections, Washington ordered the aircraft carrier *Nimitz* and its supporting ships to join the carrier *Independence* and its group heading to the Taiwan Strait area to monitor growing tensions.

China's ambitions are not the only U.S. concern in the South China Seas. Indonesia, in an action unrelated to its dispute with China over the Natunas Islands, announced in 1996 that it intended to restrict military and commercial shipping to three lanes running through the archipelago (the ones running between Sumatra and Java, between Bali and Lombok, and through the Moluccan Sea). The United States lodged an "angry protest" with the Suharto government, as Indonesia's actions would keep U.S. naval forces out of the sea-lane that runs between Java, Sumatra, and Borneo, thereby hindering the movement of its naval forces in a crisis (Skelton 1996; Passage Limits 1996). Additionally, closing the sea-lanes would add millions of dollars to the cost of shipping between Australia and Japan.

### The Persian Gulf and the Strait of Hormuz

This is, by far, the world's most critical oil chokepoint. Approximately 14 million barrels of oil per day are exported from Persian Gulf producers through the Strait of Hormuz, destined for Japan, the United States, and Western Europe. At its narrowest, the strait consists of two mile-wide channels for inbound and outbound tanker traffic, as well as a two-mile-wide buffer zone. Closure of the strait could require the use of longer alternate routes, if available, at increased transportation costs (Noer 1996, 4). U.S. trade routes numbers 18 and 28 (U.S. Pacific and Atlantic Coasts and the Gulf of Mexico to India, the Persian Gulf and Red Sea, Pakistan and Burma) are at risk in this area of the world.

The most serious concerns in the region center around Iran and Iraq, with Iran being considered the greatest long-term threat to U.S.

interests in the region. Its strategic position at the Strait of Hormuz allows Iran to control egress from the Persian Gulf into the Arabian Sea and, through there, to the Indian Ocean and the rest of the world. In early 1995, Iran deployed some 6,000 troops and heavy weapons on Abu Musa and other islands in the Strait of Hormuz, the passageway for much of the world's oil. These forces are believed to represent "an Iranian desire to control the area around the Straits of Hormuz and to intimidate the smaller countries, particularly the United Arab Emirates, which also has claims on Abu Musa" (Swan 1995). Former secretary of defense Perry said that the deployment, which also included antiship Silkworm missiles and air defense missiles, "can only be regarded as a potential threat to shipping in the area" (New U.S. 1996). In April 1996 the Iranian navy conducted a series of naval maneuvers that had the effect of slowing ship traffic through the Strait of Hormuz. The action intimidated oil-tanker owners "into holding their ships back from potentially risky passages through [the] Strait, thus temporarily raising spot oil prices and helping fuel the dramatic 'week of hell' price drop in U.S. capital markets" (Iran Ends 1996). A similar exercise took place in April 1997, with Tehran stating it proved Iran could close down the Strait of Hormuz at will (Commander 1997).

## Geographical Vulnerability and Policy Implications

With few exceptions (Nincic 1985), political scientists have paid little attention to sea-lanes of communication. Nevertheless, geopolitical approaches to international relations can be increasingly policy-relevant, highlighting challenges that must be addressed. As we have seen, the ocean trade routes and their choke points are still vulnerable; the end of the Cold War has not removed the threat to the SLOCs. While many threats exist (collision, piracy, etc), the most problematic is still the threat of war and regional instability. Now, however, the threat to the SLOCs — and to U.S. trade — comes more from the indirect threat of regional instability, rather than from the threat of a direct attack on U.S. interests.

The United States is the only nation in the world capable of protecting the "freedom of the high seas" because it is the only nation with an effective blue-water navy. As Mackinder has said: "The man-power of the sea must be nourished by land fertility somewhere, and other things being equal — such as security of the home and energy of the people — that power will control the sea which is based on the greater resources" (1942, 34). Thus, Washington increasingly recognizes that economic power is based on trade, and that trade is guaranteed on the high seas by the U.S. Navy (Coulter 1996).

The Freedom of Navigation program was established in 1979 to "protest excessive coastal claims through diplomatic channels" and the physical assertion of its "navigation and overflight rights in the disputed regions" (Department of Defense 1995, I-1). Between October 1, 1993, and September 30, 1994, U.S. military units conducted Freedom of Navigation "assertions" against some fourteen countries claiming navigation privileges "contrary to international law" (see table 5).

Washington considers the protection of its commerce, sea-lanes, and freedom of navigation rights to be so important that the mission statements of its naval fleets state that they are to "defend and protect the territory, citizens, *commerce, sea lanes,* allies and other vital interests of the United States" (emphasis added). The United States has also shown a willingness to use the U.S. military more actively to protect the freedom of navigation rights. Two recent examples are its reflagging operation of Kuwaiti oil tankers during the Iran-Iraq War, and Operation Just Cause, one of whose justifications was the fear that Noriega would inhibit traffic through the Panama Canal (Leonard 1993, 99, 102). To meet the threat to the Strait of Hormuz, in 1995 the United States created a new naval fleet. Designated as the Fifth Fleet, its mission is "deterrence and peacekeeping in the Persian Gulf and Red Sea regions."

The United States recognizes that the U.S. military may also be needed beyond the Persian Gulf to prevent "disruption of trade" in its role of helping to secure the "material well-being and prosperity" of U.S. citizens (Department of Defense 1995, 1). In mid-1995 the Clinton administration stated its willingness to escort commercial shipping anywhere in an emergency (Calder 1996, 65). It has also made progress on reaffirming freedom of navigation in the strategic energy sea-lanes from the Persian Gulf to East Asia (Calder 1996, 65).

Thus, policy needs have outstripped the ability of theory to meet them; clearly more scholarly work on the security of the world's waterways, and their implications, is needed. Several issues should be addressed in this regard. To begin with, IPE scholars should develop a

**TABLE 5.    U.S. Freedom of Navigation Assertions**

| Excessive Claim Challenged | Countries |
|---|---|
| Prior permission for warship to enter 12NM territorial sea | Burma, Cambodia, China, Egypt, India, Maldives, Sudan, Sweden |
| Excessive straight baselines | Cambodia, Djibouti, Mauritania, Philippines |
| 200NM territorial sea | Ecuador, Peru, Somalia |

*Source:* Department of Defense 1995.

stronger understanding of the changed role that manufactured-goods import trade plays in the increasingly service-based advanced industrialized economies: as fewer manufactured goods are produced competitively at home, dependence on those that are imported becomes more and more rigidly entrenched. Thus, as greater percentages of domestic economic activity in the OECD countries come to be derived from services, the United States may find itself competing with Japan and Europe for the same sources of low-priced manufactured goods, just as we competed in earlier years over access to raw materials sources.

At the same time, although most of U.S. domestic economic activity is accounted for by services, we should not lose sight of the fact that U.S. goods exports are the fastest growing sector of the U.S. economy. While several specific U.S. security concerns stemming from this increased demand on the SLOCs have already been discussed, what has not yet been fully explored is the increased demand on the SLOCs from greater numbers of the world's nations as well. As more and more nations pursue the path of export-led economic growth, the world's ocean trade routes — a *fixed commodity* — are going to experience growing competition, breeding increased global insecurity about continued access.

These two issues — the potential for increased OECD competition for sources of manufactured goods, and the consequences of increased global demand on the SLOCs — represent far more generalized forms of the security dilemma discussed thus far: competition over markets and market access is as old as capitalism itself. Understanding how this is likely to play itself out in the next century is an important academic task. Thus, the foundations of political geography have highlighted areas of theoretical research with profound policy implications in the years to come.

### The Geographical Foundations of the Service Economy: The World City

The study of global trade in services and its policy implications are somewhat hampered by the difficulties of measuring accurately the scope of the global services sector. Services such as shipping, insurance, and banking are known as *invisible* services, meaning that the costs of those services needed to conduct international trade are less apparent than are the costs associated with the buying and selling of visible and tangible products (Juda 1981, 493). Thus, figures relating to a nation's international service trade generally fail to reflect their true magnitude, as most estimates of service trade are based on extrapolations from industry-provided figures. Many international service transactions are not recorded at all: information on data and computer processing is minimal to nonexistent, and transactions of U.S. service subsidiaries located abroad are not recorded in U.S. trade data if the buyers and sellers of the service are located in the same country. Additionally, the U.S. Commerce Department records data for some 10,000 manufacturing exports, but only 40 categories of service exports are maintained. Consequently the Office of Technology Assessment has estimated that the true value of U.S. service exports may be twice that which is reported in official statistics (Price and Blair 1989, 178). Nevertheless, official U.S. statistics report that U.S. trade in services comprises approximately one-fifth of total U.S. trade (Bureau of Economic Analysis, 1998a).

The geographical implications and policy relevance of U.S. trade in services are different from those in trade in agricultural and manufactured goods. For the latter, geographical constraints included the hard, physical realities associated with sea-lanes of communication. In the case of trade in services, the implications are not rooted in the hard, physical, geographical constraints; rather, they have to do with the ability of a state to control and shape events in its *relevant geographical space* — those areas of the world that are necessary to a nation's economic, political, and military well-being. As we shall see, the nature of the international service trade, in spite of the fact that the United States is its unambiguous leader, has weakened Washington's control over both the global economy and its domestic economy.

Current IR and IPE theories provide few insights here. While there has been some focus on the control of relevant geographical space in the nuclear war literature, the decline of the Soviet threat has led IR and IPE to downplay this issue in recent years. Nevertheless, the intangible control, or dominance, of geographical space is still important, although in ways unrelated to those seen during the U.S.-Soviet nuclear era.

### The International Service Trade and the Rise of the Global City

To understand the policy implications of a large and expanding service sector, and the way they are conditioned by political geography, we must distinguish between *consumer* and *producer* services. Consumer services (retail shops, medical facilities, legal services directed to individual rather than corporate needs, and the like) are not geographically determined in the same way as producer services (advertising, corporate law, information systems, and such), since the latter are conditioned principally by population density. Relatively free of geographical constraints, consumer services are likely to be much more widely distributed. Producer services, which are the focus of this discussion, are more likely to be concentrated in important business centers (Price and Blair 1989, 175).

In recent years, capitalist institutions have increasingly emancipated themselves from national constraints. The deregulation of financial markets in the early 1980s is a recent example of corporate flight from national control, as is the development of the Eurocurrency markets. The multinational corporation (MNC), expanding significantly during the 1970s, is yet another example. Political geographers note that while manufacturing goes abroad in search of less expensive sources of labor and more profitable situations for production, it also leaves "to obtain more flexible control over operations in the light of geopolitical uncertainties" arising from "the growing bargaining power of some developing countries, . . . growing international competition, [and the] constraints of organized labor and government regulations" (Alger 1990, 103).

Producer services became an increasingly important segment of the global economy coinciding with the economic deregulations of various service industries in the 1980s, leading to a profound internationalization of global services, especially finance, by the 1990s. A system of international financial markets developed, tied to the needs of major international firms and large multinational banks—not to the needs of national governments—and, thus, increasingly free from regulation by individual states (Alger 1990, 103).

Accordingly, the world economy increasingly transcends the nation-state and must now, as Wallerstein (1984) suggests, be viewed as an "organic" whole, whose constituent parts perform differentiated functions. The dominant global service powers are now located in a few world cities. Low-technology manufacturing is now located largely in the third world, while high-technology manufacturing characterizes the advanced industrialized countries. Revolutions in technology and in research and development have made possible the single global economy. Production has been transformed by innovations in robotics so that manufacturing often occurs with relatively unskilled (and cheaper) third world labor. Robots now perform many of the upper-end manufacturing jobs, reducing the requirement for a well-educated blue-collar workforce.

While trade in both low- and high-tech manufacturing has tended to be relatively evenly dispersed throughout the third world and the advanced industrial world, global trade in producer services (in spite of its presumed independence of geography) has concentrated substantially in a few world cities that have developed to "service and sustain this expansive internationalization." While some two dozen cities are recognized as world cities, the hierarchy is dominated by New York, London, and Tokyo. These three cities, "the capitals of global capitalism, span and scan the globe in a 24-hour sequence of shifts, assisted by a constellation of regional command centers and amazing new technologies of information and monetary exchange" (Soja 1991, 366–67). While its full implications are really only being felt now, the development of the global city has been noticed and studied by political geographers since the 1970s. As early as 1973, political geographers were drawing attention to new forms of urbanization, noting that the global economy was forming into a unitary hierarchy with "global centers dominating lesser centers" (Alger 1990, 103).

The geographical concentration of trade in producer services into a few world cities demonstrates that, for all the assumptions of the nonrelevance of geographical concerns, and for all its high-technology components, global producer services are fundamentally rooted in geographical notions of *space* and *place.* This is so because (1) the *production* of services is largely *geographically determined,* and (2) the *product* of producer services (legal advice, advertising, information, etc.), while *not* geographically bound since, theoretically, it *can* go anywhere, will, nonetheless, concentrate geographically in service and manufacturing centers. Most importantly, the service product is ultimately about the control and/or organization of space and place. Each of these premises is discussed below in some detail.

### The Geography of Producer Service Production

Political geographers argue that services, especially producer services, are largely tied to place and are, consequently, much more geographically constrained than is typically imagined. Why, and how, do political geographers believe services are dependent on geographical location? This is a question with implications for whether or not the United States will retain its currently overwhelming comparative advantage in the global service sector, and it has obvious policy implications. The reasons fall into two categories: those pertaining to actual physical geographical characteristics, and those that are nongeographical in nature but which, nonetheless, derive from a nation's geographical attributes.

*Geographical characteristics.* Cities initially developed around manufacturing activities. Those that performed best, and that had suitable geographical characteristics, became export sites. Cities located on rivers or on protected seas had a primary advantage: even today we don't find major global export centers far from the water. For example, London and New York are both historically important manufacturing sites; until very recently, New York was still an important light manufacturing center (Sassen-Koob 1986, 100). In the middle of this century, as manufacturing exports began to recover after World War II, these manufacturing and export centers attracted MNC investment, initially in manufacturing, but soon also in services. Foreign firms wishing to take advantage of a profitable manufacturing location located their production in receptive host countries. At the same time, foreign firms with services to offer their compatriot MNCs located abroad as well. For example, a foreign bank would open a branch office abroad to assist conational MNCs with profit repatriation and other related financial activities.

However, as low-technology manufacturing began to migrate from the industrialized countries to the third world, where wages were lower, service corporations found that they could not follow. The skill bases required for manufacturing and for the management of global finance, advertising, and information processing were entirely different. Service corporations—domestic and foreign—found that they had to remain where they were, in the once-great manufacturing and export centers of the North.

*Derivative characteristics.*   Three additional characteristics of service economies tend to concentrate them in a few geographical areas. These are intermediate service–demand, labor-demand, and uncertainty effects.

London, New York, and Tokyo are the world's three major financial centers, and firms in London and New York show very similar location decision-making behavior. In spite of expected increased competition, they concentrate together, in part because they depend on intermediate services. This is due to the fact that more and more firms are farming out noncore activities (data entry, accounting, advertising, payroll, legal) to specialized firms.[3] The more this occurs, the more likely it is that firms—at least at the headquarter level—will remain centrally located, and near each other (Price and Blair 1989, 180).

In addition to the requirement that necessary intermediate producer services be close at hand, the producer service economy requires a specialized labor force that tends to concentrate geographically. In order to attract a highly skilled, high-quality workforce to the kinds of world-controlling service industries discussed here, world cities must also provide amenities such as world-class hotels, restaurants, entertainment, real estate, and luxury shopping (Alger 1990, 101).

Lastly, political geographers have observed that, in times of economic uncertainty and downswings, geographic concentration intensifies within the producer service sector (Mitchelson and Wheeler 1994, 88); that is, transnational corporations tend to locate with and near one another, even if they are performing very similar functions. Expansion to new, untapped areas is both risky and costly; it requires specialized investment information, and there are practical costs to maintaining technical links to the center. While the rewards of success may be significant, the costs of failure may be too great to make the risk worth taking, especially when established markets have not yet become saturated. Thus, to avoid costly failures during economic downturns, firms tend to follow similar investment and planning strategies. The lack of MNC investment in Russia, in spite of optimistic medium-term economic predictions (Thurow 1996, 41–47), can be explained by uncertainty effects, as can investor hesitation during the 1997–98 Asian financial crisis.

### The Product of Global Services and the Control of Geographical Space

Technological breakthroughs linking the world through jets, computers, and communications satellites have made capital almost instantly and globally mobile. This has, perhaps paradoxically, created a world with an even greater need for centralized control.

Much of today's information and service economy involves attempts to control economic and, thus, geographical space. One *product* of the service economy — information — is also its *input* and, unlike the service economy itself, is spread throughout the space economy; it needs to be retrieved from individual firms and consumers in order to be economically useful (Hepworth 1989, 215). Therefore, the search for control of information, fueled by market deregulation and internationalization, has led to the development of global on-line information systems. These "geographical information systems" have become increasingly valuable product commodities (Hepworth 1989, 215), allowing for the increasing control of economic and geographical space by those who, ultimately, control these information systems.

Since very few firms have the ability to manage or, often, even to understand today's global economy via their own resources, they find that they have a much better chance of doing so jointly: thus, information access becomes controlled through a centralized location. The world cities are the logical result, arising, as they did, as centers for coordinating and controlling economic activity that has now attained a global scale. Thus, the firms in the global city have not only become centers for international decision making by major firms; they have also increasingly drawn the international activities of firms outside these cities into their own orbit.

## The World City and Policy Relevance

The growth of the world city and the position of the United States in the global service economy carry a number of policy implications, particularly for continued U.S. dominance in the international system. On the positive side, as long as the dollar remains the global transaction/reserve currency (Frankel 1995), a significant percentage of global financial transactions will be processed through New York's financial services economy. And as long as global finance is concentrated in New York, other service industries will concentrate there as well. Furthermore, on the positive side, prices of producer services are higher relative to commodity prices in the richer countries, meaning that the market for producer services in the poorer countries is likely to remain limited for some time. Until the poorer countries can afford rich country prices, trade in services will remain confined to the advanced industrial economies. Within the advanced industrial economies, only a few — the world cities — have developed a comparative advantage arising from their experience and knowledge of the global market (Price and Blair 1989, 177).

Since thriving service areas attract and welcome foreign investment, this could be viewed as a plus for the nation-state. This is because foreign money invested in the United States is money *not* invested in another economy to create competition with U.S. goods and services. Kenichi Ohmae (1993, 83, 85) makes exactly this point in his discussion of the region-state (manufacturing centers spanning the borders of several states) when he talks about foreign investment (primarily Japanese) into the U.S. entertainment industry: "The result: a $10 billion infusion of new capital and, equally important, $10 billion less for Japan or anyone else to set up a new Hollywood of their own."

At the same time, while all this economic power is physically *located* in the United States, Washington cannot easily harness this power to its own policy ends — domestic or foreign. Global cities, as controllers of global services, including the all-important global financial markets, can affect government power in negative, as well as positive, ways. Regardless of their physical location, they are linked to, and identify with, the global economy, more so than with any individual states. Consequently, their needs may clash with those of their host state. The vulnerabilities for the United States may be illustrated by (1) a lessened ability to affect the international value of the U.S. dollar and

(2) increased U.S. sensitivity to financial crises throughout the international system.

*Lessened ability to affect the dollar's value.* Large multinational corporations and banks may undermine government policies as they lessen their identification with the national interests of their home country (Alger 1990, 104). We have seen this in many nonservice areas. During the OPEC oil embargo in 1973, many U.S. oil companies, enriched by dramatic price rises, identified more with their Arab hosts than they did with the depredations caused to the U.S. economy. Similarly, during the Cold War, when Washington feared that allowing Western European dependence on Soviet energy supplies would undermine national security, it threatened sanctions on those who East-West energy projects. Subsidiaries of U.S. firms in England, wishing to do business in the Soviet Union on such projects, defied U.S. interests in favor of their own.

In the service area specifically, financial deregulation and the internationalization of global capital markets (the core business of the world city) have meant that capital movements can take place almost instantaneously and can respond immediately to perceived economic strengths and weaknesses. Individual nations — even those as strong as the United States — are increasingly helpless when trying to affect global financial flows and their effects on currency values. The United States and Japan have tried since the 1980s to address the trade imbalance between their two countries. However, no manipulation of exchange rates by central bankers or political appointees in Washington has ever "corrected" these trade imbalances, as exchange rate valuation is now set almost exclusively by the currency markets in the global cities, and not by government officials in Washington or Tokyo (Ohmae 1993, 83). The attempt in June 1998 by Tokyo and Washington jointly to bolster the yen's value is further evidence of the increased ineffectiveness of currency market intervention. After the two countries spent approximately $4 billion (Sanger 1998) to prop up the value of the yen, global currency traders forced it back to its former value within a week (Will Tokyo 1998).

Similarly, there is concern over the impact the euro might have on the value of the U.S. dollar. In recent years, the dollar has benefited from being a safe haven for foreign investors, which has allowed the United States to attract foreign capital and finance borrowing at lower interest rates than it might otherwise have had to offer. The ease with which capital can now flow from one global financial center to another means that a successful euro could challenge the primacy of the dollar. A stable alternative currency could lead to rises in dollar borrowing costs for governments and companies, and the potential for reductions in U.S. economic growth (Stevenson 1998). While scenarios for the future vary from the very optimistic to the very pessimistic, some analysts fear the United States could lose up to half a percentage point of annual growth from the establishment of a credible euro, while the European economies could gain half a percentage point (Stevenson 1998).

*Increased sensitivity to financial crises.* The U.S. economy has become more sensitive to global financial crises in which it is only indirectly a participant. For example, the 1997–98 Asian financial crisis was triggered by speculative attacks by global currency traders on the Thai baht, followed by a collapse of the Indonesian rupiah. By October 1997, the baht and rupiah had each lost over 32 percent of their value against the dollar, with the Malaysian ringgit falling nearly 25 percent, and the Philippine peso dropping almost 20 percent. The United States was able to stay aloof from these events until Hong Kong announced in October 1997 that, contrary to market expectations, it would not devalue its currency. Concern over this announcement led to the collapse of the Hong Kong stock market, which was quickly followed by steep declines in stock markets around the world, including the United States, which saw the largest point drop in history in the Dow Jones Industrial Average. While the U.S. stock markets quickly recovered, persistent weaknesses in the Asian economies (from Malaysia and Indonesia to Japan and South Korea) have led to steep declines in imports from the United States, meaning that the U.S. trade deficit has increased to all-time highs. Fears about dampening U.S. exports have led to increased concerns about a future domestic economic slowdown. The internationalization of the global service economy has meant that international events have become domestic events as well.

While more theoretical work has been done recently on the world city than on the SLOCs, a more thorough political comprehension of its significance is still needed to be fully useful to policymakers. None of the work on world cities to date has been by political scientists or IPE scholars; consequently, the relationship between the world city — a profoundly *economic* entity — and the *political* power of the nation-state in the international arena is largely unexplored. While many writers expect the increasing economic might of the globalized economy to weaken the power of individual states (Ohmae 1995; Rosecrance 1996), it is, realistically, far too early to predict the collapse or emasculation of the nation-state. Historically, states far weaker than the United States have adapted successfully to other dramatic global economic changes — such as the industrial revolution — without a significant loss of national power. The issue for scholars is to determine under what conditions adaptation to profound economic changes — such as the world city and the increasingly globalized economy — may be successful. Rather than either-or theories about the future of the nation-state in the global economy (with the balance nearly always tipped in favor of global economic forces), there is a need for a more profound theoretical understanding of how national power will shape, and be shaped by, global economic forces: this is something that political scientists, with our understanding of the nature of power, should be very well equipped to do.

## Conclusion

Although the U.S. economy has recovered from the economic slumps of the early 1990s, and economic indicators are stronger than they have been in years, the lens of political geography brings two important vulnerabilities into focus. As trade grows as a component of U.S. economic activity, security of its trade routes becomes increasingly important. This is especially true when some nations have become increasingly assertive about the control of major world shipping routes, particularly through crucial choke points. While the United States has always stood ready to protect world access to oil, challenges to free navigation in the Strait of Malacca and the South China Sea may expand its security responsibilities correspondingly.

At the same time, political geography reminds us that the nature of state power is changing. Economic activity increasingly escapes the control of any one nation-state. The manufacturing multinational corporation initiated the leakage of low-wage, low-skilled jobs from the industrialized world to the less industrialized world, causing employment dislocations in the advanced industrialized countries. Global service corporations affect the national economy in a different way. Jobs are not being lost; in fact, new jobs are being created in the service sector. However, the product of the service sector is the dispersal of information, technology, and transactions throughout the domestic and international economies. What is important is that this dispersal is controlled not by national governments, but rather by private corporations, often concentrated in global cities, quite independent of national capitals.

From the examples presented here, it appears that political geography may shed light on policy constraints and choices, by illuminating two realities of international relations: (1) hard, physical geography still matters; and (2) nations — or actors within nations — seek to control their relevant economic space (with varying degrees of success). What is increasingly true for the United States is that the hard, physical geography and the relevant economic space of importance to the U.S. economy are both larger than ever before, and their control often implies novel policy approaches. Yet, IR theory, ignoring political geography, has not developed this concept very far; it would help policymakers more if it did. IR and IPE theories, formed during the Cold War, defined relevant U.S. political, military, and economic geography and space, up to — but not including — the borders of the communist world. The emerging economy of the future mitigates these borders and makes U.S. interests completely global. For the first time in its history, U.S. economic interests have been brought completely in line with its global geographical position.

NOTES

1. While it could be argued that the primary concern of *International Organization* is regimes, it must be noted that, during the 1980s when the Law of the Sea Convention took effect (which, inter alia, normalized global shipping and navigation regimes, and created the 200-NM Exclusive Economic Zone) not a single article on this topic appeared.

2. For example, compare shipping routes in Bowman (1921, 11) to current U.S. trade routes (Maritime Administration 1992).

3. Activities in support of intermediate services need not be (and rarely are) centrally located. Agglomeration effects refer to command-level activities only.

REFERENCES

Alger, Chadwick F. 1990, Jan/Feb–Mar/Apr. The World Relations of Cities: Closing the Gap between Social Science Paradigms and Everyday Human Experience. *Ekistics* 57 (340/41) (double issue): 99–115.

Anderson, John R. 1996, May 22–23. Multi-National Naval Cooperation into the Twenty-first Century. *Halifax Maritime Symposium.* http://www.dal.ca/~centre/cfps.html.

Boggs, S. W. 1951. Political Geography Lessons for Americans. In Harold Sprout and Margaret Sprout, eds., *Foundations of National Power.* Toronto: D. Van Nostrand Company.

Bowman, Isaiah. 1921. *The New World: Problems of Political Geography.* Yonkers-on-Hudson, New York: World Book Company.

Browne, Marjorie Ann. 1995, December 14. The Law of the Sea Convention and U.S. Policy. *Committee for the National Institute for the Environment.* http://www.cnie.org.

Bureau of Economic Analysis. 1998a, April. GDP and U.S. International Trade in Goods and Services, 1970–1997. U.S. Department of Commerce. http://www.ita.doc.gov/industry/otea/usfth/t05.prn.

———. 1998b, April. US Total Exports, Imports, and Balances by Area and Year. U.S. Department of Commerce. http://www.ita.doc.gov/industry/otea/usfth/t09.prn.

Cafruny, Alan W. 1985. The Political Economy of Shipping: Europe versus America. *International Organization* 39:79–120.

Calder, Kent E. 1996, March/April. Asia's Empty Gas Tank. *Foreign Affairs* 75 (2): 55–70.

Commander: U.S. Will Defend Strait of Hormuz. 1997, May 11. *Reuters.* http://www.infoseek.com/Content?arn...2B7E662D186&ud4=1&kt=A&ak=headlines.

Coulter, Daniel. 1996, May 22–23. Global Trade Routes and the Importance of Shipping (Part 2). *Halifax Maritime Symposium.* http://www.dal.ca/~centre/cfps.html.

Department of Defense. 1995, February. *Annual Report of the Secretary of Defense to the President and Congress.* Washington, D.C.: U.S. Government Printing Office.

Department of Energy. 1996, August. World Oil Transit Chokepoints. http://www.eia.doe.gov/emeu/cabs/hot.html.

Downing, John. 1996, March. China's Evolving Maritime Strategy, Part 1: Restructuring Begins. *Jane's Intelligence Review* 8 (3): 129–33.

Excerpts from the Announcement on the Cabinet. 1996, December 6. *New York Times,* A14.

Fox, William. 1985. Geopolitics and International Relations. In Ciro E. Zoppo and Charles Zorgbibe, eds., *On Geopolitics: Classical and Nuclear.* Dordrecht: Martinus Nijhoff.

Frankel, Jeffrey. 1995, July/August. Still the Lingua Franca. *Foreign Affairs* 74 (4): 9–17.

Garten, Jeffrey. 1992/93, winter. The 100-Day Economic Agenda. *Foreign Affairs* 71 (5): 16–31.

Gilpin, Robert. 1975. *U.S. Power and the Multinational Corporation: The Political Economy of Foreign Direct Investment.* New York: Basic Books.

Halstead, John. 1996, May 22–23. Navies and Foreign Policy. *Halifax Maritime Symposium.* http://www.dal.ca/~centre/cfps.html.

Hepworth, Mark. 1989. *Geography of the Information Economy.* London: Belhaven Press.

Howard, Harry N. 1962. The United States and the Problem of the Turkish Straits: The Foundations of American Policy (1830–1914). *Balkan Studies* 3 (1): 1–28.

Hughes, Barry. 1994. *Continuity and Change in World Politics: The Clash of Perspectives.* 2d ed. Englewood Cliffs, N.J.: Prentice-Hall.

Iran Ends Naval Exercises: Oil Shipments Resume through Strait of Hormuz. 1996, April 14. *Digital News Network.* http://www.pres96.com/nwi10s5.htm.

Juda, Lawrence. 1981. World Shipping, UNCTAD, and the New International Economic Order. *International Organization* 35:493–516.

Kinnas, John. 1985. Geopolitics and the 'Low Politics' Perspective. In Ciro E. Zoppo and Charles Zorgbibe, eds., *On Geopolitics: Classical and Nuclear.* Dordrecht: Martinus Nijhoff.

Leonard, Thomas M. 1993. *Panama, the Canal and the United States.* Claremont, Calif.: Regina Books.

Mackinder, Halford J. 1942. *Democratic Ideals and Reality: A Study in the Politics of Reconstruction.* New York: Henry Holt.

Maritime Administration. 1992. *United States Oceanborne Foreign Trade Routes: 1989–1990.* Washington, D.C.: U.S. Department of Transportation.

Mitchelson, Ronald L., and James O. Wheeler. 1994. The Flow of Information in a Global Economy: The Role of the American Urban System in 1990. *Annals of the Association of American Geographers* 84 (1): 87–108.

Mobil Takes Over Part of Pertamina's Equity in Natuna Gas. 1996, July 29. *The Indonesia Times—Business and Finance.* http://www.indocon.com/itolnews/past/july/mon29/b2.htm.

New U.S. Fleet Defies Iran's Terror. 1996, April 22. *Minnesota Daily Online.* http://www.daily.umn.edu/daily/1996/04/22/editorial_opinions/ofleet.col/index.html.

Nincic, Miroslav. 1985. *How War Might Spread to Europe.* London: Taylor and Francis.

Noer, John, with David Gregory. 1996. *Chokepoints: Maritime Economic Concerns in Southeast Asia.* Washington, D.C.: National Defense University Press.

Nye, Joseph S. 1990. *Bound to Lead: The Changing Nature of American Power.* New York: Basic Books.

Office of the Federal Register. 1996, October 7. Message to the Senate Transmitting the Convention on the International Maritime Organization. *Weekly Compilation of Presidential Documents.* Washington, D.C.: National Archives and Records Administration.

Ohmae, Kenichi. 1993, spring. Rise of the Region State. *Foreign Affairs* 72 (2): 78–88.

———. 1995. *The End of the Nation State: The Rise of Regional Economies.* New York: Free Press.

Passage Limits Raise Nations' Ire. 1996, April 22. *CNA.* http://web3.asia1.com.sg/timesnet/data/can/docs/cnaISSO.html.

Price, D. G., and A. M. Blair. 1989. *The Changing Geography of the Service Sector.* London: Bellhaven.

Ressa, Maria. 1996, September 22. Indonesian War Games on Oil-Rich Island Sends Message. *Cable News Network.* http://cnn.com/WORLD/9609/22/indonesia/index.html.

Rosecrance, Richard. 1996, July/August. The Rise of the Virtual State. *Foreign Affairs* 75 (4): 45–62.

Sanger, David E. 1998, June 18. U.S. Intervenes in Currency Markets to Support the Yen. *New York Times.* http://www.nytimes.com/library/financial/061898dollar-yen.html.

Sassen-Koob, Saskia. 1986. New York City: Economic Restructuring and Immigration. *Development and Change* 17:85–119.

Skelton, Russell. 1996, June 5. Jakarta Shipping Plan Sparks Anger. *Sydney Morning Herald.* http://www.smh.com.au:80/daily/archive/960605/world/960605-world.html.

Soja, Edward. 1991. Poles Apart: Urban Restructuring in New York and Los

Angeles. In J. H. Mollenkopf and M. Castells, eds., *Dual City: Restructuring New York*. New York: Russell Sage Foundation.

Spero, Joan E., and Jeffrey A. Hart. 1997. *The Politics of International Economic Relations*. 5th ed. New York: St. Martin's.

Sprout, Harold, and Margaret Sprout, eds. 1951. *Foundations of National Power*. Toronto: D. Van Nostrand Company.

Spykman, Nicholas John. 1942. *America's Strategy in World Politics: The United States and the Balance of Power*. New York: Harcourt, Brace.

*Statistical Abstract of the United States*. 1995. Washington, D.C.: U.S. Government Printing Office.

———. 1997. Washington, D.C.: U.S. Government Printing Office.

Stevenson, Richard W. 1998, April 28. In the Wings: Euro as Potential Rival to the Dollar. *New York Times*. http://www.nytimes.com/yr/mo/day/news/financial/euro-currency.html.

Swan, David. 1995, May 17. Middle Eastern Security and Strategy. *Voice of America*. http://www.voa.gov/.

Taylor, Peter J., ed. 1993. *Political Geography of the Twentieth Century: A Global Analysis*. London: Belhaven.

Thurow, Lester. (1996). *The Future of Capitalism: How Today's Economic Forces Shape Tomorrow's World*. New York: William Morrow.

U.S. Census Bureau. 1994. Imports of Goods by Principal End-Use Category: January 1994–April 1995. Report FT900 (94). Foreign Trade Division. http://www.census.gov/foreign-trade/Press-release/94_press_releases/Final_Revisions 1994/exh12.txt.

———. 1997a. Imports of Goods by Principal End-Use Category: January 1995–December 1997. Report FT900 (97). Foreign Trade Divison. http://www.census.gov/foreign-trade/Press-Release/97_press_releases/Final_Revisions_1997/exh5a.txt.

———. 1997b. US Trade in Goods and Services. *Statistical Abstract of the United States*. U.S. Department of the Census. http://www.census.gov/statab/freq/97s1307.txt.

Wallerstein, Immanuel. 1984. *The Politics of the World-Economy: The States, the Movements, and the Civilizations*. London: Cambridge University Press.

Water Resources Support Center. 1995. *Waterborne Commerce of the United States, 1994: Part 5—National Summaries*. Fort Belvoir, Va.: U.S. Army Corps of Engineers.

Will Tokyo Finally Clean House? 1998, June 27. *Economist*, 71–72.

Zoppo, Ciro E. 1985. Classical Geopolitics and Beyond. In Ciro E. Zoppo and Charles Zorgbibe, eds., *On Geopolitics: Classical and Nuclear*. Dordrecht: Martinus Nijhoff.

# C. The Relevance of Rationality

# Agreement through Threats: The Northern Ireland Case

*Steven J. Brams and Jeffrey M. Togman*

## 1. Introduction

The April 1998 agreement to end the violent conflict in Northern Ireland has given many people reason to hope that a permanent peace is finally at hand. But the settlement, however encouraging, raises as many questions as it answers. How was this seemingly intractable conflict resolved? Will the compromise endure? We address these and other questions by examining the strategic situation that embroiled the Irish Republican Army (IRA) and the British government. By utilizing a dynamic approach to game theory called the "theory of moves" (Brams 1994), we demonstrate why the IRA first suspended and then resumed its paramilitary activities, only to suspend them again, before a settlement was reached. We also draw on other major conflicts that were recently settled to indicate how farsighted leaders might prevent disruptions in their search for peace.

Some of our findings could prove helpful for those involved in future conflicts. For example, we show that threats can lead to a durable compromise, notwithstanding the common assumption that threats engender conflict rather than compromise. We argue that the use of force does not necessarily stem from a thirst for violence; in some instances it might be rational for one side to resort to force to establish the credibility of its future threats, even if that side desires peace. Our aim is not to justify such violent actions but, instead, to show how policymakers can move beyond them and parlay them into a peaceful compromise.

In this essay we apply the theory of moves (TOM) to construct a deductive model of the strategic situation in Northern Ireland, based on a 2 × 2 game. We use this game to demonstrate why certain moves were taken by both sides, and how political leaders were able to clear a path toward peace, even though the compromise outcome in this game is not what classical game theory would consider stable. We also suggest how policymakers might utilize TOM to understand future conflicts. Finally, we indicate in the appendix how the game-theoretical model we present is related to the well-known games of Chicken and Prisoner's Dilemma, based on both standard game theory and TOM.

## 2.  A Centuries-Old Conflict

On February 9, 1996, after a 17-month cease-fire, the Irish Republican Army set off a bomb in East London. Less than a week later, the London police found and destroyed a bomb that the IRA had left in a telephone booth in the West End. A few days later, another IRA bomb went off on a double-decker bus. The British government, under the leadership of John Major, asserted that it would have no official contact with Sinn Féin, the political arm of the IRA, until the paramilitary activities stopped. The government also deployed 500 additional troops in Northern Ireland. In October 1996, the IRA detonated two bombs at the British army's headquarters in Lisburn, bringing the violent conflict back to Northern Ireland for the first time since the cease-fire.

On May 1, 1997, Tony Blair became Great Britain's prime minister. His election brought a renewed sense of optimism and goodwill to the conflict in Northern Ireland. Responding to Blair's overtures, including his warning that "the settlement train is leaving, with or without them" (Hoge 1997a, A7), the IRA announced on July 19, 1997, that it had "ordered the unequivocal restoration of the cease-fire" (Clarity 1997b, 1). Soon thereafter, Sinn Féin was invited to participate in the peace talks, which reconvened on September 15, 1997.

After seven months of difficult negotiations, a power-sharing ac-cord was reached on April 10, 1998. Six weeks later, on May 23, an over-whelming 71 percent of Northern Ireland's voters approved the accord in a nationwide referendum. In an election held on June 26, voters gave 63 percent of the new Northern Ireland Assembly's seats to supporters of the accord (Hoge 1998, 4). Still, there have been sporadic incidents of violence since the referendum.

These are some of the most recent developments in the conflict over British rule in Northern Ireland. The conflict between the British govern-ment and the IRA is part of a larger struggle between Catholic Republi-cans, including Sinn Féin and IRA members, who want Northern Ireland to become part of an all-Ireland nation-state, and Protestant Unionists, who insist that Northern Ireland remain part of the United Kingdom.

While the British government has portrayed itself as a neutral party, prior to the election of Tony Blair it was more accurate to view it as a pro-Union force. Former prime minister John Major, speaking about his Conservative party in 1994, asserted, "We are a Unionist Party. We should fight for the Union" (Aughey 1994, 143). Since his election, Blair has not been as blunt about his position, but he has given no indication that he would be willing to let Northern Ireland leave the union. Indeed, Blair stated that it was unlikely that the world would "see Northern Ireland as anything but a part of the United Kingdom" (Clarity 1997a, 5).

The present conflict must be seen in the context of the centuries-old Anglo-Irish antagonism. Republicans point to the first Norman invasions of Ireland in 1169 as the start of the conflict, whereas Unionists, who favor British rule, focus on the arrival of Scottish and English settlers, beginning in 1609. The arrival of these settlers in the north, often called the "plantation of Ulster," is the source of Northern Ireland's Protestant, and mostly Unionist, majority (57 percent today).

Republicans have continually fought against British rule, most fiercely at the end of the nineteenth and the beginning of the twentieth centuries. The war of independence, from 1919 to 1921, led to the Anglo-Irish Treaty of 1921, negotiated by the British government and Sinn Féin. The treaty granted independence to the 26 southern counties of Ireland, which became the Republic of Ireland, but it gave Great Britain control over Northern Ireland. Assurances that the treaty offered to Sinn Féin that the dispute over Northern Ireland would be resolved came to naught.

After 1921 Northern Ireland remained under British control, although the Stormont regime set up by the British did enjoy a certain degree of autonomy. Until the late 1960s, the armed Republican movement in Northern Ireland met with little support or success (O'Leary and McGarry 1993, 161). Then, in the late 1960s, Catholics in Northern Ireland began a series of civil rights marches to protest, among other things, discrimination in voting, employment, and housing. The marchers appealed to the British government to protect their rights as British citizens, but they were attacked by Unionist extremists, including some in the security forces (Rose 1971, 156). Subsequently, violence spread rapidly.

In 1969 the British government sent troops to Northern Ireland in an attempt to quell the unrest. Although Britain desired to maintain the quasi independence of Northern Ireland, the conflict spiraled out of control; in 1972 the Stormont regime was suspended and replaced by direct rule from London. Attempts by the British government to control the violence during the 1970s and 1980s failed miserably. Since 1969 more than 3,200 people have been killed in sectarian fighting in Northern

Ireland (Chepesiuk 1997, 10). Furthermore, 20,000 people have been injured, with economic costs to the British government running well over $1 billion a year (Ruane and Todd 1996, 1–2).

### 3.  The Conflict from a Strategic Perspective

By 1994 Northern Ireland had experienced a quarter-century of widespread sectarian violence. In this section we present a game-theoretic view of the conflict between Sinn Féin/IRA, treated as one player, and the British government in the period preceding the 1998 peace agreement. There were, to be sure, other important actors in the conflict, including the Republic of Ireland, Unionists in Northern Ireland, and Republicans who were not associated with Sinn Féin/IRA. However, by focusing on the struggle between the British government and Sinn Féin/ IRA, we highlight the central conflict, whose dynamics we will analyze in the next section.

We consider two basic strategic stances the two sides could take. One is a hard-line stance (denoted by H). For Great Britain, this entailed a refusal to negotiate with Sinn Féin/IRA, as well as the maintenance of British rule by force. For Sinn Féin/IRA, it meant a refusal to accept any resolution short of complete independence, taking whatever paramilitary actions were necessary to undermine British rule.

Each side, as an alternative strategy, could take a conciliatory stance (denoted by C). For Great Britain, such a stance meant a willingness to negotiate a compromise solution to the conflict, including a demilitarization of its position. For Sinn Féin/IRA, C indicated a similar willingness to compromise, including halting its paramilitary activities, at least temporarily.

The choice of C or H by each side leads to four possible outcomes, or states, that can be summarized as follows:

1. *C–C.*  Compromise, resulting in a peaceful settlement.
2. *H–H.*  Violent conflict, resulting in the continuation of the "Troubles."
3. *H (Sinn Féin/IRA)–C (Great Britain).*  Capitulation by Great Britain, which unilaterally withdraws its forces.
4. *C (Sinn Féin/IRA)–H (Great Britain).*  Capitulation by Sinn Féin/IRA, which unilaterally stops its armed resistance.

We next rank these four states for both sides as follows: 4 = best; 3 = next best; 2 = next worst; 1 = worst. Thus, the higher the number,

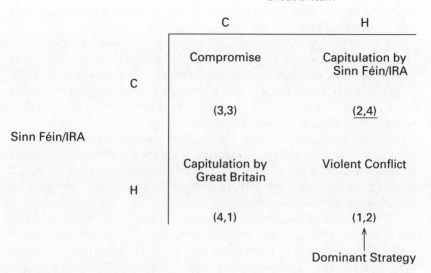

Fig. 1.    Payoff matrix of the Northern Ireland conflict

the greater the payoff to a player. These numbers, however, do not signify any numerical value or utility a player attaches to a state. Rather, they indicate only that each player prefers a higher-ranked state to a lower-ranked one.

In the payoff matrix shown in figure 1, these ranks are given by the ordered pair $(x,y)$, where $x$ is the ranking of the row player (Sinn Féin/IRA) and $y$ is the ranking of the column player (Great Britain). We offer the following brief justification of these rankings for each player, starting with the upper-left state and moving clockwise around the matrix.

*Compromise: (3,3).*    This is the next-best state for both players, involving a compromise on the issue of sovereignty.[1] For both Great Britain and Sinn Féin/IRA, the benefits of this state include an end to the violence and the possibility of long-term peace in Northern Ireland.

*IRA capitulates: (2,4).*    This is the best state for Great Britain because it has all the benefits of a compromise without having to make any concessions. It is the next-worst state for Sinn Féin/IRA because, while life in Northern Ireland achieves some level of normalcy, British rule remains in place.

*Violent conflict: (1,2).*   This is the next-worst state for Great Britain because, although it maintains control over Northern Ireland, para-military attacks continue; in addition, Britain faces pressure from the Republic of Ireland, the United States, and the European Union to bring an end to the violence. It is the worst state for Sinn Féin/IRA, because both British rule and the violence continue.

*Britain capitulates: (4,1).*   This is the worst state for Great Britain, which loses all control over Northern Ireland by withdrawing its forces; Britain is also seen as caving in to terrorism. By contrast, Sinn Féin/IRA achieves its best state by gaining independence without the need to compromise its hard-line position.

The ostensible solution to this game is the (3,3) compromise, but this is not the solution that standard game theory predicts. The reason is that Great Britain has a *dominant strategy* of H: it is a better strategy than C whatever strategy Sinn Féin/IRA chooses. If Sinn Féin/IRA chooses C, then (2,4) is better for Britain than (3,3); if Sinn Féin/IRA chooses H, (1,2) is better for Britain than (4,1).

Presuming that Britain chooses H because it is unconditionally better than C, what will Sinn Féin/IRA do? Observe that Sinn Féin/IRA does not have a dominant strategy: H is better if Britain chooses C, giving (4,1) rather than (3,3), but C is better if Britain chooses H, giving (2,4) rather than (1,2).

In a game in which all parties have complete information, we assume that Sinn Féin/IRA can anticipate that Britain will choose its dominant strategy of H. Accordingly, its best response would be to choose C, obtaining its next-worst state of (2,4) rather than its worst state of (1,2).

The strategies that yield (2,4), or capitulation by Sinn Féin/IRA, are what game theorists call a *Nash equilibrium,* because if either player departs unilaterally from its strategy associated with this state (C for Sinn Féin/IRA, H for Britain), it does worse: by changing its strategy from C to H, Sinn Féin/IRA would move the situation to (1,2), or violent conflict; by changing its strategy from H to C, Great Britain would move the situation to (3,3), or compromise. By contrast, if the players both chose C, leading to compromise, each would have an incentive to depart from C to try to achieve its best state — (2,4) for Great Britain and (4,1) for Sinn Féin/IRA.

The states of (4,1) and (1,2) are also unstable in the sense that at least one player would have an incentive unilaterally to change its strategy. Hence, (2,4) is the unique stable state in this game.

The dominance of H for Great Britain helps to explain that party's refusal to negotiate with Sinn Féin, even during the 1994–96 cease-fire. However, the actions of the IRA — commencing paramilitary activities, suspending them, resuming them, suspending them once again — belie the supposed stability of (2,4). Within the confines of classical game theory, any use of force by the IRA would seem to be irrational.

In order to account for the changes in strategy by Sinn Féin and the IRA, we next turn to the theory of moves, which allows for strategy shifts by players as they attempt to implement desired outcomes. It also allows for the exercise of threats by a player that has the power and will to carry them out if the response it seeks from the threatened party is not forthcoming.

## 4.  TOM and Threats

Game theory, as developed initially by von Neumann and Morgenstern, is an approach that is, in their own words, "thoroughly static" (von Neumann and Morgenstern 1953, 44). Classical game theory has little to say about the dynamic process by which players' choices unfold to produce outcomes, at least in strategic-form games that are defined by payoff matrices like that shown in figure 1. By contrast, TOM adds a dynamic dimension by assuming that players look ahead before making a move, switching strategies in anticipation of the possible moves of an opponent.

A key concept of TOM, and one that is very helpful in analyzing the conflict in Northern Ireland, is the notion of threat power. A player has *threat power* when it can better endure an inefficient state than can an opponent. An *inefficient state* is one that is worse for both players than some other state. Thus in the figure 1 game, (1,2) is an inefficient state, because it is worse for both players than either (2,4) or (3,3).

Consider the situation in Northern Ireland, as depicted in figure 1, and how the two sides have attempted to assert their threat power. During most of the post-1970 conflict, the IRA used its paramilitary forces to try to establish its threat power by signaling its willingness to endure the mutually harmful (i.e., inefficient) state of (1,2). Observe that by choosing H, Sinn Féin/IRA ensures that Great Britain is faced with its two worst states, (4,1) and (1,2). Presented with this choice, Britain would presumably select (1,2) over (4,1) by choosing H as well.

By asserting its threat power, Sinn Féin/IRA took a hard-line stance — but *not* because it preferred the conflict at (1,2) to capitulation at (2,4). Instead, it hoped to force the British to take a conciliatory stance. As Gerry Adams, the president of Sinn Féin, put it, "The course I take involves the use of physical force; but only if I achieve the situation where my people prosper can my course of action be seen, by me, to have been justified" (Clark 1994, 79).

Recall that Great Britain has a dominant strategy of maintaining its own hard-line position (H), which is better for it whatever Sinn Féin/IRA does. But when Great Britain implements its dominant strategy at the same time that Sinn Féin/IRA threatens Britain's two worst states with its choice of H, the result is violent conflict. This state held throughout most of the 1970s and 1980s.

One way out of this situation is for both sides to agree to move to the mutually beneficial compromise state. In the early and mid-1990s there were talks to try to arrive at such a settlement. The British position was that the IRA would have to renounce its use of paramilitary activities before formal negotiations for a resolution of the Northern Ireland conflict could begin. In essence, Great Britain was insisting that Sinn Féin/IRA move from H to C first, shifting the game from (1,2) to (2,4).

On the other hand, if Great Britain moved first to C, the situation would shift from (1,2) to (4,1), at least temporarily. Then Sinn Féin/IRA could move to C, resulting in the (3,3) compromise state. But this sequence of moves could be interpreted as Great Britain's giving in to terrorism at (4,1), which was unacceptable to the British government and also entailed the risk that Sinn Féin/IRA would not subsequently move on to (3,3). Hence, Britain insisted that Sinn Féin/IRA make the first conciliatory move.

Sinn Féin/IRA agreed to these conditions in September 1994 by declaring a "total cease-fire." This can be seen as a move by Sinn Féin/IRA from (1,2) to (2,4), which is better for both players, yielding an efficient if lopsided state. In return, Sinn Féin/IRA hoped that Britain would also switch strategies to a conciliatory stance by entering negotiations with it to resolve the conflict, leading to a final settlement at (3,3).

After Sinn Féin/IRA halted its paramilitary activities, and the situation stood at (2,4), Great Britain was not responsive: it did not enter negotiations with Sinn Féin, nor did it make any significant concessions. While (2,4) is Great Britain's best outcome, from which it would have no motivation to move, Sinn Féin/IRA still possessed the threat power to move back to (1,2). In short, the threat was that if the British government did not move to a conciliatory stance, leading to (3,3), the IRA would return to a hard-line stance, reinstating the inefficient state of (1,2).

Great Britain, under the leadership of John Major, was not willing to open negotiations with Sinn Féin unless the IRA first surrendered its weapons. Thus, the situation stood at (2,4) after the IRA declared a cease-fire in 1994. The British, by demanding that the IRA go one step further and disarm itself, sought to eliminate its adversary's threat power — that is, its power to revert to H and, once again, to inflict on Britain one of its two worst outcomes. If Sinn Féin/IRA did return to H, Great Britain would continue to implement its own hard-line stance (because it preferred [1,2] to [4,1]), which would mean a return to violent conflict at (1,2).

By refusing to move from (2,4) to (3,3) by entering negotiations with Sinn Féin during the 1994–96 cease-fire, Great Britain may have passed up an important opportunity to achieve a lasting peace. After the cease-fire, as the expression goes, the ball was in Britain's court. Yet Britain did little. The prime minister of the Republic of Ireland, John Bruton, claimed that "Britain had shown less courage, generosity and decisiveness since the paramilitary cease-fires last year than had many people in Ireland" ("Northern Ireland's Peace Process: The Nitty Gritty" 1995, 62). To most observers, Bruton seemed to be saying that Major had not been able to reciprocate the bold action taken by Gerry Adams in declaring a cease-fire and sustaining it for nearly a year and a half.

The IRA refused to disarm, prior to any settlement, for a very good reason: disarming would deprive it of the only leverage it had and would be "tantamount to surrender" (Clarity 1997c, A4). In the absence of a Republican threat, and the resolve and wherewithal to carry it out, Great Britain had no incentive to move away from its best state of (2,4).

The international commission that former U.S. senator George Mitchell chaired implicitly recognized this dynamic by recommending that all-party negotiations be conducted before the "decommissioning" of paramilitary arms. But Major rejected this suggestion and refused to enter ministerial-level talks with Sinn Féin.

In terms of our analysis, Great Britain was unwilling to move from (2,4) to (3,3). While Britain's stay-put strategy is rational in the short run because it enjoys its best state at (2,4), it is irrational if Sinn Féin/IRA is capable of reverting to (1,2), as proved to be the case. Indeed, Kevin Toolis argued that the IRA did not restart their bombing campaign "on a whim" (1996, A19). It believed, instead, that the British government betrayed promises, made in secret negotiations between 1990 and 1993, that it would be forthcoming if the IRA demonstrated good faith by renouncing violence and maintaining a cease-fire.

It was, unquestionably, Major's decision not to negotiate that persuaded Sinn Féin/IRA leaders to resume the use of violence in February 1996 (Holland 1996). Thus, after a cease-fire that lasted nearly a year and a half, the IRA resumed its paramilitary activities by commencing a bombing campaign in London, and later by extending the violent conflict to Northern Ireland, thereby returning the situation to the destructive (1,2) state.

## 5. A Path toward Peace

The IRA's restoration of its cease-fire in July 1997 offered hope that a peaceful resolution to the conflict in Northern Ireland might yet be within reach. In what follows, we analyze the moves and countermoves of Britain and Sinn Féin/IRA by applying our game-theoretic model to the 1997 efforts to attenuate the conflict — efforts that laid the groundwork for the final negotiations in 1998.[2]

Even before Tony Blair's election, it had become clear that a Sinn Féin/IRA cease-fire would have to precede any substantial conciliatory moves on the part of the British government. Like John Major before him, Blair insisted on this conciliatory move. In theory, the game we present in figure 1 can be moved from conflict at (1,2) to compromise at (3,3) via two paths. One path to compromise would involve Great Britain's changing from a hard-line to a conciliatory stance first, followed by a reciprocal change of strategies on the part of Sinn Féin/IRA. As a result, the situation would initially move from (1,2) to (4,1), and subsequently from (4,1) to (3,3). In fact, Gerry Adams tried to see if Blair might be willing to make some concessions, even before an IRA cease-fire, by showing up uninvited at peace talks on June 3, 1997, declaring that Sinn Féin had a mandate to participate (Clarity 1997e, A8).

But, as we have already noted, Great Britain could easily be seen as having caved in to terrorism if such a path were followed. Not surprisingly, Adams was not allowed to participate in the talks.

The second possible path toward peace would require that Sinn Féin/IRA change from a hard-line to a conciliatory stance first, followed by a reciprocal change on the part of Great Britain. In this scenario, the situation would initially move from (1,2) to (2,4), and subsequently from (2,4) to (3,3). While the outcome would be the same, the British government under the leadership of both Major and Blair was insistent in its demand that *this* path be followed.

With its restoration of the cease-fire, Sinn Féin/IRA made the first move, shifting the situation to (2,4). This, we believe, was a necessary condition for a peaceful resolution to be reached. But, as the breaking of the cease-fire in February 1996 proved, it was not sufficient.

Sinn Féin/IRA declared a second cease-fire in July 1997 only after it became convinced that Great Britain would respond with significant concessions that would facilitate a lasting resolution to the conflict. In terms of our model, this means that Sinn Féin/IRA was willing to move the situation from (1,2) to (2,4) — temporarily giving Great Britain its best outcome — only because it believed that Great Britain would reciprocate by taking a conciliatory stance as well, thereby moving the situation from (2,4) to compromise at (3,3).

In some respects, Great Britain's unwillingness to make such concessions during the first cease-fire made declaring a second cease-fire more daunting a prospect. Although suspicious of any new British promises of accommodation, Sinn Féin/IRA, nevertheless, chose to try again.

This second attempt was largely due to the efforts of both Republican and British leaders. For his part, Gerry Adams personalized past failures, blaming John Major for the fact that Great Britain had not reciprocated Sinn Féin/IRA's last conciliatory move. Adams did this, at least in part, because he needed to convince his fellow Republicans, especially Sinn Féin and IRA leaders, that Blair could be trusted — and that the new British leadership should not be tainted by Major's past acts. In short, the message was that Blair, unlike Major, could be trusted to move from (2,4) to (3,3).

Blair also acted quickly to assure Sinn Féin/IRA that they were now dealing with a leader who had the political will — and a majority in Parliament not beholden to Northern Ireland Unionists ("The IRA Cease-Fire" 1997) — to reciprocate a cease-fire and to push toward a resolution. Within weeks of his election, Blair went to Belfast to explain his position on Northern Ireland. If republican groups were willing to take a conciliatory stance, he promised, "I will not be slow in my response" (Clarity 1997a, 5).

The disarmament of the IRA was no longer a precondition to peace talks. As was true in the case of the first cease-fire, it was implausible to expect Sinn Féin/IRA to forfeit the threat of paramilitary activities until a satisfactory settlement was reached.

John Major's insistence during the 1994–96 cease-fire that the IRA give up its arms before participating in formal negotiations scuttled any hope of a compromise at that time. Blair, it seems, came to office far more cognizant of the fact that Sinn Féin/IRA would refuse to disarm before a settlement was reached; he also proved himself sensitive to Sinn Féin/IRA's view that one of the most important functions of its weapons was the defense of the Catholic population from Protestant attacks. Blair's peace initiative of June 1997 stipulated that disarmament would *not* be a precondition to talks, that disarmament talks should be held *simultaneously* with peace negotiations, and that *both*

Protestant and Catholic groups would, eventually, have to surrender their arms (Hoge 1997a, A7).

The issue of disarmament shaped up to be one of the most difficult obstacles to overcome. The Reverend Ian Paisley, head of the hard-line Democratic Unionist Party, complained that Sinn Féin was being offered a chance to join the peace talks without relinquishing "one weapon" (Hoge 1997a, A7). Some considered Sinn Féin to have "bombed its way to the negotiating table" (Clarity 1997a, 1, 6). But for the reasons spelled out earlier, no one expected Sinn Féin/IRA or the Unionists to disarm before a final settlement. The participants committed themselves only to "consider and discuss" the issue of disarmament (Hoge 1997c), which has yet to be taken up seriously.

Before the 1998 agreement was reached, peace in Northern Ireland seemed impossible, rather than difficult, to achieve. Much rests on what transpires in the near future. If Blair, Adams, and other leaders involved in Northern Ireland—including David Trimble, the moderate head of Northern Ireland's largest Protestant party, the Ulster Unionists—can consolidate the peace they have forged, their efforts will surely be worthy of Nobel Peace Prize consideration. Then it may be said, perhaps paradoxically, that the exercise of threats helped bring an end to the conflict.

### 6.  Game Theory, TOM, and Policy-Making

It is always difficult for adversaries to move from hard-line positions to conciliatory ones. When, after years of struggle, leaders of two hostile groups are able to find the will and to develop the trust to make such moves, a historic peace can be achieved. Such seems to have been the case in South Africa, where the prime minister, F. W. de Klerk, and the leader of the African National Congress (ANC), Nelson Mandela, found a path to peace in 1990–91. A similar reconciliation occurred in the Middle East in 1993, when the head of the Palestine Liberation Organization (PLO), Yasir Arafat, and Yitzhak Rabin and Shimon Peres, the prime minister and foreign minister of Israel, negotiated a settlement—though shaky today—between the PLO and the state of Israel.

The use of threats by the ANC and the PLO was critical in pushing the process toward a compromise. At the same time, the leaders of the South African and Israeli governments were farsighted enough to see that there was a way out of their unremitting struggles. Indeed, Mandela, de Klerk, Arafat, Rabin, and Peres were all awarded the Nobel

Peace Prize for the courage, generosity, and decisiveness they showed in persevering against formidable odds to reach a settlement.[3]

Realistically, not every international conflict will end in a durable settlement. What game theory and TOM can do is give insights into *possible* paths to peace, as well as into difficulties that may be encountered along the way.[4] Such insights can help political leaders predict both the dynamics of conflict and the conditions that can provide an escape from it.

Conceptualizing a conflict as a game elucidates the choices policymakers face and the consequences of those choices. Because the outcome of a game depends on the choices of *all* players, game theory and TOM highlight the fact that a player typically does not have a unilateral best choice, that is, a strategy that is best in all situations.

From a conventional game-theoretic perspective, Great Britain's choice of a hard-line stance (H) in the figure 1 game was its dominant strategy and so would be its expected choice regardless of what Sinn Féin/IRA does. TOM pushes this analysis farther by demonstrating that Sinn Féin/IRA possessed a threat. By incorporating this aspect into the analysis, TOM helps explain (1) why Sinn Féin/IRA opted for C, at least for a while; (2) why Sinn Féin/IRA reverted to H; and (3) why both sides eventually chose C.

To apply TOM, we suggest, as a first step, that policymakers attempt to write down the game or games they believe are being played. This may be more complicated than it sounds. Even if we limit ourselves to relatively simple two-player, two-strategy scenarios, we have found 57 different *conflict games* — games in which there is no mutually best (4,4) outcome. Because there are no outcomes in conflict games that completely satisfy both players, cooperation, while possible, may be difficult to achieve.

Without appropriate tools to analyze these games, it is by no means obvious what strategic possibilities are open to players. One needs a theory that shows which outcomes are stable — outcomes from which players would have no desire to move lest they end up, immediately or eventually, worse off. One also needs to know which outcomes are vulnerable to threats. TOM enables one to identify these properties of outcomes in the 57 conflict games, and it facilitates generalizations across all these games.

At a minimum, this theory can help policymakers distinguish better from worse strategy choices, whatever game is being played. In addition, it offers answers to such questions as: Will threats work? What kind? Which outcomes are nonmyopically stable in the sense that if players are not restricted to making just one move from an outcome, what *series* of moves and countermoves might they make to try to do better?

Emphatically, TOM cannot save players from a destructive conflict if a cooperative outcome is vulnerable to threats or is otherwise unstable. On the other hand, because TOM enables one to determine what changes would need to be made in order to bring relief to such a situation, it may suggest a path to peace. In this way, TOM can bring both realism and hope to a situation: it offers a clear-eyed view of the nature of conflict, and, at the same time, it indicates the possibilities for transforming it into a cooperative outcome.

APPENDIX: COMPARISON WITH CHICKEN AND
PRISONER'S DILEMMA

The 2 × 2 game in figure 1 that we used to model the Northern Ireland conflict combines certain properties of the well-known games of Chicken and Prisoner's Dilemma. In the figure 1 game, the row player (Sinn Féin/ IRA) has the same preferences as those found in the Chicken game, while the column player (Great Britain) has Prisoner's Dilemma preferences, as can be seen from a comparison of these three games (see fig. A1).

Both Chicken and Prisoner's Dilemma are *symmetrical games:* the players rank the diagonal outcomes the same, and the off-diagonal outcomes are mirror images of each other. In both these games, the row and column players are interchangeable, because they face the same strategic choices: what is rational for one player is also rational for the other. In the figure 1 game, by contrast, the row and column players face different strategic choices.

In Chicken, neither player has a dominant strategy, and, as a result, it is impossible to predict which of the two pure-strategy Nash equilibrium outcomes, (4,2) or (2,4), will be selected (if either). In Prisoner's Dilemma, on the other hand, both the row and column players have dominant strategies (their second strategies), yielding the unique Nash equilibrium outcome of (2,2). This Nash equilibrium, however, is inefficient, because (2,2) is worse for both players than (3,3).

In the figure 1 game, the players are in a different predicament from that posed by Chicken or Prisoner's Dilemma. Only the column player has a dominant strategy (its second strategy). According to classical game theory, the row player should anticipate this choice and should choose its own first strategy, resulting in the Nash equilibrium outcome of (2,4) that is underscored.

In none of these three games does the compromise outcome of (3,3)

|        |        |
|--------|--------|
| (3,3)  | <u>(2,4)</u> |
| <u>(4,2)</u> | (1,1)  |

Chicken

|        |        |
|--------|--------|
| (3,3)  | (1,4)  |
| (4,1)  | <u>(2,2)</u> |

Prisoner's Dilemma

|        |        |
|--------|--------|
| (3,3)  | <u>(2,4)</u> |
| (4,1)  | (1,2)  |

Figure 1 Game

*Key:* (x,y) = (payoff to row player, payoff to column player)
    4 = best; 3 = next best; 2 = next worst; 1 = worst
    Outcomes associated with Nash equilibrium strategies underscored

**Fig. A1.   Payoff matrices of three games**

constitute a Nash equilibrium. In Prisoner's Dilemma, the outcome that classical game theory predicts, (2,2), is worse for both players than (3,3), and in Chicken the two predicted outcomes—(4,2) and (2,4)— lead to a best outcome for one player but a next-worst outcome for the other. The figure 1 game gives a similar lopsided result, (2,4), but one that favors only the column player.

According to TOM, however, the compromise outcome of (3,3) in all three games can be achieved through the use of threats. Each player can threaten to choose its second strategy, associated with its opponent's two worst outcomes (1 and 2), if its opponent does not choose its first strategy when the threatener does. If this threat is credible, both players will choose their first strategies, producing the (3,3) outcome, which is clearly better for the threatened player than a 1 or 2 outcome.

As we pointed out earlier, Sinn Féin/IRA made such a threat but failed to induce (3,3) dring the 1994–96 cease-fire, because Great Britain refused to heed that threat. Sinn Féin/IRA then carried out its threat and resumed paramilitary activities, resulting once again in conflict at (1,2).

The "deterrent threat" that induces (3,3) in the figure 1 game can be undermined by a "compellent threat" (Brams 1994, chap. 5). Specifically, the column player, by sticking with its second (dominant) strategy, can compel the row player to choose between the inefficient (1,2) and the efficient (2,4). If the column player has threat power, the row player can thereby induce the choice of (2,4), which is also the unique Nash equilibrium outcome. Similarly in Chicken, if the row player has threat power, it can induce (4,2), whereas if the column player has threat power, it can induce (2,4), which are the two pure-strategy Nash equilibrium outcomes in this game.

Neither player has a compellent threat in Prisoner's Dilemma, so there is nothing to undermine a deterrent threat, on the part of either player, that can induce (3,3). While it is true that compellent threats might interfere with the choice of (3,3) in both the figure 1 game and Chicken, a deterrent threat can, in principle, work to induce (3,3) in these games. In the Northern Ireland conflict, it seems that the IRA deterrent threat, after its failure under John Major, succeeded in inducing Tony Blair to choose C, yielding the compromise (3,3) outcome.

NOTES

This essay is a revised and updated version of Brams and Togman 1998; a substantially different earlier version of this essay appeared in Brams and Togman 1996. Steven J. Brams gratefully acknowledges the support of the C. V. Starr Center for Applied Economics at New York University.

1. Various compromises that were proposed included partitioning Northern Ireland between Great Britain and the Republic of Ireland, and rule by a joint Anglo-Irish authority. To facilitate a compromise, the simultaneous surrender of weapons by the IRA and Unionist paramilitary groups was proposed by former U.S. senator George Mitchell, who chaired the international commission overseeing peace talks from June 1996 to April 1998.

2. While the 2 × 2 game we postulate, and the rational play of it based on TOM, seems to us to illustrate how a compromise could be forged, an alternative formal analysis of this conflict is given in Miall 1996 using "drama theory." In contrast to our treatment, Miall contends that there must be *preference* changes (which drama theory allows for) on the part of a number of parties in order to achieve a peaceful settlement. As we see it, however, changes in *strategies* by the players would be sufficient to resolve the conflict, given Sinn Féin/IRA has threat power. Furthermore, strategy changes, we believe, are more empirically plausible and theoretically parsimonious than preference changes.

3. The efforts of Betty Williams and Mairead Corrigan (founders of the Northern Ireland Peace Movement that was later renamed the Community of Peace People) to bring peace to Northern Ireland were also recognized by the award of the Nobel Peace Prize in 1976.

4. While this essay explores the dynamics of the Northern Ireland conflict in hindsight, see Brams and Togman 1996, published before Blair's election, and Brams and Togman 1998, published before the accord was signed, for analyses that use TOM to predict what steps might lead to peace.

REFERENCES

Aughey, Arthur. 1994. "Conservative Party Policy and Northern Ireland." In Brian Barton and Patrick J. Roche, eds., *The Northern Ireland Question: Perspectives and Policies.* Aldershot, U.K.: Avebury.

Bardon, Jonathan. 1992. *A History of Ulster.* Belfast: Blackstaff.

Barton, Brian, and Patrick J. Roche, eds. 1994. *The Northern Ireland Question: Perspectives and Policies.* Aldershot, U.K.: Avebury.

Brams, Steven J. 1994. *Theory of Moves.* Cambridge: Cambridge University Press.

Brams, Steven J., and Jeffrey M. Togman. 1996. "The Dynamics of the Northern Ireland Conflict." *Oxford International Review* 7, no. 2 (spring): 50–54.

———. 1998. "Cooperation through Threats: The Northern Ireland Case." *PS: Political Science and Politics* 31, no. 1: 32–39.

Chepesiuk. 1997. "The Weight of History: Ulster's Troubling Standoff." *New Leader* 80, no. 4 (March 10): 10–11.

Clarity, James F. 1997a. "Blair Makes Offer to Renew Contact with I.R.A. Wing." *New York Times* (May 17), 1, 5.

———. 1997b. "I.R.A. Announces a New Cease-Fire Beginning Today." *New York Times* (July 20), 1, 9.

———. 1997c. "I.R.A. Offers Support (of a Sort) for Nonviolence." *New York Times* (September 12), A4.

———. 1997d. "Sinn Féin Is Invited by Britain to Join Peace Talks." *New York Times* (August 30), 1, 6.

———. 1997e. "Ulster Talks Resume with Warning that Violence Can End Them." *New York Times* (June 4), A8.

Clark, Liam. 1994. "Contemporary Republican Politics." In Brian Barton and Patrick J. Roche, eds., *The Northern Ireland Question: Perspectives and Policies.* Aldershot, U.K.: Avebury.

Hoge, Warren. 1997a. "Blair Offers New Ulster Deal; Key Is Disarming Both Sides." *New York Times* (June 26), A1, A7.

———. 1997b. "New Truce, New Questions." *New York Times* (July 22), A8.

———. 1997c. "Sinn Féin Leader Says He Expects I.R.A. Cease-Fire." *New York Times* (July 19), 1, 5.

———. 1998. "Vote for Assembly Realigns Northern Ireland Loyalties." *New York Times* (June 28), 4.

Holland, Jack. 1996. "October Surprise!" *Irish Echo* (February 21–27), 1, 39.

"The I.R.A. Cease-Fire" (editorial). 1997. *New York Times* (July 21), A16.

Miall, Hugh. 1996. "Drama Theory and the Northern Ireland Peace Process." Preprint, Department of Politics and International Relations, Lancaster University, U.K. (June 26).

"Northern Ireland's Peace Process: The Nitty Gritty." 1995. *Economist* (November 18), 62–63.

O'Leary, Brendan, and John McGarry. 1993. *The Politics of Antagonism.* London: Athlone Press.

Rose, Richard. 1971. *Governing without Consensus: An Irish Perspective.* Boston, Mass.: Beacon Press.

Ruane, Joseph, and Jennifer Todd. 1996. *The Dynamics of the Conflict in Northern Ireland.* Cambridge: Cambridge University Press.

Toolis, Kevin. 1996. "Why the I.R.A. Stopped Talking." *New York Times* (February 21), A19.

von Neumann, John, and Oskar Morgenstern. 1953. *Theory of Games and Economic Behavior.* 3d ed. Princeton University Press.

# The Outcome of the Negotiations over the Status of Jerusalem: A Forecast

*A. F. K. Organski*

## Preface

Policymakers always demand answers to three critical questions. What will happen if things proceed as they are? How much (if at all) can the outcome be changed to come as closely as possible to what I prefer? And what actions must I take to achieve the outcome that I most prefer (i.e., who should I approach and what can I do to draw them closer to my point of view)? This essay illustrates how a critical piece of international relations theory helps to answer precisely these questions. It also illustrates the limits of such analysis. Possessing information does not help unless it is used.

This essay forecasts the outcome of a critical event in the Middle East: the results of negotiations between the Palestinian National Authority (PNA) and the Rabin administration over the final status of Jerusalem. Perhaps U.S. policymakers had a similar forecast in the back of their minds and that is why they invested so heavily on the side of the peace process shepherded by Rabin and Arafat. In any event, the forecast produced by the model utilized by this essay was startling. The findings suggest that *there would have been an agreement on the future of Jerusalem, and with Arafat's consent, Jerusalem would remain under Israeli control.* At the time, such an agreement with Arafat appeared incredible and was thus dismissed. Experts provided a plethora of reasons why it could not possibly occur.

The data for the forecast were collected in June 1995, and the analyses were performed prior to the settlement of negotiations. The original analyses were completed in July and August 1995, the results of which were presented in a preliminary version of this essay at the

American Political Science Association meeting in Chicago in the first week of September 1995. As it turned out, the original forecast accurately anticipated, by several months, the agreements that were reached in the ongoing secret negotiations between the Israelis and Palestinians. One year later the results of the negotiations were made public. This is an important point in that it establishes that the forecast we present in this chapter is not a *postdiction*. What we have is a *prediction* based on data collected prior to Rabin's death. This is an excellent illustration of the best use of counterfactual analysis, still the subject of extensive debate in both political science and history.[1] Some argue that all counterfactual claims must be based on speculation about what *would have happened* rather than on an actual set of observations. This is not the case here: the forecasts were made from data collected prior to the decisive event, and the accuracy of such forecasts is tested directly with actual events. The analysis is based upon a prediction of what *could have* happened had Rabin survived and what *could have* happened if he were no longer the leader of Israel. The first prediction cannot be directly assessed, but the second can be, and is. Given the accuracy of the latter, one can infer about the accuracy of the former. Moreover, our confidence in this analysis is strong because we use the expected utility model to generate the critical forecasts and evaluations of alternate negotiation strategies. This methodology has been successfully utilized on numerous occasions. The model's historical forecast and strategy accuracy is over 90 percent.[2] Furthermore, there is evidence that our assessment of the direction of the secret negotiations unknown at the time of the evaluation was accurate. We are confident that had Rabin not been assassinated, the analysis performed in this essay would have matched the actual, observed sequence of events.

Indeed, the research and forecast appeared voided by the assassination of Prime Minister Rabin on November 4, 1995, by a Jewish religious extremist. How could one ever find out what would have happened had Rabin lived? Despite the accuracy of the model's forecasts in other settings, it at first seemed advisable to toss the research and the forecast away and forget the whole thing.

However, almost one year later on July 31, 1996, Yair Hirschfeld revealed that in October 1995 he, representing Beilin and Peres, and Palestinian negotiators, representing the PNA, had reached agreement on several issues. Two are relevant for the present discussion: (1) the entire city of Jerusalem was to remain under Israeli control, and (2) the status quo in Jerusalem was to be altered only in cosmetic ways.[3]

The agreed alterations to the status quo were as follows.

1. All of Jerusalem (West and East) would remain under Israeli control. Jerusalem was *not* to be divided as the Likud later was to charge.
2. The capital of the Palestinian state would be the Jerusalem sub-urb of Abu Dis, which the Palestinians called part of al-Quds. The Israelis did not consider Abu Dis part of the municipality of Jerusalem, while the Palestinians did. Both could truthfully claim their preferences had been achieved.
3. The Palestinians would recognize West Jerusalem as the capital of Israel, and the Israelis would recognize al-Quds as the capital of the Palestinian state. The issue of sovereignty over East Jerusa-lem would not be conclusively resolved.
4. It was agreed that the Palestinians would have free access to the Temple Mount and that the Palestinian flag would fly there. Therefore, Palestinians could claim that the Temple Mount was Palestinian.

Yair Hirschfeld and Ron Pundaq were the academics that had nego-tiated the foundations of the Oslo agreement three years earlier, on which the peace process is based. According to Hirschfeld, on the Pales-tinian side the "highest level of the PNA" supported and encouraged the talks. On the Israeli side, these understandings were reached with the knowledge and support of Beilin and Peres. The agreements were con-solidated in a paper that was signed by Yossi Beilin and Abu Mazin. Hirschfeld noted that the constant charge of the Likud that Labor had agreed to partition Jerusalem was false, and that it was a grave political mistake not to make the agreement public before the election. Such an announcement would have revealed that the Likud's charge that Labor had agreed to the division of Jerusalem was false. In his view, had Peres agreed to do so Labor would have won the election, and Netanyahu and the Likud would not have come to power.

We consider the revelation of the agreement on understandings between the Abu-Mazin and Yossi Beilin a validation of our forecast. The expected utility model accurately anticipated the decisions that made it possible for Arafat to agree that Jerusalem remain under Israel's control and for the Israelis to agree to minor concessions.

## Introduction

As noted in the preface, this essay reports a forecast of the results of the negotiations over the future status of Jerusalem. Two analyses are involved. The first examines the bargaining process carried out by the Palestinians and Israelis, assisted by the United States. The second estimates the degree of international acceptance of the terms of the settlement by a small number of critical third parties. These international players will not participate directly in the negotiations, but they have a special interest and influence over Jerusalem's fate. They should be important actors in shaping the reaction of the wider international community.

It has long been our feeling that negotiations and the decision making inseparable from it are the weakest area of policy studies. Here we examine the dynamics that make players in major negotiations insist on their positions or be willing to change them. We focus the examination on a series of negotiations of wide interest, the settlement of Jerusalem.

The issue of Jerusalem was left by the Declaration of Principles together with other scabrous issues to the end of the peace process after other vital problems were resolved.[4] This is still some time away. Clearly one could expect that some of our data would change as the negotiations approach and players begin bargaining in earnest. In a sense, though not formally on the agenda, negotiations have already begun. Critical actors, by words and actions, have for some time been positioning themselves for the bargaining to come. One could give an extensive list of such moves. Israelis and Palestinians have been maneuvering to change "the facts on the ground" for a long time; Arafat confronted King Hussein on the latter's assertion of his special responsibility to Muslim religious places; on that occasion the Israelis signaled their preferences for Jordan; the Vatican after decades has moved to establish diplomatic relations with Israel; Western Europe decided not to participate in the Israeli government-sponsored celebration of the 3,000th anniversary of Jerusalem's founding; the U.S. congressional leadership has urged that the United States move its embassy from Tel Aviv to Jerusalem; and the Israeli and American government leaderships have demurred. The initial sparring over the negotiations could not be clearer.

## The Model

The model we use to forecast these negotiations, often called the expected-utility model,[5] has been described in more technical detail elsewhere.[6] This section provides only a basic description of the model.

The fundamental assumption underpinning its logical structure is that all actors in the negotiations are rational, expected-utility maximizers and adjust their actions in response to their perceptions of gains to be made and losses to be incurred. The model is based on several well-established microeconomic and political theories. First, it utilizes Black's median voter theorem, treating the stakeholders in a bargaining situation as voters, who cast their "votes" or exert their influence strictly according to their preferences over a range of alternatives.[7] The outcome of negotiations is an aggregation of these votes, with certain restrictions. Second, the model utilizes Bank's theorem about the monotonicity between expectations and the escalation of political disputes. In short, this theorem helps the model distinguish between negotiated settlements and conflictual outcomes. The farther apart are the votes of two actors on an issue, the more likely is a conflict to emerge.

The model utilizes these theorems to compute the change in actors' positions on an issue over time, producing three important tools for the analysis of policy negotiation. First, it provides a point forecast, or a forecast of outcomes within a very narrow range, of the overall outcome for an issue. Second, on the basis of its calculations of each actor's expected utilities (the payoff they expect to receive given the casting of their vote), it produces a detailed map of all the pushes and pulls that are the substance of the bargaining process in any set of negotiations. Finally, the model forecasts the outcome when all players act according to their perceptions, attempting to maximize their gains and minimize their losses. Each actor decides whether to make demands on the other and whether to compromise or yield when facing demands. It is therefore possible to locate all of the decisions that every player has made throughout the negotiation.

This latter point should be stressed. It is possible to locate all the instances in the bargaining process where players have failed to make demands because they misperceived what they could do and therefore did not act. Such knowledge permits analysts to simulate what *would have happened* had the opportunities been exploited. This information, in turn, provides the basic data that make it possible to construct detailed strategies of when and how to intervene in the process and maximize the probability of obtaining specific goals. For the purposes of the two analyses undertaken by this essay, we are not exploring whether the outcomes could be changed and thus did not construct strategies to that end. We make reference to this aspect of the model only at the end of the second analysis and in passing.

One final point: the model is dynamic. It follows the sequence of player interactions and repeats the process we have just described for every round of negotiation. It ceases to iterate when it calculates that the costs of negotiations are higher than the benefits to be derived from continuing. We should note incidentally that the length of negotiations can be finessed, however, and the model can be instructed to continue analyzing beyond the point where it would have stopped.

## The Data

Any analyst examining the bargaining process must begin by asking the questions "What do the players want?" "How badly do they want it?" and "Are they powerful enough to get all or part of what they want?" These are precisely the data used by the expected-utility model. We obtained data from estimates provided by an expert on the issue.[8] The expert was asked: (1) *who* are the actors, (2) what are the *preferences* of each actor on the issue under discussion, (3) how *salient* is this specific issue to each of the players, and (4) how *powerful* are they in relation to one another?

We should define what a group (actor, player) is for the purposes of this research. The definition is quite precise. A group is any number of individuals (e.g., a city, a business, a nation, or set of nations) who have access to the decision-making process and exercise influence over it. The restriction is that all members of the group must share a common set of preferences, have a common pool of resources and influences used during negotiations, and assign the same level of importance to the issue.

The choice of actors for this forecast of the negotiations is straightforward. There are three major actors in the coming bargaining process: the Palestinians, represented by Arafat; the Israelis, represented by Rabin; and a U.S. moderator, acting as an adviser and catalyst to the parties. The Palestinian and Israeli groups are estimated to have at least some influence on the decision in the coming negotiations. The choice of giving as full representation as possible to Palestinian and Israeli actors is due to the fact that the peace process has been structured as primarily their affair.

The second piece of data is the estimate of the *power* each group holds on this issue. Power, of course, is relative. One can only have power over someone else, and the power one exercises *always* requires the use of resources. It is possible therefore to estimate the power of an actor by the size of the resource pool the actor has available to it. The values, therefore, appropriately represent estimates of the relative sizes of resource pools or capabilities. This is a simple accomplishment. One identifies the most powerful actor in the set and assigns it the value of 100. The pool of resources of all other actors are seen as proportions of the pool of the most powerful actor. Therefore, if the most powerful actor is 100 and another is 25, then the second actor is estimated to be one-fourth as powerful as the first. In the data above, Rabin is estimated as the most powerful actor (i.e., having the most resources on this issue), which seems reasonable because so far as Jerusalem is concerned, he controls most of the assets on the ground. The United States and Arafat are close behind. The United States is estimated to have the edge on Arafat because, among other things, on any issue Rabin is far more likely to yield to the United States than to Arafat.

The values recorded under *salience* are again estimates of how important the issue is to each actor, that is, how much of their resources they are willing to employ to pull the solution to their preferred position. The value, therefore, is an estimate of the percentage of its available resources that the actor would employ to get its way on the issue. One should keep in mind that in the real world, actors contending on an issue are also engaged in many other issues, and the more powerful players are also often preoccupied with many issues pulling them in opposite directions. Not surprisingly, the issue of Jerusalem is estimated as highly salient to most of the Israeli and Palestinian actors, and one would expect its salience to rise even further when negotiations actually begin. Still, there are clear differences that actors attach to this issue. The United States, for example, can be expected to call on 80 percent of its power on this issue, while for Hamas and the Likud this is *the* issue, and they are willing to bring all of the resources to bear in this situation.

Finally, *preferences* are what players wish the outcome to be, not what they think they can achieve. The preferences of each group are recorded on a scale that stretches from 0 to 100. All of the significant points on the scale are given a substantive meaning. Table 1 defines the continuum of preferences available to actors on this issue.

**TABLE 1.   Preference Continuum for the Disposition of Jerusalem**

| | |
|---|---|
| 0 | Status quo: Jerusalem united under Israeli sovereignty |
| 10 | East Jerusalem remains under Israeli control, but the Palestinians are represented with municipality of the city with some arrangement that they can vote separately. The Holy Places are open, and extraterritoriality applies to the religious institutions. |
| 25 | Power-sharing in East Jerusalem under Israeli sovereignty |
| 35 | Holy Places under international control |
| 50 | Israeli sovereignty over West Jerusalem and Jewish areas over the Green Line (Arab areas under Palestinian control) |
| 60 | City under UN control |
| 75 | City divided into two capitals along the Green Line |
| 100 | Jerusalem united under Palestinian rule |

A set of approximately 30 actors was centrally involved in the Israel-Palestine negotiations. Data collected on power, position, and salience for each of these actors is reported more fully elsewhere.[9] In this work we will concentrate on the interaction between the key actors Arafat, Rabin, the United States, and the Likud, who were the veto players in these negotiations. Yet, it is important to note that the actions of all the players and their moves shape the course of the bargaining for the veto players. We concentrate on the latter to simplify the presentation and because no major changes are induced by the more complex presentation.

## The Bargaining over Jerusalem's Status

Before proceeding, we should caution that we are not forecasting that the negotiations *would* occur. We are forecasting what would have happened during negotiations on the status of Jerusalem with the three key players: Rabin, Arafat, and the United States. This forecast rests on the assumption that other obstacles in the way of the peace negotiations have been resolved. Given the obvious determination of the Israeli government to reach a solution, this appears to be likely but by no means assured.

We begin with the key result of all our analyses, our forecast of the terms of the settlement over the future status of Jerusalem. The model forecasts that the final settlement will be Jerusalem under Israeli control, but with the incorporation of Palestinians in the city council. The Holy Places will be open, as they are now. This is the position of Prime Minister Rabin throughout the negotiations. The resulting equilibrium is unexpectedly stable for what has been described by all knowledgeable observers as a very difficult negotiation over an extremely contentious issue. From our analysis, the issue is resolved quickly after the first round of negotiations.

The negotiations are completed within four rounds, which is a moderately lengthy process. This is a plausible estimate of the time required, but it should be noted that a *round* in the context of this model does not correspond to a precise interval of time — it is a loose analytic device to indicate the passage of time as actors' positions change. Thus, we cannot establish the exact meaning of *moderately long*. The settlement between the Palestinians and the Israelis thus should prove more straightforward than generally believed at present. As the second analysis will show, the greater difficulties are likely to be found at the international level after settlement has been established.

Before proceeding to examine the bargaining process in greater detail, we should note two critical points in regard to the number of rounds of negotiation. The analyses of the negotiation, as well as the analysis of international acceptance of the results, reveal that at various points in the bargaining process participants will have opportunities to shorten the duration of negotiations and alter the outcome. But they do not see the opportunities, and they slip by. As noted earlier, we did not pursue here what *would have* happened had the actors seized the missed opportunities. Such efforts are part of the work in progress. In the parlance of those who use this model for analytic purposes, the analysis and forecast in this chapter is the "base case forecast," one that reveals the bargaining process and the outcome if things are allowed to follow their natural course.

### The Bargaining Dynamic

Let us now turn to the critical aspects of the bargaining over Jerusalem. The actual forecast is based upon the interaction of a much broader set of players, but for the sake of simplicity and demonstration of the model, we focus here on the behavior of three players: Prime Minister Rabin, Chairman Arafat, and the United States. Rabin and Arafat are the only two players who can speak for their own side. Among the groups on each side representing the principal disputants, Rabin and Arafat are the only ones who can stop the negotiations or who can authoritatively veto the result (i.e., they are *veto players* in the lexicon of the model). None of the other actors has such an ability: not Peres, nor the Likud, nor the Islamic Jihad, nor even Hamas. As we have seen, all of these players are important for a stable outcome, but we judge Rabin and Arafat to have the final say. Our choice of the United States requires no lengthy explanation. The United States has been critical from the beginning of the peace process, and it is the sponsor of the talks. The pattern of bargaining and the critical moves of the central actors in the drama of the Jerusalem negotiations are presented in figure 1.

The figure depicts the central events of our story. As negotiations open, Arafat and Rabin are very far apart on what the future status of the city should be. The United States is much nearer to Rabin, but qualitatively its position represents a first significant step in the alteration of the status quo. The United States' position allows power to be shared between the Palestinians and the Israelis in East Jerusalem even though Israel has sovereignty over the entire city. In contrast, Rabin prefers Israeli control over Jerusalem. The forecasted outcome is at Arafat's position, which advocates that the city be divided into two

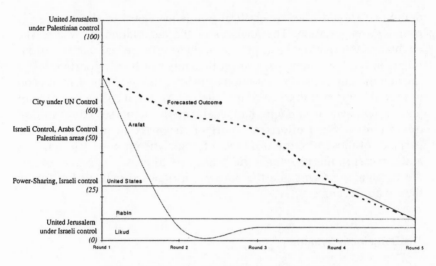

**Fig. 1.    Preferences of principal actors over time**

capitals along the Green Line. In this round there are clear, significant differences dividing *all* actors, which suggests that the equilibrium is very unstable.

The model ceases iterating at the fifth round. At that point, a settlement of the issue of Jerusalem's future has been reached. Palestinian and Israeli actors, as well as the United States, share Rabin's own preference.

The first major break in the disagreement separating the major players comes in the very first round of negotiations, when Arafat shifts from his demand that Jerusalem be again divided into two cities. Having made the move, Arafat remains at his new position throughout the negotiations and seeks repeatedly to bring other players to his position. This first break in Palestinian ranks provides a signal of what the solution will probably be like. The Arafat shift is so dramatic and important that we will use it, at the end of this review and before we launch our second analysis, to illustrate the depth of insight the model provides the analyst, helping to make sense of the *mano a mano* over the peace process.

We should also mention briefly the role of the United States. The United States holds on to its initial position that Israel should be sovereign in Jerusalem, but that in East Jerusalem power should be shared between Israelis and Palestinians. In the broader analysis (where all relevant actors are included), as long as the United States resisted, a number of Palestinian and Israeli actors (the IDF, Labor, Hamas, etc.) also held out for that solution. When the United States finally moves at the demand of Rabin, all these holdouts move as well. Arafat's and the rest of the PLO contingent's earlier move gives political cover to the U.S. acceptance of Rabin's demand.

One can only speculate about some of the possible reasons for the United States holding out as long as it did and why it eventually shifted its position. It may be that, in part, the United States believed that its original position would have provided greater stability after a settlement was reached; and it was correctly concerned, as it turns out, about the international reception the settlement would receive. As the leader of the world, it has the task of working for the global acceptance of the final settlement.

Rabin does not change his position through the entire negotiation. There are a number of possible ways to account for his firmness. Political reasons may be present. One could argue that the more hawkish position of the Likud on Jerusalem may be a factor, because distancing his own position from the status quo would leave the Likud free to portray itself as the only defender of Israeli interests in the future of the city. Such a view is not really persuasive since other Labor party leaders have taken such positions. Instead, it seems plausible that Rabin (similar to President Reagan in other situations) determined what the solution *ought* to be and simply was unwilling to bend on this conviction. Be this as it may, the Palestinian-Israeli negotiation should conclude with agreement that the reality of power in Jerusalem should be changed only in minor ways.

## Arafat's Change in Position

Here we discuss the motivations for Arafat's dramatic shift in round 1 of the negotiations. We think the interaction presents us with an opportunity to illustrate the level of precision and detail about the bargaining process that the model produces for the analyst. We deal only with Arafat's shift in position, but the information we present is produced by the model for every pair of actors (every actor bargaining with every other actor).

The model reveals that Arafat *perceives* that both he and the Likud stand to lose, though the Likud would be the heavier loser in a confrontation. The model's calculation of Arafat's expected utility is $-1.719$ and the Likud's is $-1.774$. Because both would lose, neither is anticipated to make a move against the other. This, however, is not the view of the

Likud. The Likud perceives that both actors would benefit from a confrontation, but that it would have a slight edge (where the expected utility for Arafat is 0.463 and for the Likud is 0.493). Believing it will gain a clear advantage, it has reason to confront Arafat, expecting to gain the amount indicated by its expected utility for the move. The expected utility for Arafat is negative. Arafat expects to lose the amount of his expected utility, −1.719. Arafat's anticipation of loss is far more than he thinks the Likud will ask, and, assuming rationality, he must follow the least costly course and accept the Likud's demand.

The relation of Arafat and the Likud is only half of the picture. In Palestine, Arafat has two enemies rather than one. In this round of negotiation, Arafat's yielding to the Likud should be viewed in light of what the model tells of the expected dynamic between Arafat and Hamas. Arafat perceives correctly that he and Hamas are at a standoff. If demands are made, both stand to lose, and Arafat thinks Hamas would lose more (where Arafat's expected utility is −0.157 and Hamas's is −0.430). Hamas, on the other hand, see itself yielding if Arafat were to make a demand because Hamas believes that, in a confrontation, Arafat would win a minor gain while Hamas itself would lose far more than Arafat would ask (with an expected utility for Arafat at 0.013 and for Hamas at −0.274). Because each actor perceives itself as a loser in a confrontation with the other, neither should be expected to initiate demands. The result is that in this case Arafat's judgment is correct. Hamas is not anticipated to confront him directly.

How are we to interpret the simulated dynamic we have just described? Any observer of the Israeli-Palestinian scene would readily understand why Arafat should choose to yield to the Likud. Arafat has three bitter threats to his own security and power: the Likud, Hamas, and their allies. He correctly views Hamas as unable to threaten him directly for the time being. When he discovers he has misperceived the Likud's ability to attack him, he defuses the danger by yielding. Arafat's capitulation at one stroke deprives the Likud of a much-needed enemy, and it contemporaneously undermines the Likud's image as the defender of Israeli interests in Jerusalem against a Palestinian threat. His taking such a position cannot help but have an effect against the Likud in the coming Israeli elections. In every way his "yielding" on Jerusalem protects his most cherished asset, his leadership position. In short, he does no more than he has already done in negotiating the Principles for Peace. He preserves his power.[10] Hamas, the avowed opponent of Arafat, takes an opposite strategy. There are at least three links in the chain connecting what Hamas does and what it hopes to achieve. Terror against Israeli civilians is designed to turn the elections against the Rabin government and help elect the Likud, which will halt (or renege on) the negotiations. This, in turn, will discredit Arafat and, Hamas hopes, remove him from power. There is a clear alliance of interests between the Likud and Hamas, and Rabin and Arafat.[11] All leaders everywhere want power. For some leaders, gaining and retaining power is the only goal.[12] Viewed in this perspective, Arafat yielding to the Likud is not as strange as it may have first appeared.

### The Issue of International Acceptance of the Settlement

The resolution of this issue is contingent not just on the response of local actors, but also on the response of the international community. This raises the important question, How will the international community and its major players receive the Palestinian-Israeli agreement? Will the status of Jerusalem again become an issue after the settlement?

We shall proceed in the same fashion and use the same scale as in the first analysis. The set of international actors includes some representatives from the region with important ties to the city. The actors in question are Saudi Arabia, Jordan, and Egypt. The set also includes three actors beyond the region: the Vatican, world Jewry, France, and the United Kingdom. The religious interest of the Vatican in Jerusalem is too obvious for discussion, and the same can be said of the world Jewry. We include two secular powers, France and the United Kingdom, because they are leaders in Europe. France is Catholic, and the United Kingdom Protestant. We also include the United States because, as the world's leader, it will inevitably be involved in the debate following a settlement over a city so important to three major world religions.

One could object that including the United States, due to its involvement in the negotiations and its result, its double counting. But the U.S. case is complicated. The United States at all times would have two roles, as a participant in the negotiations and as an observer. It is clearly a participant in, a resource to, and a catalyst for negotiations. However, it is also a leader of the international community and therefore at the same time has a separate, oversight role. We capture this audience role to the negotiation by adjusting the estimates of the power, salience, and preferences of the United States. The new values reflect the fact that in this setting, dealing with an issue largely, though not entirely, involved in world religions with roughly two billion adherents, U.S. power is probably less than it was as party to the group negotiating a settlement. The lowering of the value of the U.S. preference seeks to capture its desire to play the role of the defender of the terms of the settlement. Other

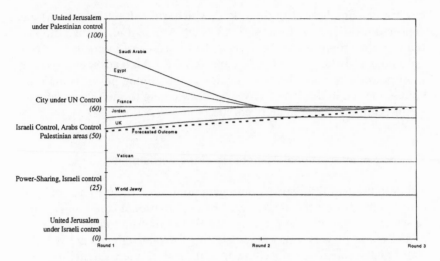

**Fig. 2. Preferences of international actors on the Jerusalem negotiations over time**

portions of the U.S. government than those involved in the negotiation would become involved, and their preferences would be close to, but still lower than, the original U.S. position. Finally, we have raised the salience of the United States slightly on the assumption that, as negotiations and their aftermath approach, the debate will become more intense. Figure 2 reports the results of the analysis in the same manner as before.

It is fairly clear from figure 2 that this key group in the international community rejects entirely the very foundations of the bargains struck in the Israeli-Palestinian negotiations with U.S. assistance. France, Saudi Arabia, and Jordan prefer, in effect, that Israeli sovereignty over Jerusalem be annulled and the city put under international control. Great Britain would rather see Israelis control Jewish areas in East Jerusalem and Palestinians control Palestinian areas. The Vatican expectedly prefers that Holy Places be under international control. Only the United States prefers changes in the status quo without undermining the Israeli sovereignty over the city.

It is very reasonable to assume that if these actors cannot be persuaded to accept at least the general outline of the settlement, the rest of the international community will have a similar reaction. In such a case the struggle for a settlement may be followed by an equally long struggle for acceptance. One can foresee a very lengthy tug of war.

One final note: Even the very exploratory analysis we have done reveals a number of missed opportunities open to participants to maximize their preferences and alter the outcome. The United States had ample opportunities to get France, the United Kingdom, Saudi Arabia, and Jordan to come to its position. The reader will recall that such information offers the occasion to simulate the course of events that would occur if the opportunities had been exploited. We executed such a simulation, and the result was dramatic. Had the United States perceived that it was possible for it to move all actors (except the Vatican) to its own position in the third round and again in the fourth round of the bargaining process, the first step in the process of creating international acceptance of the settlement might well have begun.

## Conclusion

This essay outlines what would have been the settlement over the final status of Jerusalem if Rabin had not been assassinated. If the Israelis and Palestinians had reached the final negotiations stage with Rabin in command of the Israeli government, Jerusalem would have remained under Israeli control but there would have been slight modifications to the status quo. The Palestinians would have made their capital a suburb of Jerusalem and would have obtained a number of concessions of great symbolic value to them. A real equilibrium would have been achieved. Both sides could and would have claimed victory.

The results of the analysis are strongly supported by the revelation of results of the secret exploratory talks between representatives of the Palestinian National Authority and the Israeli government. Time will tell what differences the death of Prime Minister Rabin and subsequent events will make on the settlement over the final status of Jerusalem.[13]

Before the assassination of Rabin, a key factor would have made the settlement in regard to Jerusalem possible — Arafat's early agreement to Rabin's position. In retrospect we can see that Arafat would have made the concession in exchange for a number of important gains. He would have obtained the evacuation of the Israelis from the West Bank, the recognition of a Palestinian state, and the face-saving provision that would have made it possible for him to claim that Jerusalem was also the capital of the Palestinian state. Very important politically, the settlement permitted him to stay ahead of Hamas.

However, the international community would have reacted strongly and negatively to the settlement. Experts have considered the attempt to settle differences between Palestinian and Israeli authorities over the future of Jerusalem a difficult and contentious problem. But our analysis indicates that the contentiousness on the issue would have been far greater in the world community. Leaders of countries and religions with emotional, philosophical, and religious ties to the Holy Places in the Old City would have rejected, at least at first, the terms of the settlement. The United States would have had to work very hard to turn things around, and it would have had a number of chances to do so, by exploiting some of the opportunities it was revealed to have missed in our analysis. Clearly, in the short term, the settlement on the ground would not have managed to settle the issue. For a protracted period, the tug of war over Jerusalem would have continued on the international plane.

NOTES

Kenneth Organski passed away while this volume was in preparation. Final revisions to the article were made by Jacek Kugler, of Claremont Graduate University.

The author wishes to thank two institutions that have helped with this work. The Earhart Foundation once again has been critical in helping financially and in other ways to make this research possible. The Center of Political Studies, our longtime intellectual home, has made major contributions to this project. Finally, we wish to express our thanks to Decision Insights, Inc., for permission to use their model in this analysis.

1. A more complete discussion on this point is beyond the scope of this essay. A balanced set of views on the value and limitations of counterfactual reasoning can be found in James Fearon, "Counterfactuals and Hypothesis Testing," *World Politics* 43, 1991, 169–95; David Sylvan and Stephen Majeski, "A Methodology for the Study of Historical Counterfactuals," *International Studies Quarterly* 42, 1998, 79–198; Philip E. Tetlock and Aaron Belkin, *Counterfactual Thought Experiments in World Politics: Logical, Methodological, and Psychological Perspectives* (Princeton: Princeton University Press, 1996).

2. For a fairly thorough review of the model's success see Bruce Bueno de Mesquita, "A Decision Making Model: Its Structure and Form," *International Interactions* 23, no. 4, 1997, 259–64; Bruce Bueno de Mesquita, David Newman, and Alvin Rabushka, *Red Flag over Hong Kong* (Chatham, N.J.: Chatham House Publishers, 1996), 165–90; for a recent assessment see Jacek Kugler and Yi Feng, eds., *The Expected Utility Approach to Policy Decision Making: Assessments, Forecasts and Strategies,* special issue, *International Interactions* 23, no. 3–4, 1997.

3. There were other understandings that dealt with the settlements that are beyond the scope of the analysis performed in this essay.

4. The relevant passages in the Declaration of Principles, from the Ministry of Foreign Affairs, Government of Israel, *The Declaration of Principles,*

September 1993, read as follows: *"2. Permanent status negotiation will commence as soon as possible, but not later than the beginning of the third year of the interim period . . . 3. These negotiations shall cover remaining issues, including Jerusalem, refugees, settlement security arrangements, borders, relations and cooperation with other neighbors and other issues of common interest."*

5. This name is slightly misleading in that the forecasting tool used for this essay utilizes both game-theoretic and decision-theoretic calculations.

6. See Kugler and Feng 1997.

7. Duncan Black, *The Theory of Committees and Elections* (Cambridge: Cambridge University Press, 1958).

8. The expert in this case is a specialist in the Middle East and has provided data repeatedly for forecasts on a variety of issues. The use of a single expert is not problematic. Stanley Feder, "Factions and Policon: New Ways to Analyze Politics," *Studies in Intelligence Studies,* 1987, 41–57, shows that multiple experts produce similar analytical results even when they seemingly do not agree on the values assigned each actor or the number of actors involved. Indeed *slightly* different data do not generate substantive differences in the forecast.

9. See A. F. K. Organski and Ellen Lust-Okar, "The Tug of War over the Status of Jerusalem: Leaders, Strategies and Outcomes, *International Interactions* 23, 1997, for details on the data collection.

10. Steven Spiegel, *The Other Arab-Israeli Conflict* (Chicago: University of Chicago Press, 1985); A. F. K. Organski, *The 36 Billion Dollar Bargain* (New York: Columbia University Press, 1990).

11. Serge Schmemann, "My Enemy's Enemy," *New York Times,* August 23, 1995, 1.

12. The issue of the ideologue and opportunist elites is central to politics. It is connected to fundamental assumptions of power and security (see Bruce Bueno de Mesquita and A. F. K. Organski, *People, Preferences, and Power,* forthcoming). Margaret Thatcher gave a vivid view of the opportunist leader: "Prime Minister Andreotti . . . apparently an indispensable participant in Italian governments represented an approach to politics that I could not share. He seemed to have a positive aversion to principle, even a conviction that a man of principle was doomed to be a figure of fun. He saw politics as an eighteenth century politics saw war: a vast and elaborate set of parade grounds maneuvers by armies that would never actually engage in conflict but instead declare victory, surrender, or compromise as their apparent strength dictated in order to collaborate on the real business of sharing the spoils."

13. A different analysis forecasts that outcome; see Organski and Lust-Okar 1997, 333–50.

# Conclusion

# Policy Relevance and Theoretical Development in International Relations: What Have We Learned?

*Joseph Lepgold*

How useful *should* theories of international relations (IR) be to policy-makers? How useful *can* IR theory be, since theories are judged by primarily intellectual criteria in addition to their practical utility? Twenty-five years ago, a symposium issue of *World Politics* explored the question of policy-relevant IR theory from various epistemological and practical perspectives;[1] since then, with only a few key exceptions, students of IR have largely ignored the issue.[2] The dearth of reflection on this issue is puzzling and unfortunate. We have returned to it in this volume for two reasons. First, as Miroslav Nincic notes in his introductory essay, if theoretically oriented scholars were to pursue an understanding of IR with little regard for practical relevance, the link between IR theory and its empirical relevance would grow ever more tenuous. Increasingly arid and inconclusive academic debates would be a likely consequence. Second, world politics is at a historic transition point between Cold War bipolarity and a less hierarchical, polarized international systemic environment. While this has created opportunities for policymakers to re-think basic assumptions and perhaps strive for new objectives, it has also produced much uncertainty about what the future will bring. At times, new issues and actors seemingly overwhelm one's ability to make sense of the major trends and their implications. In periods of major flux, policy-makers might well want intellectual guidance about strategic choices and the consequences of such decisions. If IR theory can be useful, it should be able to rise to these challenges. The contributors to this volume believe that it is time to reassess whether and how our intellectual products can help the actors we write about, and at what cost — if any — to the field's theoretical development.

One answer to the questions posed at the beginning of the previous paragraph might be as follows: Theory is a set of causal proportions that are generalizable across space, time, and perhaps substantive issue areas. Because such propositions are designed to explain general patterns of behavior and specify the initial conditions that activate them, they can reveal little in detail about individual cases. Yet policymakers often want to know such detail and tend to feel more comfortable with in-depth studies of specific cases than they do with generalizable arguments.[3] This line of reasoning suggests that IR theories should *not* be judged by their practical usefulness, because policymakers are not inclined to use them. It thus matters little if many IR theorists are motivated by a desire for better policy,[4] since those who make policy are not buying what theorists are offering. IR theorists should therefore focus on developing a "pure" science of IR, let their academic peers judge the worth of their work, and not worry about whether or how it is applied in policy-making.

Yet another answer to these questions also seems plausible. Policymakers can in principle use IR theory to identify strategic situations, explore outcomes they wish to achieve, or identify and assess options for achieving them. Clinton and Bush administration officials, for example, have embraced the theoretical argument that democracies are inherently peaceful in dealing with other democracies. They believe that for a status quo country such as the United States, the more democracies the better. This proposition in part underpins efforts to liberalize Russia, enlarge NATO, and help rid Africa of dictatorships — none of them easy or cheap objectives. Similarly, U.S. officials during the Cold War found theoretical arguments about nuclear strategy and coercive diplomacy useful in thinking through some of the problems they faced,[5] and the political economy literature on structural adjustment provides a good example of fruitful synergies between scholars and practitioners.[6] More generally, if a need for mental economy pushes people to adopt choice heuristics — rules of thumb that obviate the need to consider fully a wide range of options — they might see theory as a tool to make such principles self-conscious. Whatever one's intellectual assumptions are, from this point of view, it is better to be conscious of them than to leave them implicit and immune to scrutiny. From this perspective, policymakers might be more averse to theory as a *term* than to the *underlying notion* that generic knowledge about strategies can help them better achieve their objectives.[7]

The essays in this volume find support for both of these positions. On the one hand, there is less overt demand for theory from IR practitioners than is found in many domestic areas of public policy, where social science regularly informs policy choices. On the other hand, there are reasons to explore whether and how the theory-practice gap in IR can be narrowed. Logically, it would seem that intellectually powerful theory *should* be useful to officials, if only to discipline their intuitions. It is more counterintuitive in some ways that policymakers do *not* find theory useful than the reverse.

In an effort to understand this paradox, our contributors have examined two major issues. One concerns how various groups of IR professionals — ranging from the most abstract theorists to policymakers — actually interact. The other concerns the logic and substantive fruits of theoretical inquiry in this field. In analyzing these questions, they have found that narrowing the theory-practice gap can be difficult. Some things foreign policy practitioners want to know can be difficult to infer from abstract arguments, and some theorists are interested in phenomena that do not have obvious empirical referents or cannot be manipulated by policymakers. The criteria of science and engineering are not the same, in this field as in others. This was not always the case. Earlier in this century, much IR writing was done by practitioners for other practitioners: "In the Anglo-Saxon world of the 1920s and 1930s . . . enlightened men, of learning and leisure, moved in and out of the worlds of academia, government, and politics without observing too closely the boundaries between them."[8] These boundaries have hardened as the study of politics has become more self-consciously scientific, especially in the United States. Perhaps, then, something about the contemporary academic packaging rather than the particular contents of IR theory has inclined policymakers to resist it.

There seems, in short, to be a sociology-of-knowledge dimension as well as an epistemological or logic-of-inquiry aspect to the challenge of finding, creating, or framing IR theories that are useful in practical terms. To understand how and when officials can fruitfully use theory, we must reflect on what it means to generalize in this field and how various groups of people who specialize in IR can use different types of knowledge. I thus conclude this volume by addressing five questions: (1) How profound is the theory-policy gap in IR? (2) How, if at all, can such a gap be narrowed? (3) *Should* it be narrowed? (4) How can the rational-choice research program contribute to narrowing it? (5) What needs next to be done to make IR theory as useful as it can be to policymakers?

## How Profound Is the Theory-Policy Gap in International Relations?

The prevailing view is that a wide gap separates IR theorists from practitioners, at least in the United States. Epistemological considerations reinforce the sociology of the field to create this result. As Miroslav Nincic notes in the introduction to this volume, theorists and practitioners tend to write for different audiences and in different journals. *International Organization* and *World Politics* rarely feature work by practitioners, while *Foreign Policy* is written mainly for and by IR practitioners. While a few journals and writers try to straddle this divide[9] — for instance, such journals as *Survival* and such writers as Joseph Nye — doing so tends to be uncomfortable, since the vocabularies and audiences are so distinct. Journals that "work heroically back and forth across the [theory-practice] divide" tend not to have a firm footing in either the academic or policy community.[10]

This gap is the product of a secular trend in the evolution of the social sciences — particularly political science, since most IR theory is situated there. As the study of politics and strategic interaction has become more rigorous, the standards of value in the scholarly and policy communities have become more distinct. Only well-trained social scientists can understand much of today's "academic" IR literature; as in the natural sciences, theorists believe that only their academic peers have the competence and shared objectives necessary to evaluate their work.[11] One analyst at RAND noted that he found not only the articles but also many of the *titles* of articles in the major political science journals to be unintelligible. Young scholars, moreover, learn quickly that only by publishing in the "right" academic journals will they build their professional reputations and gain tenure in most university departments. This tendency has intensified as the academic job market has tightened over the last generation.

Consequently, much IR theory does not speak to policymakers, as that is not its purpose. Neorealism, for instance, is deliberately couched as a systemic argument that explains only the external constraints on national units, not how those units are likely to respond to such pressures. System structure, of course, is not a variable that policymakers can readily manipulate. Yet scholars who aspire to broad generalizations and theoretical elegance may have little incentive to provide insight about manipulable variables. Conversely, as Arthur Stein notes in his essay, the kind of research that *would* often interest policymakers is often harder to model, has less general implications, and is therefore less likely to interest theorists. Practitioners, however, care primarily about the ways in which policy instruments actually operate. What, for instance, are the consequences of giving or withholding economic or military aid, withdrawing one's ambassador diplomatic recognition, and so on?[12] In his essay, Joseph Lepgold contends that contingent generalizations about such matters are precisely what IR theory needs, as a way to attenuate debates that have become imprecise and unproductive.[13] Such work would also tell officials more about more of the cases they were likely to see. But the academic IR field has not rewarded precise, contingent propositions as much as it should, and they are not as well represented in the literature as they might be.

Evidence suggests that the theory-practice gap in IR is not only wide but growing. A quick count of IR articles in the *American Political Science Review* in the volumes for the years 1944, 1964, and 1994, for instance, reveals that perhaps 7 or 8 of 9 articles in 1944, perhaps 2 of 4 in 1964, and at most 1 of 4 in 1994 could be understood by a policy practitioner without some advanced theoretical and methodological training in social science. A similar trend is evident in other American social science journals and scholarly books. Furthermore, at least some policymakers may care even less about interacting with theorists than they did before 1989.[14] The Cold War, after all, drove much of the scholarly agenda of security studies, including such issues as the effectiveness of deterrence, the impact of nuclear weapons, and the degree to which various distributions of power internationally are stable.

One can, however, view the disjunction between IR theorists and practitioners in another way. At least in the United States, Lepgold contends that there are four IR groups, distinguished by their proximity to specific policy problems. While each group encompasses distinct literatures and activities, together they create a potential transmission belt that runs from "pure theory" to "pure policy-making." When people talk about a "chasm" that separates theory and policy in IR,[15] they ignore two groups situated between general theorists and working foreign policy officials. These are (1) theorists and area studies scholars who work on particular, issue-oriented IR puzzles, such as crisis bargaining and the effectiveness of structural adjustment policies; and (2) researchers who analyze specific policy-relevant cases, such as the nature of U.S.-Iraqi bargaining prior to the Persian Gulf War, and the degree to which IMF-mandated programs have worked in specific places. In his essay, Ernest Wilson similarly notes that IR groups have varying interest in specific policy problems, with the most applied having the most direct impact on practitioners' thinking.[16] Specifically, Lepgold's two intermediate groups correspond to people that produce what Miroslav Nincic calls "policy-relevant theory," as opposed to "basic theory" and "ideographic policy analysis" (see fig. 1 in "Policy Relevance and Theoretical Development").[17] Since there is less distance between any two of these adjacent groups than across the entire theory-practice spectrum, a series of bridges exists — and presumably can be strengthened — across much of it.

From this perspective, whether one sees a bridgeable gap or a vast chasm between theorists and policymakers depends on where one sits along this continuum and the detail with which one examines it. The distance can appear unbridgeable at either end: general theorists and policymakers often speak languages that are unintelligible to the other. This explains why many practitioners' eyes glaze over when the word *theory* is mentioned.[18] But policymakers *do* value "well-founded empirical propositions"[19] — the kind of knowledge that case-oriented researchers produce, often using specific theories from puzzle-oriented work. Think-tank symposia exemplify these links, since they typically bring together those with policy experience and academic theorists. The National Research Council sponsors brainstorming sessions at which scholars describe current theories and evidence in their areas of expertise, officials discuss their problems, and together they think through how the U.S. government might better deal with such issues.[20] There are, in brief, more working connections among various types of IR professionals with differing mixes of applied and theoretical interests than is often supposed.

Despite such possibilities for mutually profitable interaction, much contemporary IR theory seems to be simply irrelevant to policy issues, if by *policy* we mean "social problems to which some practical urgency attaches."[21] Many theorists rarely (if ever) have the kind of exchanges just described: they produce their work without reading the policy literature or talking to policymakers, and seem to regard that kind of interaction as a distraction. Similarly, many diplomats and military professionals spend their careers isolated from the IR theoretical literature. How — if at all — can this situation be changed? I next discuss what we have learned about this issue in the process of producing this book.

### How Can the Theory-Practice Gap Be Narrowed?

A central conclusion of this volume is that there is no single standard or measure of policy relevance in IR, and therefore no one way to improve the theorist-practitioner relationship. What is relevant depends on what practitioners want to know and how much theorists can enlighten them. This inference is less banal than it may at first appear. It is often assumed that theory is useful only if it provides foreknowledge of key events or important thresholds in ongoing relationships. John Lewis Gaddis thus concludes that IR theory is useless, since no existing theory anticipated the end of the Cold War.[22] Even though such a view is misleading, it is understandable. The fact that few people anticipated or even considered seriously until the late 1980s that the Cold War could end was certainly costly, if not intellectually embarrassing for IR as an academic field. And because other social scientists, notably econometricians, earn stature by the importance and accuracy of their predictions, one might believe that IR theorists should also be evaluated on that basis. While an ability to predict behavioral outcomes is an attractive feature of any social theory (as I suggest below with respect to rational choice work), it is by no means the only way in which theory can speak to policy issues. Any discussion of how the theorist-practitioner gap could be narrowed must also consider other types of relevance.

In their essays, Miroslav Nincic and Lepgold discuss various ways IR theory can aid officials. Theory can help people identify how different actors (themselves included) are framing questions, which can help them clarify others' goals and the nature of their own assumptions. It can help policymakers identify the contextual variables that define strategic situations, allowing them to assess whether or to what degree the conditions favoring a certain strategy are present. For example, policymakers who might consider using preventive diplomacy to contain an incipient ethnic war might want to know if that instrument fits the situation. By focusing on the factors that give rise to the fears of ethnic groups and the role that confidence-building measures might play in alleviating them, Donald Rothchild's essay offers an analysis that could help answer that question. Theory can also clarify the range of possibilities in strategic situations — that is, it can be used to identify how certain strategies can be expected to work, with what results and likely risks, and to achieve what goals. In addition, theory can illuminate the direct and indirect consequences of policy choices, including the opportunity costs of alternative options. Put differently, theory can help people see where they are (or where they are heading), who they are dealing with, what they might want to do, and, given their objectives, what they should instrumentally do. Enlightenment in achieving *any* of these purposes can be considered "policy relevance."

This suggests that the relationship between IR theorists and policy practitioners might be better understood if the issue of policy relevance were reframed. Instead of asking, "Can IR theory be useful?" one could ask, "What kinds of policy insight can theory provide, when are decision makers likely to want it, and how much do they want or need that kind of insight?" As Wilson notes in his essay, officials need current information and analysis, conceptual guidance about choices, political support, and what he calls "contextualization"— a sense of what situation they face, who the key actors relevant to outcomes are, and so on.[23] In other words, they need virtually every kind of help just enumerated at one time or another. Academicians, and especially those who enter government temporarily, might perform a valuable role simply by flagging these possibilities at appropriate times. Doing so might refute the first view of policy relevance summarized at the outset of this conclusion: that the whole notion of useful IR theories is oxymoronic, since there is no apparent practitioner demand for IR theory. If the multiple uses of theory were internalized within bureaucracies, think tanks, and university faculties, overt demand for it might increase.

Robert Lieber's essay in this volume illustrates a number of these points. He claims that the U.S. political system has numerous Madisonian features that are typically masked during crises but reappear during tranquil periods, including a public that is indifferent or hostile to foreign policy issues and a Congress that is prone to micromanage their day-to-day execution. These characteristics make it difficult for presidents to pursue coherent external strategies and legitimate them to the public.[24] The end of the Cold War, Lieber argues, has seen a recrudescence of these features, which were largely masked from the 1940s to the early 1990s. While Lieber's argument is unlikely to generate precise predictions, it could sensitize U.S. officials to various aspects of the domestic context they face, and particularly to how those features are interrelated. It also highlights less obvious implications. Because the U.S.-Soviet rivalry had an ideological and social dimension, with elites in each country claiming that their system better provided for people's welfare, the Cold War helped catalyze broad political support in the United States for an expanded welfare state, stronger civil rights protections, and expanded educational opportunities for those less well-off. Lieber argues that the end of the Cold War contributed to Liberalism's American demise by weakening an international motivation to pursue such policies.[25] More generally, the absence of a unifying external threat has already diminished the leverage and stature of the presidency, with implications for the kinds of domestic coalitions presidents need in order to make foreign policy and the political risks they are likely now to face in trying to keep coalitions together.[26]

I have argued that because there is no single standard of theoretical "relevance" in IR, this volume offers no one-size-fits-all formula for improving the theorist-practitioner relationship. Various types of theoretical generalizations can be useful, depending on the circumstances. Nevertheless, several of our contributors offer a more specific recommendation. They believe that so-called mid-range theory would most often be useful to practitioners, and several of the substantive applications in this volume — those by Emily Goldman, Donna Nincic, Eric Larson, and Bruce Jentleson — illustrate such theory. Mid-range theories

eschew all-encompassing generalizations in favor of an emphasis on spe-
cificities of context. They allow scholars to focus on comparable cultural, institutional, or strategic characteristics across cases.[27] As Bruce
Jentleson notes in his essay, mid-range theories often have the practical
advantage of pointing to particular features of the strategic context and
specific manipulable variables. He reports that U.S. officials who partici-
pated in the early stages of the Middle East Arms Control and Regional
Security talks in the early 1990s found that specific propositions about
international cooperation helped them work through the conditions that
might be conducive for bridging long-standing antagonisms and security
rivalries. This parallels a point long made by Alexander George: the
route to policy-relevant IR theory is through contingent generalizations
rather than universal laws. The former are closer to the ground than the
latter and thus more focused on the reality with which policymakers
must deal.[28]

Seen in this light, narrowing the theorist-practitioner gap requires
that scholars notice when theoretical insights can be strategically useful
to officials. For example, policymakers may find theory most useful in
making day-to-day adaptations in an ongoing line of action: because the
stakes and risks attached to any one action here are often fairly low,
some experimentation with different kinds of knowledge and guidance
may be feasible. For all of its drama, inaugurating a Middle East initiative is atypical of foreign affairs activity, most of which involves adjusting policy at the margins.[29] During his time in the government, Ernest
Wilson found that officials spent about 90 percent of their time fitting
current policies to new circumstances. Only 10 percent was devoted to
mapping new strategies.[30] If mid-range theories were to specify more
precisely the international (or domestic, as need may arise) context in
which policy must operate, this sort of task could be better grounded.
Lepgold thus suggests careful, explicit specification of the empirical conditions and theoretical assumptions that define mid-range models.

Yet even truly useful theory may go unused, since easy communication between theorists and policymakers is likely to be rare. While the
two groups have more opportunities for dialogue than is often realized,
their professional cultures and incentives are very different. This problem tends to inhibit a genuine understanding of each other's curiosities
and expertise. Theorists gain stature when they define and solve problems that are intrinsic to scientific disciplines;[31] to policymakers, such
criteria are irrelevant. Professional schools of international affairs may
increasingly seek faculty that combine some real-world experience with
a theoretical knowledge of IR,[32] on the assumption that tomorrow's
practitioners need to see how general principles and actual experience

are linked. Such faculties, though, do not typify those found in American universities, which emphasize discipline-oriented achievements. If anything, political science is moving in the direction taken by economics a generation ago: toward greater formalization and less attention to empirical content. Social scientists, then, will likely continue to focus on developing more-or-less abstract models, at times intrigued by the policy implications of their work, but rarely driven by them. If so, narrowing the gap(s) between the academic and practitioners in IR will require sustained effort, perhaps with only minimal or intermittent payoff. Is such effort worthwhile? I turn next to this issue.

## Should Sustained Efforts Be Made to Narrow the Theory-Practice Gap?

The reader is by now aware that the overt demand for what we have called "useful" IR theory is fairly thin and may be growing thinner. This raises an obvious question: Is sustained effort to broaden it worthwhile? The contributors to this volume believe that it is, for two reasons. From the perspective of IR theory, a concern for policy relevance will often be beneficial. It will serve to keep academic work from focusing on trivialities and help to keep the field's principal concepts tied to clear empirical referents. From a practitioner's point of view, whatever her specific policy and political objectives, a better understanding of the strategic environment within which policy must operate is almost always preferable to a murky understanding of that context. Just as anyone who believes that health is preferable to illness would want an empirical science of medicine for instrumental purposes,[33] so, setting aside the costs of inquiry, most people with an interest in effective policy would want to understand cause and effect in IR as precisely as possible. What needs to be done to make theory better on its own terms thus seems to be in the interest of the entire IR community, broadly defined.

Theory might also, however, be useful to policymakers in two less direct ways. First, it can address issues policymakers had not thought to ask about but would probably want to consider if those issues were brought to their attention. For example, officials might assume that the diffusion worldwide of new military technologies makes it highly likely that other countries' military organizations will become more effective, thus reducing the United States' relative advantage. While some such diffusion is probably inevitable, Emily Goldman shows in her chapter that to affect military performance, the acquisition of new technology must be accompanied by compatible innovations and learning within the organizations acquiring the new tools. As she put it, "ideas not compatible with prevalent values, norms, and institutional infrastructure of a social system will not be adopted as rapidly and emulated as completely as innovations that are compatible."[34] Policy analyses that incorporate these variables could lead to conclusions quite different from those that ignored such factors. Of course, it may not be in anyone's interest to probe such issues during the decision process. But the normal competitiveness of viewpoints within a bureaucracy as pluralistic as America's makes it likely that some actor would introduce such analysis if she were reminded that it was pertinent. Theory, then, can lead policymakers to ask better or different questions than those with which they began.

Second, theory can also be useful when it tells officials things they did not want to hear. Assume, in the example just cited, that no official was interested in considering the organizational argument, because each agency had signed on to a logrolling agreement whereby any significant diffusion of dual-use technology — whatever its eventual consequences — was used to justify an increase in everyone's procurement and R&D budgets. An argument such as Goldman's could still be useful in affecting policy if some set of defense officials, noting that overinvestment in procurement during a prior budgetary cycle was now forcing undesired cuts in the budget, insisted that future analyses of technological diffusion must examine how organizations within the recipient country were likely to use the knowledge they had acquired. If the organizational argument were never made and disseminated, it would be impossible for anyone's consciousness to be raised.

For all these reasons, sustained effort to narrow the theory-practice gap in IR seems to be worthwhile. Not only can policymakers use theory in indirect as well as direct ways; compelling general arguments about international affairs, if couched in a reader-friendly form, can help enlighten at least those citizens who follow public affairs, and they can help define an agenda for possible future action even if policymakers are not receptive to them when they are made. If the justification for any field is strengthened by an ability to inform important policy choices,[35] there appears to be little reason *not* to try to narrow the gap.

Such a conclusion does, however, raise a concern that is important to many scholars: If mid-range generalizations are in greater demand from policymakers than general theory, and this demand began significantly to drive scholars' research activities, would the scope of theoretical propositions be reduced to an unacceptably low level? In other words, would the generation or refinement of general theory suffer as a result? Many academics commonly assume that the answer to this question is yes. Yet there are several reasons to believe that they are too pessimistic. First, as Nincic noted, a demand for policy-relevant theory is likely to reduce the comprehensiveness of theoretical generalizations only if a very narrow definition of "relevance" is employed.[36] If, for instance, one defined *policy relevance* as knowledge about how one manipulates very specific tools under very particular conditions, such analyses would indeed amount to virtually case-specific description. Some practitioners no doubt do define practicality in these terms,[37] and they may dismiss even moderately abstract work as useless. But there is no reason for the field as a whole to overreact to this phenomenon. Any scholarship that has clear implications about manipulable variables or the properties of strategic situations can speak to policy issues, even if the propositions are couched in general terms. Generic propositions about the conditions under which deterrence works, the conditions under which economic sanctions can be effective, or the functions of international regimes, for example, can in principle help officials in the ways discussed in this volume. In short, policy-relevant theory need not be at the ground level of decision makers' daily experience in order to be useful to them.

Another reason to doubt that a greater demand for mid-range generalizations would drive away basic theorists has to do with the sociology of the field. Some scholars are more comfortable with abstraction than others, and these individuals will presumably continue to seek the tangible and intangible rewards of discipline-based achievement regardless of what their more applied colleagues do. There is room in virtually every scientific field for applied as well as basic work, with both types of research seen as legitimate. Why should this not be true of IR? If one sees the different comparative advantages within the various IR professional communities as a basis for mutually profitable exchange instead of competition, there is every reason to think that basic research will continue to flourish even if the demand for work that is more directly policy-relevant increases.

### Does the Rational-Choice Research Program Speak to Policymakers?

Let us consider a question that has aroused controversy within political science during the last decade: Can work in the rational-choice tradition speak meaningfully about real-world issues? Formal models are based on a theory that presumes consistent and transitive preferences over outcomes, an absence of motivated biases that could inhabit purposive behavior, and individuals who regularly act so as to maximize their expected utility, once they have ordered the policy options they have identified. Such work begins with a general theoretical argument and can move directly to empirically specific inferences, depending on the particular model employed. The intermediate level of policy-relevant theory (what Lepgold calls Groups II and III) is thus bypassed. In this volume, the Steven Brams and Jeffrey Togman essay on the dynamics of conflict in Northern Ireland and the A. F. K. Organski essay predicting an outcome of the struggle over Jerusalem provide examples of this approach.

As is apparent from its use in many disciplines, rational choice work can offer a powerful analytical tool. Advocates of this approach claim that if actors know the preferences and power of those with whom they deal, the rational choice approach clarifies strategic options, the consequences of choosing the various options, and an actor's best choice, given that situation. In addition, by providing a general theory of strategic interaction, rational choice work offers the possibility of situating within a common intellectual framework any situation or case in which the parties are behaving strategically. Organski and Kugler thus outline what a settlement over the final status of Jerusalem would have consisted of had Israeli prime minister Yitzhak Rabin lived: Jews would have continued to control the city, but the Palestinians would have been given enough symbolic concessions for them to be bought off. Brams and Togman show that the Irish Republic Army miscalculated its moves by assuming that conciliation backed up by a threat of renewed violence would push Britain to a settlement; resolving the conflict was impossible so long as the factions were willing to resume paramilitary operations.

Advocates of rational choice make bold claims about its policy relevance. Brams and Togman claim, for example, that the theory of moves (a part of game theory) can tell officials when threats will work, what kinds of threats will work, and the consequences of acting on faulty information. More generally, they argue that without an explicit theory of strategic interaction, policymakers cannot know what strategic possibilities are open to them and which moves will lead to stable outcomes.[38]

Nevertheless, two problems — one epistemological, the other sociological — make it unlikely that large numbers of policymakers will soon accept these claims. Formal approaches can require consumers to take a good deal on faith. Analytic assumptions holding that states or internal factions are operationally coherent and that actors consistently optimize across transitive preferences in complex situations may take such liberties with the actual facts of a situation a policymaker knows intimately that the conclusions offered by such work may have little meaning to her. Of course, demanding that the analysis reflect such specific features of the context vitiates the approach: its power and operation require extreme parsimony. But, to use Miroslav Nincic's words, "[these] simplifications [can] play havoc with the truth of the premises employed."[39] One either accepts the simplification for purposes of the analysis or one does not, but there is little room for compromise in between.

A second, related problem has to do with the professional cultures and training. As an academic field, IR is not united by any methodological or epistemological approach. Political science as a field has become steadily more rigorous in the last few decades, but many in the discipline remain comfortable with epistemological and research approaches closer to the humanities. As a consequence, those with a historical or legal orientation continue to find it difficult to communicate with their more social science–oriented colleagues. As a result, the mathematical reasoning required to understand formal models of any sophistication comes only with difficulty to many people in the profession.

An obvious way to deal with this situation is to tolerate a good deal of pluralism. Scholars and practitioners who believe that formal models clarify the basic nature of strategic situations — or at least that some models produce this result some of the time — should use them. Others who reject the simplifying assumptions and technical demands of this approach will ignore them. At the same time, formal theorists could look for ways to make their major conclusions accessible to more traditional scholars, and traditionalists who are not unalterably opposed to the approach might be prepared to meet them halfway. We have three grounds for this conclusion. First, just as one need not know how to fix a car to drive one, one need not understand fully the mathematical reasoning behind the deductions to appreciate their policy implications. Second, the possibility for a strong connection between a general theory of strategic interaction and the needs of policy consumers should not be discounted, since the track record of success has apparently been quite good in some places.[40] Such a theory, if it did come to be widely accepted, could benefit policy consumers of theoretical work by simplifying their search for a model that fits their particular problem. Third, one need not rely exclusively on formal models for them to be useful; they can be supplemented by empirical elaborations that correspond more closely to reality.[41] This in fact illustrates a more general point: a variety of types of knowledge can serve varying policy uses. A game model can perhaps clarify one's basic strategic options, but policymakers might only be convinced that such knowledge was valuable in thinking through a problem if they were shown that the differences among the many policy options they have identified could be grouped into a small number of basic strategic options. In this case, theory would help to organize the "facts" a decision maker takes seriously, rather than providing definitive solutions to her problem; but the effect is to provide some degree of enlightenment she might otherwise not have had.

### Next Steps

Because there are so many types of IR theories at varying levels of abstraction and a number of distinct policy ways that they can be used in policy-making, no single collection can discuss every important link between theory and practice. To further strengthen the case for policy-relevant theory, at least two further types of illustrations or analysis are needed.

One would involve detailed case studies of past policy deliberations to determine what kind of knowledge or analysis was used (or needed) at various points and whether theory could have helped to meet that need. In diagnosing Mikhail Gorbachev's objectives and plans in the mid-1980s, for instance, one might try to reconstruct how U.S. policy-makers tried to determine the range of possibilities for dealing with a man who was evidently a very new type of Soviet leader. What kinds of inferences or analogies did they use? Could an existing theory have sharpened these inferences or pointed to other, less obvious possibilities? Could an argument about reciprocity in IR, to take one example, have helped to clarify the value of concessions each party expected, and on what schedule?[42] In deciding whether to intervene in Somalia in 1992, would American leaders have acted differently if they had had before them a powerful formal model outlining the expected consequences of their various options?

Delving into the past to see how theory *might* have helped policy-makers in various types of situations could show theorists how to offer better advice in the future. As is the case with most people, policymakers need help in disciplining their (often perceptive) everyday intuitions. People's social inferences are often driven by easily constructed, ad hoc theories, rather than by objective data or intersubjectively accepted arguments. As a result, they often see patterns not present in the actual data and overlook chance or situational factors that may have contributed to outcomes.[43] Systematically derived hypotheses and replicable evidence could provide a more reliable knowledge base for helping policymakers do their jobs.

A second, more ambitious way to analyze the theory-practice connection in IR would bring practitioners into a collaborative project to simulate various kinds of decisions and reenact actual policy deliberations.

Although some contributors to this volume have served temporarily in government, all are academicians by training and inclination. As a result, each of us have had to make guesses about what kinds of information and advice decision makers need or would use. In the early stages of this type of enterprise it may be necessary to get one's own house in order, taking stock of what the field has to offer intellectually and then trying to match it to substantive issues and decision makers' needs. We believe that this book has taken that first step. A logical next step is systematically to ask the actual policy consumers what they need and how they would use it if it were available, and then to find out how satisfied they have been with the results. If the retail slogan "the customer is always right" is itself correct, academic theorists at some point need to determine who outside of university faculties is buying or might buy their product, and how that set of consumers might better be satisfied.

NOTES

I thank Miroslav Nincic for his helpful comments on an earlier draft of this conclusion.

1. See *World Politics* 24, supplement (spring 1972).

2. Notable exceptions include Alexander L. George, *Bridging the Gap: Theory and Practice in Foreign Policy* (Washington, D.C.: U.S. Institute of Peace, 1993); Philip Zelikow, "Foreign Policy Engineering: From Theory to Practice and Back Again," *International Security* 18, no. 4 (spring 1994).

3. Zelikow, "Foreign Policy Engineering," 145.

4. Michael Nicholson, *Causes and Consequences in International Relations* (London: Pinter, 1996), 171.

5. Greg Herken, *Counsels of War,* expanded ed. (New York: Oxford University Press, 1987), 207–10.

6. Examples include Stephen Haggard, ed., *The International Political Economy and Developing Countries* (Aldershot, Hauts, Great Britain: Edward Elgar, 1995); Tun-jen Chang and Stephen Haggard, *Newly Industrializing Asia in Transition: Policy Reform and the American Response* (Berkeley: Institute of International Studies, University of California, 1987); Joan M. Nelson, *Migrants, Urban Poverty, and Instability in Developing Nations* (Cambridge: Center for International Affairs, Harvard University, 1969).

7. George, *Bridging the Gap,* xvii–xviii.

8. William Wallace, "Between Two Worlds: Think Tanks and Foreign Policy," in Christopher Hill and Pamela Beshoff, eds., *Two Worlds of International Relations: Academics, Practitioners, and the Trade in Ideas* (London: Routledge, 1994), 140.

9. Christopher Hill, "Academic International Relations: The Siren Song of Policy Relevance," in Hill and Beshoff, eds., *Two Worlds of International Relations,* 7.

10. Ibid.

11. Miroslav Nincic, "Introduction: Scholarship and the Contours of Policy Relevance," this volume.

12. Arthur A. Stein, "Counselors, Kings, and International Relations: From Revelation to Reason, and Still No Policy-Relevant Theory," this volume.

13. Joseph Lepgold, "Scholars and Statesmen: Framework for a Productive Dialogue," this volume.

14. Edward A. Kolodziej, "What Is the Challenge, and Will We Accept It?" *Mershon International Studies Review* 38, supplement 1 (April 1994), 175.

15. See, for example, Joseph Kruzel, "More a Chasm than a Gap, But Do Scholars Want to Bridge It?" *Mershon International Studies Review* 38, supplement 1 (April 1994), 178–81.

16. Ernest J. Wilson III, "How Social Science Can Help Policymakers: The Relevance of Theory," this volume.

17. Miroslav Nincic, "Policy Relevance and Theoretical Development: The Terms of the Trade-off," this volume.

18. George, *Bridging the Gap,* xviii.

19. Kruzel, "More a Chasm than a Gap," 180.

20. Wilson, "How Social Science Can Help Policymakers."

21. Nincic, "Introduction."

22. John Lewis Gaddis, "International Relations Theory and the End of the Cold War," *International Security* 17, no. 3 (winter 1992–93), 5–58.

23. Wilson, "How Social Science Can Help Policymakers."

24. Alexander L. George, "Domestic Constraints on Regime Change in U.S. Foreign Policy: The Need for Policy Legitimacy," in Ole R. Holsti, Randolph M. Siverson, and Alexander L. George, eds., *Change in the International System* (Boulder: Westview, 1980).

25. Robert J. Lieber, "Domestic Political Consequences of the Cold War's End: The International Impact on America's Foreign Policy Capacity," this volume.

26. This argument is elaborated in Alan C. Lamborn and Joseph Lepgold, "Foreign Policy Analysis, Linkage Politics, and the U.S. Case," manuscript, April 1997.

27. Peter Mair, "Comparative Politics: An Overview," in Robert E. Goodin and Hans-Dieter Klingemann, eds., *A New Handbook of Political Science* (Oxford: Oxford University Press, 1996), 316, 330.

28. George, "Summary and Conclusions," in *Bridging the Gap,* 135–45.

29. For a classic statement of this position, see Charles E. Lindblom, "The 'Science' of Muddling Through," *Public Administration Review* 19 (1959), 79–88.

30. Wilson, "How Social Science Can Help Policymakers."

31. Nincic, "Introduction."

32. Wilson, "How Social Science Can Help Policymakers."

33. Robert A. Dahl, *Modern Political Inquiry,* 5th ed. (Englewood Cliffs, N.J.: Prentice-Hall, 1991), 137.

34. Emily O. Goldman, "Military Diffusion, the Information Revolution, and U.S. Power," this volume.

35. Nincic, "Introduction."

36. Nincic, "Policy Relevance and Theoretical Development."

37. Ibid., 27.

38. Steven J. Brams and Jeffrey M. Togman, "Agreement through Threats: The Northern Ireland Case," this volume.

39. Nincic, "Policy Relevance and Theoretical Development."

40. See Lepgold, "Scholars and Statesmen."

41. Michael Nicholson, *Formal Theories in International Relations* (Cambridge: Cambridge University Press, 1989), 11. See also Robert Bates et al., *Analytic Narratives* (Princeton: Princeton University Press, 1998).

42. See Joseph Lepgold and George Shambaugh, "Who Owes Who, How Much, and When? Modeling Reciprocity in International Relations," June 1997, draft manuscript.

43. Susan T. Fiske and Shelley E. Taylor, *Social Cognition,* 2d ed. (New York: McGraw-Hill, 1991), 376–77.

# Contributors

Steven J. Brams is Professor of Politics, New York University.

Emily O. Goldman is Associate Professor of Political Science, and Director of the International Relations Program, University of California, Davis.

Bruce W. Jentleson is Professor of Political Science, University of California, Davis, and Director of the UC Davis Washington Center.

Jacek Kugler is Professor of Politics and Policy, Claremont Graduate University.

Eric V. Larson is a Policy Analyst with RAND.

Joseph Lepgold is Associate Professor of Government, Georgetown University.

Robert J. Lieber is Professor of Government, Georgetown University.

Donna J. Nincic is Lecturer in Political Science, University of California, Davis.

Miroslav Nincic is Professor of Political Science and Department Chair, University of California, Davis.

Kenneth Organski was Professor of Political Science, University of Michigan.

Donald Rothchild is Professor of Political Science, University of California, Davis.

Arthur A. Stein is Professor of Political Science, University of California, Los Angeles.

Jeffrey M. Togman is Assistant Professor of Political Science, Seton Hall University.

Ernest J. Wilson III is Professor of Government and Politics, and Director of the Center for International Development and Conflict Management, University of Maryland.

# Index

Abu Mazin, 345
Abu Musa, 307
Achen, Christopher, 86
Acheson, Dean, 141
Adams, Gerry, 332–36
Addis Ababa, 246
Adeleke, Ademola, 258
Adelman, Howard, 247
Afars, 253
Afganistan, 166
Africa, 14, 114, 118, 237–38, 241, 252, 257, 364
African Crisis Response Force (ACRF), 259
African National Congress (ANC), 246, 248–49, 251–52, 254, 336
AID Project, 114, 157, 161
Albright, Madeleine, 166, 168, 295
Alger, Chadwick, 298, 311–13
All Amhara Peoples' Organization, 248
Allison, Graham, 272
American foreign policy. *See* policy, U.S. foreign
American Political Science Association, 1, 117, 137, 344
*American Political Science Review,* 79, 117, 367
American political system, 153
American Revolution, 156
Amhara, 253
Angola, 245, 255, 258
Arabian Sea, 307
Arabic leaders, 79

Arab-Israeli peace process, 154
Arafat, Yasir, 336, 343, 345, 348–55, 357
Arrow's impossibility theorem, 65
Arusha, 245
Asian Regional Forum, 143
*Asia Survey,* 117
Association of Professional Schools of International Affairs (APSIA), 109, 110
Association of Southeast Asian Nations (ASEAN), 143
*Atlantic Monthly,* 117
Austria, 242
authority, political, 13
Axelrod, Robert, 117

Bacevich, A. J., 267
Bacon, Francis, 50
Baker, James (U.S. Secretary of State), 142
bargaining, 237
Barnett, Michael, 136
basic theory (BT), 22, 36, 37, 39, 40, 41, 42, 43, 44, 78
Bates, Robert, xvi
Beijing, 305
Beilin, Yossi, 345
Ben David, Joseph, 16, 45
Bennett, Andrew, xvi
Blair, A. M., 310–11, 313, 315
Blair, Tony, 326–27, 336
Bosnia, 116, 138, 154, 159–61, 165, 174, 184–89, 191, 193–207, 209, 211, 213, 241, 255, 260

Bosnia (*continued*)
  peacekeeping operation in, 13,
    174–75, 188–89, 191, 200–201,
    207–8, 211
Bosnia-Herzegovina, 184
Botswana, 237
Brams, Steven, 15, 16, 325, 339, 375
Bretton Woods, collapse of, 52
Brzezinski, Adam, 51
Buchanan, Pat, 159
Bureau of Economic Analysis, 297,
    303, 310
Bureau of Intelligence and Research
    (INR), 111, 113
Bureau of Mines, 121
Burton, John, 333
Burundi, 245, 254, 258, 261–62
Bush, George, 138, 158–59, 162, 295
  administration, 184, 364
Buthelezi, Mangosuthu, 252
Buyoya, Pierre, 259

Cafruny, Alan, 298
Campbell, Donald, 52
Canada, 303
Carnegie Commission, xv, xvii
Carnegie Endowment, 114
Carr, Canon Burgess, 246
Carter administration, 163
case studies, x, xvi
CBMs (confidence-building mea-
    sures), 143–44, 240, 247
Central Intelligence Agency (CIA),
    124, 166
  officials, 81
CFC gases, 96
Chemical Weapons Convention, 155,
    160
Chicago Council on Foreign Rela-
    tions (CCFR), 158, 189
Chicken Dilemma, 326, 338–40
China, 138, 155, 162, 167, 295, 305
Choucri, Nazli, xvii, 119
Christopher, Warren, 138, 140–41,
    143, 162
Civil War (U.S.), 12, 156

Clarity, James, 326, 333–36
Clinton, Bill, 12, 109, 138, 140–41,
    158, 159, 161–62, 166, 168, 183–
    84, 191, 194, 198, 213
  administration, 130, 138, 141, 155,
    160–61, 165, 184–85, 200–201,
    206–7, 209, 211, 295, 364
Clough, Michael, 115
CNN, 118, 120, 124
Cohen, Benjamin, 134
Cohen, Eliot, 267, 277
Cold War, 12, 13, 53–55, 61,62, 77,
    80, 109, 112, 118, 119, 122, 130–
    32, 138–43, 145, 153–60, 162–64,
    166, 168–69, 241, 267, 270, 271,
    295–96, 307, 316, 319, 363–64,
    367–70
Commerce Department (U.S.), 310
Commission on Global Governance,
    90
communication, 2, 15
Comprehensive Test Ban Treaty, 155
conciliation, xi
Conference on Security and Coopera-
    tion in Europe (CSCE), 143
Conference on Security and Coopera-
    tion in the Middle East
    (CSCME), 143
conflict(s), xv, 55, 57, 143, 238, 247,
    325, 335
  ethnic, xiv, 14, 53, 118, 131, 167,
    237, 239, 253
  interethnic, 14
  international, 14, 15
  religious, xiv
Congo, 258
Congress (U.S.), 115, 155, 157–58,
    160–61, 163–64, 168, 185, 211
Constitution (U.S.), 156
Contract with America, 159
cooperation, xi, 57, 145
Council of Economic Advisors, 50
Council on Foreign Relations, 109,
    114
crisis, xi
crisis management, xi, xvi

Croats, 184
CSBMs (confidence- and security-building measures), 144
Cuban missile crisis, 52, 53, 112

Damascus, 141
Davis, Major Norman C., 273
Dayton agreement, 198
decision making, x, 3
Declaration of Independence, 156
Declaration of Principles, 346
democracy, 33, 114, 115, 118, 138, 141
Democratic Unionist Party, 336
democratization, 34
Democrats, 4, 191, 201–2
Department of Defense, U.S. (DoD), 113–15, 118, 145, 164, 308
Department of Energy (U.S.), 120, 305
Depression, Great, 156
Dessle, Davis, xvi
Destler, I. M., 115
deterrence, xi, xii, xvi, 23, 57, 61, 78, 112, 132, 141
Deutsch, Karl, 1, 16, 61
Diesing, Paul, 183
DiMaggio, Paul, 279–80
diplomacy, 4, 141
   coercive, xi, xvi
   preventive, xi
Dole, Bob, 159, 165
Downing, John, 305
Dukakis, Michael, 138
Dulles, John Foster, 141

East Rand townships, 254
Economic Community of West African States (ECOWAS), 258–59
Egypt, 142, 144, 162, 167, 355
Eisenhower, Dwight, 162
E-issues, 119–22, 125
elite power-sharing regimes, 248–49
Eritrea, 256
Ethiopia, 248, 251–53, 259
Ethiopian People's Revolutionary

Democratic Front (EPRDF), 251, 253
ethnicity, xv
   ethnic elite(s), 238, 241
   ethnic group(s), 238
   ethnic leaders, 241, 243
   ethnic relations, 237
   ethnic violence, 23
   interethnic violence, 238
Europe, 53, 139, 143, 159, 166, 270, 299
   chaos in, 55
   Eastern, 114, 163
   integration of, 53
   Western, 114, 346
European Economic Community, 52
explanation, xi, x, 24, 26, 29, 286
Exxon, 121, 306

Farrell, Theo, 272
fascism, 155
FCC (Federal Communications Commission), 124
Feaver, Peter, 274
Federalist No. 10, 156
Federalist No. 51, 156
Flexner, Abraham, 41
Forbes, Steve, 159
force, 4
Ford Foundation, 54
forecasting, xv
*Foreign Affairs Journal,* 22, 81, 117, 137
*Foreign Policy Journal,* 22, 81, 117
Foreign Relations Committee (U.S. Senate), 160, 161–62
Fox, William, 32, 299
France, 24, 25, 26, 355–57
Freedman, Jeffrey, xvi, 16
Freedman, Milton, 27
Freedom of Navigation program, 308
Fukuyama, Francis, 117

G-7, 155
Gambari, Ibrahim, 257
Garten, Jeffrey, 295, 301

GATT, 165, 298
General Motors, 58
George, Alexander, xvi, 3, 4, 5, 9, 16,
    22, 34, 80, 112, 129–31, 142, 145,
    210, 371
Germany, 139, 161–62, 167
    Nazi Germany, 159
Ghali, Boutros, 258
Ghana, 244
Gilpin, Robert, 296
Gingrich, Newt, 27
*Global Governance,* 80
Globalization, 124
Goldhamer, Herbert, 50
Goldman, Emily, 14, 268, 272, 276,
    281, 370, 372–73
Goldstein, Judith, 131
Goodman, Louis W., 110
Gorbachev, Mikhail, 377
Graham, Phil, 194
Great Britain, 15, 24, 25, 26, 326–35,
    337–38, 356, 375. *See also* United
    Kingdom
    government, 326–28, 334
Greece, 165, 168
Green Line, 352
Greer, Scott, 6, 7, 16
Gregorian, Raffi, 277
Gulf Crisis, 170
Gulf of Mexico, 306
Gulf states, 142
Gulf War, 35, 77, 159, 170, 179, 196,
    205, 281, 295, 367

Haiti, 77, 159–60, 165, 203–4, 212
Hamas, 351, 353–55
Hardin, Russell, 239
Harknett, Richard, 268, 277
Hassan (crown prince of Jordan), 143
Havel, Václav, 129–30
Helms, Jesse, 161, 198
Hepworth, Mark, 314
Herken, Gregg, 62
Hirschfeld, Yair, 344–45
Hoge, Warren, 326, 336
Holbrooke, Richard, 165

Holsti, Kal, 134
Hong Kong, 82, 317
House of Representatives (U.S.), 158
Hughes, Barry, 297
Huntington, Samuel P., 117, 140, 272
Hussein (king of Jordan), 346
Hussein, Saddam, 59, 166
Hutu, 249, 254
    hard-liners, 245
    ideologues, 240

Idiographic Policy Analysis (IPA), 22,
    25, 40, 44, 81
Implementation Force (IFOR), 161
India, 273
Indonesia, 305–6, 317
inflation, 58
Information Agency (U.S.), 12
Inkatha Freedom Party (IFP), 248,
    254
Institute of Peace, 122
institutionalism, 94
Intel, 58
intelligence, xv
Intergovernmental Authority on
    Development (IGAD), 257,
    259
International Monetary Fund (IMF),
    367
*International Organization,* 79, 80,
    137
International Political Economy
    (IPE), 296, 298–99, 308, 310, 319
International relations theory (IR
    theory), xi, xiv, xvi, 11, 45, 77,
    78, 84, 89, 116, 130, 133, 142,
    319, 363–66, 369–72
International Science and Technology
    Center (ISTC), 96, 97
*International Security,* 80, 117, 137
International Studies Association, 137
*International Studies Quarterly,* 79
intervention(s), 13, 14
    U.S. military, 13
Iran, 35, 96, 167, 276, 307
    mullahs, 60

Iran-Iraq War, 308
Iraq, 35, 60, 166, 255, 276
  politics, 60
Ireland, Northern, 15, 82, 165, 325–36, 340, 375
Ireland, Republic of, 328, 331
Irish Republican Army (IRA), 15, 325–26, 328–40, 375
Islam, 38
Israel, 22, 142, 144, 162, 167, 273, 336, 344
  Israelis, 344, 346, 348, 350–52
  Israel-Jordan negotiations, 142
  Israel-Lebanon negotiations, 142
  Israel-Palestinians negotiations, 142
  Israel-Syria negotiations, 142
Israeli-Palestinian "Declaration of Principles" (DOP), 140
ivory tower(s), 10, 11, 45

Japan, 139, 155, 159, 162, 167, 304, 306, 317
Java, 306
Jensen, Kenneth, 110, 122
Jentleson, Bruce, 12, 370–71
Jerusalem, 16, 343–46, 349–58, 375
  East Jerusalem, 351–52, 356
  West Jerusalem, 345
  Al-Quds, 345
Jervis, Robert, 242
Johannesburg, 254
Johnson, Lyndon Baines, 162, 181
Jordan, 167, 346, 355–57
*Journal of Democracy,* 117
Juda, Lawrence, 298, 309
Justice Department, 124

Kagan, Robert, 165
Kansas Events Data Systems (KEDS), 185–86
Kaplan, Abraham, 44, 75, 76
Kaplan, Robert, 117
Katlehong, 254
Katzenbach, Edward L., Jr., 272
Kaysen, Carl, 53
Kennan, George, 139, 163

Kennedy, Edward, 191, 198
Kennedy, John F., 159, 162–63
Kenya, 249–51
Keohane, Robert, 131
Kerry, Bob, 191
Keynes, John Maynard, 66
Kier, Elizabeth, 272
King, Kay, 110
Kissinger, Henry, 51, 141
Klare, Michael T., 110
de Klerk, F. W., 336
knowledge, xi, xii, xiii, xiv, 6, 59, 131
Kolodziej, Edward, 145
Korea, 159, 179–81, 209, 212, 304
  North, 96, 165, 168, 276
  South, 168, 273, 306, 317
Korean War, 52, 163, 166, 205
Krepinevich, Andrew, 267, 283
Kristol, William, 165
Kruzel, Joseph, 145
Kumaratunga, Chandrika, 249
Kuwait, 166

Labor party (Israel), 345, 353
Lagon, Mark, 154
Lakatos, Imre, 29, 30, 78
Lake, Anthony (U.S. National Security advisor), 141
Lake, David, 23
Lal, Deepak, 67
Larson, Deborah, xvii
Larson, Eric, 13, 370
Latin America, 139
*Latin American Research Review,* 80
Lauren, Paul G, xvi
League of Nations, 52
Lebanon, 181, 203, 205, 206, 209–10
Legro, Jeffrey, 272
Lemarchand, René, 243, 246, 254
Lenin, Vladimir, 30
Lepgold, Joseph, 11, 16, 366–67, 369, 371, 375
Levitt, Barbara, 275
Liberation Tigers of Tamil Eelam, 249
Liberia, 242, 257
Lieber, Robert, 13, 370

Likud, 345, 350–51, 353–55
Linberg, Leon, 121, 122
Lindblom, Charles, 2, 16
Lisburn, British army headquarters in, 326
London, 312–13, 327
    East London, 326
Lugar, Richard (U.S. senator), 161
Lusaka Protocol (of 1994), 245, 255
Lynn, John, 270, 274

MacKinder, Halford, 14, 307
Madison, James, 156
Madrid Middle East peace conference, 142
Maghreb states, 142
Major, John, 326–27, 335, 340
Malaysia, 305, 317
Mandela, Nelson, 336
Mansfield, Edwin, 271
March, James G., 275
Marshall Plan, 139
Mattes, Robert, 249
Mauritius, 237, 248
McGarry, John, 327
McNeill, William, 274–75
Mead, George Herbert, 3
Mearsheimer, John, 61
mediation, xi, 255
Mediterranean, 97
Meehan, Eugene, 1, 16
de Mesquita, Bruce Bueno, xv, xvii, 15, 16, 65
Mexico, 303
    loan guarantees, 155
Middle East, 140, 142, 143, 159, 162, 164–65, 305, 336
Middle East Bureau, 121
Middle East Multilateral Arms Control and Regional Security Negotiations (ACRS), 12, 130, 142–44, 371
military-technical revolutions (MTR), 282
Mills, Wilbur, 163
Milosevic, Slobodan, 240

Milstein, Jeffrey, 181
Mitchell, George, 333
model, conceptual, xi
model, Munich-syndrome, 86
Mogadishu debacle, 138
Mohr, Lawrence, 282, 284–86
Moi, Daniel arap, 250
Moodie, Michael, 274
Morgenthau, Hans, 22, 30, 39, 133, 242
Morocco, 142
Morrow, James, 92
Moscow, 96, 139
Moynihan, Daniel Patrick, 191
Mozambique, 256, 258
Mueller, John, 53, 67
Muslims, 184

NAFTA, 113, 158–59
Namibia, 250, 256
Napoleonic revolution, 272, 283
Napoleonic wars, 26
Nash equilibrium, 15, 338–39
National Defense Research Council, 63
nationalism, xv, 270, 272
National Research Council, 114, 368
national security, 54, 120
National Security Council (NSC), 12, 113, 116, 118
    NSC-68, 139
    staff, 141
National Union for the Total Independence of Angola (UNITA), 245
NATO, 59, 90, 155, 161, 197, 278, 364
Natunas Islands, 305–6
Ndadaye, Melchior, 245
Near Eastern Affairs (NEA), 137
negotiation(s), 15, 97, 98, 237, 243
Netanyahu, Benjamin, 345
New Republic, 117
Newsom, David, 110–12, 119, 145
New York, 312–13
Nigeria, 248
Nincic, Donna J., 15, 182, 370

Nincic, Miroslav, 78, 81, 117, 154,
     182, 240, 307, 363, 367, 369, 375
Niou, Emerson M. S., 117
Nitze, Paul, 139
Nixon, Richard, 162
Nolan, Janne, 274
Northeast Asia, 82
Nozick, Robert, 63
nuclear deterrence, 23
nuclear proliferation, xiv, 61, 62, 155
Nuclear Regulatory Commission, 121
Nujoma, Sam, 250
Nye, Joseph, xvii, 23, 267, 296
Nyerere, Julius, 259, 261

OECD countries, 96, 309
Ogarkov, Nikolai, 282
Ohmae, Kenichi, 315–17
O'Leary, Brendan, 327
Oman, 142
OPEC, 316
Operation Desert Shield, 157
Operation Desert Storm, 157
Ordeshook, Peter C., xvi, 45, 117
Organization of African Unity
     (OAU), 143, 254, 257–58
Organization for Security and Co-
     operation in Europe (OSCE),
     143
Organski, Kenneth, 15, 16, 375
Oromo Liberation Front, 248
Oslo agreement, 140, 345
Oval Office, 55
Owens, William, 267

Paarlberg, Robert, 154, 169
Pakistan, 306
Palestinian Liberation Organization
     (PLO), 336, 353
Palestinian National Authority
     (PNA), 16, 343–45, 357
Palestinians, 22, 140, 344, 346, 348,
     350–52, 357
Panama Canal, 304, 308
Pan Am flight 103, bombing of, 167
Pearl Harbor, 166

Pentagon, 163
Peres, Shimon, 143, 336, 351
Perot, Ross, 158
Persian Gulf, 154, 164, 304, 306–8
Philippines, 305
policy, consequences of, 14
policy, foreign, xi, xii, xiv, 2, 3, 9–13,
     35, 54, 60, 62–65, 80, 109–12, 121,
     129, 131, 134–35, 138–39, 145,
     153–58, 164, 169, 295–96, 302
policy, national security, 14
policy, U.S. defense, 14
policy, U.S. foreign, xv, 13, 14, 58,
     133, 154, 169, 237, 295–97
policy, U.S. security, 62
policymaker(s), xi–xv, xvii, 2, 5–7, 9,
     11–13, 15, 33, 34, 51, 53–62, 66,
     75, 76, 78, 80–81, 83, 87–89, 91–
     92, 97, 99, 109, 111–15, 117–19,
     122, 124–26, 129, 131, 134, 140,
     145, 155–56, 181–82, 209, 267–
     69, 272, 277–78, 286–88, 319,
     337, 343, 363–65, 368, 371, 373,
     375–76
Policy Planning Office, directorship
     of, 12
   staff, 109, 139
policy relevance, 3, 9, 12–13, 21, 55,
     57–59, 65, 75, 89, 129, 145, 254,
     369, 372, 374
   policy-relevant theory (PRT), 22,
     23, 25, 36–40, 42–44, 51, 53, 75,
     81, 89, 99, 145, 174, 212, 367,
     373–74, 377
   policy-relevant work, 9, 36, 38, 43,
     63
*Political Science Quarterly,* 80
Posen, Barry, 272
poverty, 4
Powell, Walter, 279–80
power, 6, 10, 12
prediction, 24, 26
preferences, 88, 92, 94, 134
   societal, 3
President's Science Advisory Council,
     63

Prisoner's Dilemma, 326, 338–40
Program on International Policy Atti-
    tudes (PIPA), 187–89, 207–10
proportional representation (PR), 251
Protestant Unionists, 326
Przeworski, Adam, 58, 260
Putnam, Robert, 154

Rabin, Yitzhak, 16, 336, 343–44,
    348–55, 357, 375
    administration, 343
Radio Free Europe/Radio Liberty
    (RFE/RL), 123, 124, 125
Radio Mille Collines, 240
Ralston, David, 271, 275
RAM, 120
RAND Corporation, x, 13, 115, 366
Reagan, Ronald, 154, 206, 353
    administration, 163
    rearmament program, 54
realism, 77, 133
reciprocity, 237, 240
Red Sea, 306, 308
relations, contextual, 33, 34
relations, instrumental, 33
Renshon, Stanley, xvii
Republicans, 4, 27, 138, 159–60, 191,
    201–2
    Republican presidents, 160
Resende-Santos, 271
Revolution in Military Affairs
    (RMA), 14, 267–68, 278, 281–
    83, 288
Rio Treaty, 160
Roberts, Michael, 282
Robinson, Thomas W., xvii
Rodionov, General, 166
Rogers, Clifford, 275, 281, 287
Roland, Alex, 283
ROM, 120
Root, Michael, 3, 16
Rose, Gregory, 117, 327
Rosner, Jeremy, 116
Rothchild, Donald, 14, 23, 369
Rubin, Barry, 140

Russia, 155, 159, 162, 165–66, 242,
    275, 304, 314
Rutkowski, Anthony M., 124
Rwanda, 116, 160, 240–43, 245, 249,
    254, 258, 260–62

Sagan, Scott, 271
Salim, Salim Ahmed, 257
Sarajevo, 189
Saudi Arabia, 142, 167, 355–57
Savimbi, Jonas, 245
Schelling, Thomas, 80
Schlesinger, Arthur, 155
Schwartau, Winn, 277
Scott, W. Richard, 272
sea-lanes of communication (SLOCs),
    15, 295, 297–98, 300, 303, 307,
    309, 317
Sebenius, James, 97
security, U.S. national, 15
security dilemma(s), 14, 23, 39, 237,
    239–41, 253, 257, 259–60
Serbia, 240
    Serbs, 184
*Sharia* (Islamic) law, 253
Sierra Leone, 261
Silkworm missiles, 307
Simon, Herbert, xv, xvii
Singer, J. David, 61
Sinn Fein, 15, 326, 328–37, 339
Smoke, Richard, 3, 4, 5, 16, 22
Snyder, Jack, 124, 272
Somalia, 179, 181, 203–5, 207, 209–
    10, 242, 257–59
    Somalia crisis, 138, 160
Soroos, Marvin, 121
South Africa, 246, 248–49, 253, 336
South China Sea, 304–6, 318
Southeast Asia, U.S. policy in, 59
South West Africa People's Organiza-
    tion (SWAPO), 250
sovereignty, 53, 260
Soviet Union (USSR), 54, 55, 60, 61,
    110, 153–54, 157–58, 162, 278
Sprout, Harold, 14, 298

Sprout, Margaret, 14, 298
Sputnik, 166, 168
Spykman, Nicholas, 14, 302
Sri Lanka, 249
Stabilization Force (SFOR), 161
START II Treaty, 160
statecraft, xi, xiv, xvi
State Department (U.S. Department of State), xv, 12, 110–13, 118, 121, 125, 135, 138–40, 161–62
    planning staff, 130
Stedman, Stephen, 248
Stein, Arthur, 11, 58, 366
Stevenson, Richard, 316–17
Strait of Hormuz, 304, 306–8
Strait of Malacca, 304, 305, 318
strategy, xi, xii
Stokman, Frans N., xvii, 16
Stormont regime, 327
Sudan, 246, 252, 254, 257
Sullivan, Brian, 282
Sumatra, 306
Syria, 162
system, international, 14
Szabo, Stephen, 110

Taiwan, 273, 305
Tanzania, 259
Tehran, 307
Tel Aviv, 346
Temple Mount, 345
terrorism, 53
Teune, Henry, 58
theory, 133
    decision, 63, 64, 66
    empirical, 4, 24, 31, 32
    game, x, xvi, 15, 64, 65, 134
    microeconomic, 15
    organizational, 14
    rational choice, 45, 78, 81–83, 87, 92, 134
    structural-realist, ix, x
    substantive, 9
    theory and policy gap, ix, x
    theory design, xv

theory of moves (TOM), 15, 325–26, 331, 336–39
theory of relevance, 10
Thompson, W. Scott, 110, 122
Tigray, 253
Toffler, Alvin and Heidi, 267, 274, 283
Togman, Jeffrey, 15, 375
Tokoza, 254
Tokyo, 312–13, 316
Trimble, David, 336
Truman, Harry, 67, 162, 181
    Truman Doctrine, 168
Tunisia, 142
Turkey, 165, 168
Tutsi, 243, 245, 249, 254, 259

Ulster, plantation of, 327
UNESCO, 95
United Arab Emirates, 307
United Kingdom, 326–27, 355, 357. *See also* Great Britain
United Nations (UN), 52–53, 90, 161, 254, 256
    Security Council, 159
    U.S. mission to, 136
United Nations Assistance Mission for Rwanda (UNAMIR), 259
United Nations Operation in Mozambique (ONUMOZ), 256
United States, 23, 35, 53, 60, 61, 63, 76, 77–80, 90, 99, 118, 119, 124, 153–56, 158, 161–65, 167, 169–70, 191, 193, 195–96, 201–3, 209, 258, 267, 269, 271, 277, 295, 299, 302–3, 315, 317–18, 346, 349–50, 352–53, 355–56, 358, 366
    democracy, Madisonian features of, 13
    economy, 58
    elections, 53
    policymakers, 60
    presidents, 32
University of Maryland (College Park), 187–88

University of Toronto, 117
U.S. Census Bureau, 300–301
U.S. Information Agency, 113, 123
    USIA project, 114, 157, 161
U.S.-Soviet Basic Principles Agreement (BPA), 144
USTR, 124

Van Evera, Stephen, 272
Vatican, 346, 355–57
Vietnam, 59, 141, 145, 157, 159, 163–64, 179–81, 196, 205, 209, 212, 305
    era, 155
    war, 52
Vladivostok, 305
Voice of America, 123
Vosloorus, 254

Wallerstein, Immanuel, 297, 311
Waltz, Kenneth, ix, xvi, 30, 39, 268, 271
war, xi, 57, 58
Warsaw Pact, 278, 288
Washington, D.C., 12, 95, 109, 115,
    117, 125, 182, 185–87, 189, 302, 307–8, 315–16
Watergate, 157, 164
White House, 63, 109, 113, 140, 185
Wilson, Ernest, 12, 119, 124, 367, 369, 371
Wolfers, Arnold, 95, 243
*World Politics,* 79, 137, 363
World Trade Center bombing, 167
World Trade Organization (WTO), 155
World War I, 13, 156 — 57, 242
World War II, 53, 63, 155–57, 159, 162–63, 178–79, 205, 296
Wright, Quincy, 275

Yankelovitch, Daniel, 115
Yeltsin, Boris, 166
    presidency of, 166
Yugoslavia, 161, 163, 262

Zaller, John R., 183
Zelikow, Philip, 9, 16
Zenawi, Meles, 251
Zimbabwe, 244, 249, 256